Reading David Foster Wallace between philosophy and literature

Manchester University Press

Reading David Foster Wallace between philosophy and literature

edited by Allard den Dulk, Pia Masiero, and Adriano Ardovino

MANCHESTER UNIVERSITY PRESS

Copyright © Manchester University Press 2022

While copyright in the volume as a whole is vested in Manchester University Press, copyright in individual chapters belongs to their respective authors, and no chapter may be reproduced wholly or in part without the express permission in writing of both author and publisher.

Published by Manchester University Press
Oxford Road, Manchester M13 9PL

www.manchesteruniversitypress.co.uk

British Library Cataloguing-in-Publication Data
A catalogue record for this book is available from the British Library

ISBN 978 1 5261 6354 7 hardback
ISBN 978 1 5261 7232 7 paperback

First published 2022
Paperback published 2023

The publisher has no responsibility for the persistence or accuracy of URLs for any external or third-party internet websites referred to in this book, and does not guarantee that any content on such websites is, or will remain, accurate or appropriate.

Typeset
by New Best-set Typesetters Ltd

Contents

Notes on contributors   vii
Acknowledgements   xi

Introduction: David Foster Wallace between philosophy and literature – Allard den Dulk, Pia Masiero, and Adriano Ardovino   1

Part I: General perspectives

1. Absorbing art: the Hegelian project of *Infinite Jest* – Adam Kelly   19
2. Stages, Socrates, and the performer stripped bare: David Foster Wallace as philosopher-dramatist – Jeffrey Severs   48
3. 'A matter of perspective': 'Good Old Neon' between literature and philosophy – Adriano Ardovino and Pia Masiero   68
4. The influence of Christopher Lasch's *The Culture of Narcissism* on David Foster Wallace – Paolo Pitari   89

Part II: Consciousness, self, and others

5. 'What all she'd so painfully learned said about her': a comparative reading of David Foster Wallace's 'The Depressed Person' and Fyodor Dostoevsky's *Notes from Underground* – Allard den Dulk   113

6 *Infinite Jest*'s 'trinity of You and I into We': Wallace's 'click' between Joyce's literary consubstantiality and Wittgenstein's family resemblance – Dominik Steinhilber 138
 7 Solipsism, loneliness, alienation: David Foster Wallace as interpreter of Wittgenstein – Guido Baggio 160
 8 'This is just my opinion': modelling a public sphere in *The Pale King* – Daniel South 180
 9 Pioneers of consciousness: hypothesis for a diptych – Lorenzo Marchese 200
10 The problem of other minds in 'Good Old Neon' – Matt Prout 219

Part III: Embodiment, gender, and sexuality

11 'I am in here': David Foster Wallace and the body as object – Clare Hayes-Brady 241
12 'The interstices of her sense of something': David Foster Wallace, the quest for affect, and the future of gendered interactions – Mara Mattoscio 259
13 'You are loved': race, love, and language in early Wallace – Lola Boorman 279
14 'They remain just bodies': on pornography in David Foster Wallace (1989–2006) – Chiara Scarlato 297
15 'Something staring back at you': an anamorphic reading of *Infinite Jest* – Angelo Grossi 314

Index 333

Notes on contributors

Adriano Ardovino is a Full Professor of Theoretical Philosophy at 'G. d'Annunzio' University of Chieti-Pescara. His teaching and research interests include German idealism, phenomenology, hermeneutics, post-structuralism, aesthetic theory, philosophy of religion, and philosophy of literature. He has published numerous articles on those areas as well as books and translations. In 2018 he organized the first international conference on David Foster Wallace in Italy ('David Foster Wallace between Philosophy and Literature', 'G. d'Annunzio' University).

Guido Baggio is Assistant Professor of Theoretical Philosophy at the Department of Philosophy, Communication and Performing Arts, University of Roma Tre. He is the author of three monographs on George Herbert Mead, Jean-François Lyotard, and David Foster Wallace. He also published several contributions on pragmatism, philosophy of psychology, and cognitive science in collective volumes and international journals.

Lola Boorman is a Lecturer in American Literature and Culture at the University of York. Her work focuses on twentieth- and twenty-first-century American literature and she is currently writing a book about the relationship between grammar, politics, and literary form entitled *Make Grammar Do: Grammar and Twentieth-Century American Fiction*.

Allard den Dulk is Senior Lecturer in Philosophy, Literature, and Film at Amsterdam University College and Research Fellow at the Faculty of Humanities of the VU University Amsterdam (The

Netherlands). He is the author of *Existentialist Engagement in Wallace, Eggers and Foer: A Philosophical Analysis of Contemporary American Literature* (2015). Currently, he is working on a book tentatively titled *Wallace's Existentialist Intertexts: Comparative Readings with the Fiction of Kafka, Dostoevsky, Camus and Sartre*. For more information and publications see www.allarddendulk.nl.

Angelo Grossi received his PhD in American literature from Ca' Foscari University of Venice in 2018, with a dissertation that explores David Foster Wallace's work through the interpretative prism of film theory. His fields of interest are intermediality, film theory, American postmodern and post-postmodern fiction, and poetry.

Clare Hayes-Brady is an Associate Professor of American Literature at University College Dublin. She is the author of *The Unspeakable Failures of David Foster Wallace* and the editor of *The Journal of David Foster Wallace Studies*. She has published and presented widely on contemporary literature, communication, gender and the body, with an interest in moments of liminality and extremity, especially illness and death and the role of narrative in clinical encounters.

Adam Kelly is Associate Professor of English at University College Dublin. He previously taught at the University of York and was a postdoctoral fellow at Harvard University. He is the author of *American Fiction in Transition: Observer Hero Narrative, the 1990s, and Postmodernism* (2013). He is currently completing his second monograph, *American Fiction at the Millennium: Neoliberalism and the New Sincerity*. From 2022 to 2026 he is Principal Investigator on the project "Imaginative Literature and Social Trust, 1990–2025," funded by the Irish Research Council.

Lorenzo Marchese is Assistant Professor in Comparative Literature at University of Palermo. His research focuses on issues such as theory and practice of contemporary fiction, comparative literature (with particular regard to the novel-essay), works of Primo Levi and Cesare Pavese. He is the author of the books *L'io possibile: L'autofiction come paradosso del romanzo contemporaneo* (2014) and *Storiografie parallele: Cos'è la non-fiction?* (2019).

Pia Masiero is Associate Professor of North American Literature at Ca' Foscari University of Venice. Her research interests include modernist and contemporary literature, literary theory at the intersection of cognitive sciences and second-generation post-classical narratology. She has published on, among others, Philip Roth, William Faulkner, David Foster Wallace, George Saunders, Alice Munro, Jorge Luis Borges, Roberto Bolaño.

Mara Mattoscio is a Postdoctoral Researcher at the 'G. d'Annunzio' University of Chieti-Pescara. She is the author of *Corpi affetti: Il Sudafrica di Nadine Gordimer dalla pagina allo schermo* (2018, AIA Book Prize Honourable Mention 2020) and the editor, together with Megan C. MacDonald, of a special section of *Feminist Media Studies* on 'Gender, Migration, and the Media' (2018). She has published extensively on Anglophone postcolonial literature and film, with a special focus on the intersections of race and gender, and on South African and diasporic writing in a comparative perspective.

Paolo Pitari obtained his joint PhD in American literature at Ca' Foscari University of Venice and at LMU Munich. He was awarded research grants by the JFK Institute of Freie Universität Berlin and by the DAAD.

Matt Prout recently completed his PhD thesis, *David Foster Wallace and Scepticism*, at the University of Bristol. He has published articles on Wallace in *Critique: Studies in Contemporary Fiction* and *Journal of Modern Literature*. His next research project looks at the representations of philosophical practice in contemporary autofiction.

Chiara Scarlato is a Postdoctoral Fellow in Theoretical Philosophy at the 'G. d'Annunzio' University of Chieti-Pescara. She is the author of a monograph on David Foster Wallace (*Attraverso il corpo: Filosofia e letteratura in David Foster Wallace*, 2020) and she has published and presented widely on issues concerning the philosophy of literature.

Jeffrey Severs is Associate Professor of English at the University of British Columbia. He is the author of *David Foster Wallace's Balancing Books: Fictions of Value* (2017) and the co-editor of *Pynchon's Against the Day: A Corrupted Pilgrim's Guide* (2011). His articles have appeared in *Critique*, *Modern Fiction Studies*, *MELUS*, *Textual Practice*, and several other journals.

Daniel South holds a PhD in English and Related Literature from the University of York, and is an Associate Fellow of the Higher

Education Academy. His thesis explored how four contemporary novelists address the relationship between literature and the public sphere in the internet age. He has reviewed for the *Journal of American Studies*, co-edited a recent issue of *Alluvium*, and has a chapter forthcoming in a new collection on Zadie Smith.

Dominik Steinhilber is a postdoctoral researcher at the University of Konstanz. His dissertation concerned itself with the American epic novel in the Ulyssean tradition, in which he investigated Wallace's *Infinite Jest* and Thomas Pynchon's *Gravity's Rainbow* with regard to their response to James Joyce's *Ulysses*. His research interests include digitization, postmodern and contemporary literature, and transatlantic intertextuality. He is currently working on a project investigating alternative ecologies in American dark romanticism.

Acknowledgements

This volume was born in the aftermath of the first full-fledged international conference on David Foster Wallace in Italy. It took place at the University of Chieti-Pescara back in 2018 (18–21 April) and was titled 'David Foster Wallace between philosophy and literature'. That gathering was very thought-provoking and spawned a further conversation that mustered other scholars interested in David Foster Wallace's disciplinary in-betweenness.

This edited collection is the result of that long and enriching conversation. We would like to thank our colleagues – specifically, Roosje van der Kamp, Chiara Scarlato, and Amanda Swayne – for their advice and assistance in putting together this volume.

Introduction: David Foster Wallace between philosophy and literature

Allard den Dulk, Pia Masiero, and Adriano Ardovino

> Literature (among other things) is 'exemplary': it always is, says, does something other, something other than itself, an itself which moreover is only that, something other than itself. For example or par excellence: philosophy.
>
> Jacques Derrida, 'Passions'

> Nothing is more important though than the construction of fictional concepts, which will teach us at last to understand our own.
>
> Ludwig Wittgenstein, *Culture and Value*

> This is what I see. Can you see it too?
>
> Toril Moi, 'The Adventure of Reading'

This collection aims to show that David Foster Wallace's work originates from and functions in the space between philosophy and literature. Indeed the philosophical dimension of his work is not a mere supplement or decoration, a finishing touch to perfect his literary writing. Nor is it the other way around: a pre-established truth which Wallace sees the literary merely serving to illustrate. Rather Wallace intertwines the two discursive modes in a never-ending process of reciprocal cross-fertilization. By suggesting that Wallace's texts, characters, story-worlds, linguistic and formal choices, plots and concepts should be read as between philosophy and literature, we are not imposing a preconceived methodology or theoretical context on his oeuvre that univocally homogenizes each individual reading in the collection; rather, our approach offers an investigative perspective, allowing for a variety of theories and methods that shed light on the constitutive in-betweenness of his work.

What does it mean to say that Wallace's work originates from and functions in the space between philosophy and literature? In this introductory chapter we will first briefly address Wallace's relation to and career switch between philosophy and literature. Then we will look at the general relation between these two discursive modes – not by going back to Plato and Aristotle (a path already well-trodden in discussions of the relation between literature and philosophy) but by briefly outlining three aspects in which philosophy and literature both differ and overlap, firstly, as activities or practices; secondly, with regards to their instruments, which is to say, their forms of language and communication; and, thirdly, with regards to their purposes, or the experiences and possible understandings they generate. In all three aspects the discursive modes we call philosophy and literature offer different ways of interacting with, articulating, and apprehending the world that present many zones of contact but do not fully dissolve into one another.[1] Again this brief overview should not be seen as a unifying methodology or theoretical framework. Rather it is a general sketching out of different ways in which the philosophical and literary modes may be seen to differ from and overlap with each other, and which thus also allow texts, authors, and readers to operate 'in between' them and bring aspects of their varying practices, languages, and purposes to bear on each other. There is perhaps no better example of this fruitful cross-pollination than the work of David Foster Wallace. Below we will outline first this theoretical framework, then the chapters making up this collection and the thematic groupings in which we have decided to present them.

It is widely noted that David Foster Wallace's oeuvre develops along philosophical lines and themes, presenting not so much a sustained conceptual or theoretical reflection but rather an expression and experience of some of the most pressing existential issues in contemporary Western life. The possibility of pursuing this kind of immersive experience seems to have been an important reason why Wallace switched from philosophy to literature during his academic career. After studying mathematical logic and philosophy of language from 1980 to 1985, Wallace abandoned academic study of philosophy to devote himself to literature. Wallace later explained this shift in terms of no longer feeling the 'click' he had initially experienced in 'proof-completions, or maybe algorithms': he realized that 'the click existed in literature, too' and that he was 'able to get it in fiction' after he stopped getting 'the click from math logic' (McCaffery, 2012: 35). Literature 'felt like it was using 97 percent of me', he also observed, compared to philosophy's use of only '50 percent' (Lipsky, 2010: 261). We could speculate about which tendencies in himself Wallace may have been referring to with these percentages. One could argue that the activity of philosophizing, with its argumentative leanings, might be experienced as more monological and directed towards rational closure, and thus mainly occupied with – or even fortifying of – the self: the enjoyment of one's own mind in having crafted a persuasive argument. The activity of literature, on the other hand, might feel comparatively open, dialogical, and vulnerable (the 'success' of one's description being more ambiguously reliant on the response of the reader) – and, as such, more self-forgetting and other-directed. While these are generalizations, these latter qualities are indeed thematized, advocated, and instantiated throughout Wallace's literary work.

So far most scholars who have situated Wallace's work at the intersection of philosophy and literature have resorted either to a reconstructive perspective dictated by Wallace's own biographical-intellectual trajectory or read philosophy and literature as two distinct and partly incompatible traditions – the former more abstract, rational, and universal, and the latter more vital, emotional, and particular (and often hierarchically related: with philosophy preceding and explaining literature). These approaches are certainly legitimate, but the chapters in our collection have in mind and attempt to work towards another interpretative approach – one that moves beyond the distinctiveness of the discursive realms of the philosophical and the literary, with their corresponding analytical tools and vocabulary, to approach Wallace's work instead as originating from and constituted by the space between philosophy and literature. For Wallace philosophy and literature are co-originating ways of confronting reality: philosophical works, styles, and concepts trigger literary experiences, while literary works, styles, and genres trigger philosophical questioning. Both appear within and amplify each other from the start.

In this Introduction our aim is not to theorize the relation between philosophy and literature. That would inevitably imply some disciplinary bias or impose some sort of methodology – perhaps indebted to 'philosophy of literature' or to 'literary theory' – regarding how best to conceive of such a relation. Our contributors, like we ourselves as editors, come from different disciplinary backgrounds that we cannot and do not want to absorb into one view.[2] Wallace's trajectory as a writer calls for attention to how this relationship was entrenched in his unique way not only of being a writer but of living. The intermingling and cross-fertilization of philosophy and literature belongs to Wallace's way of apprehending the world and making meaningful sense of it through his writing. Analogously, we as readers and scholars are called less to systematizing his work than to attending to the different ways in which it enables access to the potentials of this fertile in-between space.

Philosophy and literature are primarily activities, that is, they both envelop sets of discursive practices possessing their own formational rules produced by the historical and social contexts in which they emerged and developed. As such they manifest within particular orders of discourse, employ specific conceptual tools, and express themselves in recognizable writing styles. Western philosophical practice – with its recognizable themes, language, and resources – has a long history. Before Plato it had other names. Indeed, much more than definitions, discourses, practices, and institutions, philosophy and literature are forms of experience and expression, of apprehending and articulating the world.

Against this broad backdrop Wallace's fictional and non-fictional corpus helps to foreground that the relationship between philosophy and literature, and the fluid in-between space their intersection creates, takes at least three different forms or can be seen from three different perspectives: firstly, it can be understood as a discursive practice, a language game that arises from and blends different sources and desires, from the (personal, biographic) particular to the (speculative, conceptual) universal, secondly, it is a specific linguistic form, a discourse that inhabits the intersection of literary writing and philosophical inquiry, and thirdly, it is an experience and exchange that can substantially transform the author, text, and reader constituting the discursive project in question.

The first perspective calls us to keep in mind that philosophy and literature are activities or practices with both authors and readers as participants (or users). Philosophy was institutionalized, as a practice and as a discipline, with the birth of institutions such as the university in the Middle Ages and the profession of philosophy in the nineteenth century: indeed, whereas Descartes was a mathematician and Kant taught geography, with Hegel the figure of the professor began to crystallize in a definitive way, socially and politically. Recent decades have seen a partial return to (or increased visibility of) philosophical practices with communal dimensions external to academic discourse and discourses that are not strictly scientific, but more personal and linked to the experience of individuals. This process could also be said to include an increased prevalence of philosophical connections in literary discourses, or rather, greater stylistic contamination and greater hybridization of content.

In turn it was only in modern times that the word *literature* stopped designating all culture and knowledge related to writing (which is the meaning of its Latin root, *litteratura*) and began referring to a specific writing practice recognizable in well-defined texts bearing a certain artistic value (the so-called *belles lettres*, placed next to the *beaux arts*). Distribution of these texts and their compositional styles into rather stable genres and the shaping of institutionalized approaches and disciplines to study these particular practices – such as literary history, criticism, and theory – later followed.

Though it is certainly true that the practices of (and as we will see below, the languages and objectives relating to) philosophy and literature changed and acquired distinctive tonalities over time, they have none the less continued to nourish each other – from a period well before Plato to our contemporary era. Therefore the following questions (still) resonate with us today: what do we do when we engage with – that is, write and read – philosophy and/or literature? Is it possible – or perhaps, as authors such as Richard Rorty have suggested, even necessary – to do philosophy through literature? Is it possible to produce literature that does not merely engage with philosophical themes but enters into a more essentially 'philosophical' mode? Do quintessentially philosophical issues exist? Or should we rather say that the crucial issues concerning our existence are the same across the two disciplinary boundaries and that the differences between them reside only in their respective institutional structures and languages? Different literary forms – from poetry to drama, from epistolary writing to allegorical tales – have been employed as part of philosophical practice, with results that are counted as great philosophical achievements; this makes the development of philosophical thought difficult to separate from literary practice in a definite, abstract way. On the other hand, the literary tradition – from ancient epics to the contemporary novel, passing through tragedy and poetry – has reached great heights in presenting human experience as motivated by and pulsating with core existential questions, and thus cannot be isolated from philosophical practice either.

This brings us to the second aspect or perspective, namely the languages of philosophy and literature, which constitute their existence as mainly verbal communications: the songs of poets and rhapsodists, the words of actors, dialogue, speech, written texts, etcetera. As mentioned above, such forms and genres and their communicative strategies and participants (authors and audiences) shape the intersection of the philosophical and literary in manifold ways.

If, on the one hand, it is true that philosophical inquiry has often made use of markedly literary forms, giving birth to a veritable 'literary philosophy', on the other it is similarly indisputable that literary practice has always been distinctively open to linguistic experimentation. In the boundless formal diversity of genres and texts – from poetry to the modern novel – and its endless staging of what Wittgenstein would call specific 'language games', the encounter between an author who narrates a world, oneself, and the human condition, and a reader who incorporates and transforms that narrated world through her own distinctive interpretation takes place within a formal space that activates a profound and intense first-person engagement. Words, in the literary context, are the necessary, irreplaceable vehicle for this engagement; their role is not merely instrumental or accessory. This linguistic specificity, stemming from both convention and experimentation, is always tightly interwoven with ambiguity and suspension. As such it has traditionally signalled the principal distinction between literary narrative and philosophical argumentation. Literature is, in all respects, a field in which knowledge is transformed into stories. The centrality of the narrative dimension and of fictionality, that is, of the invention and articulation of imaginary worlds, brings us to the third aspect or perspective of the fertile cross-pollination of philosophy and literature.

The third aspect regards the purposes of philosophy and literature: the experience of them and their possible transformation of our understanding of the themes and problems with which they deal. Through the literary text readers fine-tune their abilities to detect and understand the most idiosyncratic aspects of existence and the values and backgrounds that sustain them. The role of the imagination is crucial here, because it connects individual and intersubjective experience with the question of what is verisimilar or not, of what is fantasy or falsification, and foregrounds the many paradoxes of existence that Wallace explores and revels in. Obviously imagination is crucial for philosophers too. As Kant famously maintained, imagination coincides with neither knowledge nor ethics but supports both. In a work of art, however, the imagination is arguably unfettered from preceding understanding or subsequent action, connecting the aesthetic subject – be it artist or viewer – to the artistic object itself.

If we consider Wallace's oeuvre we cannot help but acknowledge the centrality of the imagination, from both a philosophical and a literary perspective. Wallace's work illustrates how far literary imagining can go and invites us to test this imagining extra-textually. If we assume that a literary text (unlike most traditional philosophical texts) necessarily revolves around: firstly, the continuous and non-linear modification of expectations while writing or reading; secondly, the dynamic negotiation between feeling and writing or reading; thirdly, the activation of what is inside and outside the text (a separation that runs along porous and ever-changing lines); fourthly, the (re)configuration of the different experiences and discourses the text initiates; and, finally, fifthly, the progressive establishment of an imaginative becoming which takes the shape of, or makes room for, an other (the author, the reader) – then it becomes clear that the imagination plays a role in each of these steps of writing, reading, narrating, and listening. In this sense it becomes important not to fully equate theoretical and definitional philosophical discourses, which inevitably offer (though to varying degrees) abstract reflections on this or that issue, with literary discourses offering an experience and understanding dependent on the lived experience prompted by the text. Whereas the former wants and needs to operate with models, the latter is rooted in an actual – if fictional – experience stemming from a specific and individualized deictic field.

The contributions to this volume explore these subtle and fluid interconnections between the philosophical and the literary as they manifest in Wallace's work. Their scholarly engagements with this multi-layered and kaleidoscopic interrelation mirrors the many negotiations and interpretations at work in Wallace's writing, especially with regard to the three elements of practice, language, and experience or understanding sketched out above. The chapters collected here explore how Wallace's literary practice is both linguistically peculiar and experience-oriented, demonstrating – we hope – the relevance of an in-between approach.

Given his early predilection for philosophical studies, Wallace opted for a fiction practice that mingled philosophical jargon with literary writing, giving rise to texts centring on markedly philosophical issues – from solipsism to freedom, free will to time – but deploying markedly literary strategies. Wallace was intrigued by a mode of writing that borrowed philosophical technicalities; he created a rich interpenetration across the divide of fiction and non-fiction, always on the lookout for ways to interrogate and engage with the existential predicaments of contemporary life. Indeed his textual experimentation was recognizably experiential, resulting in multi-layered reader involvement. In this sense his work turned philosophy into a first-person, fully embodied matter.

Wallace wanted to 'reaffirm' that fiction is 'about what it is to be a fucking *human being*' and constitutes a 'living transaction between humans' (McCaffery, 2012: 131), 'that writing is an act of communication between one human being and another' (Wallace, 1997: 144). These statements reiterate how, for Wallace, philosophy and literature are interrelated. Wallace's fiction aims to contribute to our philosophical understanding of concrete human existence, not by offering conclusive truths but by requiring the reader to 'put in her share of the [work]' (McCaffery, 2012: 138), by negotiating through the problems and perspectives it presents. As such Wallace's oeuvre represents an original and relevant philosophical discourse, turning literature into philosophy and using philosophy as the inner propeller of literary practice. This 'in-betweenness' represents the propulsive force of Wallace's work.

The chapters in this volume approach Wallace's textual richness and multi-layered in-betweenness starting from different perspectives and privileging one or more of the aspects mentioned above. Together they represent a multifaceted engagement with the philosophical-literary in-betweenness of Wallace's oeuvre, eschewing a monolithic interpretation of what philosophy and literature are and paying close attention to Wallace's fictional and philosophical ideas without subsuming them under one, broad philosophical framework. The volume aims to explore the myriad ways in which Wallace mobilizes the philosophical dimension not merely as a supplement or embellishment but as a discursive mode that is always already intertwined with the literary through a never-ending process of reciprocal cross-fertilization.

Through a series of fresh readings of Wallace's oeuvre the chapters that follow will offer a plurality of interpretations of and responses to the open question regarding Wallace's engagement with philosophy and literature. We decided to organize this multiplicity of approaches into three parts. The first one provides general perspectives on the building blocks of David Foster Wallace's macro text – his aesthetics, interest in performativity, formal choices, sociology, and ethics – that extend beyond the precincts of the primary texts they employ as case studies. The second and third parts delve in more focused ways into two thematic blocks: 'Consciousness, self, and others' and 'Embodiment, gender, and sexuality'. Both thematic blocks have already elicited conversation in Wallace scholarship, but both are far from being exhausted.

In 'Absorbing art: the Hegelian project of *Infinite Jest*', Adam Kelly argues that the project of reading Wallace's fiction between philosophy and literature 'means passing through Hegel', whose role has been largely neglected in Wallace scholarship so far. Kelly maintains that Hegel is key to understanding what has been called Wallace's 'socialist phenomenology', that is, his belief in human beings as 'always already existing in a norm-based relation to one another'. Kelly's aim is to mobilize Hegelian categories – most notably that of absorption (*Aufhebung*) – to map some crucial aesthetic principles and effects structuring Wallace's masterpiece. Kelly's reading of *Infinite Jest* focuses mainly on James Incandenza's filmography and especially on Joelle van Dyne's viewing of the film *Pre-Nuptial Agreement of Heaven and Hell*. Joelle's attitude becomes the key to demonstrating how the notion of absorption – and, more specifically, what Kelly calls 'refractive absorption' – is 'an important principle in Wallace's broader aesthetic project', which reads sincerity as 'a social achievement that required a new aesthetic form'.

Jeffrey Severs's 'Stages, Socrates, and the performer stripped bare: David Foster Wallace as philosopher-dramatist' reflects on Wallace's writing about performance, not so much in the mannerisms of actors and other artists (and their audiences) but, more subtly, in the ways dramatic form has seeped into the very texture of Wallace's way of handling philosophy. According to Severs, Wallace consistently stages philosophical performances that take one of two forms: 'scenes of dialogue that mark a twist on the Platonic dialogues and their dramatic staging of philosophical conflict' or 'moments that conjure ... a particularly abject stage performer' and allow Wallace to demonstrate his awareness that there is ultimately no way to escape 'the artifices of performance' – a stance he tries to explore from within the space of performing vulnerability.

Ardovino's and Masiero's '"A matter of perspective": "Good Old Neon" between literature and philosophy' argues that Wallace's most famous short story thematizes what literature is about according to David Foster Wallace. Ardovino and Masiero follow the tripartite layers structuring the short story – centred on the respective protagonists of Neal, David Wallace, and David Foster Wallace – to demonstrate the centrality to its development of imagination, which, in Wallace's competent hands, becomes both the space of caring and an empty space of suspension in which truth about the other may dwell.

Paolo Pitari's 'The influence of Christopher Lasch's *The Culture of Narcissism* on David Foster Wallace' demonstrates Lasch's influence on Wallace to be much broader and deeper than has yet been acknowledged. Pitari patiently reconstructs the consistent agreement between the two writers with respect to three different areas: sociology, literary criticism, and philosophy. Well beyond the somewhat unsurprising overlappings that emerge from a comparison of Lasch's book with 'E Unibus Pluram', Pitari tries to unearth how these shared concerns shape Wallace's criticism of contemporary fiction and more broadly underpin his sociology and ethics.

The second section, devoted to 'Consciousness, self, and others', opens with Allard den Dulk's '"What all she'd so painfully learned said about her": a comparative reading of Wallace's "The Depressed Person" and Dostoevsky's *Notes from Underground*'. As suggested by its title, Den Dulk's chapter outlines the aspects Wallace cherished in Dostoevsky which seeped into his own work: namely 'Dostoevsky's analysis of the societal problems of his time and exploration of alternatives' and his 'ability to cast these theoretical ideas into fiction and still create stories and characters that are real, human, and lifelike'. In both Dostoevsky's and Wallace's texts the main problem of the narrative revolves around the narrator's excessive self-consciousness, which results in a solipsistic sickness that can be addressed only through empathetic understanding of the other – which both narrators resist but both texts can be seen to encourage in the reader. This is the blueprint for Wallace's conception of the relation between philosophy and literature: literary exploration of philosophical themes above and beyond conceptual and theoretical means that are meant to be realized through readers' experience.

In *'Infinite Jest*'s "trinity of You and I into We": Wallace's "click" between Joyce's literary consubstantiality and Wittgenstein's family resemblance', Dominik Steinhilber offers a persuasive comparative reading of Joyce and Wallace via Wittgenstein. Steinhilber deftly mobilizes two interrelated concepts – the aesthetic of the trinity and the theological concept of consubstantiality, employed by Joyce in *Ulysses*, to read *Infinite Jest*. According to Steinhilber, Wallace situates Joyce's trinity and literary version of consubstantiality in dialogue with Wittgenstein's public language game philosophy, offering this combination as an antidote to both solipsism and endless deconstruction. Steinhilber explores the ways in which Wallace stages possible countermeasures to solipsistic dysfunction in the Incandenza family and how, more broadly, his view literary practice infused with philosophical elements reconceptualizes the vital relationship between author and reader.

The association of Wallace to Wittgenstein is well known but always worth reflecting upon. Guido Baggio's 'Solipsism, loneliness, alienation: David Foster Wallace as interpreter of Wittgenstein' proposes a rather original take on Wittgenstein, arguing against the default interpretation of Wallace's indebtedness to Wittgenstein that claims Wallace managed to fight and overcome the abyss of solipsism thanks to the Austrian philosopher. Baggio contends that Wallace did not win the battle against solipsism through Wittgenstein – or through any other literary or philosophical discourse, for that matter.

Rather, according to Baggio, solipsism is what actually wins out in Wallace's work.

Daniel South's '"This is just my opinion": modelling a public sphere in *The Pale King*' reflects on one of Wallace's main interests in the second half of his career: the public sphere. More specifically, South strives to illuminate the kind of political writing we can find in *The Pale King*, which he presents as a blueprint of Wallace's more general take on political-philosophical inquiry. Via fiction writing, literature can (and should) play an important role in reversing the hyper-partisan tones of current political conversations and inject the public sphere with dialogue, nuance, and complexity – the nuts and bolts of literary aesthetics. Habermas provides South with an interpretative framework for detecting elements of the public sphere in Wallace's posthumous novel. South highlights how Wallace paradigmatically stages his belief in the interconnections among individual agency and societal structures, the limits of the former and overwhelming presence of the latter, while affirming 'literature as a potential curative for the contemporary public sphere's ills' – not so much by writing as by reading.

In his chapter 'Pioneers of consciousness: hypothesis for a diptych', Lorenzo Marchese highlights the stories 'Incarnations of Burned Children' and 'Another Pioneer' as emblematic of Wallace's attention to negativity and psychological despair in his late work. Marchese's parallel close readings consider the two stories as a narrative diptych that illustrates 'Wallace's narrative approach to analysis of the intermittent relation between self-consciousness and the limits of communicative language'. The two stories concern burned children, and stage, despite their many differences, a shared outcome deriving from misunderstanding and idiocy. Marchese fruitfully reflects on the incommunicability of consciousness that the two short stories present, drawing on but taking distance from Thomas Nagel's reflections on the issue of other minds. Marchese shows that both children may be considered pioneers who show the limits of empathy and identification, and consequently, of language and discourse.

In 'The problem of other minds in "Good Old Neon"', Matt Prout mobilizes Wittgenstein's treatment of this much-vexed issue to discuss how Stanley Cavell's tackling of the problem of other minds – which draws heavily on Wittgenstein – can shed light on

Neal's predicament, which lies at the centre of Wallace's short story. Most notably, Prout's reading employs Cavell's notion of 'crucifying the intellect' and his notion of 'acknowledgment' to illuminate the many dangers and enticements of sceptical thinking.

Clare Hayes-Brady's '"I am in here": heads and bodies in David Foster Wallace' opens the third part of this volume, which is devoted to 'Embodiment, gender, and sexuality'. Hayes-Brady's chapter sets out to address how linguistic experience is rooted in our bodily existence. More specifically she explores 'the ways in which our embodied experiences, as represented in Wallace's writing, shape and often foreclose our linguistic engagement with the world'. Using the lens of affect theory, Hayes-Brady offers a fine-grained analysis of the opening of *Infinite Jest* and 'Brief Interview #20' to demonstrate how the body and embodied experience are antecedent to communication.

Mara Mattoscio's '"The interstices of her sense of something": David Foster Wallace, the quest for affect, and the future of gendered interactions' offers a feminist reading of affect theory that takes Lauren Berlant's notion of 'cruel optimism' as its point of departure. Mattoscio focuses on two short stories as key texts for exploring Wallace's interest in gendered and sexed relationships: 'Datum Centurio' and 'Octet', both from *Brief Interviews with Hideous Men*. Both texts are read as explorations of 'the socio-structural nature of affects' and of what Mattoscio dubs Wallace's 'wry pessimism'. Mattoscio understands these texts as presenting Wallace's invitation to the readers 'to "invest" in their own structural affective inadequacies in attempt to track apparently irretrievable emotions down in the "interstices" of our gender-constrained world'.

In '"You are loved": race, love, and language in early Wallace', Lola Boorman offers a much-needed reflection on how the pervasive references to love and communication in Wallace's work (and corresponding scholarship) are shaped and transformed when race enters the conversation. The primary texts that Boorman considers, and which should be viewed as just the first stage of a reflection worth further expanding, are 'Girl with Curious Hair' and *Signifying Rappers*. Analysis of these early texts paves the way for us to understand Wallace as espousing 'a model of political consensus and universality in his later writing'. Boorman first reflects on Wallace's employment of race 'to develop a logic of distance and separation' in 'Girl with Curious Hair' and 'Lyndon', via James Baldwin's take on love in *The Fire Next Time*. She then maps Wallace's transition to a more profound awareness of 'the limitation of his exploration of difference in his early writing' in *Signifying Rappers*.

Chiara Scarlato proposes an intriguing reflection on pornography – a rather pervasive theme in Wallace's work. The chapter argues that Wallace uses the addictive and entertaining practice of viewing pornography as a sort of reverse mirror that allows him to reflect on another, more authentic form of intimacy between author and reader: what Scarlato dubs 'anti-Entertainment' and contends is Wallace's antidote to solitude. '"They remain just bodies": on pornography in David Foster Wallace (1989–2006)' traces this thread by making reference to archival documents concerning Wallace's unpublished 1989 commissioned piece for *Playboy*, fictional works – namely *Infinite Jest* and the two stories 'Adult World (I)' and 'Adult World (II)' – and the non-fictional essay 'Big Red Son'.

Angelo Grossi's '"Something staring back at you": an anamorphic reading of *Infinite Jest*', which closes the third part and thereby the volume, reflects on how Wallace's novel 'thematizes a radical questioning of the philosophical dualities implied in the Cartesian subject by evoking two rival models of modern visuality – Renaissance perspectivalism and the baroque'. According to Grossi, Wallace mobilizes baroque visual rhetoric both thematically and formally to disrupt the utilitarian liberal ideology that dominates the novel. To explain this mobilization Grossi turns to Lacan's mature concept of the gaze, highlighting how it resonates with Wallace's blurring of the boundaries between the autonomous (liberal) subject and (passive, inert) object.

Notes

1 For a classical analysis of the various dimensions relating to discursive practices see Foucault, 1972. Therein Foucault presents a crucial analysis of 'the system of emergence of objects, the system of the appearance and distribution of enunciative modes, the system of the placing and dispersion of concepts, the system of the deployment of strategic choices' (79).

2 For another nuanced and comprehensive attempt to work in this vein – though one still recognizably rooted in the approaches of analytical philosophy – see, for example, Lamarque, 2009.

References

Derrida, J. (1995). *On the Name*. Stanford CA: Stanford University Press.
Foucault, M. (1972). *The Archeology of Knowledge & The Discourse on Language*. New York NY: Pantheon Books.
Lamarque, P. (2009). *The Philosophy of Literature*. Oxford: Blackwell.
Lipsky, D. (2010). *Although of Course You End Up Becoming Yourself: A Road Trip with David Foster Wallace*. New York NY: Broadway Books.
McCaffery, L. (2012). 'An Expanded Interview with David Foster Wallace', 21–57. In Stephen J. Burn ed., *Conversations with David Foster Wallace*. Jackson MS: University of Mississippi Press.
Moi, T. (2011). 'The Adventure of Reading: Literature and Philosophy, Cavell and Beauvoir', in *Literature & Theology* 25:2, 125–40.
Wallace, D. Foster. (1997). *A Supposedly Fun Thing I'll Never Do Again: Essays and Arguments*. New York NY: Back Bay Books.
Wittgenstein, L. (1998). *Culture and Value. A Selection from the Posthumous Remains*, ed. G. H. von Wright. Oxford: Blackwell.

PART I

General perspectives

1

Absorbing art: the Hegelian project of *Infinite Jest*

Adam Kelly

Heads, bodies, minds, and words

'I am seated in an office, surrounded by heads and bodies' (Wallace, 1996: 3). Thus begins *Infinite Jest* in the perspective of Hal Incandenza, the 18-year-old protagonist we encounter being interviewed for admission to the University of Arizona on a tennis scholarship. That we first find Hal amid 'heads and bodies' rather than among 'people' is an immediate signal that something is wrong. Some vital connection between the outer appearance of others and the intimation of their inner human lives has become opaque to Hal. Moreover it seems that Hal's inner life may be equally opaque to others: 'I am in here', runs the famous assertion, rather odd and desperate, that constitutes the whole of the novel's second paragraph (3). As the interview progresses, we witness Hal endeavouring to 'appear neutral', not attempting 'what would feel to me like a pleasant expression or smile', and leaving the talking to those present to support him (3). Hal's tennis prowess is undoubted and his academic track record has been 'off the charts' (6). But following recent test scores that one interviewer describes as 'subnormal', the admissions panel wants, understandably, to hear an explanation from the boy they are planning to admit (3). And so, as his silence becomes ever more excruciating and with his supporters banished from the room, Hal is left with little option but to speak. When he finally does so, among the first things he tells the panel is the following:

> 'I am not just a boy who plays tennis. I have an intricate history. Experiences and feelings. I'm complex. I *read*. ... I'm not a machine. I feel and believe. I have opinions. Some of them are interesting. I could, if you'd let me, talk and talk. Let's talk about anything. I believe the influence of Kierkegaard on Camus is underestimated. I believe Dennis Gabor may very well have been the Antichrist. I believe Hobbes is just Rousseau in a dark mirror. I believe, with Hegel, that transcendence is absorption.' (11–12)

Hal tries to convince his interviewers of his 'intricate' and 'complex' inner life by declaring his beliefs about some of the most famous figures in the history of philosophy.[1] Of these figures, scholars have already established the importance to Wallace of Søren Kierkegaard and Albert Camus, two major existentialist thinkers (Boswell, 2003: 137–45; Den Dulk, 2015). Thomas Hobbes and Jean-Jacques Rousseau, two renowned political philosophers, have not yet featured so prominently in Wallace criticism, but one can surmise that their conjoining here points to their shared status as philosophers of the social contract. This was a political philosophy that the last-named figure, Georg Wilhelm Friedrich Hegel, explicitly aimed to move beyond. With his philosophy of unfolding Spirit or *Geist* – his term for the realization of self-conscious freedom in human ideas, norms, and practices – Hegel set out to describe the conditions necessary for the historical reconciliation between subject and object, self and other, inner and outer worlds. It is precisely this set of oppositions that the opening scene of *Infinite Jest* presents in a state not of reconciliation but of stark contradiction.

While his role in Wallace scholarship has to date been minimal, Hegel will be a central figure in the present chapter.[2] I will argue that reading Wallace's fiction 'between philosophy and literature', as this collection seeks to do, means passing through Hegel, whose science of logic and philosophy of history provide an alternative route to the 'deep necessity' that Wallace initially sought in analytic logic and math (Chodat, 2017: 244), and whose phenomenology posits an essential role for aesthetic expression in the progression of *Geist*. Joining a chorus of scholars, Robert Chodat observes that Wallace's turn away from 'the visionless medium of logic and mathematics' led him to embrace the later Wittgenstein (246). While I do not dispute this well-established fact, I maintain that Hegel stands as a key communitarian predecessor for what Chodat (following John Haugeland) calls Wallace's 'socialist phenomenology' (259) – his representation of humans as always already existing in a norm-based relation to one another. Moreover I argue that Hegelian thought offers a highly fruitful approach to the specific role that aesthetic concerns play in Wallace's philosophical fiction. Although Wallace did engage with Hegel, my explication does not depend on that engagement; rather I introduce Hegelian categories as a way to clarify some of the key aesthetic principles and effects of *Infinite Jest*.

The chapter thus sets out from the phrase Hal attributes to Hegel: 'transcendence is absorption'. I focus particularly on the term *absorption*, which I contend is both a keyword in *Infinite Jest* and an important principle in Wallace's broader aesthetic project. That project has been understood, by me and others, in close relation to the idea of sincerity, and this chapter offers an account of why Wallace saw sincerity as a *social achievement* that required a new *aesthetic form* – rather than viewing it simply as a voluntaristic ethos of individual being, speech, or action (a common interpretation of Lionel Trilling's canonical definition of sincerity as 'a congruence between avowal and actual feeling' (in Trilling, 1972: 2)). The social and aesthetic crisis of sincerity that Wallace perceived as characterizing his own time – an analysis he laid out most forcefully in the *Infinite Jest*-era essays 'E Unibus Pluram: Television and U.S. Fiction' (Wallace, 1997: 21–82) and 'Joseph Frank's Dostoevsky' (Wallace, 2005: 255–74) – is a crisis that his major novel aims to identify, represent, and move towards resolving. *Infinite Jest* thus harbours ambitions to fulfil for its historical moment the role Hegel attributed to Greek tragic drama, the historical emergence of which he considered a sign 'that a great crisis in the basic institutions of that society had arisen and could not be resolved' (Pippin, 2014: 34). In Wallace's case absorption offered a thematic and formal principle through which to seek a resolution of the sincerity crisis. In the chapter's second section I turn to the relationship between art and absorption, engaging the work of the Hegelian art historian Michael Fried in order to think about absorption's history as well as its pros and cons as an aesthetic ideal. In the third section I examine how absorptive themes play out in *Infinite Jest*'s presentation of the work of the book's primary artist figure, Hal's father James Incandenza. I read Incandenza's filmography as an oscillating engagement with absorption that tries (and fails) to employ absorptive techniques in service of an art of sincere communication. This description makes evident the connection to Wallace's own project, and in the chapter's final section I offer a close reading of one particular Incandenza film – more precisely, one character's viewing of that film – that I argue provides the closest thing in *Infinite Jest* to a model for what sincere artistic communication looks like. This model in turn presents a potential basis for the reconciliation – for the reader, if not for Hal Incandenza – of the contradictions presented in the novel's opening scene.

'I believe, with Hegel, that transcendence is absorption', Hal says aloud in that opening scene (Wallace, 1996: 12). Or does he? Before analysing the meaning of this phrase, we must observe that, at this precise moment, the scene's most striking contradiction is revealed, as we learn that the words we are reading in Hal's voice are not what his interviewers hear. '*Sub*animalistic noises and sounds' (14) are what they profess to have heard instead, while what they see is something horrifying: 'I look out. Directed my way is horror. I rise from the chair. I see jowls sagging, eyebrows high on trembling foreheads, cheeks bright-white' (12). The first-person monologue we have been reading as Hal's speech to the panel is suddenly shown to bear no relation to the 'vision of hell' these men claim to behold (14). Like his forebear Prince Hamlet, Hal Incandenza evidently has that within which passeth show, but the creeping madness that others observe in Hamlet has here been scaled up to the level of a full-blown crisis in presentation and communication, summarized by Hal's repeated remark 'I cannot make myself understood' (10).

Critics have offered a number of narrative explanations for Hal's communicative crisis at the beginning of *Infinite Jest*, the scene that in fact occurs chronologically latest in the novel. Hal's inability to make himself understood might be due to his withdrawal from marijuana, a painful process we witness through many of the novel's closing scenes. It might be a severe manifestation of his escalating depression, equally evident over these final pages. It might be the result of his ingestion of 'the incredibly potent DMZ', a drug with effects that are described as 'almost ontological' (170). The crisis might even stem from Hal's exposure to the film cartridge 'Infinite

Jest' at the hands of the Quebecois terrorists who are on the verge of capturing him at the end of the novel.[3] 'Infinite Jest', colloquially known as 'The Entertainment', is a film so absorbing that no one who views it can turn it off or turn away. And this description highlights the connection among all these plot possibilities: their shared reliance on the trope of absorption. Marijuana and DMZ are substances absorbed by the subject, with the consequence that the subject loses touch with the objective world. Clinical depression, as represented not only in Hal but even more powerfully in the figure of Kate Gompert, is characterized in the novel by acute absorption in the self rather than the world. Conversely, exposure to 'Infinite Jest' leads not to self-absorption but to absorption wholly in the object, to the radical extent of complete self-forgetting. Absorption in all these forms heralds a crisis in the relationship of subject to object: at one extreme, complete absorption in the subject; at the other, complete absorption in the object, with no mediation between the two. Subsequent appearances of the word 'absorption' in the novel seem only to underscore its association with damagingly polarized states of being.[4] With this in mind, to believe that 'transcendence is absorption' looks like a serious error on Hal's part – absorption would appear to equate not to transcendence of the contradictions in the opening scene but rather to their deepening. Yet Wallace's novel will in fact be driven by the project of reclaiming and redeeming absorption – in a form I will term *refractive absorption* – as a positive and potentially transformative force.[5]

As Hal intuits, Hegelian thought is the key to this project of reclaiming and redeeming absorption. Hegel's signature term *Aufhebung*, usually rendered in English as 'sublation', has also on occasion been translated as both 'transcendence' and 'absorption' and contains both of these elements as 'moments' within it. Hence the phrase 'transcendence is absorption' gestures most obviously to Hegel's dialectical story of unfolding *Geist* – a story in which the contradiction between two concepts or states is transcended through their absorption into a synthesis, with the concepts or states preserved but their polarity overcome. Without this movement of transcendence through absorption, we are left only with polarized stasis, and with a failure in what the Hegel scholar Robert B. Pippin calls 'the conditions of social subjectivity necessary for mutual intelligibility' (2014: 29). But how is the stasis to be overcome? How are the conditions of mutual intelligibility to be discovered? One answer that Hegel offers is the answer Wallace pursues: the overcoming and discovery can happen through the mediation of art.

Dubbed 'the father of art history' by the leading twentieth-century art historian E. H. Gombrich, Hegel's story of the development of art emphasizes how it traces and contributes to the coming to self-consciousness of *Geist*. 'Things in nature are only immediate and single', Hegel writes in the *Aesthetics*, 'while man as *Geist* duplicates himself, in that (i) he is as things in nature are, but (ii) he is just as much for himself; he sees himself, represents himself to himself, thinks, and only on the strength of this active placing himself before himself is he *Geist*' (Hegel, 1975: 30–1). As Pippin explains, man's [sic] need to represent himself in order to understand himself means that 'there is a deep connection between understanding meaningful conduct, actions, and expressions of persons and understanding expressive meaning in artworks' (Pippin, 2014: 49). In each case – the carrying out of an action, the speaking of words, or the creation of a work of art – the animating 'inner' intention can be understood only retroactively through the 'outer' deed or work itself, and then only in a context of broader communal recognition. What I intend to do, say, or make is inextricable from the social interpretation of my deed, words, or work.[6] Unless this social interpretation can be entirely predicted in advance, a gap or uncertainty will remain in the connection between intention and deed. In the case of *Infinite Jest*'s opening scene, more than any contingent plot development (depression, drug use, film watching) it is the symbolic failure to bridge the gap between inner intention and outer deed – owing to a dearth in 'the conditions of social subjectivity necessary for mutual intelligibility' – that accounts for Hal's communicative crisis.

In Hegel's modernity art becomes the model for what a realized intention looks like, and a successful artwork achieves a special status 'as the achievement of a speculative identity of inner and outer' (21). This grants art a powerful historical role, because it means that 'the externalization of our ideas about ourselves in artworks is essential, not merely exemplifying' (41). This new view of art prepared the ground for a shift in the arts themselves away from a primary concern with beauty – the imitation of natural or classical models – towards an overriding concern with meaning.[7] While Romantic artists were inspired by these ideas, it was modernist art – created against the background of disintegrating social values and discredited grand narratives – that began to require from its beholders a kind of interpretation and judgement that – as Kant as well as Hegel had argued – could be rendered only in response to an aesthetic work. *Infinite Jest*, a fractured work created in a fractured modernity, sets out to elicit aesthetic judgement of this kind by means of the trope of absorption.

Hegel's treatment of the thematic and instrumental role of absorption in the story of man's 'represent[ing] himself to himself' in art emphasizes two dimensions: absorption's expression in the content of an artwork and in the relationship of the artist to their work.[8] *Infinite Jest*, by contrast, is most interested in the theme of absorption with regard to the *reader* of literature or *beholder* of art. It is through its treatment of absorption in this sense that the novel attempts to address Hal's symptomatic crisis and to set out its own aesthetic and ethical project to overcome the contradictions of its moment and restart the stalled historical dialectic.[9] In the second half of this chapter we will see the project of aesthetic absorption critically framed through the films of Hal's father, James Incandenza. But first we must ask some basic questions that bear upon the relation between artistic practice and readerly absorption. What does it mean to create an absorbing work of art? What might be the risks and opportunities in doing so? What aesthetic techniques serve the ends of absorption? And how might the absorptive aesthetics of a novel like *Infinite Jest* relate to its project to heal the divisions between subject and object, inner and outer, self and world?

Absorbing art

In approaching questions like these I have found it useful to turn away from the traditions of literary criticism – in which readerly absorption has generally been considered only through its interruption, for instance in the alienating devices of Brechtian theatre or postmodernist meta-fiction – and towards scholarship on the visual arts. In a series of studies beginning with his now-classic 1980 book *Absorption and Theatricality: Painting and Beholder in the Age of Diderot*, the art critic and historian Michael Fried uses the term *absorption* to describe an ideal relation between an artwork and its beholder. Fried's initial thesis, briefly summarized, is that in French painting of the 1750s and 1760s there emerged, simultaneously and in combination, a *practical* concern with the representation of states of absorption and a *theoretical* concern with the status of the beholder. Fried reads a wide array of paintings through the comments about them made by critics at the time; employing this historicist method, he shows that painters like Chardin and Greuze, along with critics like Diderot, promoted an 'anti-theatrical' aesthetics which 'treated the beholder as if he were not there' (Fried, 1980: 4). In Diderot's criticism, any implicit acknowledgement of the beholder represented a theatrical appeal for his or her attention, which had the converse effect of weakening the painting's hold on the beholder and therefore its aesthetic self-sufficiency as a painting. The converse goal of anti-theatricality was initially served by Chardin and Greuze depicting figures fully absorbed in their daily lives and seemingly unaware of the beholder standing before the painting. As French painting developed over the following century, major artists including David, Géricault, Courbet, and Manet, all forced to confront 'the primordial convention that paintings are made to be beheld' (93, 157, 178), could continue to defeat theatricality only by turning to ever more elaborate and complex techniques. Fried's subsequent works then trace 'the dialectical vicissitudes and modifications of the Diderotian paradigm up through its abandonment or rather its radical reconfiguration in the art of Manet and his generation' in the 1860s, at which point we have reached the dawn of modernist art (Fried, 2010: 2).

Although not always explicitly framed in this manner by Fried, his story about eighteenth- and nineteenth-century French painting intersects significantly with two contemporaneous strands of European thought and culture: the growing worries in romantic circles concerning the (in)sincerity and (in)authenticity of life in modern societies; and the development of aesthetic theory in the German Idealism of Kant, Schelling, and Hegel. In the Romantic tradition, represented by figures including Diderot and Rousseau, the notion of absorption was understood normatively as an authentic identification with one's social role or activity, whereas theatricality 'would be to act without such identification, to perform an activity controlled and directed by an anticipation of what others expect to occur, as when subjects are posed in a painting in classic poses assumed to connote heroism or fidelity' (Pippin, 2005: 578). Meanwhile the normative underpinnings of German aesthetic theory – its concern with the truth or falsity of artworks as models for social being – are brought out by statements such as the following from Hegel's *Aesthetics*, which, though it does not employ the word 'absorption' with respect to the relationship between artwork and beholder, is nonetheless concerned with outlining in proto-Friedian terms what that relationship should ideally look like:

> Producing effects is in general the dominating tendency of turning to the public, so that the work of art no longer displays itself as peaceful, satisfied in itself, and serene; on the contrary, it turns inside out and as it were makes an appeal to the spectator that tries to put itself into relation with him by means of the mode of portrayal. Both, peace in itself and turning to the onlooker, must indeed be present in the work of art, but the two sides must be in the purest equilibrium. If the work of art in the severe style is entirely shut in upon itself without wishing to speak to a spectator, it leaves us cold; but if it goes too far out of itself to him, it pleases but is without solidity or at least does not please (as it should) by solidity of content and the simple treatment and presentation of that content. (Hegel, 1975: 619)

In *Infinite Jest* the film career of James Incandenza will display this oscillation between work that is 'entirely shut in upon itself without wishing to speak to a spectator' and work that 'goes too far out of itself' in order to entertain and please (alongside a third mode, an aggressive attempt to dominate the audience). Wallace's detailed representation of Incandenza's artistic output can therefore be read productively with regard to this Diderotian-Hegelian-Friedian aesthetic model of absorption, theatricality, sincerity, and authenticity. It should simultaneously be read, however, against the historical background of Wallace's own emergence as a writer and, in particular, his relation to postmodernist aesthetics. And here Fried's example is again helpful.

Like Wallace, Fried emerged to public consciousness with an eye-catching critique of postmodernism, albeit one articulated at the dawn of postmodernism's reign rather than (as in Wallace's case) at its moment of eclipse. Fried's 1967 article 'Art and Objecthood' defended the American modernist colour field painting of Morris Louis, Jules Olitski, and Frank Stella against the emerging minimalist (Fried calls it literalist) sculpture of figures like Tony Smith, Robert

Morris, and Donald Judd. These sculptors saw painting 'as an art on the verge of exhaustion' and in their own artistic practice placed new emphasis on 'presence', 'experience', 'situation', and 'objecthood', repositioning the ontological basis of the artwork in the beholder's experience rather than in the artist's manipulation of his medium (Fried, 1998: 149). This literalist espousal of objecthood and concomitant privileging of the beholder 'amounts to nothing other than a plea for a new genre of theater', Fried writes, 'and theater is now the negation of art' (153).

As has been well established by scholars, the reader's experience is importantly privileged in Wallace's fiction, and in a manner that would seem overtly 'theatrical'. Yet this apparent theatricality (in the sense of appealing directly to the reader) is in fact undertaken to the end of defeating theatricality (in the sense of artistic inauthenticity). This gives Wallace a position in the development of twentieth-century American fiction equivalent to the one Edouard Manet holds in Fried's narrative of eighteenth- and nineteenth-century French painting. For Fried the century-long anti-theatrical battle to sustain 'the fiction of the beholder's nonexistence' came to necessitate a completely new approach, which involved Manet painting figures looking out of the painting towards the beholder, yet without making a wholly intelligible appeal to the beholder (Fried, 1980: 153). Fried calls this Manet's 'facingness' technique, and it saw him 'systematically avoid or subvert absorptive or potentially absorptive motifs' in the service of interrogating (rather than appealing to) the beholder (Fried, 1996: 405). American modernist painting took up this tradition of interrogation, Fried believed, whereas in minimalist sculpture the mode of interrogation was replaced by the mode of appeal. Which is to say that Fried saw postmodernism, as it would come to be called, as an historical error – a sacrifice of the principles of aesthetic conviction and autonomy to the ends of flattering the views and sensibility of the beholder.

Wallace, by contrast, saw postmodernism as a historical necessity: a salutary engagement with its time, and therefore a paradigm that needed to be overcome rather than ignored or reversed. If postmodernism had become 'theatrical', it had not started out that way but rather had failed to develop sufficiently in response to subsequent developments, primarily the incorporation of ironic modes of communication into contemporary television and advertising alongside the increasing commercialization of everyday life. This is the argument of 'E Unibus Pluram', an essay that culminates by calling for a 'weird bunch of *anti-rebels*' who would ameliorate the situation by risking the appearance of outdatedness in their writing: 'Dead on the page. Too sincere. Clearly repressed. Backward, quaint, naïve, anachronistic' (Wallace, 1997: 81). These renowned lines risk making the problem of creating new art after postmodernism sound simply like a question of ethos or attitude, of the willingness to return to past models in the service of 'single-entendre principles'. As I am not the first to point out, however, the relative simplicity of this message contrasts with the vast complexity and highly wrought technical sophistication of *Infinite Jest* and Wallace's later fiction. The reason for this contrast between medium and message is that, in Hegelian terms, the achievement of sincerity in contemporary art has to pass through complexity in order to attain the recognition it requires to be itself. In a complex world in which 'the conditions of social subjectivity necessary for mutual intelligibility' (Pippin, 2014: 29) are uncertainly available, sincerity cannot know itself without such recognition, and the artist must address his or her audience as a partner in the search for certainty and meaning. This requires a rethinking and reworking not only of theatricality but of absorption too – something that becomes clear in the novel's presentation of other artworks, most notably the films made by Hal's father, Professor James O. Incandenza, Jr.

The medium is the message

Judged according to the qualities Wallace regularly called for in contemporary art – passion, communication, intimacy, sincerity – the work of James Incandenza would seem to constitute a rather spectacular failure, and critics have uniformly regarded it as such. In keeping with his initial description as 'tall, ungainly, socially challenged and hard-drinking', Incandenza – whose suicide precedes the main action of *Infinite Jest* by approximately five years – is depicted as silent and withdrawn during his few appearances in flashback scenes from the narrative present (Wallace, 1996: 64). Marshall Boswell describes him as 'a cold, closed figure with serious paternal resentment, a man who has been trained to hide his emotions behind cold logic and surface objectivity', and goes on to claim that 'his films seamlessly reflect these psychological defenses' (Boswell, 2003: 162). Based on 'JAMES O. INCANDENZA: A FILMOGRAPHY' (Wallace, 1996: 985 n24), the eight-and-a-half-page endnote that reads, as Boswell avers, like 'an extended parody of the postmodern canon' (Boswell, 2003: 162), it would be difficult to argue with this assessment of the films and the filmmaker. Yet it is also true, as Mary Shapiro has observed, that the progression of the filmography 'tells the only story that serves to illuminate the circumstances directly leading to Incandenza's suicide' (Shapiro, 2020: 26), with the films moving from 'serious attempts to understand the world, particularly through experiments in optics', to 'increasingly autobiographical attempts to understand only his own life' (27). And it is likewise true, as David Hering notes, that the descriptions in the filmography – often collated from dubious sources and harbouring critical intent – do not always match up with the way the films are described ekphrastically in the main text of the novel (Hering, 2016: 104).

Taking both the filmography and ekphrastic textual descriptions into account, Incandenza's output can be said to oscillate among a number of modes, ranging from relatively realist early-career documentaries to work (such as the *Found Drama* series) that appears to be, in Hegel's phrase cited earlier, 'entirely shut in upon itself without wishing to speak to a spectator'. More common in Incandenza's oeuvre are films that address the viewer in a heavily theatrical manner, but not in a way that achieves the Hegelian ideal of art as 'a subject-subject relation, not some sort of subject-object relation' (Pippin, 2014: 86). The achievement of a sincere 'subject-subject relation' in art is always under threat: 'if "theatricalized"', Pippin adds, 'that social relation is presented either in terms of submission to a collective subjectivity (in effect a self-objectification or an internalization of what "they" want) or as an attempt by the artist to dominate or overwhelm and so objectify the artwork's audience' (87). Thus in genre works by Incandenza such as *Very Low Impact* and *Blood Sister: One Tough Nun* we get submission to the norms of entertainment and the desires of the audience, 'an internalization of what "they" want'. And in films like *The Joke*, *The Medusa vs. the Odalisque*, and *Cage III – Free Show*, we see an aggressive attempt to dominate, overwhelm, and objectify the audience of the film (often by depicting them *in* the film).

Incandenza's life and film career end with his sixth and final attempt to make 'Infinite Jest', the cartridge that will surface as the lethal 'Entertainment'. As Lee Konstantinou has observed, 'The Entertainment' is not only (as its nickname suggests) 'the ultimate expression of the recursive logic of U.S. consumer culture' (2016: 187); it is also an über-experimental work that accomplishes the historical avant-garde's mission 'to end art as an institution and to break down the barriers ... that prevent art from changing consciousness' (188). In the Friedian terms set out above, 'Infinite Jest' is both intensely theatrical and intensely absorptive. On the one hand, it is difficult to imagine a work more clearly designed to appeal to the subjectivity of its beholder, given that it has been created for a single beholder, Incandenza's son Hal, as 'a magically entertaining toy to dangle at the infant son still somewhere alive in the boy, to make its eyes light and toothless mouth open unconsciously, to laugh' (Wallace, 1996: 839). On the other hand, 'Infinite Jest' is wholly absorptive: indeed, its capacity to absorb is so extreme that no one who sees it can ever become unabsorbed again. Such lethal absorption was far from Incandenza's aim in making the film, which was – he professes late in the novel in his posthumous incarnation as the wraith – 'to contrive a medium via which he and the muted son could simply *converse*' (838). While Wallace italicises the final word of this line, '*converse*' – an emphasis which is in keeping with his vision of art as communication – I want to suggest that it is equally crucial that Incandenza envisages this act of conversation as requiring a new 'medium'. If a new medium proves necessary for 'Infinite Jest' the film/post-film, then it raises a larger question for *Infinite Jest* the novel: might it be that for an artwork to heal the divisions between subject and object, self and other, inner and outer worlds, a new medium will have to be contrived to achieve that purpose?

Here Wallace's invocation of the avant-garde is indeed of equal importance to his more widely noted critique of the entertainment industry. Yet while Konstantinou is right to see 'Infinite Jest' in relation to the aims of the historical (i.e. early) avant-garde, I would argue that of even more relevance for Wallace is what avant-garde art became after it had been widely acknowledged institutionally as the leading edge of artistic practice. In the most canonical accounts of the avant-garde, beginning with Clement Greenberg's landmark

1939 essay 'Avant-Garde and Kitsch', the movement emerged in nineteenth-century Europe in response to the decay of bourgeois society and 'the first bold development of scientific revolutionary thought' (i.e. Marxism). It then turned away, in the twentieth century, from 'subject-matter or common experience' towards 'pure' preoccupation with the medium of each particular art form (Greenberg, 2000a: 49, 50). In Greenberg's view this development was justified by the fact that, in a society still capitalist rather than socialist, 'by no other means is it possible today to create art and literature of a high order' (51). In Greenberg's later writing the focus on capitalism dropped away, and heightened attention to medium became the only means of sincere art-making. With Romanticism artistic sincerity had been envisaged as a direct communication of sentiment, so that 'the medium was a regrettable if necessary physical obstacle between the artist and the audience, which in some ideal state would disappear entirely to leave the experience of the spectator or reader identical with that of the artist' (Greenberg, 2000b: 62). By contrast – and in line with Hegel's counter-Romantic emphasis on mediation – modernist sincerity came to mean formalism: in an age when 'the conditions of social subjectivity necessary for mutual intelligibility' (Pippin, 2014: 29) were breaking down, the medium turned out to be the one thing an artist could successfully *mean*. In his *Aesthetics* Hegel writes that 'the work of art stands in the middle between immediate sensuousness and ideal thought. It is not yet pure thought, but, despite its sensuousness, it is no longer a purely material existent either' (Hegel, 1975: 38). For modernist critics like Greenberg and Fried it was precisely from this 'medium' position between ideality and materiality that avant-garde art could do its absorptive work. The downside, as thinkers such as Pierre Bourdieu and Stanley Cavell have acknowledged in different ways, is that avant-garde art becomes 'a field of restricted production' (Bourdieu, 1993: 115) in which 'artist and audience are out of touch' (Cavell, 2002: 185), with fewer and fewer potential beholders knowing enough about these media to be absorbed in modern art.

James Incandenza is described in *Infinite Jest* as an 'après-garde' artist. Beyond the evident humour of this phrase, it throws an interesting light on his attempts to 'contrive a medium', since it suggests that neither the avant-garde project of medium-specific absorption nor the postmodernist embrace of intermedial theatricality will be sufficient to achieve his communicative goals, including the attempt to reach his son Hal. It is important, I would argue, to take those goals seriously: rather than interpret Incandenza's output as simply indexing his biographical weaknesses and failures, we should see the filmmaker as facing a parallel conundrum to Wallace – the question of how to communicate sincerely in an increasingly complex world and at a highly fraught aesthetic conjuncture. To pursue the implications of this parallel between the two artists, the final section of this chapter will concentrate on a single film from the Incandenza oeuvre, one whose effects are likely to come as close as possible to those of 'The Entertainment' (the content and form of which cannot be analysed in detail, because it cannot be viewed without an experience of absorption that destroys the possibility of critical detachment). This comparison seems appropriate because the film in question – Incandenza's mid-career *Pre-Nuptial Agreement of Heaven and Hell* – features at its heart a work of sculpture at which, according to the historian Simon Schama, 'we stare and stare ... as we stare at no other sculpture ever made' (Schama, 2009: 125).

The ecstasy of refractive absorption

The sculpture in question is *The Ecstasy of St Teresa*, completed in 1652 by the Italian artist Gianlorenzo Bernini. Held in the Cornaro Chapel in Rome's Santa Maria della Vittoria, the baroque altarpiece depicts the moment when God penetrated Teresa of Ávila through the intercession of an angel with a golden spear. In her diary the nun recalled this moment in vivid terms: 'The sweetness of this intense pain is so extreme that there is no wanting it to end' (qtd in Schama, 2009: 114). Expressing this intensity in sculptural form, *The Ecstasy of St Teresa* has gone on to become one of the most celebrated works in the history of art. Yet its inescapable power has not protected Bernini from the criticism of later artists and critics. As Schama recounts of the altarpiece: 'It's magic. And that was precisely why, after his death, Bernini would be attacked by artists such as Sir Joshua Reynolds for being a cheap sorcerer, a specialist in theatrical trickery, who – for the sake of wowing the worshipper – had, unlike Michelangelo, debased the purity of his chosen material' (81–2). In emphasizing the beholder's experience over the purity of its subject matter and medium, *The Ecstasy of St Teresa* constitutes, in Michael Fried's terms, an eminently theatrical artwork.[10] And not only in Fried's terms: in her book *Bernini: Art as Theatre* (2013) Genevieve Warwick shows how Bernini's engagements with the Roman theatre – including writing and acting in plays – shaped his now more celebrated work in sculpture. Schama comments on this theatricality in its connection with the beholder's experience of Bernini's earlier *David*. 'There's never a time when Bernini isn't conscious of the spectator, who becomes not just a silent starer, but an actively engaged participant, moving around the piece and seeing it work in different ways from different perspectives', he writes. 'Centuries on, this understanding of sculpture as presenting not one but multiple images to us, each in a state of mutating motion as we move about it, might seem a truism; but in the 1620s it broke all previous conventions. Bernini had discovered a way to make marble movies' (Schama 2009: 92).

This invocation of the 'marble movie' returns us to *Infinite Jest*. *The Ecstasy of St Teresa* appears in Wallace's novel at four points, three of which have to do with the sculpture's role in Incandenza's *Pre-Nuptial Agreement of Heaven and Hell*. In the filmography endnote the plot of *Pre-Nuptial Agreement* is described as follows: 'God and Satan play poker with Tarot cards for the soul of an alcoholic sandwich-bag salesman obsessed with Bernini's "The Ecstasy of St. Teresa"' (Wallace, 1996: 988 n24). In the main text of the novel the sculpture is discussed twice from the point of view of Joelle van Dyne. The first time Joelle is freebasing cocaine and her experience is narrated thus:

> The 'base frees and condenses, compresses the whole experience to the implosion of one terrible shattering spike in the graph, an afflated orgasm of the heart that makes her feel, truly, *attractive*, sheltered by limits, deveiled and loved, observed and alone and sufficient and female, full, as if watched for an instant by God. She always sees, after inhaling, right at the apex, at the graph's spike's tip, Bernini's 'Ecstasy of St. Teresa', behind glass, at the Vittoria, for some reason, the saint recumbent, half-supine, her flowing stone robe lifted by the angel in whose other hand a bare arrow is raised for that best descent, the saint's legs frozen in opening, the angel's expression not charity but the perfect vice of barb-headed love. (235)

Absorbing art 35

Figure 1.1 Gianlorenzo Bernini, *The Ecstasy of St Teresa*, Santa Maria della Vittoria, Rome.
Photograph by Dnalor 01 (19 March 2005). Wikimedia Commons.
CC BY-SA 4.0

Joelle – who is the university girlfriend of Incandenza's son Orin and gets nicknamed the P.G.O.A.T. ('Prettiest Girl of All Time') by his peers – wears a veil in the novel, her face having reportedly been accidentally disfigured by acid thrown in rage at her father by her mother. Joelle's cocaine high in this scene restores her beauty not as the isolating factor it had formerly been (her 'almost grotesquely lovely' quality left her 'almost universally shunned' (Wallace, 1996: 290)) but as a source of fullness, of Godlike attention and love. The feeling is paradoxical – she feels simultaneously 'observed and alone' – and so intensely sweet and painful that it suggests comparison with St Teresa's ecstatic encounter. That encounter is rendered at the culmination of the passage through a dense and provocative ekphrastic description that emphasizes a phallic quality in the 'bare' and 'barb-headed' arrow brandished by the angel, a heavily eroticized Cupid figure.

At this point in the novel the reader might not connect Joelle's drug-fuelled vision of Bernini's sculpture with its role in Incandenza's filmmaking – after all, the two references have appeared in unrelated scenes many pages apart, and Incandenza's art is generally presented, as we have heard, as cold, distant, and unerotic. Much later, however, we discover that Joelle's knowledge of *The Ecstasy of St Teresa* has developed (and may even have begun) through her viewing of *Pre-Nuptial Agreement of Heaven and Hell*. This information arrives in a passage when Joelle is thinking through Incandenza's films and how she saw in their surface coldness 'flashes of something. Very hidden and quick. Almost furtive' (Wallace, 1996: 741). These 'flashes' are then explored in a lengthy passage that describes Joelle's viewing of *Pre-Nuptial Agreement*, a passage in which Bernini's sculpture appears in the novel for the final and most substantial time:

> But it wasn't even the subjective identification she felt, watching, she felt, somehow, for the flashes and seeming non-seqs that betrayed something more than cold hip technical abstraction. Like e.g. the 240-second motionless low-angle shot of Gianlorenzo Bernini's 'Ecstasy of St. Teresa', which – yes – ground *Pre-Nuptial ...*'s dramatic movement to an annoying halt and added nothing that a 15- or 30-second still shot wouldn't have added just as well; but on the fifth or sixth reviewing Joelle started to see the four-minute motionless shot as important for what was absent: the whole film was from the alcoholic sandwich-bag salesman's POV, and the alcoholic sandwich-bag salesman – or rather his head – was on-screen every moment ... except for the four narrative minutes the alcoholic sandwich-bag salesman stood in the Vittorio's [sic] Bernini room, and the climactic statue filled the screen and pressed against all four edges. (742)

Joelle's understanding of what this shot signifies is explained as the passage continues:

> The statue, the sensuous presence of the thing, let the alcoholic sandwich-bag salesman escape himself, his tiresome ubiquitous involuted head, she saw, was the thing. The four-minute still shot maybe wasn't just a heavy-art gesture or audience-hostile herring.

> Freedom from one's own head, one's inescapable P.O.V. – Joelle started to see here, oblique to the point of being hidden, an emotional thrust, since the mediated transcendence of self was just what the apparently decadent statue of the orgasmic nun claimed for itself as subject. Here then, after studious (and admittedly kind of boring) review, was an un-ironic, almost *moral* thesis to the campy abstract mordant cartridge: the film's climactic statue's stasis presented the theoretical subject as the emotional effect – self-forgetting as the Grail – and – in a covert gesture almost moralistic ... – presented the self-forgetting of alcohol as inferior to that of religion/art. (742)

This challenging passage brings together many of the themes I have been discussing in this chapter: art, absorption, mediation, self-forgetting, self-transcendence. 'I believe, with Hegel, that transcendence is absorption', Hal tells us in the opening scene, and here, 730 pages later, we have the novel's most explicit discussion of the relationship between absorption and transcendence with regard to an artwork. Bernini's sculpture, an eminently theatrical work, is here viewed not from several perspectives, as in Schama's description of the sculpture's intended effect, but from a single perspective, in stasis. Bernini may have made a 'marble movie', but here that movie is reduced to one, static, four-minute shot. Note that these 'four narrative minutes' where the statue fills the screen come to operate like a photograph, thereby achieving – albeit in an unusual manner – what Fried calls 'a certain essentially photographic distance from the film experience, a distance by virtue of which the automaticity of the avoidance of theatricality ... is forestalled or undone' (Fried, 2008: 13).[11] While the theatrical effect of Bernini's statue might thereby seem to be accentuated, the multimedial element of this extended moment offers a complicating factor. Indeed, the moment involves the interaction among a whole range of traditionally separate arts: sculpture (Bernini's altarpiece), photography (the four-minute static shot), cinema (Incandenza's film), television (Joelle views the film on a small screen at home, rather than in the cinema space that is the traditional site of film theory), poetry (the reference to Blake's *The Marriage of Heaven and Hell* in the film's title), and prose fiction (Wallace's *Infinite Jest*). While Wallace necessarily falls short of 'contriv[ing] a medium' for the representation of this moment, he goes almost as far as one could imagine in refracting the moment through a series of media that modernist criticism in the

Greenberg–Fried mode has typically construed as in competition with one another.[12] It is this multiply mediated quality that reveals the oblique 'emotional thrust' of the moment to Joelle, even if she does not exactly experience that thrust herself. But perhaps the 'thrust' (the echo of the angel's arrow surely not coincidental) should not in fact be experienced by the beholder, since this would risk reducing the moment to the norms of melodrama, perhaps the most theatrical of genres in its overt intent to stir audience emotions.[13] Indeed, rather than accentuating the theatricality of Bernini's statue, Incandenza's technique would appear intended precisely to defeat that theatricality by inducing absorption – if not emotion – in the viewer in the same way that it induces absorption in the alcoholic sandwich-bag salesman whose point of view we inhabit (and simultaneously escape) for the duration of the shot.

But here Joelle's description of the conditions in which she views Incandenza's films becomes important. Of the 'flashes of something' she remarks: 'She noticed them only when alone, watching, without Orin and his rheostat's dimmer, the living room's lights up high like she liked them, liked to see herself and everything else in the room with the viewer – Orin liked to sit in the dark and enter what he watched, his jaw slackening, a child raised on multichannel cable TV' (Wallace, 1996: 741). Here we have two models of watching. One of them – Orin's – seems the height of absorption; the other, Joelle's, is very different. Even though she is watching the alcoholic sandwich-bag salesman undergo a kind of absorptive 'self-forgetting' in front of Bernini's statue, Joelle herself is *not* engaged in absorptive self-forgetting in front of Incandenza's film. The medium is of particular importance here, since by watching alone on a small screen Joelle has the option of turning up the lights and refusing the invisibility of herself and everything else in the room.[14] Rather than wholly enter the film, she can retain perceptual awareness of herself and her surroundings as she watches the statue on the screen. This could indeed be described as an experience of 'mediated transcendence of self', rather than an experience of fully absorptive self-forgetting.

Marking the difference between these two experiences constitutes, I would argue, an important engagement by Wallace with the notion of *self-consciousness*. To the Romantic sensibility, self-consciousness is primarily understood as self-alienation, with the threat of inauthenticity and theatricality established by any acknowledgement of others as minded, desiring beings whose thoughts and actions pre-empt and shape the thoughts and actions of the self. We can see this sensibility expressed in famous statements such as the following by Rousseau: 'The Savage lives within himself; sociable man, always outside himself, is capable of living only in the opinion of others and, so to speak, derives the sentiment of his own existence solely from their judgment'; and likewise in Diderot's claim that his art criticism is informed by the distinction between 'a man presenting himself in company and a man acting from motivation, between a man who's alone and a man being observed' (qtd in Pippin, 2005: 581, 576). This is a sensibility expressed in much of Wallace's fiction and non-fiction too, but it is one that *Infinite Jest* seeks to counter. Here it is again crucial that Joelle, in the cocaine passage, describes feeling simultaneously 'observed *and* alone', as if the romantic picture of self-consciousness as self-alienation could be overcome by another view. This other view – the view Wallace could be said to be working towards in his representation of Joelle's viewing experience – resembles what Pippin calls *reflective absorption*, which he explains in terms of the absorption–theatricality dialectic as follows:

> A reflective embodiment is not one that in some way *thematizes* one's role and thereby distances oneself from it, but reflection is meant in the original Kantian sense of apperception, as *adverbial*. An apperceptive awareness of a room is not a direct awareness of a room *and* a second-order self-consciousness *of* one's perceptual state as a new, dual object. (This misunderstanding is the source of the unavoidable self-alienation worries). Rather one perceives the room *self-consciously*, aware in perceiving the room that one is in a perceptual state (not an imagined or remembered state) as one perceives but not aware of two intentional or separate objects. The idea would be to understand reflective absorption as *an intensification of such absorption*, not a thematizing and ultimately theatricalizing distance. ... That sort of theatricalizing might be said to occur only when something like the normative structure of such mindedness begins to break down, fails to sustain allegiance, becomes a *reflected object of inquiry*, not a *mode of life*. (Pippin, 2005: 592)

Pippin is commenting directly here on Fried's reading of the nineteenth-century German painter Adolph Menzel, whose realism aimed to counter Romantic self-alienation by inducing reflective absorption. As David Hering has persuasively argued, however, 'reflection' is a vexed term in Wallace's aesthetics, connoting mirror tropes that lead not to apperceptive awareness but to inescapable recursive loops back to the character, the author, and the surface of the text. In Hering's four-stage model of Wallace's engagement with motifs of reflection, Orin Incandenza's mode of watching films would offer a good example of the third stage, narcissism: 'the absorption of the character in the text within the reflective image, be it a mirror or screen' (Hering, 2016: 86–7). The fourth stage, 'refraction', a motif 'often in deliberate conflict with the preceding three', marks a breakthrough as 'a specifically communicative gesture between character and character, text and reader or authorial presence and reader' (87). Such a breakthrough 'reframe[s] looking and watching as a communicative, dialogic gesture' (87), and Hering summarizes the contrast between reflection and refraction as one between '"looking at" (as one does to a mirror) and "looking into" (as one does to another's eyes)' (94). While it never leaves reflection wholly behind, refraction directs the intentionality of the gaze towards self and other simultaneously.

Bringing together Hering with Hegel and Fried, I would argue that Joelle's mode of watching *Pre-Nuptial Agreement* is best described as 'refractive absorption'. The multimedial quality of the film's presentation, combined with Joelle's account of how she chooses to watch it, transfigures both the theatricality of Bernini's sculpture and the absorptive self-forgetting of the film's protagonist, precisely via an example of 'mediated self-transcendence'. In contrast to Hal's failed reading of other texts and other minds throughout the novel – in the opening scene he 'look[s] out' rather than looking into, and 'Digests things' rather than responding to communicative acts (Wallace, 1996: 15) – we can see Joelle as a model for the reader of *Infinite Jest*. Chodat may be right to condemn James Incandenza's films as '"subjective facts" wholly without "objective self-evidence"' (Chodat, 2017: 297), but that division between subject and object can be healed, and the aesthetic experience made whole, by the refractively absorbed Joelle, who realizes the text's 'flashes' of communication through a mediated absorption that does not equate to total self-forgetting. While Incandenza's aim to converse with his son Hal by contriving the medium of 'Infinite Jest' ended in failure, Wallace's hope was that the medium of *Infinite Jest* would provide that healing experience of refractive absorption for the novel's reader.[15]

But attempting to induce such a state in the reader – to make them feel simultaneously 'observed and alone' – was a delicate task, and one that for Wallace was forever threatened by a writer's tendency to anticipate the reader's response and to look for overly theatrical or overly absorptive effects on that basis. In the AA strand of *Infinite Jest* this problem is described as 'Sincerity with an ulterior motive', which is 'something these tough ravaged people know and fear' because such 'sincerity' results in a kind of performative theatricality that undermines the therapeutic prospects of both speaker and listener (Wallace, 1996: 369). This worry about the art and artifice of sincerity would become an overriding concern of later Wallace stories such as 'Octet' and 'Good Old Neon', which ask how and to what extent the desires of the other should be taken into account by the self, both in aesthetic creation and in social interaction. These questions are necessarily unanswerable in advance, because – as with Mark Nechtr's hobby of archery in Wallace's early novella 'Westward the Course of Empire Takes Its Way' – the aim can be judged successful only if the target is hit. The proof is in the aesthetic execution, and the execution can be judged only *ex post facto*. If sincerity is an art, then the art of sincerity must derive as much from the outside as from the inside. Intention is realized in recognition; sincerity is achieved only in the other's response.

Notes

1 The exception is Dennis Gabor, the inventor of the hologram, although part of Wallace's point may be that any philosophy that does not take technological change seriously is inadequate. Holography's influence on Hal's dead father, the filmmaker James Incandenza, is a likely reason for Hal's dark thoughts about Gabor.
2 A few glancing references: Gregory Phipps (2010: 75) begins his essay on *Infinite Jest*'s John Wayne by citing Hegel, while David Morris (2001) uses Wallace's novel as an exemplary text in his treatment of addiction in Hegel. Andrew Warren notes that Wallace read Marx's 'Contribution to the Critique of Hegel's *Philosophy of Right*' for a class at Harvard (2018: 173) and makes a connection between Hegel's critique of 'interdependence' and O.N.A.N.'s 'Interdependence Day'

(182). Jeffrey Severs makes multiple allusions to Hegel's importance for Wallace, particularly the dialectic of lord and bondsman from *The Phenomenology of Spirit* (2017: 54–5, 86). Addressing the passage I have quoted above, Jon Baskin briefly glosses Hal's reference to Hegel as simply an initial therapeutic signal that the novel's aim is 'not to settle such disputes but to help its reader come to consciousness of and therefore be able to move beyond them' (2019: 55).

3   For a consideration of evidence for each of these explanations (he prefers the first one), see Carlisle, 2007: 480–2. Following the convention in Wallace scholarship, to distinguish the film cartridge from the novel in which it appears I refer to the former as 'Infinite Jest' and the latter as *Infinite Jest*.

4   When readers are first informed of Hal's marijuana habit, for instance, we are told that his mother and uncle 'know nothing about Hal's penchants for high-resin Bob Hope and underground absorption' (Wallace, 1996: 51). Later, during the Eschaton scene, Hal's drug use will lead to him failing to intervene in the escalating chaos of the game: 'Hal, now leaning forward, steeple-fingered, finds himself just about paralyzed with absorption … almost incapacitated with absorption' (340). Absorption in drug use is also associated with other characters, most notably Joelle van Dyne, who, when we first meet her, is embarking on a suicidal binge with crack cocaine: 'She is now a little under two deliberate minutes from Too Much Fun for anyone mortal to hope to endure. Her unveiled face in the dirty lit mirror is shocking in the intensity of its absorption' (238). The phrase 'Too Much Fun' also hints at the absorptive role played by entertainment (not only 'The Entertainment') in the novel, most tragically in the death of Hugh Steeply's father, whose all-consuming obsession with the television show M*A*S*H led to his 'withdrawal from life' (640). And absorption likewise characterizes the worst forms of depression in *Infinite Jest*, as in the *It* that haunts Kate Gompert, whose 'depressed self *It* billows on and coagulates around and wraps in *Its* black folds and absorbs into *Itself*' (695).

5   Severs and Chodat have addressed the role of absorption in Wallace's work, the former focusing on absorption in labour and the latter on absorption in listening and tennis. While I have found their comments illuminating, the thematic approach taken by both critics does not attend to the distinction between *pure or total absorption* and *refractive absorption* that I will argue is crucial to Wallace's aesthetics. My use of the term 'refractive' builds on David Hering's engagement with reflection in Wallace's fiction, discussed below.

6   'Bodily movements bear meaning as deeds (they have an "inner" meaning) in the same way that sensible objects like paintings can be said to bear

meaning as artworks. In both cases the intention is only "realized" as the intention it determinately is *in* the deed or in the work, *as* that deed or work counts as this or that *to* a community at a time; before that realization, it is only provisionally and putatively the determinate intention or meaning' (Pippin, 2014: 20).
7 'Hegel was lecturing on art just before the treatment of art began shifting from "aesthetics" to the "philosophy of art" (i.e. from the sensible appreciation of beauty to art's interrogation of its own nature and possibility)' (Pippin, 2014: 8). In this new era 'the romantic categories, even the whole notion of the beautiful, all seem simply beside the point' (48).
8 For example Hegel writes admiringly of the freedom from sin and guilt in Correggio's 1528 statue of Mary Magdalene: 'she is unconscious of those times, absorbed only in her present situation [*nur vertieft in ihren jetzigen Zustand*], and this faith, this sensitiveness, this absorption [*Versinken*] seems to be her entire and real character' (Hegel, 1975: 868). He writes with similar approbation of the artist who 'is united directly with the subject-matter, believes in it, and is identical with it in accordance with his very own self. The result is then that the artist is entirely absorbed in the object [*Dann liegt die Subjektivität gänzlich in dem Objekt*]' (604).
9 The claim that *Infinite Jest* shows history itself to be stalled is not one I have the space to substantiate here (it is taken up in the monograph-in-progress from which this chapter is drawn). Phipps gets close to my view in his summary comment that in the America of Wallace's novel 'freedom is not, as in Hegel's philosophy, a continuously expanding manifestation of historical progress, but is rather a unidimensional extreme in an increasingly unstable dialectic movement' (2010: 75).
10 Indeed, in *The Moment of Caravaggio* Fried briefly cites Bernini as the epitome of the baroque theatricality against which Caravaggio's absorptive painting attempted to struggle (2010: 122).
11 The idea that film automatically avoids (rather than attempts to overcome) theatricality is a complicated one, which appeared first in 'Art and Objecthood' and was then developed by Stanley Cavell in *The World Viewed* (1973), a work that likely influenced Wallace.
12 Addressing comments Wallace made in an interview, Philip Sayers argues that they 'suggest a convergent model for the different media, wherein the differences "at the level of sign-types, forms, materials of representation, and institutional traditions" ... do not give rise to diverging goals (as in the medium specificity thesis) but rather to different techniques for the achievement of a similar set of goals, a "kind of weird intimacy" numbering among them' (2014: 112, the first embedded quotation is

from W. J. T. Mitchell's *Picture Theory: Essays on Verbal and Visual Representation*, 1994). While this interpretation is clearly pertinent to *Infinite Jest*, I would argue that in the description of the still shot from *Pre-Nuptial Agreement* the different media are not converging so much as interacting in a dialectical manner, where each frames the others depending on the order of priority one chooses to see. This is not, in other words, a postmodern moment of intermediality, but nor is it a modernist moment of medium specificity.

13 Incandenza's later films are described by Joelle as 'narratively anticonfluential but unironic melodrama' (Wallace, 1996: 740). The lack of narrative confluence would seem here to clash with the lack of irony, in a way that turns the 'emotional thrust' into a cognitive experience that can be accessed only on rewatching.

14 This directly challenges the premises of the canonical treatment of film in the absorption–theatricality tradition, Cavell's *The World Viewed*: 'A screen is a barrier. What does the silver screen screen? It screens me from the world it holds – that is, it makes me invisible' (1973: 24).

15 Here the fact that Wallace needs to imagine his model reader as an 'other' – whose recognition of mediated but potentially sincere communication serves to realize that sincerity – is accentuated by Joelle's gender difference from her author. Fully considering this significant issue – which opens onto the enormous can of worms that is Wallace's presentation of gender norms, female characters, and female sexuality in his fiction – is unfortunately beyond the scope of the present chapter. Any such consideration would have to address the fact that *The Ecstasy of St Teresa* is a sculpture by a man of the penetration of a woman, which in turn becomes the subject of contemplation by a man in Incandenza's film. It would also have to acknowledge that the female viewer of the film itself, Joelle, stars in many of the director's other films, most notably 'Infinite Jest', in which she plays a veiled mother apologizing to the camera lens. Finally, such a consideration would have to address the fourth appearance of *The Ecstasy of St Teresa* (this time not by name) in the novel. In this scene St Teresa's expression in the altarpiece is described by a female AA speaker as 'the sort of pinched gasping look of neurologic concentration that marks a carnal bliss beyond smiles or sighs' (373), which the speaker compares to the expression of her 'totally paralyzed and retarded and catatonic' (371) sister after the sister has been 'incestuously diddled' (374) nightly by their father. In the speaker's story much of the blame for this horrific situation lies with her 'rabidly Catholic wacko foster mother' (371), who kneels and worships below a photograph of Bernini's statue every day. In contrast to Joelle's conclusions about the role of Bernini's statue

in *Pre-Nuptial Agreement*, it is much less clear in this troubling scene that 'religion/art' exists in a higher realm than 'the self-forgetting of alcohol' (742). If nothing else, these differing responses reiterate the point that the beholder's relation to an artwork is, for Wallace, at least as important as the intent of its creator. For critical engagements with Wallace and gender see Hayes-Brady, 2016: 167–91; Holland, 2017; Kelly, 2018.

References

Baskin, J. (2019). *Ordinary Unhappiness: The Therapeutic Fiction of David Foster Wallace*. Stanford CA: Stanford University Press.

Boswell, M. (2003). *Understanding David Foster Wallace*. Columbia SC: University of South Carolina Press.

Bourdieu, P. (1993). 'The Market of Symbolic Goods', 112–44. In Bourdieu, *The Field of Cultural Production: Essays on Art and Literature*. Cambridge: Polity Press.

Carlisle, G. (2007). *Elegant Complexity: A Study of David Foster Wallace's Infinite Jest*. Austin TX: Sideshow Media Group.

Cavell, S. (1973). *The World Viewed: Reflections of the Ontology of Film*. Cambridge MA: Harvard University Press.

Cavell, S. (2002). *Must We Mean What We Say?*. updated edition. Cambridge MA: Cambridge University Press.

Chodat, R. (2017). *The Matter of High Words: Naturalism, Normativity, and the Postwar Sage*. Oxford: Oxford University Press.

Den Dulk, A. (2015). *Existentialist Engagement in Wallace, Eggers and Foer: A Philosophical Analysis of Contemporary American Literature*. London and New York NY: Bloomsbury.

Fried, M. (1980). *Absorption and Theatricality: Painting and Beholder in the Age of Diderot*. Chicago IL: University of Chicago Press.

Fried, M. (1996). *Manet's Modernism; or, The Face of Painting in the 1860s*. Chicago IL: University of Chicago Press.

Fried, M. (1998). *Art and Objecthood*. Chicago IL: University of Chicago Press.

Fried, M. (2008). *Why Photography Matters as Art as Never Before*. New Haven CT: Yale University Press.

Fried, M. (2010). *The Moment of Caravaggio*. Princeton NJ: Princeton University Press.

Gombrich, E. H. (1984). 'The Father of Art History', 51–69. In E. H. Gombrich. ed., *Tributes: Interpreters of Our Cultural Tradition*. Ithaca NY: Cornell University Press.

Greenberg, C. (2000a). 'Avant-Garde and Kitsch', 48–59. In Francis Frascina. ed., *Pollock and After: The Critical Debate*. 2nd edition. London: Routledge.

Greenberg, C. (2000b). 'Towards a New Laocoon', 60–70. In Francis Frascina. ed., *Pollock and After: The Critical Debate*. 2nd edition. London: Routledge.

Hayes-Brady, C. (2016). *The Unspeakable Failures of David Foster Wallace: Language, Identity, and Resistance*. London and New York NY: Bloomsbury.

Hegel, G. W. F. (1975). *Aesthetics: Lectures on Fine Art*. 2 volumes, trans. T. M. Knox. Oxford: Clarendon Press.

Hering, D. (2016). *David Foster Wallace: Fiction and Form*. London and New York NY: Bloomsbury.

Holland, M. K. (2017). '"By Hirsute Author": Gender and Communication in the Work and Study of David Foster Wallace', in *Critique* 58:1, 64–77.

Kelly, A. (2018). '*Brief Interviews with Hideous Men*', 82–96. In Ralph Clare, ed., *The Cambridge Companion to David Foster Wallace*. Cambridge: Cambridge University Press.

Konstantinou, L. (2016). *Cool Characters: Irony and American Fiction*. Cambridge MA: Harvard University Press.

Morris, D. (2001). 'Lived Time and Absolute Knowing: Habit and Addiction from *Infinite Jest* to the *Phenomenology of Spirit*', in *Clio* 30, 375–415.

Phipps, G. (2010). 'The Ideal Athlete: John Wayne in *Infinite Jest*', 75–88. In David Hering, ed., *Consider David Foster Wallace: Critical Essays*. Austin TX: Sideshow Media Group.

Pippin, R. B. (2005). 'Authenticity in Painting: Remarks on Michael Fried's Art History', in *Critical Inquiry* 31, 575–98.

Pippin, R. B. (2014). *After the Beautiful: Hegel and the Philosophy of Pictorial Modernism*. Chicago IL: University of Chicago Press.

Sayers, P. (2014). 'Representing Entertainment in *Infinite Jest*', 107–25. In Marshall Boswell, ed., *David Foster Wallace and 'The Long Thing': New Essays on the Novels*. London and New York NY: Bloomsbury.

Schama, S. (2009). *The Power of Art*. London: Bodley Head.

Severs, J. (2017). *David Foster Wallace's Balancing Books: Fictions of Value*. New York NY: Columbia University Press.

Shapiro, M. (2020). 'The Textually Aware Text: Recursive Self-Consciousness in *Infinite Jest*'s Filmography', in *Orbis Litterarum* 75:1, 24–33.

Trilling, L. (1972). *Sincerity and Authenticity*. Oxford: Oxford University Press.

Wallace, D. Foster. (1996). *Infinite Jest*. Boston MA: Little, Brown.

Wallace, D. Foster. (1997). *A Supposedly Fun Thing I'll Never Do Again: Essays and Arguments*. London: Abacus.

Wallace, D. Foster. (2005). *Consider the Lobster and Other Essays.* Boston MA: Little, Brown.
Warren, A. (2018). 'Wallace and Politics', 173–89. In Ralph Clare, ed., *The Cambridge Companion to David Foster Wallace.* Cambridge: Cambridge University Press.
Warwick, G. (2013). *Bernini: Art as Theatre.* New Haven CT: Yale University Press.

2

Stages, Socrates, and the performer stripped bare: David Foster Wallace as philosopher-dramatist

Jeffrey Severs

David Foster Wallace never wrote a play or a film or TV script, as far as we know, but in his fiction he loved working with – to wildly varying degrees of seriousness – the techniques and effects of the playwright and scriptwriter. Most prominent among these is his rendering of rapid-fire, often hilarious dialogue, rife with spiralling speeches in distinctive voices, free of intervening prose descriptions, and sometimes posed on the page in transcript form. Such features led the adaptor John Krasinski, in the film version of *Brief Interviews with Hideous Men*, to convert short-story pages more or less directly into dramatic script pages (with merely so-so results in transferring the narrative's richest meanings, I would say). Wallace was deeply interested in representing and analysing performance in the work of rappers, porn stars, and especially the actors in the countless examples of (both real and made-up) films, TV shows, and commercials in his fiction and non-fiction oeuvre; but he was even more interested in the tendencies toward performance in everyday life that those professional actors – many of them experts at the paradoxical art of 'act[ing] natural' – inspired in audiences (Wallace, 1997: 25). Much of Wallace's analysis of performance, especially in the fiction, meshes with his mid-career concern for irony and sincerity – in effect concerns with (mere) performance and its presumed opposite, authenticity – and the ways abundant, highly cultivated

Stages, Socrates, and the performer stripped bare 49

media self-presentations infiltrated the minds of average people, distorting sex, beauty, politics, and so on. As a summary line says in 'E Unibus Pluram: Television and U.S. Fiction', 'Can we deny connections between an unprecedentedly powerful consensual medium that suggests no difference between image and substance, on one hand, and stuff like the rise of Teflon presidencies ... [and] the popularity of "Vogueing" to a cynical synthesized command to "Strike a Pose"?' (Wallace, 1997: 63–4).

In this chapter, though, I argue that there is another, less obvious strain in Wallace's writing about performance. This recurrent, quite subtle idiom invokes technologically unmediated live theatre, sometimes of ancient vintage, and, most importantly, demonstrates that being a philosopher for Wallace is an art frequently, if not always, tied to performances of a certain exacting and humbling kind. While readers of Wallace's work as philosophical fiction are naturally drawn to its philosophical arguments, I examine here the forms – primarily the dramatic form – he consistently uses or alludes to when portraying philosophy-in-action, philosophy being spoken into existence, both by people who would call themselves philosophers and by those who would not. I ground my readings in moments from across Wallace's oeuvre (though concentrated in *Brief Interviews*, with some attention paid as well to *Infinite Jest* and *The Pale King*) that occupy one or both of two major domains: firstly, expertly crafted scenes of dialogue that mark a twist on the Platonic dialogues and their dramatic staging of philosophical conflict, particularly when it involves the sophistry Wallace found dominating postmodernity; and, secondly, moments that conjure not just performance but a particularly abject stage performer, showing that Wallace, while seeing no ultimate escape from the artifices of performance, would at crucial moments strategically strip performers down to a state of naked vulnerability. In crucial moments of powerful idea-making where he relies on theatrical metaphors, opposes live stage performance to the kind that TV and film offer, and plays with definitions of the performer to unseat an ensconced idea, Wallace is, I argue, a philosopher-dramatist.

I draw throughout from the literary and philosophical framework offered by Martin Puchner's *The Drama of Ideas: Platonic Provocations in Theater and Philosophy*, which begins by arguing that Plato, famously said to have given up theatre to turn to philosophy, continued operating fundamentally as a playwright, in what have often been taken (especially in the common understanding) as monological treatises shorn of their crucial theatrical features. Puchner argues that the Platonic dialogues demonstrate that philosophy and performance are inextricably linked and that ideas only ever emerge out of drama, decrying the 'antitheatrical and undramatic tendency' (Puchner, 2010: 6) of so much philosophical writing in centuries since that intended, wrongheadedly, to honour Plato's seeming attacks on theatre (which were actually calls for radical innovation, Puchner says). 'The Greek root *thea* [as in *theatre*] is to be found in the word *theorein*, which denotes theoretical contemplation', Puchner writes (6). Ranging across examples from Platonic dialogues to modern writers in many genres, including Nietzsche, Kierkegaard, Wilde, Shaw, Brecht, Beckett, Camus, Murdoch, Deleuze, and Badiou, Puchner shows that philosophy's inherent drama survives and thrives in writing – drama, philosophy, and some fiction – that often reanimates Socrates and his speeches and gestures, to diverse purposes. Puchner claims dramatic Platonism as the source of modernist theatre's radical innovations, while also challenging Bakhtin's much-used theories of novelistic dialogism in ways that I apply to understanding dialogue in Wallace's work.

Wallace, I suggest throughout, fits into the broad, very long tradition Puchner identifies of writers who draw upon Plato's ancient techniques of philosophical theatre and theatrical philosophy without necessarily endorsing Platonic conclusions about metaphysics (and with some of these writers turning Platonic drama to wholly anti-Platonist purposes, as Puchner says of Deleuze, Badiou, and others). Wallace, deeply appreciative of post-structuralism's claims, was of course no Platonist or even a casual fan of Plato's metaphysics: in 'E Unibus Pluram' he speaks derisively of the illusory 'Platonic Always' in which writing teachers expected his work to be set (Wallace, 1997: 44); in 'The Empty Plenum' he criticizes the 'trick' of a 'specious Platonic universalism' that insists there is 'some transcendentally existent feature common to every' instance of a thing (Wallace, 2012a: 110); and in 'Authority and American Usage' he touts Derrida's rebuttal to another 'specious' claim, 'at least as old as Plato's Phaedrus', that 'speech is language's primary instantiation' (Wallace, 2005: 84). As I detail below, though, amid all the scepticism of Plato that Wallace expressed in essays, he makes ample use in his fiction (particularly *Brief Interviews*) of Plato's images and tropes, the stuff of Plato as literary figure. As I detail, too, there is strong evidence that Wallace saw the Platonic dialogues as highly useful reflection points for contemporary sophistry and its taste for the mere rhetorical performance of truth.

Wallace criticism that has invoked performance has done so without drawing out the special mode of rigorous theatrical philosophizing I notice and without distinguishing screen performance from theatre performance, as I find it paramount to do. Frank Louis Cioffi wrote in 2000 of 'Narrative as Performance' in *Infinite Jest* and, contrasting the passively consumed title film and the actively read novel, defined 'performing' very broadly: Wallace 'draws the reader in with his own virtuoso, *tour de force* performance', while the novel also 'forces the reader to perform', to consult endnotes and sources, to 'cocreate[] the world of the novel … in the manner of a stagehand', with Cioffi along the way connecting Wallace's techniques to Brecht's alienation (Cioffi, 2000: 162). I agree with Cioffi's assessment, among the first to demonstrate what in the twenty years since his article has become a Wallace critic's commonplace: that his writing incites active reading. But I also see major value in analysing more of Wallace's works using a much narrower definition of performance, to address the particular power he granted the theatrical, the kind of action that occurs on stages and often involves direction, improvisation, costumes, and props. In the same vein I leave to others consideration of Wallace through linguistic theories of performativity grounded in, for instance, J. L. Austin's classic *How to Do Things with Words*, which Wallace likely knew, along with the Derridean critique of it in 'Signature Event Context', in *Limited Inc*. This subject of performative language is first touched on by Wallace in *The Broom of the System* when Rick says pleadingly to Lenore, 'Only by actually uttering certain words does one really *do* what one *says*. "Love" is one of those words, performative words' (Wallace, 1993: 285).

Let me turn my attention to specific Wallace texts by discussing the first of my domains of philosophical performance: dialogue. Philosophy in Wallace's fiction most often means not explorations and explanations wrought into his narrative prose or the narrator's voice but the speech of characters, who dramatically mount, whether in monologue or dialogue, philosophical ideas – and who often, indeed, pontificate. Consider LaVache at Amherst College, a philosophy student who tutors in Hegel (in exchange for drugs) and lectures Lenore on Wittgenstein, or the rambling quasi-spiritual discourse of Reverend Sykes, or the performed intelligence of graduate students (descendants of LaVache) who name-drop Foucault and other theorists to support their misogyny in 'B.I. #28'. A simple explanation for Wallace's preference for seeing philosophers (and wannabe-philosophers) speak and perform is his wish to avoid ponderous writing untrue to his famous desire to inject readability and warmth into postmodern experimentation. 'I tend to think of fiction as being mainly about characters and human beings and inner experience, whereas essays can be much more expository and didactic', he replied in 2006 to an interviewer who said his fiction was surely 'philosophical'. Wallace continued, 'If some people read my fiction and see it as fundamentally about philosophical ideas, what it probably means is that these are pieces where the characters are not as alive and interesting as I meant them to be' (Karmodi, 2011). Wallace made philosophical fiction 'alive and interesting' by having vivid, flawed characters speak, perform, express conflict, live out their ideas, and quite often misuse their philosophical training to nihilistic, unethical, or spiritually vacant ends – all of which activates readers' own thinking far more effectively than sage, always-correct pronouncements might.

But 'alive and interesting' only scratches surface complexities in Wallace's rendering of philosophical dialogue, particularly in the famously one-sided 'Brief Interview' stories, where, in the unnatural environment of the documentary and psychologically exploratory interviews that seem to be Q's project, Wallace is able to combine the cultivated and performative aspects of a familiar media format and the more substantive and unguarded soul-searching that the Hideous Men end up doing. This soul-searching has the long shadow of Plato, Socrates, and the Sophists on it. As I have argued elsewhere, *Brief Interviews* sees Wallace toying constantly (and, again, not at all didactically) with Plato's materials, from the ability to stop time in the ring of Gyges narrative in *The Republic* ('B.I. #59') to the image of one's 'other half' in *The Symposium* ('Adult World') (Severs, 2017: 151–3). But the relationship to Plato to be most fully explored in the context of philosophical performance is *Brief Interviews*' sinuous structural allusion to the dialogue form itself, in which Plato

Stages, Socrates, and the performer stripped bare 53

pits Socrates against the Sophists in order to have the latter at least begin to find their own way to key definitions and self-contradictions. For context let me quote Wallace's only extended commentary on the Platonic dialogues, which *Rolling Stone* published among statements on the new millennium in December 1999, six months after *Brief Interviews* appeared. His statement can be taken as a key to that collection's philosophical roots.

> Everyone is extremely conscious of manipulating how they come off in the media; they want to structure what they say so that the reader or audience will interpret it in the way that is most favorable to them. What's interesting to me is that this isn't all that new. This was the project of the Sophists in Athens, and this is what Socrates and Plato thought was so completely evil. The Sophists had this idea: Forget this idea of what's true or not—what you want to do is rhetoric; you want to be able to persuade the audience and have the audience think you're smart and cool. And Socrates and Plato, basically their whole idea is, 'Bullshit. There is such a thing as truth, and it's not all just how to say what you say so that you get a good job or get laid, or whatever it is people think they want'. (Wallace, 1999–2000: 47)

The quotation makes clear that Wallace saw a strong connection between the performers his fiction lampooned and the ancient Sophists seen in verbal combat with Socrates across the Platonic dialogues. In these battles Wallace sees the Sophists appealing not to their interlocutors or to a standard of truth but to 'the audience'. In consonance with Wallace's summary of this disregard for truth in favour of rhetoric and audience appeal, Puchner notes the consequence of the Greek Sophists' 'relativistic teaching' (Puchner, 2010: 30): 'argumentative skill became an end in itself, a tool to be used in order to gain an advantage. Since the sophists had forsworn the search for truth, they ... seem to believe at least implicitly that no certainty can ever be reached and no true knowledge established', Puchner concludes, only winners and losers in 'a battle of wits' (31).

Such sophistry is legion among the often very witty and combative Hideous Men, mostly in reference to intimate relations (or getting laid, as Wallace puts it), from the seducer with the shrivelled arm and the chicken-sexing sadist to the slick, rhetoric-slicing faker of 'B.I. #2' (the earliest interview and apparently the originating moment for Q's whole quest to go cross-country documenting men). The speaker in 'B.I. #2' makes 'the God's honest truth' a meaningless refrain as he plays the fearful victim in their break-up (Wallace, 1999: 92). But, far from content with this surface-level exposure of hypocrisy and verbal manipulation of moral certainty, Wallace makes the innovative gambit in *Brief Interviews* of giving the stage over *entirely* to sophistry – to show how much more overwhelming this long-standing impulse has now become, but also, more pointedly, to force the role of Socratic hole-poking on to the reader. Socratic questioning and the Socratic method come down to the modern day – especially in pedagogy – as the generalized fruit of the Platonic dialogues, and Wallace's allusion in the 'B.I.' stories is not so much to the specifics of any Platonic texts but to this whole, durable philosophical practice. I would not go so far as to allegorize Q as Socrates – though, as Puchner points out, 'Socrates' death casts a shadow over every single one of Plato's dialogues. Even though Socrates' death [in effect for seeking truth] is not mentioned in many dialogues, author and readers cannot but be painfully aware of it', and *The Apology*, about Socrates' sentencing to death, was Plato's first philosophical work after he gave up writing tragic plays (Puchner, 2010: 9). The apparent death of Q in the chronologically final interview, 'B.I. #78' (Wallace says mysteriously in an interview that 'something *really* bad' happens to her (Stein, 2012: 90)), casts similar shadows on *Brief Interviews*; that attack seems to be an outcome of her search for truth among Hideous Men and is crucial to understanding the book's stance on both all the misogynistic violence it contains and Q's erasure from her own project. The broader point to make about Q as occluded character is akin to what Zadie Smith shrewdly says regarding *Brief Interviews*' characters: Wallace's 'stories [are] turned outward. It's *our* character that's being investigated' (Smith, 2009: 273). Nowhere in Wallace's extensive experimenting is this precarious conversion of reader into central character more clear or forceful than in the case of Socratic Q.

Because Wallace has so deftly and ostentatiously structured these particular dialogues as philosophical theatre, I follow Puchner's lead and resist taking up Bakhtin's theory on the novel's dialogism and its absorption of all other genres (like drama), a theory that has proved so useful to interpreting novels in general and Wallace's in particular. Adam Kelly, for instance, expertly deploys Bakhtin's dialogism to define how Wallace works as a novelist of ideas, showing how his three novels' elevated philosophical dialogues – LaVache and Lenore, Marathe and Steeply, and Glendenning and company in the elevator – all develop richly multivalent thinking by making each of the novels 'a forum for competing ideas' on selfhood, pleasure, government, etc. (Kelly, 2014: 5). As Kelly notes, in Bakhtin's history of forms the Socratic dialogues (or primarily the early ones, more driven by real dialogue than the more monological later ones) become proto-novels of a sort, but inferior in their multi-voiced search for truth to Bakhtin's *telos* of Dostoevsky's fully 'polyphonic' novel (Kelly, 2014: 6). But by using Socratic dialogue to investigate *Brief Interviews* and gravitating towards Puchner's forceful retort to Bakhtin's account of the nineteenth-century novel as the absorber of all other genres, I hope to explain the uniqueness of this collection and Wallace's methods. Bakhtin, according to Puchner, makes the novel the 'upstart genre [that] triumph[ed] over its more established rivals' (Puchner, 2010: 124). But why, Puchner asks, should drama's representation of embodied dialogical conflict not be seen as a preserved, distinctive, and vital force for the dynamic interplay of philosophizing voices across literature and in philosophy itself? Puchner notes, too, that Bakhtin, in his effort to have the novel triumph, has a rather narrow conception of drama's range, taking terms like 'heteroglossia' that 'resonate very clearly with dialogue and drama' and 'seek[ing] to wrest them from this domain' (Puchner, 2010: 124). Citing novels with ample dramatic inserts like *Moby-Dick*, *Ulysses* (in its 'Circe' chapter), and *This Side of Paradise*, as well as novels of dramatized ideas by Dostoevsky and Mann, Puchner suggests that we might see in such moments not 'the incorporation of drama by the stronger novel' but the 'invasion of the novel by a newly resurgent drama', which had its deep origins in those alleged proto-novels by Plato (Puchner, 2010: 125). In this context it is also worth noting that Wallace himself criticized Bakhtin's idea of polyphony, if along different lines: in a footnote of 'Joseph Frank's Dostoevsky' he seems to agree with the biographer that Bakhtin, because he wrote under Soviet ideological pressure to de-emphasize religious ideas, unduly exaggerated the '"polyphonic" characterizations [and] "dialogic imagination" that supposedly allowed [Dostoevsky] to refrain from injecting his own values into his novels' (Wallace, 2005: 269 n25).

While I cannot bring Puchner's case to bear on Wallace's novels in this space, I do find this idea of drama's distinctive, unassimilable contributions to an aesthetic as intensely hybrid as Wallace's the perfect lens for understanding *Brief Interviews* (far more integrated a narrative than a conventional short-story collection) and larger swaths of his work. Nowhere in Wallace's corpus is his insistent inhabiting of dramatic form more prominent and rich than in *Brief Interviews*' 'On His Deathbed, Holding Your Hand, the Acclaimed New Young Off-Broadway Playwright's Father Begs a Boon', a surreal, 'Circe'-esque play-as-story, complete with stage directions. It invites connection to the 'Brief Interviews' through allusions to their vocabulary (the refrain about a child's powers of 'bewitchment' recalls 'B.I. #59', for just one example) and the father's ample (physical and emotional) hideousness. In addition, 'Deathbed' reframes the silenced, invisible Q's relationship to her interviewees. Thinking about the book's unity, Wallace wanted the varied, formally irregular narrative units of *Brief Interviews* to 'play off one another' and have 'certain leitmotifs weave through them' (qtd in Max, 2012: 248), and in 'Deathbed' the playwright son makes dramatically visible the unstable combination of roles (interviewer, reader, transcriber) readers can easily forget about with Q (in part for regressive gendered reasons) as they become used to filling in her blanks or pass over them altogether for the next hideous speech. The son in 'Deathbed', the target of his father's vicious attacks embedded within a moment of last rites, goes entirely unmentioned in the many stage directions about grotesquely awful medical procedures (several focused on his ailing eyes, for this story is Wallace's brilliant rendition of a raging, eye-gouged Oedipus, though one who – as a conniving strategy to gain pity – claims it is his son who has all the power and must be rebelled against). Then suddenly, a page from the end, the son is not just expected for his daily hospital visit with his wife and children but has apparently been there all along, holding his father's hand: 'YOU [cruelly]: But Father it's me. Your own son. All of us, standing here, loving you so' (Wallace, 1999: 281). The son is explicitly 'You', the reader (something always only implicit with Q), but he even seems to be (we slowly realize, unable to be sure) the author of the very drama of cruel filial projection and counter-projection we are reading, perhaps even having off-Broadway success with it. For his part the father, as rendered, is exactly the kind of sophist Wallace's *Rolling Stone* piece calls out: the father believes no emotion or relationship is authentic and all is mere rhetorical performance, an idea in line with his wholly transactional view of family bonds. He in fact credits his dramatist son with a '*coup de theatre*' (280) not for his plays (not as brilliant as critics think, the father says), but for performing every day of his upbringing a belief in his own lies about loving his parents. Life is entirely a cynical battle of wits and appearances that this adept playwright/performer/son has supposedly played to the hilt, from infancy forward.

Still more pointedly, though, it is the raving and probably deluded father's claims and slip-ups about ancient Greek language, drama, and philosophy, beyond his many resonances with Oedipus, that point careful readers to Wallace's broader use of performance as an anti-sophist and thus Socratic project. In addition to the Latin and French this highly intelligent man deploys, the *Hamlet* line he spontaneously quotes, and the Aquinas and Nietzsche he cites, he seems especially attached to ancient Greece and its dramatic literature, absurdly calling out his Pulitzer-winning son for needing 'weeks of slack-jawed labor' in college to read an English translation ('not even Sophocles' Greek', he laughs (274)) of the *Oresteia*, oblivious to the fact that his son was probably not just reading but studying the text's art and ways of staging, adapting, or imitating it. For it is theatre and performance as philosophically rich art – and not just lies of affection covering sincerely held hatreds – that this father cannot understand, despite his scholarly acumen (resonances with the failed Hal/Himself relationship in *Infinite Jest* are manifold).

Wallace often uses errors with etymology and grammar to illustrate a character's flawed or overly technical thinking (see my readings of Hal and Joelle in *Infinite Jest* in this regard (Severs, 2017: 113–15, 128)). In 'Deathbed' Wallace has the father continue in his utterly transactional views of life and his excoriation of the 'gift' his talented son is said to have: 'The Attics called one's particular gift or genius his *techno*. Was it *techno*? Odd for "gift." Do you decline it in the genitive?' (Wallace, 1999: 275). We are signalled by his later confession that he misnamed the author of the *Oresteia* – Aeschylus, not Sophocles – to see that he is, with *techno*, not simply confused over grammar but missing whole realms of lived, familial wisdom that a technical view of grammar papers over. *Techno* does not mean 'gift or genius' in any direct way, but τέκνον (usually transliterated as *teknon*) does mean 'child', the gift of progeny this father has utterly misperceived. Wallace obliquely suggests as well that this deluded father is thinking of or misunderstands *technē* (τέχνη), often translated as art or craft (and in line with 'genius'), a concept that would help him understand the richness in his son's artistic skills. *Technē* is a central, complex subject in Platonic dialogues such as *Gorgias*, and Wallace leads us to think about it when it appears in a mangled explanation of a TV haloing phenomenon – 'what we're transfixed by is artificial & mediated by imperfect *technē*' (Wallace, 1999: 253) – in the wild parody of Greek gods in the story directly preceding 'Deathbed', 'Tri-Stan: I Sold Sissee Nar to Ecko'. The father misremembering '*techno*' also evokes, like that earlier jab at TV, techno-logy and its growth into modernity's god, a trend consonant with this father's instrumentalizing and transactional view of life. Drugs, pain, delirious visions, a scholar's misprision – whatever the sources of the father's deathbed speech and slip-ups, Wallace uses his brazen performance, and its network of allusions to Socratic philosophy, to achieve something much more complex and devastating than simply indicting another unethical, ignorant character. *Brief Interviews*' theatre of ideas leads its audience of readers to find their own way to Socratic questions and perhaps even wisdom.

In other moments of meta-theatricality, *Brief Interviews* produces my second major domain of Wallace as philosopher-dramatist, one significantly overlapping with the grotesque father of 'Deathbed': the abject and naked performer. This performer – invoked fleetingly and brought to a point of reckoning on an implied stage – yields for Wallace meanings somewhat more transparent and palatable than in 'Deathbed'. The naked performer appears in 'Octet', which famously attempts to transcend the self-consciousness of typical postmodernist meta-fiction. But in trying to achieve that transcendence, 'Octet', at the last desperate moment, shifts its generic terrain and relies on tropes of meta-*theatre*. In the final pages of the last Pop Quiz, the narrating voice ponders an uncertain solution to the problem of insincerity faced by 'you', a 'fiction writer': some bracingly direct and honest communication with the reader (Wallace, 1999: 145). 'The trick to this solution is you'd have to be 100% honest. Meaning not just sincere but almost naked. Worse than naked – more like unarmed. Defenseless' (154). Wallace almost always elaborates, of course, and later the image of nakedness is, as it were, fleshed out: 'you' 'will have to puncture the fourth wall and come onstage naked (except for your hand's hat) and say all this stuff to a person' (157). Multiple theatrical metaphors appear here: to 'puncture the fourth wall' is an idea based in self-conscious versions of the performing arts but widely applied to all sorts of meta-artworks; yet, having found this sort of meta-theatre an already tired move of previous meta-fiction, 'Octet' goes a step beyond it by adding a stripped, audience-approaching performer holding a hat/hand over his privates. There is also a subtle, implicit contrast between this naked performer-writer and Johnny Carson, who is emblematic of televised performance and appears in the story's final footnote for his ironic 'Carson Maneuver' at jokes that have failed with the audience (159 n17). Implied here is a hope that there is distance between Carson's antics and the 'good deal more urgent and real' plea of the naked performer who embodies the fiction writer's attempt at sincerity (159). In another connection of performers, the idea that the 'hand's hat' is the only prop in this naked theatre calls back to the humbled X in 'Pop Quiz 6(A)', who tells his secret thoughts to Y after 'coming hat in hand to Y for a sympathetic ear', with the phrase 'hat in hand' evoking a bygone, folksy era of doffing hats to show earnest humility (143). The '[s]elf-evident' (144) Q for X is whether he will in the end perform his false love for his dead father-in-law to his relatives or try to be sincere about his ugly narcissism, as he was with his empathic friend Y. By connecting X to 'Pop Quiz 9' in this way, Wallace suggests that the naked-but-for-his-hat writer-performer faces a complex task: he cannot easily abandon (and perhaps should not abandon) all social niceties of lying, all social 'clothing'.

My question is: why must this sincere, naked performer still come on a stage and be a performer at all, especially if the goal of this final moment is to avoid being 'coy or performative or sham-honest-so-she'll-like-you' (154)? Why not another metaphor altogether for this all-important approach to the reader and exception to irony? Or why not let the writer's nakedness be, like so many other metaphors for communication in *Brief Interviews*, more directly evocative of sex, if not sex of the creepy seducer's sort that dominates the collection? From the perspective on *Brief Interviews* I have established, the answer to all these questions is that this anti-performative writer still must be a part of Wallace's rigorous imagery of live theatre, where true philosophical breakthroughs seem often to occur for his characters, even as Wallace expresses such antagonism for mass-media performances and everyday acting. In other words Wallace can never leave performance completely behind, along with complex questions, like those facing X, of how lying about his sincere feelings might be the best way to serve familial love. 'Octet' is often read as representative of Wallace's anti-irony mission, and there are parallels between my suggestion that performance is still unexpectedly present in its climactic moment of sincerity and the ideas of iconoclastic critics who, sceptical of his association with a movement towards sincerity, have seen Wallace never fully abandoning ironic distance, just pressing it to a breaking point. A. O. Scott, for example, writes in a perceptive 2000 omnibus review (including *Brief Interviews*) that Wallace the alleged anti-ironist retained a deeply ironic mode and actually wished somehow 'to be at once earnest and ironical', at once (in two evocations of the complex performance dynamics in play) 'straight man and clown, grifter and mark' (Scott, 2000). After reading this review Wallace wrote in the margin of a later story's draft, 'AO Scott saw into my character' (qtd in Max, 2012: 255), itself a punning evocation of a naked exposure (or perhaps transparency of the soul) combined with the writer's retention of control over the artifice of literary character.

All this thinking about sincerity and naked bodies, around and through performance, occurs in a far more folksy and appealing idiom in 'Octet' than in 'Deathbed', of course. But with that nakedness – as well as phrases about sincere people who seek only to be liked being 'obscene' and partaking of 'obscenely naked direct interrogation' (Wallace, 1999: 154) – Wallace points subtly to the more horrifying, unwilled exposure of bodies that occurs elsewhere in the philosophical theatre of *Brief Interviews*. I have in mind here the male victim of sexual abuse in 'B.I. #46', who very obliquely recounts his own anal violation with a liquor bottle by invoking Viktor Frankl's *Man's Search for Meaning* and, in an utterly disturbing act of projection, telling Q that women who are rape victims should find a humanizing worth in that trauma. As with 'Deathbed's' ambiguous mixture of a hateful father and the son who may have scripted him, readers must piece together from various clues whose brutal experience 'B.I. #46' is actually about, where the rage is emanating from, and where their complicated empathy should lie. Evoking the depths of his trauma, this interviewee says to Q, 'See now it's showtime, now's when you find out what you even *are* to yourself' (122). 'Showtime', a glib metaphor awful for its glibness, is one more grim part of Wallace's philosophical theatre, as well as a radical repurposing of a term common to anaesthetizing entertainment culture. Later the man refines what kind of self-realization and authentic choice he means with the word 'showtime': '[M]ost people are so smug and knee-jerk and walking around asleep they don't even know it's something you have to actually choose for yourself that only has meaning when all the like props and stage-settings that let you just go around smugly assuming you're not a thing are ripped away and broken' (123). For this beaten man, the dictum to 'choose for yourself' to be human, and thus not be reduced to a thing, is a profoundly personal call from a moment in which he was nakedly vulnerable to attack (and for Wallace, weaving together motifs, this man sets up the more often critically examined efforts of the 'Granola Cruncher', in 'B.I. #20', to maintain her humanity during a rape). By contrast to the phrase 'choose for yourself', 'So decide' (Wallace, 1999: 160), after the naked stage performer emerges at the end of 'Octet', is an outwardly directed moment of choice for the reader or audience. But both are moments of philosophical clarity on the central Wallace subject of choosing, and both depend fundamentally on images of the stage, of a harrowing and therefore authenticating performance of selfhood. Moreover, 'choose for yourself', when fully understood as this brutalized victim's advice to himself, resonates deeply with Wallace's brilliant line in his Kafka essay: 'the horrific struggle to establish a human self results in a self whose humanity is inseparable from that horrific struggle' (Wallace, 2005: 64).

Let me close this consideration of what can be generative about performance in Wallace by taking a step back from Socratic connections to examine what happens when theatrical and filmic performances intersect and acting becomes a self-conscious, supposedly avant-garde art form, a career choice. The abject, stripped performer on a stage, a trope in which Wallace placed his faith, has things in common with more modern forms of theatre than those I have invoked thus far: the existential theatre of Beckett (whose character Hamm, among others, 'Deathbed''s father vividly recalls), as well as Antonin Artaud's Theatre of Cruelty. But often, when Wallace represents characters who are explicitly engaged in professional avant-garde projects in the kind of theatre of abjection I have argued is subtly and fleetingly present in *Brief Interviews*, the results are often parodic objects of pretension and unfulfilled artistry. Such moments are frequently evocative of all that Wallace called out in postmodernists, and not at all these clarifying moments of finding that self that is coterminous with struggle. In fact, to self-consciously embrace the role of performer in an ongoing artistic way, regardless of whether it is for screen or stage, seems to doom Wallace's characters: note all the long-term addicts, from Stokely Darkstar and Joelle van Dyne to James Incandenza himself, who act in Poor Yorick film productions in *Infinite Jest*. James's works often interweave theatre and film or devise films that are set at plays (*The Medusa and the Odalisque* is one example), but usually the kinds of generative philosophical performance I have extracted from *Brief Interviews* fall prey to the camera's mediation, become a mannered act, or dissolve into feeble, non-rigorous art.

Consider Incandenza's efforts in 'Found Drama', called 'probably the historical zenith of self-consciously dumb stasis' in his already rather static work (Wallace, 2006: 398). In these 'conceptually unfilmable' efforts that ostensibly combine highly minimalist theatre with film (989 n24), James draws out the idea that everything is performance: he throws a dart at a randomly torn-out page from the phone book and calls 'whatever happens to the protagonist with the name you hit' in the next ninety minutes the (unfilmed) drama, after which 'you go out and have drinks with critics who like chortlingly congratulate you on the ultimate in Neorealism' (1028 n145). Found Drama comes to James on a night he is 'sloppy-blotto' with Lyle (375). 'Dumb stasis' indeed: Wallace clearly suggests Found Drama is not art at all, exemplary of postmodernism's sterility and James's excuse-strewn, lazy pathway back into the addiction and excess that art, for Wallace, ought to mitigate.

In *The Pale King*, a book squarely focused on the boring, dramaless everyday, the conscious use of avant-garde theatrical techniques is less maligned, yet still not as artistically productive as the uncanny performances Wallace arranged for unassuming figures in *Brief Interviews*. In an imagined play that Tom McCarthy aptly says invokes 'the entirety of Beckett's drama' (McCarthy, 2011), an IRS examiner describes the 'totally real, true-to-life', and 'unperformable' play he aspires to write. 'The setting is very bare and minimalistic', just the office of an examiner at work. Eventually the audience will all get up and leave, and only then 'the real action of the play can start', though the writer 'could never decide on the action, if there is any' (Wallace, 2012b: 112). The lack of action and drama is the philosophical point of this Beckettian theatre, but one sees here perhaps Wallace's meditation on the pitfalls of composing (and aspiring to compose, amid much apparent writer's block) the potentially quite alienating *Pale King*, rather than a full modelling of his own dramatic intentions in the book. With the novel incomplete, it is impossible to tell how this play's ideas about the REC as a stage set might have connected with, in §14, the framing of the many interview fragments, including apparently Fogle's whole narrative, as the product of a documentary film. The description of that filming sounds similar to the actionless play: 'It's an IRS examiner in a chair, in a room. There is little else to see' (107). While I have throughout drawn a distinction between films and live theatre, documentary – with its association with truthful and unvarnished self-presentation by comparison to fictional films, and its potential to shade into things like Fogle's narration – might have in a completed *Pale King* done similar work to the images of minimalist theatre I have mined for their philosophical potential.

Wallace seems to have been at his best and most comfortable with avant-garde dramatic intertexts when he could, as with Socrates' shadowy presence in *Brief Interviews*, bend (foreign) philosophical theatre to his own contexts and ends, part of a pattern Lucas Thompson identifies of Wallace 'rework[ing]' his global influences, levelling their geographic distinctiveness so they could be used mainly 'to defamiliarize his Americanness' (Thompson, 2019: 3). Throughout *Infinite Jest*, but primarily in Marathe and Steeply's dialogue, Wallace tropes on Peter Weiss's Beckett- and Artaud-inspired play, *The Persecution and Assassination of Jean-Paul Marat as Performed by the Inmates of the Asylum of Charenton under the Direction of the Marquis de Sade*, or *Marat/Sade*. Thompson and Andrew Warren have each made apt arguments about the philosophical significance of *Marat/Sade* to the Marathe/Steeply debates, with Warren arguing that Steeply embodies the play's discourse on individuality and freedom (Warren, 2018: 176), and Thompson claiming that Wallace's use of M and S initials implies 'that Marathe's views correspond to Jean-Paul Marat's position on violence and revolutionary zeal, while Steeply's character aligns with [Sade's] cynical pragmatism' (Thompson, 2019: 18). But from the perspective on abject, deeply embodied performance I have developed here I would emphasize the way in which Wallace's wheelchair-bound Marathe – as one of Wallace's most agile philosophical performers, voicing so many of the book's themes of suspect worship, instant gratification, and failed American discipline – refashions the basic dramatic presence of Weiss's Marat, who speaks from his medicinal bath and gives voice and embodiment to what Robert Cohen calls 'Weiss's obsession with the body in pain' (Cohen, 1998: xiv). More critical work might be done on Wallace's version of Weiss's obsession with the body in pain, as well as on how Sade's behind-bars, mentally ill players at Charenton serve as a model for Wallace's mongrel cast at AA meetings and the many jester-patients of the Ennet House common room. These are all examples of how grotesque dramas of ideas, not just ideas themselves, guided Wallace.

Thompson and Warren also leave out of their consideration of Weiss's influence on *Infinite Jest* Wallace's more direct allusion to *Marat/Sade* in Himself's productions, an allusion that, like Found Drama, illuminates anew the pitfalls of performance for Wallace when it becomes self-conscious and affected. Here, Himself's use of his camera to turn a stage performance into a film *about* a stage performance seems to have lethal effects on the production of what Wallace elsewhere calls 'nourishing' art (Miller, 2012: 60). The filmography endnote entry on James's appropriation of Weiss's play and Peter Brook's well-known 1967 film adaptation reads:

> Fictional 'interactive documentary' on Boston stage production of Weiss's 20th-century play within play, in which the documentary's chemically impaired director (Incandenza) repeatedly interrupts the inmates' dumbshow-capering and Marat and Sade's dialogues to discourse incoherently on the implications of Brando's Method Acting and Artaud's Theatre of Cruelty for North American filmed entertainment. (Wallace, 2006: 993 n24)

A 'cerebral hemorrhage' follows, someone is thrown into Marat's medicinal bath, and 'Incandenza becomes ill all over the theatre audience's first row', a merger of addictive life and alleged art that nourishes no one and figures as a precedent for a title film that mysteriously, in trying to reach its audience through representation, becomes an addictive, real-life killer (993 n24). Weiss's illuminating philosophical rumination on pain devolves into the Poor Yorick crew's own real pain, their unredemptive found drama and cruelty to themselves. Finally the Brando mention reminds us of his biggest follower, in art and in everyday gestures – James's father – and suggests that among the addictions he passed along to son and grandson may be an attachment to method-acting one's way through life, purporting to seek the real but actually inhabiting a philosophical and emotional cloud. The better alternative for all Incandenzas would be to use art's powerful distancing effect to represent and see clearly the cruel, horrific struggle of selfhood – as we readers are able to do at many points in Wallace's oeuvre, but especially so when performance is not self-consciously inhabited as such.

'Life for him had the quality of a performance', D. T. Max writes in his biography of Wallace (Max, 2012: 13) as he was nervously preparing to interview for college, an experience Max says he would later fictionalize in the opening of *Infinite Jest*. As the fiction career he began during those college years developed further, including some portrayals of Sophist-like interviewees along the way, Wallace would prove that if performing was an inevitable part of life, it could be – it needed to be – shaped into a philosophically potent resource. *The Pale King* is largely set in the mid-1980s, but its 'Author's Foreword' remarks on connections to the meaning of performance in the twenty-first century in which Wallace wrote: 'one disadvantage of addressing you here directly and in person in the cultural present of 2005 is the fact that, as both you and I know, there is no longer any kind of clear line between personal and public, or rather between private vs. performative' (Wallace, 2012b: 80). By 2005 the divide between private and performed may have been obliterated, largely by the on-screen entertainment culture and performed sophistry that had been the dominant concerns of Wallace's work at least up through *Brief Interviews* (and into many parts of *Oblivion* too). But by *The Pale King* he saw value and new opportunity in reconstructing, in key moments, the perceptive apparatus of a generation born in and around the 1930s and not raised with television performance as a monumental cultural fact, such as Fogle's father and the accounting substitute. Of the latter's philosophical lecturing Fogle observes, 'when he put the first transparency on the overhead projector and the room's lights dimmed, his face was lit from below like a cabaret performer's, which made its hollow intensity and facial structures even more pronounced' (220). The substitute teacher is one of several other theatrical, philosophizing speech-makers in Wallace's works that the critical paradigm I have described here might be extended to cover, for throughout his career Wallace's sense that philosophical fiction ought to exploit a drama of performed ideas remained consistent. Along the way the features of that theatre – its props and costumes, its performers' physicality, the way he scripted it on the page, and the means by which it catalysed in readers an abiding Socratic wisdom – were all quite brilliantly deployed and transformed.

References

Cioffi, F. (2000). '"An Anguish Become Thing": Narrative as Performance in David Foster Wallace's *Infinite Jest*', in *Narrative* 8:2, 161–81.

Cohen, R. (1998). 'Introduction', vii–xxiv. In Peter Weiss, *Marat/Sade, the Investigation, The Shadow of the Body of the Coachman*, ed. Robert Cohen. New York NY: Continuum.

Kelly, A. (2014). 'David Foster Wallace and the Novel of Ideas', 3–22. In Marshall Boswell, ed., *David Foster Wallace and 'The Long Thing': New Essays on the Novels*. London and New York NY: Bloomsbury.

Max, D. T. (2012). *Every Love Story Is a Ghost Story: A Life of David Foster Wallace*. New York NY: Penguin Books.

McCarthy, T. (14 April 2011). '"The Last Audit". Review of *The Pale King* and *Fate, Time, and Language: An Essay on Free Will*, by David Foster Wallace'. *New York Times*.

Miller, L. (2012). 'The Salon Interview', 58–65. In Stephen J. Burn, ed., *Conversations with David Foster Wallace*. Jackson MS: University Press of Mississippi.

Puchner, M. (2010). *The Drama of Ideas: Platonic Provocations in Theater and Philosophy*. New York NY: Oxford University Press.

Scott, A. O. (20 February 2000). 'The Panic of Influence'. *New York Review of Books*.

Severs, J. (2017). *David Foster Wallace's Balancing Books: Fictions of Value*. New York NY: Columbia University Press.

Smith, Z. (2009). *Changing My Mind: Occasional Essays*. New York NY: Penguin.

Stein, L. (2012). 'David Foster Wallace: In the Company of Creeps', 89–93. In Stephen J. Burn ed., *Conversations with David Foster Wallace*. Jackson MS: University Press of Mississippi.

Thompson, L. (2019). 'David Foster Wallace's Germany', in *Comparative Literature Studies* 56:1, 1–30.
Wallace, D. Foster. (1993). *The Broom of the System*. 1987. Reprint. New York NY: Avon.
Wallace, D. Foster. (1997). *A Supposedly Fun Thing I'll Never Do Again: Essays and Arguments*. New York NY: Black Bay Books.
Wallace, D. Foster. (1999–2000). 'The Party 2000', 47. *Rolling Stone*, 830/831, 30 December 1999, 6 January 2000.
Wallace, D. Foster. (1999). *Brief Interviews with Hideous Men*. Boston MA: Little, Brown.
Wallace, D. Foster. (2005). *Consider the Lobster and Other Essays*. New York NY: Little, Brown.
Wallace, D. Foster. (2006). *Infinite Jest*. 10th Anniversary ed. New York NY: Back Bay.
Wallace, D. Foster. (2012a). *Both Flesh and Not: Essays*. New York NY: Little, Brown.
Wallace, D. Foster. (2012b). *The Pale King: An Unfinished Novel*. 2011. New York NY: Back Bay.
Warren, A. (2018). 'Wallace and Politics', 173–89. In Ralph Clare, ed., *The Cambridge Companion to David Foster Wallace*. Cambridge: Cambridge University Press.

Internet sources

Karmodi, O. (13 June 2011), '"A Frightening Time in America": An Interview with David Foster Wallace', in *NYR Blog*. https://tinyurl.com/eutpx6bv (accessed 30 June 2021).

3

'A matter of perspective': 'Good Old Neon' between literature and philosophy

Adriano Ardovino and Pia Masiero

> One of his recent stories ends in the finality of this half sentence: Not another word. But there is always another word. There is always another reader to regenerate these words.
>
> Don DeLillo 'Informal Remarks from the David Foster Wallace Memorial Service in New York on 23 October 2008'

> You think that because you understand 'one' that you must understand 'two' because one and one makes two. But you forget that you must understand 'and'.
>
> Sufi story

Whose 'other words'?

'– in other words David Wallace trying, if only in the second his lids are down, to somehow reconcile what this luminous guy had seemed like from the outside with whatever on the interior must have driven him to kill himself in such a dramatic and doubtlessly painful way –' (Wallace, 2004: 181).

'Good Old Neon' is heading to its close: we are in its final (almost) two-page-long paragraph, deep in the folds of the stunning revelation that changes everything we have assumed since the beginning, forty pages earlier. We'll have to return to this final paragraph in due course. Still this sentence allows us to begin entering and mapping the labyrinthine maze of David Foster Wallace's most famous short story and some of the stakes at play, both literary and philosophical.

Let us begin with a minor grammatical detail, a matter of utmost importance that articulates the gist of it all: 'in other words' – which promises to come to the point of the whole narrative, to present its core basic impulse – is given parenthetically. On a very basic level we are here confronted with a narrative deflection attempting to refine what has already been said: a clause that bespeaks the need to fine-tune the telling while interrupting it. This implies that linearity does not clarify matters; something else, something more is needed.[1] Throughout the short story the proliferation of attempts to clarify – represented syntactically by relative, attributive, or incidental clauses – signals an obsession with finding the right words to honour reality.[2] This transversal issue, typical of Wallace's macro-text, is coupled with the awareness of its own impending inevitable failure. Incremental, maximalist sentences – we are analysing an exemplary one – aiming at an unattainable precision are the formal correlative of the never-ending, inevitable need for *other* words to describe how things are, especially in most emotionally charged moments of our lives. The very fact that we always need other words, which, typically, interrupt our first-level train of thought, *both* proves our failure *and* attests to this need to find other words – which, in an endless loop, cannot but again fail. As 'Good Old Neon' repeatedly reminds us, this is because of the incommensurability between feelings and the language we have to articulate them: 'one-word-after-another-word English ... is all we have' (151). Therefore failing is so intrinsic to our being humans that it loses its relevance in favour of a reflection on *how* we fail, consciously or unconsciously, authentically or not. Hayes-Brady suggests that 'the interpretive gap ... exists only because of the inevitably incomplete nature of communication, and so, counter-intuitively, the necessary failure of communicative exchange- functions as proof against solipsistic tragedy' (Hayes-Brady, 2016: 10). And so one wonders: might not the ultimate trajectory of this short story be an invitation to consider literature as the quintessential form of authentic failure – a failure acknowledging that other words, the words of others,[3] should be looked for and imagined and spoken and listened to and read and written again and again? Can we not read the 'Not another word' that famously closes the story as the silencing of those who are trapped in the awareness 'that you can't ever truly know what's going on inside somebody else' (Wallace, 2004: 181) and yet argue against trying and failing again through literary (and not philosophical) endeavours? In other words can we not read this imperative silencing as a need to suspend rationality, i.e., firepower, that allows for an empty space in which another truth can be heard?

Back to the opening quote: the tentativeness contained in such words as 'trying', 'somehow', 'seemed', 'whatever' is counterbalanced by the force of the modal 'must have' and the adverb 'doubtlessly', which point to the certainty that a definite reason explaining this luminous guy's decision to kill himself exists and that there are physically unobjectionable facts everyone can easily relate to and recognize as truthful. Significantly, 'must' is present only three times in the whole short story: when Neal tries to read and interpret his sister's reactions (149 and 172) and here, where the foundation of David Wallace's engagement with Neal's story is described. Significantly, 'must' and 'trying' go hand in hand for both Neal and David Wallace: the reconciliation of outward appearances and interior landscapes may be tentative ('*somewhat* reconcile') but is none the less a necessity that transcends direct experiences and hinges upon what is emotionally recognizable.

Furthermore the *subject* of the gerundial form 'trying' is David Wallace, who is, at the same time, the *object* of Neal's telling. Here we touch the core of the narratological skeleton of the short story: it is a first-person narrative offered in the final paragraph as attributable to a David Wallace. Readers, therefore, face a referential tangle in which the first-person narrator names himself as the narrated and are consequently asked to reconfigure what they have read so far, to try to reconcile what seems like a Möbius strip: the narrator (partially) recedes into the background, bringing to existence (a version of) his creator who thus crosses diegetic boundaries and becomes imaginatively reflected upon. As we will see in a moment, the situation is much more complex than this, but it is sufficient to say here that the short story is predicated upon an inherent – possibly unresolvable – narratological recalcitrance, which constitutes one of the many paradoxes readers must confront.[4] The paradoxical nature of the short story's primary theme – fraudulence, the discrepancy between appearance and essence and the amplification of the former at the expense of the latter – is formally mirrored and thus becomes a theme rich in literary and philosophical branchings. The name David Wallace[5] indicates that we should at least peripherally consider this 'in other words' meta-fictionally, as a pointer to the short story's formal structure – an indication of the source of the text we are reading.

The entire short story thus can be read against an interpretative horizon constituted by the diegetic relationship between Neal–David Wallace (and their respective, shifting roles), the extradiegetic relationship between David Foster Wallace and the reader, the inherently metaleptic David Wallace himself, and the pervasive second-person pronoun *you*. All these textual and extratextual positions, each with its own specific perspectival underpinnings, take on a paradoxical duplicity – a multi-layered reiteration or refraction that is extremely challenging to navigate, let alone master. The difficulty is amplified by the issue of the story's being posthumous, which represents the thematic centre of the text: 'Good Old Neon' presents a (philosophical) reflection on (literary) language as the quintessential embodiment of being-posthumous in all its different facets, namely, words after the end versus words at the end, from the end (to the beginning), about the end.

The pages that follow will unpack the three layers that constitute the narratological skeleton of the short story and propose an in-depth analysis of the distinguishing features of each in the chronological order in which they enter the fictional stage. The reader encounters Neal, who speaks and imagines, David Wallace, who stares and imagines, and David Foster Wallace, who writes and imagines. In our interpretation, the reader reaches this third layer ready to consider a further inflection of the notion of imagination that pertains to the short story as a whole.

While we delve into these three layers we will consider why a reflection on the shifting referents of the second-person pronoun is necessary to understand the dynamics of the text and why Neal's posthumous positioning and its inherent privileges – first and foremost omniscience – opens up a reflection on the kind of authorship Wallace is interested in. Being-posthumous turns out to provide a frame, an interpretative key, that juxtaposes knowledge with invention.

In our reading Wallace's short story ultimately stages a meditation on how literary imagination may counterbalance and somehow undo the ending – opening up the possibility of endlessness, so to speak. Our overall argument is that the kind of imagining activated here is the essence of literature itself. This statement is rooted in our close-reading experience: we experienced the short story as thematizing, indirectly, what literature is all about according to David Foster Wallace. This aboutness concerns, crucially, the possibility of caring and compassion, past the pervasiveness of fraudulence and past the manipulative attitude that fraudulence entails. This possibility is predicated upon a recalcitrance to disentangling once and for all the ambiguity of the final paragraph: everything is in the hands of the author, who shapes the ending of this short story in such a way as to open a breach of wonder and a breach to wonder that is sufficiently empty as to resonate with meaning.

Neal's narrating and imagining

The tripartite textual structure of the short story may be summarized through key verbs: Neal, speaking, narrates and sees; David Wallace, thinking, imagines Neal as narrating and seeing; David Foster Wallace, writing, imagines David Wallace imagining Neal narrating.

Neal takes textual shape around the act of narrating;[6] he is assertive, articulate, assured in his self-perception and presentation. The opening sentence 'My whole life I've been a fraud' does not allow for any doubtful undertone. Neal's assurance is manifest in the control he exerts over his narrative: he repeatedly anticipates what will come next (the scene of his death and what it feels like to die); he does not fail to remark that he has kept his narrative promise (once he actually reaches the scene of his death); he comments on what his listeners might be thinking about the long preamble before the promised death scene. His attention to his listeners is monological even when he conjures an intradiegetic or extradiegetic 'you' – be it himself, the reader, his sister, or David Wallace. Fraudulently oriented towards triggering a certain behavioural reaction, Neal listens complacently to the sound of his own voice; he summons others in a 'piece of high-powered machinery' that refers both to the vehicle of movement-towards-death (car) and the vehicle of a narrative-towards-life (story). This posthumous portrait of himself requires a dialogic context to measure both its verisimilar narrative trajectory and its relevance beyond the self as mere narrator: to move past internal self-referential musings and become communicative and true.

'English is all we have to try to understand [what we think we are talking about when we say 'my life'] and try to form anything larger or more meaningful and true *with anybody else*' (151, emphasis added). The second-person is as much required as the first-person (more on this in a moment) to shape a form that might be experientially more relatable. This in short is the reason why the deictics concerning our own embodied selves are activated ('*we*'re sitting *here* in *this* car') and why '*this* isn't even really about *me*' (152) – but, through David Wallace, about potentially every inhabitant of our post-industrial times.

This posthumous portrait of himself passes through writing (his suicide note) and his abstention from writing. Both are measured against the yardstick of fraudulence: the note to his sister is presented as somehow immune from fraudulence because of its intrinsic 'last-testament urgency' (171), whereas the note to Dr Gustafson is presented as impossible to rescue from fraudulence – 'I knew that in the note I'd spend a lot of time trying to seem as if I was being honest but really just dancing around the truth' (170). Writing is none the less peripheral to Neal's portrait and relegated to being a residue of what he is *telling us* – as he specifies in reference to the suicide note to his sister: 'I simply said, without going into anything like the level of detail I've given you, ... that I was killing myself because I was an essentially fraudulent person' (173 emphasis added).

Neal finally, and crucially, imagines. Neal imagining himself imagined by someone might easily be taken as the perfect instantiation of a narcissistic impulse: conjuring up someone who is so engorged in figuring himself (Neal) out that he invents an immersive first-person monologue. And yet, at this climactic moment, our reading experience registered a difference which allowed us to glance past the narcissistic loop: the story also permits a reading which recognizes in David Wallace an authenticity that defies Neal's manipulative strategy. He is presented as someone capable of looking at Neal with the sole purpose of understanding his existential predicament as a fellow human being – as an other mind, which is intrinsically opaque but can be reached thanks to a compassionate, imaginative gaze. This reading – David Wallace as having a life untouched by Neal's manipulation – depends on his being portrayed as someone struck by a discovery – Neal's suicide – that urges him to find a narrative to honour a life that cannot be 'imagined as happy and unreflective and wholly unhaunted by voices' (181), a narrative that turns bafflement into caring. Neal invests this final imaginative foray with a thrust that allows the shift from philosophical understanding to literary exploration. He summons someone to whom he can ascribe the only trait that, in his fraudulence, he has forfeited: a decentring subject capable of listening who possesses a gaze which conjugates penetration and discernment with care.[7] We will return to this possible reading alongside the other – fraudulent – one later when we consider the potential of the conversation in the car. Preliminarily let us suggest that, among the many dialogical situations that Neal evokes (with his foster parents, his sister, his therapist), the conversation in the car mobilizes compassionate listening; there the narrative machinery is not exploited for manipulative effects, or rather for fake authenticity, but is offered for the other's awareness and evaluation.

Once we reread the short story taking up the interpretative invitation to attribute everything to David Wallace, not a single word of the monologue changes in the literal sense. As we will see, what changes is how David Wallace's engagement comes to appear a highly religious gesture – in the etymological sense, as *re-legens* (reading again and more deeply) and *re-ligans* (binding together again and more tightly).

David Wallace appears at the end of Neal's monologue. Crucially, he neither writes nor narrates, that is, he duplicates neither the quintessential identity of the author nor that of the (surface) protagonist. His 'act of imagining Neal's life is portrayed as a purely mental event largely beyond his control and unchecked by any considerations of craft or audience' (Kocela, 2018: 68). David Wallace enters the stage in the guise of someone who experiences a series of happenings. He is narrated as doing things that have some kind of relationship with imagining, understood in the full sense of sentimental acts and respective mental experiences that rest on factual fragments – scanning the photo, reading about the incident. David Wallace 'blinks', 'tries to imagine', has thoughts-feelings-memories-impressions, 'tries to reconcile' outside and inside, 'is fully aware', 'tries very consciously to prohibit, having emerged from years, [experiencing] a part of him commanding the other part' (Wallace,

2004:181). Even the final verb – commanding – can easily be read as bespeaking an internal intentional stance securing the possibility of imagining. David Wallace tries, and tries, and then tries again – but, crucially, he does not write a single word.

If David Wallace is the centre of this narrative of the (other) self, then that centre is the act of imagining; Neal's narrating and David Foster Wallace's writing are subsumed into David Wallace's imagining. To put it in other words: David Wallace mobilizes his mental and emotional abilities to conjure up someone else's particularized self. This kind of imagining is the essence of literature itself: an imagining (the author's) that activates another imagination (the reader's) and produces a form of understanding (of the self and the other) both in the person who authored the narrative and in the person to whom the narrative was addressed. Literary imagining moves away from narcissism – in which the kind of image of oneself projected is paramount – into religious communication (in the etymological sense suggested above) and caring. 'Good Old Neon' stages this movement by redirecting the reader's attention towards David Wallace, a fictional version of the author who is crucially engaged in what we might consider pre-authorial activities. Paradoxically Neal seems to be much more engaged in authorial activities than David Wallace: he is always claiming authorship of his fraudulent narratives, which are intended to please; of his insights concerning other people's reactions; and of the consequent vicious repetitions these insights spawn. It is thus paramount to focus on David Wallace and delve deeper into his central role.

David Wallace's staring and imagining

In the many readings this short story has elicited, the spelling out of the name David Wallace is always indicated as a key moment. By conjuring up his presence Neal's long rant undermines the stability of the text as the reader has appraised it so far: a straightforward, first-person stream-of-consciousness-like narrative couched in a highly conversational tone. At the beginning of this final paragraph Neal strives to get at the essence of what he has been trying to say, returning to the central and overarching paradox of time – 'the reality is that dying isn't bad, but it takes forever. And that forever is no time at all' – and reducing it to 'a matter of perspective'. The concluding two-pages-long sentence endeavours to explain 'the big picture', stating that the 'back-and-forth between us' is only seemingly endless but actually happens in the time needed to stir a pot, pack some pipe tobacco with a thumb, roll cat hair off a blouse, inhale before starting to speak, or blink while idly scanning photos. Most of these gestures belong to characters Neal has already mentioned in his narrative – Fern, his stepfather, Angela Mead, Melissa Betts – except for the last one (blinking), which refers to David Wallace, whose name appears here for the first time in the story. Whereas the other gestures are indeed brief, it is difficult to think of 'seeing my photo and trying, through the tiny little keyhole of himself, to imagine what all must have happened to lead up to my death ... like what sorts of pain or problems might have driven the guy to get in his electric-blue Corvette and try to drive with all that O.T.C. medication in his bloodstream' (180) as occurring in the short moment marked by David Wallace's blink: blinking/scanning versus seeing/imagining are for us, embodied readers, different ways of engaging with reality that are impossible to conflate.[8]

We are furthermore caught off guard because, in the short space of five lines, the narrative centre shifts from the first-person (*my* photo, *my* death) to the second-person (*your* stepfather), then to the third-person (*the* guy, *his* Corvette, *his* bloodstream). The powerful first-person voice that has been in charge so far seems to collapse and vanish into the third, never to return. This pronominal shift, however, may be interpreted as *not* interrupting the flow of Neal's speaking but manifesting the strongest form of his authority: he continues narrating in a different guise, looking at himself through David Wallace's perspectival positioning. We prefer this reading to the other possible one, in which Neal's presence evaporates because of David Foster Wallace's alleged need to unveil his imagining activity via his fictional self. The main reason for our preference is twofold: the tone and style remain the same, but Neal's posthumous positioning entails both omniscience and the (likely) resolution of his manipulation. As we will see in a moment, this positioning triggers a reflection on what literature is all about.

The pronominal shift is not simply a transitory distancing effect, which we have already witnessed ('you're thinking here's this guy going on and on and why doesn't he get to the part where he kills himself …' 169); it rather seems to be a complete change in the narrative situation that shifts it from first-person to (pseudo-)figural.[9] Neal leaves behind his narrating-I and becomes an external narrator who positions David Wallace's internally focalized perspective on himself. This is a figural narrative of sorts for two reasons: because Neal's omniscience and extradiegetic positioning are specifically ascribed to Neal's afterlife existence (whereas the omniscience of the typical external narrator is axiomatically posited), and because the focalizer's gaze is reflectively directed towards the narrator himself. This figural narrative is partial and not absolute, since the narrator's idiom, Neal's, is recognizable: despite the pronominal shift, the voice is seamlessly his. Neal's move results in a subtle and illuminating mirroring effect: subtle because the words remain the same, illuminating because now those (same) words are filtered through another's (external) point of view. Neal is thus offered an image of himself that he may accept as a gift that exists beyond his entrenched need to manipulate it and control others' reactions. It could obviously be argued that this is his umpteenth manipulative move; however, in our reading, what is important is the evocation of an alterity, which, as such, has its own independent (narrative) take on reality. In other words David Foster Wallace creates the textual conditions for a character whose fraudulence has wrecked his life to experience the potentially healing gift of someone else's narrative (that is, literary) decentring.[10] Both readings – the one in which Neal keeps narrating in a different guise and the one in which Neal disappears because Wallace cannot hide behind his fictional self any more – provide the reader with a different, embodied perspective. The need to manipulate remains a given to be coped with in any case, but we are invited to entertain the possibility of relinquishing our mental powers and allowing for the potential existence of another (paradoxical) perspective. This opening too is religious in nature, as it accepts the manifestation of alterity.

The centrality of imagination is reiterated and magnified here and takes the shape of an experience of imaginative compassion: Neal imagines David Wallace as having compassion for him → David Wallace imagines because he has compassion for Neal → David Foster Wallace, a writer who conceives literature as an inherently compassionate gesture, imagines himself as David Wallace while imagining Neal imagine himself from the outside, by someone who does not know him. David Wallace's imaginative trajectory takes the form of letting Neal speak faithfully about his fraudulent posture, but it takes him past his need to manipulate. This, as we said earlier, is presented as an attempt. David Foster Wallace presents David Wallace's attempt as the quintessence of literature, just as he presents Neal's narcissism as intrinsic to authoriality. David Foster Wallace, furthermore, has David Wallace, that is, his fictional self, both described and seen from the outside and understood from the inside through Neal's posthumous positioning. One way or another these imaginings bear the seeds of failure. If, as we have suggested, literature is quintessentially a form of failure, this piling up of imaginative failures reinforces the invitation to make room for other words that provide a different perspective.

That the focalizer bears the name David Wallace implies that this narrative move both provides the reasons to envision (and thus reconfigure) the first-person narrative as embedded and signals the authorial self as the object of representation. This reading has nothing to do with the 'troubling trend' of taking 'the "Wallace" as character for a bona fide surrogate of David Foster Wallace' that Cory Hudson is worried about (Hudson, 2018: 298); it has everything to do with addressing the consequences of using this name and not any other possible one. Neal's rendering is in keeping with the main tenets of a figural narrative, that is, privileged access to a character's interiority in the very terms by which that character apprehends itself. This is the typical effect of the story's narrative situation, which, despite the third-person pronoun, depends on internal colouring (by the focalizer). The fact that David Wallace is a fictionalized version of the real author creates a refraction and gives the text its peculiar circular (and paradoxical) aspect: Neal imagines all the people that inhabit his world because this is part and parcel of feeding his basic need to be approved and loved – and he goes as far in his narcissistic trajectory as to imagine occupying the mind of the would-be author. In a reading that privileges the seamless, recognizable quality of Neal's voice, and thus does not posit his disappearance, the story's narrative emerges as belonging to Neal's unique way of apprehending the world. However, once we accept the proposal to read 'this whole seemingly endless back-and-forth between us' (180) as anchored in David Wallace's own subjective, imaginative horizon, we must read the depiction of the (fictional) authorial self, David Wallace, as self-projected. In one way or another we are presented with a doubling that concerns the opaque relationship between inside and outside and the related issue of one's self-perception.

Fraudulence – the most glaring theme of the story – potentially infects everything that happens within it: fraudulence is the unassailable core of Neal's perception of himself, whether we take him to be a first-order character or we take him to be the instantiation of David Wallace's hypothesis on the 'luminous guy' (second-order character). It is also what we might experience as readers who have been led to believe in Neal's first-order existence.

The text, however, also allows for a reading that deflects and diffuses this fraudulence – or at least creates the possibility of other (authorial) words regarding its meaning. It is now time to consider authorship (and its gifts) more closely.

David Foster Wallace's writing and imagining

Neal's narrating position turns the 'matter of perspective' into a matter of authorship too. The invitation to read the story again after its final reconfiguration extends well beyond the issue of ascription to this or that character's imagination and constitutes a reflection on how 'individuals generate subject-dependent constructs of their world through their mental representations and verbal descriptions' (Nünning, 2001: 209) – that is, it is a way to foreground the need to attend to the 'obscure invitation' to reconsider 'the persistence of the author', to echo Benjamin Widiss's title. We would like to expand David Hering's idea that Wallace's metafictional texts, starting with 'Octet', 'can be described as Wallace performing a mediation of his own prior style, an interrogation of and escape from the voice which, until this point, he has possessed' (Hering, 2016: 33). What 'Good Old Neon' makes collaterally clear is that David Foster Wallace *de facto* stages two authorial characters – the first through his afterlife positioning, the second through his name.

Whether we approach it via Cavell, as Matt Prout does in Chapter 10 below, or via Borges's essay on Zeno as Hudson proposes, the central theme of other minds is given a further turn of the screw once we add the issue of literary authorship to the mix. The latter veers the story toward a reflection on the different tools philosophy and literature have at their disposal to address this theme and its branchings. Interestingly, the two authorial personas the story presents manifest themselves through distinct features belonging to their authorial function: omniscience, on the one hand, and compassionate imagination, on the other. Both correspond to the kind of author David Foster Wallace is interested in being. This interest precedes 'the premise that [Wallace's] ideas on the moral usefulness of literature were partly modeled on the widely accepted assumption that novel reading augments the so-called "empathy-altruism hypothesis"' (Staes, 2012: 410): any consideration about what might happen after reading should not deviate us away from reflecting on the act of writing, which is predicated not upon speaking but upon lending a voice.

Let's say we agree with Hudson's final remarks, namely, that 'perhaps it would be more correct to read the short story as an exhaustive attempt to demonstrate the impermeability of the bounds of consciousness' (Hudson, 2018: 304): at the philosophical level, the problem of other minds remains unsolvable. And yet, at the literary level, it is safe to say that the story is a successful piece of literature for the following reasons. Firstly, because the fact that it is 'unable to get anywhere, to reach a formal conclusion about Neal' does not preclude our engagement with the kind of (mental) life Neal is imagined to have – be it projective or not. Secondly, because it is not – and here too we agree with Hudson – 'a metafictional experiment that illustrates a storyteller's ability to mediate a meaningful relationship between two people' but a literary experiment into what a literary author can do – not so much to tell us the truth about Neal but to provide a springboard by which we might engage experientially with what David Foster Wallace deemed one of the illnesses of our present era. To do so, it moves past its metafictional scaffolding into a 'perspective structure' (Nünning, 2001: 207) that trades in the stuff we are made of – the first-person singular.[11]

As we have seen with regard to the last two pages of the story, a figural narrative allows access to a character's interiority; the worldview we are presented with belongs to that interiority and is coloured by it, even if it is not presented via the first-person pronoun. This similarity – in terms of immersive effects – poses a simple question: why has David Wallace not chosen a figural narrative to hypothesize Neal's predicament along the same lines as the one he used to have Neal describe himself? Why has David Foster Wallace preferred to hide his first-order narrating namesake not partially (within the folds of a figural narrative) but absolutely?

The text itself supplies a very strong argument to explain why David Foster Wallace opted for a first-person narrative and not a third-person, internally focalized one. When Neal evaluates the effects of his suicidal note, he comments:

> what a fine and genuine-seeming performance in a drama it would make if only we all had not already been subject to countless scenes just like it in dramas ever since we first saw a movie or read a book, which somehow entailed that real scenes like the one of my suicide note were now compelling and genuine *only to their participants* and to anyone else would come off as banal and even somewhat cheesy or maudlin. (176, emphasis added)

The narrative choice of the first-person to shape David Wallace's imaginative re-creation of 'what must have driven' this luminous guy to kill himself is the best (narrative) way of reducing the risk of triteness: present these reasons as they felt to Neal himself from within and parasitically project a ventriloquized voice. One could argue that the standard payoffs of a figural narrative typically centre on the possibility of employing what Dorrit Cohn aptly called 'stylistic contagion' (Cohn, 1978: 33), the blurring of the extradiegetic narrator's and diegetic focalizer's positions and the consequent sliding of the former's voice towards the idiosyncratic features of the latter. And yet, the counterargument to this narratological alternative is exactly what makes 'Good Old Neon' such an engaging text: taking the 'genuine-only-to-their-participant' notion literally in the only formal way possible – through the first-person pronoun, but using a character whose name inherently suggests a metaleptic crossing.

As we have already suggested, this appropriation – which can be read on one level (DW's) as the result of the attempt to wear someone else's shoes empathetically, and on another (DFW's) as the result of an inventive and compassionate literary exploration of emotionally charged materials – should be interpreted alongside the use of the second-person pronoun. It is its employment with multiple referents that makes this multi-level machinery much more than a metafictional device.

The 'genuine-only-to-their-participant' argument moreover directs us towards an interpretative hypothesis that might shed further light on the highly dialogic nature of Neal's alleged monologue. The 'you' evoked in the very first paragraph of the story – 'You get the idea' (Wallace, 2004: 141), 'You know what I mean' (142) – might be interpreted as an instantiation of David Wallace as the privileged listener to Neal's invented telling. The successfulness of David Foster Wallace's imaginative foray into having David Wallace understand Neal (and be understood) would thus require both evocation of the first-person pronoun and projection of his own fictional self – first as the privileged recipient of that telling, then as the I's perfect double, i.e., someone who wants to commit suicide in the very moment in which he is doing it. Then finally, as his own posthumous and thus knowledgeable self-created creator.

This trajectory is textually manifested in a second-person pronoun that starts off referring to some sort of generic listener or reader and becomes progressively the 'you' in the car with Neal on his fatal last drive – 'his' referring crucially to both Neal and his own dialogic projection. This progressive sliding towards a precise spatio-temporal field – the Corvette – reconfigures the story as a meditation on the explorations of the self as other that literature allows. This is successful only in so far as the others always implied – i.e. readers, 'you'[12] – feel they have been offered imaginable experiential positions for themselves too. This implicit invitation to imagine according to our own experience moves in a precise discursive direction which, broadly speaking, goes from allocution to interlocution, from the mere creation of a rhetorical effect through an impersonal reference to the diegetic materialization of a specific interlocutor. This movement towards interlocution begins to emerge rather early in the short story and – it might be argued – paves the way for David Wallace's own appearance. It is easy to think of a generic reader as being bored by the preliminaries concerning the death scene ('this part is ... probably boring you', 147) or as relating to the cliché of the velocity of thinking ('knowing how fast thoughts and associations can fly through your head', 150), but the situation changes when eleven pages into the story we read: 'so if I'm saying that words and sequential time have nothing to do with it you're wondering why we're sitting here in this car using words and taking up your increasingly precious time ...' (153). The second-person pronoun allows David Foster Wallace to turn an abstract dialogical device into a metaleptic move that mobilizes the 'what-it's-likeness' principle and asks readers to envision themselves driving with Neal and belonging to an inclusive we/us.

Two details in the handwritten manuscript of the story at the Ransom Center reinforce the importance of this dialogic component. Firstly, the dialogic 'endless back and forth between us' was originally Neal's 'endless talking'. Secondly, in the manuscript version, the eventual sentence 'high beams don't work in the fog, they only make the fog worse. Much like this – you can go ahead and try them' is interrupted as follows: 'Much like this – i.e., the fog in the car they're riding in. Narrator becomes the reader. He is hitchhiker in car. "I'd say don't do it but it'd be too late."' A further sentence adds, 'He's driving – he picks up hitchhiker – now he is hitchhiker' (Wallace, container 24.2, HRC).

These two details are worth pondering: the first change signals a clear shift from what Bres and Nowakowska call 'intralocutionary dialogism (or autodialogical)' to 'interlocutory' dialogism. Neal's endless talking is self-referentially directed towards himself – 'you' notwithstanding – whereas 'the back and forth between us' suggests a leaning toward an other that is different from the self. 'What interlocutionary dialogism adds is (i) that the consideration of the interlocutor is meant to shape the response of the other, and above all (ii) that the speaker keeps anticipating the response that he imagines, and that this imagined response in its turn influences his speaking.'[13] It is always slippery to speak about authorial intentions, but it seems safe to say that the change (at least) suggests a rather clear direction. This (interlocutionary) direction is confirmed by the free-wheeling associative notes, which revolve around the notion of becoming: the driver/narrator picks up a hitchhiker/reader, then the latter becomes the former. As we have seen, in the published version the 'you' is presented as being in the car and driving toward his death. The fog presented in the annotation as invading the car is the objective correlative of the blurred and tentative substance of this becoming. As Greg Carlisle ironically puts it, 'On my first reading, I didn't realize I was sitting in a car and that the narrative was not really about the narrator' (Carlisle, 2013: 76).

In 'Good Old Neon' the Corvette stands for the 'piece of high-powered [*textual*] machinery' (Wallace, 2004, 169 emphasis added) through which authors, characters, and readers can engage in thinking about what matters with imaginative compassion. Crucially, the meaning of the claims appearing relatively early in the story that 'despite appearances this isn't even really about me', followed closely by 'why it had the impact it did on who this is really about' (152), is left ambiguously hovering above the entire narrative; it touches upon the very essence of fictional attempts at understanding both oneself and the other. The conversation in the car thus becomes the ultimate conversation, i.e., the conversation that contemplates meaningfulness when life is at its end. In 'this car', while 'you' are on 'your' way to commit suicide, David Foster Wallace via David Wallace has Neal narrate all that has happened to him in the hours before that ride and on the ride itself, has him tell you about your own ride after making the most important decision of your life, has him reflect on both the decision made and the deed still to be done. The positive consequences of this fictional mirroring are manifested when death still seems one of the possible outcomes of the car ride of the 'two' protagonists: 'But it *wouldn't have made* you a fraud to change your mind. It *would be* sad to do it because you somehow have to' (180, emphasis added). Neal is already dead; Neal is still alive and as such becomes the representative of all those who suffer the same syndrome, which is described as the signature of our age. 'The fog of the future' through which the bumper of the Corvette cuts in the authorial note that contains 'THE END' of the story and Neal's death (179) – and which invades the car in the annotation we have already touched upon – is the existential emblem both of the paradox of time and of human existence.

This tripartite reading of the story situates an interlocutionary 'back and forth between us' at the pulsating centre of the whole narrative, but Neal's shifting position gives it the authority of knowledge: the author not only invents a fiction to imagine himself through the fiction of someone else's imagination but privileges this imagination as posthumous, i.e., omnisciently authorial. If David Foster Wallace is the one who writes, Neal seems to be the one who speaks to himself or about himself (up to the end); but he speaks to himself only in so far as he imagines the way in which David Wallace imagines him. On the other hand, crucially, David Wallace injects into his imagining of Neal both the latter's confrontation with the meaning of his existence in his long pre-suicidal reckoning and his description of himself from his post-mortem position. David Wallace thus imagines for Neal an authoritative gaze which moves beyond imagining into omniscient knowing. Neal's afterlife description of David Wallace as disentangling himself from the mires of his own weak confidence (and becoming a writer, someone who keeps trying and caring) thus acquires the confirmation of a superior truthfulness, so to speak. The truthfulness here defended seems to concern literature itself: is not literature, after all, a continuous probing of the question of the human mind – the other's mind and one's own? Can we conclusively say that Neal's imaginative itinerary is complete and controlled, whereas David Wallace's is tentative and compassionate since it allows Neal to speak in his own voice – a voice that bespeaks a fraudulent need to control? Can we say that it is precisely in letting Neal be the kind of man he is that David Wallace offers him a possible way out because Neal discovers himself as the inventor of a compassionate other, in spite of his fraudulence?

This amounts to saying that only the imaginative or fictional dimension allows for a kind of authenticity not possible in the real life, mired in fraudulence and manipulation, that Wallace depicts in his texts. Yes, 'we are all trying to see each other through these tiny keyholes', but we should not forget that the door 'does have a knob', that is, 'the door can open' (178). 'Good Old Neon' asks us to entertain the idea that, for Wallace, literary imagination may well be the only authentic way of addressing existential complexity: literature opens an imaginative door and legitimizes an understanding that trades in philosophical paradoxes, implies their employment, and fosters their acceptance. Authorial omniscience – paired with its diegetic mirror, the afterlife – rules not in real lives but in invented lives. But exactly what invented literary lives can do for our real lives has not yet been written, because, as this short story emblematically stages, it is a matter not of choosing one perspective and one word but of accepting that there are always other perspectives, other words.

Notes

Although this chapter is the result of a close and mutually enriching collaboration, Pia Masiero is the author of pages mid 75–85, Adriano Ardovino of pages 68–mid 75.
1. It is worth mentioning that the first draft of the short story, which was written by hand and is archived at the Ransom Center in Austin, stops

mid-sentence just before this point, which thus becomes the first new addition to the second typescript version – a possible indication that the author himself felt the need to try again.
2. This obsession is furthermore signalled by the massive employment of the word 'etc.' (around 25 occurrences) and of the expression 'or, whatever' in the text. Both underscore the ever-present gap between experience and articulation, feeling and telling.
3. The words of others include those of people, David Wallace for example, who have to use words to say 'not another [useless, empty, negatively rational] word'.
4. If only in the peripheral space of a note, we consider it necessary to emphasize the pervasive presence of paradoxes throughout the text: we count 23 uses of the word or its derivatives in the story, describing at least 15 different kinds of paradoxes. Besides explicit references to canonical names, such as Kant, Russell, Berry, or Gödel, the text is obsessed with logical, linguistic, temporal, psychological, affective, and perceptual paradoxes which take the technical form of antinomies, contradictions, reductions to absurdity, or infinite regressions. One way or another, a traditionally philosophical theme is subsumed into a narrative discourse that amplifies it: every aspect of life and death in the story is textually staged as touched by what defies cognition or understanding and what defies experience, which is to say, by the clash between the surface of things and their essence. This leitmotif incorporates relinquishment of the mental faculty that aims to subsume materials resisting logical linearity (in sequential and rational terms) into a multilinear narrative in which paradoxes are not solved or dissolved but put to work. Paradoxes, disentangled from the philosophical need to define them, narratively become the manifestation of what is quintessentially other and yet can coexist with the self and be accepted and cherished. Once they become part and parcel of the narrative, paradoxes drift away from the potential risk of self-referential abortive loops and become the door to accessing the narrative of a life and its defeat and death – which, despite this failure, is not paralysed and still but rather imaginatively, if paradoxically, active. The readerly and scholarly attention 'Good Old Neon' has drawn attests that all this can be narrated, successfully, in forty-odd pages.
5. It is worth mentioning that the name David Wallace is repeated nine times in this final paragraph, whereas the name Neal appears in the whole short story just twice – in a context which suggests doubling and refraction, namely through inverted commas and parentheses: '"But if you're constitutionally false and manipulative and unable to be honest about who you really are, Neal" (Neal being my given name ...)' (153).

6 We prefer the verb *to narrate* because Neal's posthumous positioning provides him with an awareness that goes well beyond mere telling or speaking.
7 We are here employing but reinterpreting the words that Neal attributes to Beverly-Elizabeth: 'She said she'd never felt the gaze of someone so penetrating, discerning and yet so totally empty of care' (165).
8 David Foster Wallace often reflected on the amazing number of thoughts inhabiting our minds at any given moment in time, noting that, when it comes to the actual articulation of thoughts, we often stumble on the obvious fact that language takes time – as our reading of Neal's/David Wallace's alleged musings attests and as Neal himself is perfectly aware of (152).
9 A figural narrative situation is a third-person narrative in which the events of the story are presented by an external, typically inaudible narrator and filtered by a focalizing internal character.
10 Insisting on this possible reading does not mean we are not aware of the fact that Wallace's macro text shows this (narrative) decentring itself to be always susceptible to narcissistic rabbit-holes.
11 The foundational reference to the first-person singular depends upon us interpreting the notion of experience in its most basic sense, which Galen Strawson defines as 'what-it's-like-ness'. In a note he explains, '[a] personalized ostensive definition will do: one says to each reader "You know what it is like from your own case, as you burn your finger, listen to Beethoven, give birth, and so on"' (Strawson, 1994: 69).
12 See Monika Fludernik's two contributions on second-person narratives (1993, 1994).
13 'Ce qu'ajoute le dialogisme interlocutif, c'est (i) que cette prise en compte de l'interlocuteur vise à façonner la éponse de l'autre; et surtout (ii) que le locuteur anticipe sans cesse sur cette réponse qu'il imagine, et que cette réponse imaginée influence en retour son discours' (Bres and Nowakowska, 2006: 24, our translation).

References

Bres, J. and Nowakowska, A. (2006). 'Dialogisme: du principe à la matérialité discursive', 21–48. In Laurent Perrin, ed., *Le sens et ses voix*. Université de Lorraine: CREM.

Carlisle, G. (2013). *Nature's Nightmare. Analysing David Foster Wallace's Oblivion*. Los Angeles CA: Sideshow Media Group Press.

Cohn, D. (1978). *Transparent Minds. Narrative Modes of Presenting Consciousness in Fiction*. Princeton NJ: Princeton University Press.

Fludernik, M. (1993). 'Second-Person Fiction: Narrative "You" as Addressee and/or Protagonist', in *AAA: Arbeiten aus Anglistik und Amerikanistik* 18:2, 217–47.
Fludernik, M. (1994). 'Second-Person Narrative as a Test Case for Narratology: The Limits of Realism', in *Style* 28:3, 445–79.
Hayes-Brady, C. (2016). *The Unspeakable Failures of David Foster Wallace. Language, Identity, and Resistance.* London and New York NY: Bloomsbury.
Hering, D. (2016). *David Foster Wallace: Fiction and Form.* London and New York NY: Bloomsbury.
Hudson, C. M. (2018). 'David Foster Wallace Is Not Your Friend: The Fraudulence of Empathy in David Foster Wallace Studies and "Good Old Neon"', in *Critique*, 59:3, 295–306.
Kocela, C. (2017). 'The Zen of "Good Old Neon": David Wallace, Alan Watts, and the Double-Bind of Selfhood', 57–72. In Beatrice Pire and Pierre-Louis Patoine, eds, *David Foster Wallace. Presences of the Other.* Brighton: Sussex Academic Press.
Nünning, A. (2001). 'On the Perspective Structure of Narrative Texts: Steps toward a Constructivist Narratology', 207–24. In Willi van Peer and Seymour Chatman, eds, *New Perspectives on Narrative Perspective.* Albany NY: State University of New York Press.
Staes, T. (2012). 'Rewriting the Author: A Narrative Approach to Empathy in *Infinite Jest* and *The Pale King*', in *Studies in the Novel* 44:4, 409–27.
Strawson, G. (1994). 'The Experiential and the Non-experiential', 69–86. In Tadeusz Szubka and Richard Warner, eds, *The Mind-Body Problem.* Oxford: Blackwell.
Wallace, D. Foster. (2004). *Oblivion.* New York NY: Back Bay Books.
Widiss, B. (2011). *Obscure Invitations. The Persistence of the Author in Twentieth-Century American Literature.* Stanford CA: Stanford University Press.

Archival sources

Wallace, D. Foster. (undated). 'Good Old Neon', *Handwritten drafts*, David Foster Wallace Papers, container 24.2, Harry Ransom Center, University of Texas (TX).

4

The influence of Christopher Lasch's *The Culture of Narcissism* on David Foster Wallace

Paolo Pitari

This chapter argues that Wallace's texts exhibit an outstanding alignment with Christopher Lasch's *The Culture of Narcissism* (1979), both in content and – most significantly – in the logic by which the two authors come to analogous conclusions regarding their central sociological, literary, and philosophical concerns. The aim is to show the extent and significance of the conceptual alliance between Wallace and Lasch. This comparative analysis will lead to a strong suggestion of Lasch's direct influence on Wallace, but the chapter will not focus on the problem of influence; rather, the focal point will be the *content* of the alliance and how it illuminates certain aspects of Wallace's thought in relation to the cultural discourse of our time.

We already know something of the connection between *The Culture of Narcissism* and Wallace. We have at the Harry Ransom Center (HRC) Wallace's annotated copy of Lasch's book, to which Hering briefly refers in *David Foster Wallace: Fiction and Form* (2016). And we have Holland's 'The Art's Heart's Purpose' (2013), which demonstrates 'a remarkable alignment' (Holland, 2013: 66) between *Infinite Jest* and Lasch's book. The importance of *The Culture of Narcissism* to Wallace studies is thus no mystery, and it is even unsurprising, given that narcissism was recognized as a fundamental predicament in Wallace ever since Boswell's *Understanding David Foster Wallace* (2003).

But the present chapter argues that the alignment between Wallace and Lasch remains largely underappreciated. Its nucleus is an interpretation of contemporary narcissism as the manifestation of self-hatred, not self-love, and this is why Wallace underlined – in his archival copy of Lasch's book – this extensive definition of narcissism:

> narcissism represents the psychological dimension of this dependence. Notwithstanding his occasional illusion of omnipotence, the narcissist depends on others to validate his self-esteem. He cannot live without an admiring audience. His apparent freedom from family ties and institutional constraints does not free him to stand alone or to glory in his individuality. On the contrary, it contributes to his insecurity, which he can overcome only by seeing his 'grandiose self' reflected in the attentions of others, or by attaching himself to those who radiate celebrity, power, and charisma. For the narcissist, the world is a mirror.
>
> (Lasch, 1979: 10)

This chapter will make multiple references to new findings in Wallace's archival copy of *The Culture of Narcissism*, but these are mostly elaborated in notes, because their function is to confirm what emerges from the more primary comparative textual analysis of Lasch's and Wallace's works. The chapter is divided into three sections, one for each area of consonance, and all references are selected to demonstrate the alignment between Wallace and Lasch as thoroughly as possible. The first section establishes parallels between the sociology in *The Culture of Narcissism* and 'E Unibus Pluram', highlighting how Wallace's essay reiterates the logic and content of Lasch's work almost verbatim. The second section looks at the principles uniting the two authors' views on literary fiction, showing that Lasch anticipated early versions of Wallace's criticisms of metafiction and solipsistic writing. This section builds on the first, because both Wallace and Lasch constructed their literary ideals from their approaches to sociology. Finally, the third section uncovers the fundamental philosophical alliance uniting the two authors. Wallace and Lasch grounded their sociology and literary ideals on their philosophical beliefs. Accordingly, the chapter closes by paying attention to their shared worldview and makes an argument for the profundity of their alignment, suggesting that adaptation of Lasch's framework in the existential crisis of the contemporary played a key role in the development of Wallace's literary project.

Lasch's sociology and 'E Unibus Pluram'

'E Unibus Pluram' (1993) largely follows *The Culture of Narcissism* in content, structure, and language – so much so, in fact, that one may even hypothesize a certain amount of direct appropriation. Firstly, Wallace's essay argues that today's media generates loneliness because it 'purveys and enables *dreams*, and most of these dreams involve some sort of transcendence of average daily life' (Wallace, 1997b: 39, emphasis original). These dreams 'are unsubtle in their whispers that, somewhere, life is quicker, denser, more interesting, more ...' (39). Thus they imply that our lives lack worth and make the prospect of seclusion ever more appealing, further provoking this vicious cycle: we choose loneliness to avoid shame, loneliness reinforces the shame, shame induces loneliness, etc. This vicious cycle is one of the essay's greatest concerns, and Lasch anticipates it by writing that 'the media give substance to and thus intensify narcissistic dreams of fame and glory' (Lasch, 1979: 21), that these dreams 'make it more and more difficult for [anyone] to accept the banality of everyday existence' (21), and that this shame destroys self-esteem – resulting in narcissism as a social phenomenon.

Consequently, Wallace's essay denounces how these dreams equate meaning with 'watchableness': in today's culture, 'true actualization of self would ultimately consist in ... becoming one of the images that are the *objects* of this great herd-like watching' (Wallace, 1997b: 56). For Wallace, our culture makes self-actualization dependent both on one's complete separation from the herd and on the herd's recognition of one's value. Other people must be both shunned and feared: to be *object* of the herd's watching, one must separate oneself from the herd; but, to feel self-actualized, one depends entirely on the herd's recognition. *The Culture of Narcissism* too examines this tremendous engine of loneliness: Lasch writes that the media 'encourage the common man to identify himself with the stars and to hate the "herd"' (Lasch, 1979: 21), and that this creates 'dependence on the vicarious warmth provided by others combined with a fear of dependence, a sense of inner emptiness' (33).[1]

Within the culture of narcissism, the gaze of others becomes judgemental, and its power determines our value. The social environment becomes hostile, and one cannot help but become lonely and fearful of others. Accordingly, 'E Unibus Pluram' states that 'the most frightening prospect ... becomes leaving oneself open to others' ridicule ... .Other people become judges; the crime is naiveté. The well-trained viewer becomes even more allergic to people. Lonelier' (Wallace, 1997b: 63). Likewise, Lasch affirms that today's 'experiences of inner emptiness, loneliness and inauthenticity ... arise from the warlike conditions that pervade American society' (Lasch, 1979: 27).

As a result, contemporary despair takes the form of hyper-self-consciousness: people become terrified of others and so begin to obsessively judge themselves, hoping thus to avoid external judgment. Narcissism arises not as a pathological form of self-assurance but as a pathological form of self-doubt. Wallace calls this 'the metastasis of self-conscious watching' (Wallace, 1997b: 34), where 'human beings ... become vastly more spectatorial, self-conscious' (34). Correspondingly, Lasch declares that 'a number of historical currents have converged in our time to produce not merely in artists but in ordinary men and women an escalating cycle of self-consciousness' (Lasch, 1979: 90).

For both authors, that is, narcissism is hyper-self-consciousness that becomes concrete in the form of fearful self-absorption. In fact 'narcissism', 'hyper-self-consciousness', and 'despair' all refer to the same condition. 'E Unibus Pluram' states that 'personal anxiety ... has become a national phenomenon with national consequences' (Wallace, 1997b: 53), and 'for us civilians, who tend to own mirrors' (53), these consequences are rather familiar. Likewise *The Culture of Narcissism* describes how 'the new Narcissus gazes at his own reflection, not so much in admiration as in unremitting search of flaws, signs of fatigue, decay' (Lasch, 1979: 91).

Crucially, both authors criticize the social structure for its consequences on individual lives.[2] 'E Unibus Pluram' diagnoses the culture of narcissism, and its central focus on irony is coherent with this essential intent. For both Lasch and Wallace irony is the narcissist's mode of self-defence, and this is why irony becomes pervasive in the culture of narcissism. Wallace states that today we 'view ridicule as both the mode of social intercourse and the ultimate art-form' (Wallace, 1997b: 63) and that this attitude establishes our narcissistic shell against 'the most frightening prospect [of] leaving oneself open to others' ridicule by betraying passé expressions of value, emotion, or vulnerability' (63). In doing so he again reiterates *The Culture of Narcissism*: 'by creating an ironic distance, [the narcissist] takes refuge in jokes, mockery, and cynicism ... . In this way he attempts to make himself invulnerable to the pressures of the situation ... . The posture of cynical detachment becomes the dominant style of everyday intercourse' (Lasch, 1979: 95).

Even Wallace's famous citation from Lewis Hyde's *Alcohol and Poetry* (1979) – 'irony has only emergency use. Carried over time, it is the voice of the trapped who have come to enjoy their cage' (Wallace, 1997b: 67) – finds another echo in Lasch's work: 'escape through irony and critical self-awareness is in any case itself an illusion; at best it provides only momentary relief. Distancing soon becomes a routine in its own right ... . Self-created roles become as constraining as the social roles from which they are meant to provide ironic detachment' (Lasch, 1979: 96).

Views on contemporary fiction

We have seen how 'E Unibus Pluram' mirrors the logic of *The Culture of Narcissism* even in analysis of its most fundamental concern, irony. But what is most surprising (given Lasch's expertise in history and sociology) is how the essay's criticism of contemporary fiction also finds a precedent in Lasch. Wallace criticizes today's writers because they 'render their material with the same tone of irony and self-consciousness' (Wallace, 1997b: 52) that constitutes contemporary narcissism. Lasch criticizes them because they 'suffer from the same crisis of self-consciousness that afflicts the man in the street' (Lasch, 1979: 96). Wallace stresses that self-conscious irony detaches contemporary fiction from its obligation of social engagement, making it 'free to plunge into reflexivity and self-conscious meditations on aboutness' (Wallace, 1997b: 34). Lasch decries how the crisis of self-consciousness distances literature from meaningfulness: 'novelists and playwrights call attention to the artificiality of their own creations and discourage the reader from identifying with the characters' (Lasch, 1979: 96–97). Wallace insists that the end of metafiction is complete detachment from the world, purely solipsistic writing about writing: 'that American subspecies into fiction writing starts writing more and more about' (Wallace, 1997b: 34). Lasch does the same: 'by means of irony and eclecticism, the writer withdraws from his subject but at the same time becomes so conscious of these distancing techniques that he finds it more and more difficult to write about anything except the difficulty of writing. Writing about writing then becomes in itself an object of self-parody' (Lasch, 1979: 97). Finally, Wallace criticizes such writers from an ethical perspective: they are guilty of narcissism because their 'sole aim is, finally, to wow, to ensure that the reader is pleased and continues to read' (Wallace, 1997b: 79). Lasch again does the same: 'these writers ... try to charm the reader instead of claiming significance for their narrative. They use humor ... to ingratiate themselves, to get the reader's attention without asking him to take the writer or his subject seriously' (Lasch, 1979: 18).[3]

This consonance in their views on fiction surpasses the confines of 'E Unibus Pluram', indicating the extent and significance of Lasch's impact on Wallace's entire oeuvre. That Wallace denounced meta-fiction as the mode of expression of 'all the weary ironists' (McCaffery, 2012: 49) – the place where 'postmodern irony and cynicism becomes an end in itself' (48) – has been well noted. Indeed, Wallace found that meta-fiction 'gets empty and solipsistic real fast' (40), inevitably resulting in self-exhaustion because of a lack of content. His patricidal homage to John Barth – 'Westward the Course of Empire Takes Its Way' (1989) – seeks to expose precisely these dynamics.[4] What is less known, however, is that Lasch anticipates Wallace even here. Lasch does not use the term 'meta-fiction', but he does refer precisely to John Barth as paradigmatic of authors who 'attempt an escape through irony and self-awareness [that] is itself an illusion' (Lasch, 1979: 96), and he moreover accuses such writers of producing frivolous work: 'having called attention to himself as a performer, the writer ... waives the right to be taken seriously, at the same time escaping the responsibilities that go with being taken seriously' (20).

Like Lasch, then, Wallace insists that writers must go back to writing 'serious' literature. This is the driving force of his ethical literary criticism. For Wallace, authors of 'the literature of self-consciousness' (Kennedy and Polk, 2012: 18) are problematic because they 'treat formal ingenuity as an end in itself' (McCaffery, 2012: 29), which manifests their narcissism. They focus on 'formal stunt-pilotry ... serving the rather darker purpose of communicating to the reader "Hey! Look at me! Have a look at what a good writer I am! *Like* me!"' (25, emphasis original). They seek 'merely and always to *engage*, to *appeal to*' (Wallace, CB2012b: 53, emphasis original). This is exactly how Lasch describes the literature of narcissism: 'the writer thus attempts to charm the reader instead of trying to convince him' (Lasch, 1979: 20) to take anything seriously; he seeks only 'to seduce others into giving him their attention, acclaim, or sympathy and thus to shore up his faltering sense of self' (21).

In consequence Wallace maintains that 'there is a fundamental difference between expressive writing and communicative writing' (O'Brien, 2012: 114). Expressive writing assumes that whatever you say is 'interesting because, you, yourself, say it' (114). Therefore, it is solipsistic, 'alienating and unpleasant' (114); it feels 'as if someone is going through all the motions of communicating with you but in actual fact you don't even need to be there at all' (114). Instead, communicative writing knows 'that writing is an act of communication between one human being and another' (Wallace, 1997b: 144); it attempts to '*give* the reader something' (McCaffery, 2012: 50), to establish 'a real full human relationship' (34) with her. This is why it can work as an 'anodyne against loneliness' (Kennedy and Polk, 2012: 16) and be 'nourishing, redemptive' (McCaffery, 2012: 22).

In accordance with this framework, in 'Certainly the End of Something or Other' (1998), Wallace criticizes John Updike, Norman Mailer, and Philip Roth as 'Great Male Narcissists' (Wallace, 2005: 51): pinnacles of 'the most self-absorbed generation since Louis XIV' (51) since their fiction expresses 'radical self-absorption' (53) and gives voice to the 'anomic self-indulgence of the Me Generation' (54). This argument too is already present in *The Culture of Narcissism*, where Lasch refers to 'confessional writers' (Lasch, 1979: 18) and explicitly names Mailer and Roth. Lasch states that their fiction's 'only claim to the reader's attention is that it describes events of immediate interest to the author' (18), that they are guilty of 'self-indulgence' (18), that they are full of 'the narcissist's pseudo-insight' (18), and that their narcissism is so substantial as to be a form of solipsism: 'the writer no longer sees life reflected in his own mind. Just the opposite: he sees the world, even in its emptiness, as a mirror of himself' (21).

The fundamental philosophical alliance between Wallace and Lasch

The sociological and literary consonances mapped above arise from a fundamental philosophical alliance between Wallace and Lasch. What they postulate about the role of literature in contemporary society is premised in their sociology. In turn their sociology is predicated on a shared philosophical position about what human life is and should be. This is why this final section focuses on their philosophy and addresses convergences in their attitudes towards the delusion of self-sufficiency, the need to worship, the ultimate primacy of individuality, and the relationship between self and other. This philosophical exploration grounds the larger argument of the chapter regarding the depth and significance of the overlaps in their work.

Both Lasch and Wallace make a psychological argument that, at its core, is philosophical; or rather, that depends entirely on their vision of what a human being is and – most importantly – should be. *The Culture of Narcissism* warns against the dangers inherent in the tendency to exalt and conjoin psychotherapy and the ideals of self-sufficiency and self-interest. In this context it defines 'the final product of bourgeois individualism' as the 'psychological man': 'plagued by anxiety, depression, vague discontents, a sense of inner emptiness, the 'psychological man' of the twentieth century seeks neither individual self-aggrandizement nor spiritual transcendence but peace of mind, under conditions that increasingly militate against it' (Lasch, 1979: 13).

Lasch sees self-contempt as feeding narcissism: the kind of self-absorption that results from feeling empty, frightened, and worthless. The narcissist is someone who seeks relief from suffering in entirely individualistic fashion. This is why *The Culture of Narcissism* criticizes contemporary psychotherapy: it considers it to reinforce the illusion of self-sufficiency that generates the suffering in the first place. In this regard Lasch draws from Peter Marin's 'The New Narcissism' (1975) to argue that contemporary therapies 'teach that 'the individual will is all powerful and totally determines one's fate'; and that this orientation ultimately intensifies the "isolation of the self"' (9). He also denounces 'post-Freudian therapies' (Lasch, 1979: 13) – and here he cites Gail Sheehy's *Passages: Predictable Crises of Adult Life* (1976) – because in them 'the ability to manipulate ... "life-support systems" now appears to represent the highest form of wisdom' (49).

Wallace makes the same argument throughout his oeuvre, in both his non-fiction and his fiction. Our 'great despair and stasis' (Wallace, 1997b: 49) derive from how our culture encourages us 'to fly solo' 56); suffering originates from the elevation of 'enlightened self-interest' (Wallace, 1996a: 428) to our more cherished value.

The illusion of self-sufficiency is the primary cause of narcissism. We believe everything is in our hands and so become anxiously self-absorbed. An example of these beliefs about 'psychological man' is Wallace's understanding of timidity as narcissism: 'I think being shy basically means being self-absorbed to the extent that it makes it difficult to be around other people' (Lipsky, 2010: 16). Likewise the individual in *This Is Water* (2005) who finally commits suicide is himself an example of the 'psychological man': he despairs because he is incapable of overcoming his default setting of self-absorption.[5]

Most significantly, Wallace's *fiction* repeatedly represents the image of 'psychological man' presented by Lasch's criticism of psychotherapy. In *The Broom of the System* (1987), 'Wallace seems to impale modern psychotherapy' (Dudar, 2012: 9). The short story 'Here and There' in *Girl with Curious Hair* (1989) represents two exes in a 'fiction therapy' that doesn't seem to help them at all. *Infinite Jest* (1996) includes various scenes of psychotherapy – none of which brings its characters close to insight. Similarly, all the interviews in *Brief Interviews with Hideous Men* (1999) are reports from psychotherapy sessions that produce no redemption. The collection also contains the short story 'The Depressed Person', which may be Wallace's most paradigmatic representation of 'psychological man': the depressed person's interactions with 'her Support System' (Wallace, 2000: 41) are manipulative, and precisely echo Lasch's comments about 'post-Freudian therapies and the ability to manipulate life-support systems'. Even Wallace's description of the story in the ZDF interview recalls Lasch: Wallace considers the story a representation of 'popular Freudianism, a compendium of all the worst and most painful features of the popular psychology movement in the US' (Wallace, 2003).

Finally the collection *Oblivion* (2004) and the novel *The Pale King* (2011) also advance scepticism about psychotherapy. The short story 'Good Old Neon' follows a man who manipulates his therapist before killing himself, while the novel tells of Meredith Rand, who develops a seemingly pathological relationship with her therapist that leads to a suspicious marriage. It is therefore clear that both Lasch and Wallace insist on the dangers inherent to the contemporary alliance between psychotherapy and the (illusory) ideals of self-sufficiency and self-interest.

Wallace disavows utilitarianism – the doctrine that actions are right if they are useful – seeing this orientation to advance the attitude that 'pleasure becomes a value, a teleological end in itself' (McCaffery, 2012: 23). In this sense he associates utilitarianism with the problem of contemporary nihilism because of an inextricable correlation between our condescension towards belief and our elevation of personal pleasure to ultimate value: that is, utilitarianism can become popular only in a society that has lost faith in the authority of traditional beliefs and the meaningfulness they bestowed upon human life. For Wallace the problem with the 'authority vacuum' (62) this produces is that it ultimately makes life meaningless: without traditional 'guides to *why* and *how* to choose' (Wallace, 1997b: 76), we are bound to despair.[6]

Thus Wallace argues that life acquires meaning only when individuals consciously choose to give themselves to something larger than the self. This is what makes a meaningful life possible: 'we're absolutely dying to give ourselves away to something' (Lipsky, 2010: 81). In fact we do this naturally, as Wallace famously puts it in *This Is Water*: 'everybody worships. The only choice we get is *what* to worship. And an outstanding reason for choosing some sort of god or spiritual-type thing to worship … is that pretty much anything else will eat you alive' (Wallace, 2009: 100–2).

Wallace thinks that to live is to worship. We have no choice but to worship. The ironist worships the brain. The utilitarian worships personal pleasure. Yet the mistake of the ironist and the utilitarian is that they believe themselves beyond worship and therefore worship *unconsciously* – that is, they are slaves to their own minds, and this traps them in suffering. Instead to live the good life is to be aware of the human need to worship and to choose an appropriate object accordingly. Such awareness makes freedom possible: only one who knows they must choose can choose in the best of ways.

This fundamental ethical ideal is also expressed in Lasch's *The Culture of Narcissism* – in a passage about 'modern therapies' and their 'rugged individualism' underlined by Wallace, which introduces precisely this ideal of committing to something larger than the self. Here Lasch writes that modern society 'gives no thought to anything beyond its immediate needs', that it seeks only 'the immediate gratification of every impulse' (Lasch, 1979: 13), and that

> it hardly occurs … to encourage the subject to subordinate his needs and interests to those of others, to someone or some cause or tradition

outside himself. 'Love' as self-sacrifice or self-abasement, 'meaning' as submission to a higher loyalty – these sublimations strike the therapeutic sensibility as intolerably oppressive, offensive to common sense and injurious to personal health and well-being. (13)

Lasch's commitment to criticizing contemporary individualism and decrying the loss of traditional beliefs out of need to worship anticipates Wallace's own ethics. In this sense Wallace must have found inspiration in *The Culture of Narcissism*, given that Lasch reiterates this point throughout the book. For example he denounces 'the erosion of the capacity to take any interest in anything outside the self' (Lasch, 1979: 87); he praises the traditional ethics that 'required the athlete or soldier to submit to a common discipline, to sacrifice himself for the good of a higher cause' (116); he decries how traditional ethics today 'suffers the general erosion of organizational allegiance in a society where men and women perceive the organization as an enemy' (116); and finally – in another passage underlined by Wallace – he criticizes how, 'since "the society" has no future today, it makes sense to live only for the moment, to fix our eyes on our own "private performance," to become connoisseurs of our own decadence, to cultivate a "transcendental self-attention"' (Lasch, 1979: 6).

Wallace reiterated throughout his career this attitude towards the impossibility of living a good life without worshipping something larger than the self. Before him, Lasch did the same.

Wallace denounces not only the illusion of self-sufficiency but also the illusion of selflessness. Individuality is primary in his philosophy, and this is what ties him to existentialism.[7] *This Is Water* (2005) is his most explicit expression of the primacy of individuality: 'the only thing that's capital-T True is that you get to *decide* ... to *choose* how you construct meaning from experience' (Wallace, 2009: 94, 54).

Wallace insists that we need to restore a 'community of relationships' (Wallace, 1997b: 26), but, in order to do so, we must accept individual responsibility for choosing to give ourselves away to the community: 'how we construct meaning [is] actually a matter of personal, intentional choice, of conscious decision, ... a matter of my choosing to do the work' (Wallace, 2009: 28, 44). Appeal to community thus must not obscure the primacy of individuality. In this sense Wallace seeks a third way between the two pathological and illusory extremes of self-sufficiency and selflessness. The individual's responsibility is to learn 'how to exercise some control over *how* and *what* you think' (53) and so achieve 'real freedom' (121). Yet, at the same time, real freedom appears only when one consciously chooses to give oneself away to a 'good' ideal outside the self. This is how Wallace reconciles the needs of both individuality and community: they are two sides of the same coin of human life, and to fail to recognize either is to live in falsehood and thus to suffer.

Wallace most effectively represents the pathology of these two extremes in *Infinite Jest*, where Steeply voices the American ideal of 'enlightened self-interest' (Wallace, 1996a: 428), self-sufficiency, and utilitarianism criticized by the novel and it is Marathe who represents the opposite extreme, arguing (in words resembling Wallace's) that we are all 'worshippers at the temple' (108), that 'our attachments are our temple' (108), and that you must 'choose your attachments carefully ... with great care' (108). These words undeniably anticipate *This Is Water*, and yet Steeply is right when he accuses Marathe of totalitarianism. Marathe's terrorism seeks 'moral eugenics' (Wallace, 1997b: 320), 'the National Socialist Neofascist State of Separate Quebec' (320) – a kind of 'Cuba with snow' (320), where you will 'ski immediately to your nearest reeducation camp, for instructions on choosing' (320). These accusations may seem comical, but, as Wallace noted, 'Wittgenstein believed that the most serious and profound problems and questions and issues could be discussed only in the form of jokes' (Wallace, 2003) – and Wallace applied this principle throughout *Infinite Jest*, by combing the comic and the profound. Moreover, in the novel's story-world, Steeply's accusations are unambiguously true: Marathe is part of the deadliest terrorist group in North America, which seeks to decimate the American population.

Wallace even strengthens Steeply's thesis by creating Gerhardt Schtitt. Like Marathe, Schtitt voices Wallace's traditional ideals. He teaches the significance of 'permanent values' (82), of 'honor and discipline and fidelity to some larger unit' (82), of 'learning to sacrifice the hot narrow imperatives of the Self ... to the larger imperatives of a team' (82), of not surrendering to 'this flat and short-sighted idea of personal happiness' (83) because 'without ... something bigger. Nothing can contain meaning. Lonely' (83). But like Marathe, Schtitt too borders on fascism: he is 'patriarchal' (82), has 'proto-fascist potential' (82), and advocates 'training for citizenship' (82) as service to a 'State' and 'Law' (82) that are not coincidentally capitalized.

In his 1996 'Bookworm' interview Wallace said that Schtitt is 'really the only one there who to me is saying anything that's even remotely non-horrifying, except it is horrifying because he's a fascist' (Wallace, 1996b). What he meant was that Schtitt's (and Marathe's) ideals are fascist because they are not accompanied by the self-scrutiny and self-doubt that constitute what in 'Authority and American Usage' (1999) Wallace calls 'a true Democratic Spirit' (Wallace, 2005: 72). In other words, for Wallace, the only ethical path is to do justice to the needs of both individuality and community and, therefore, to accompany the call to commit to something larger with inviolable respect for individual freedom, responsibility, and the self-reflexivity these demand.

This ethical path is present in *The Culture of Narcissism* as well. Just as Wallace found affirmation in Lasch's book of the need to worship, so too he found a similar warning against selflessness. This is another passage that Wallace underlined: 'the left has too often served as a refuge from the terrors of the inner life ... political movements exercise a fatal attraction for those who seek to drown the sense of personal failure in collective action' (Lasch, 1979: 15). Therefore, in Lasch, Wallace found rejection of both extreme individualism and extreme collectivism and affirmation of a third way which would respect both the primacy of the individual (the terrors of the inner life) and the need for community (the need to worship and self-sacrifice).

To close, a look at *The Minimal Self* (1984) – where Lasch makes the philosophical postulates of *The Culture of Narcissism* most explicit – will help us delve deeper into the fundamental philosophical alliance between the two authors. Like *The Culture of Narcissism*, *The Minimal Self* criticizes the Enlightenment illusion of self-sufficiency as the origin of narcissism. But here Lasch also explicitly specifies that views such as Morris Berman's cosmic connectedness in *The Reenchantment of the World* (1981) and Gregory Bateson's holistic consciousness in *Steps toward an Ecology of Mind* (1972) deny the incontrovertible truth of 'the "independent self so dear to Western thought"' (Lasch, 1984: 54).

The independent self is the foundation of individual freedom and moral responsibility. It is the foundation of *This Is Water*, of existentialism. For both Lasch and Wallace, without the independent self, the traditional ethics and values of humanism collapse. And the independent self is not the self-sufficient self; rather, it is what guarantees freedom of choice to all human beings. The self-sufficient self is an illusion of autarkic individuality not situated in (and therefore restricted by) a specific socio-historical situation. We must do away with the illusion of self-sufficiency, but we cannot afford to lose the independent self. Those who advocate selflessness present a 'simpleminded case for "cultural revolution"' (57) that doesn't recognize the truth of individuality. This failure establishes another pathological extreme. The final section builds on this distinction.

The distinction between self and other

For both Lasch and Wallace the ethical imperative to do justice to both individuality and community rests on a deeper ontological and epistemological truth: the distinction between self and other. This distinction entails both difference and recognition: to distinguish itself from the other, the self must recognize the other as other (i.e., as another self). *The Minimal Self* explicitly maintains that 'the distinction between the self and the not-self is the basis of all other distinctions' (Lasch, 1984: 184): 'the axiomatic principle without which mental life cannot even begin' (163) and 'the source of our intellectual mastery of the world around us' (164). This distinction is the foundation of Lasch's vision of individuality – how we orient ourselves in the world depends upon it – and so is also 'the source of our existential uneasiness' (164): we see ourselves as free to act upon the other and therefore feel the burden of responsibility, the terrors of the inner life.

This distinction between self and other is a central focus of Sartrean existentialism. It is therefore unsurprising that it is pivotal for Wallace as well.[8] The story of Norman Bombardini in *The Broom of the System* is the most direct fictionalization of Lasch's words. Bombardini's wife 'is leaving' (Wallace, 1997a: 83) and so, in despair, he enters a restaurant with the aim of eating and growing to infinite size until he fills the entire universe: 'for I am now hugely alone ... I'm going to grow and grow, and fill the absence that surrounds me' (83).

Bombardini constructs this plan on the basis of his belief that the distinction between self and other is the fundamental law of reality. He explains to Rick and Lenore, the two protagonists, 'the transparently true fact that for each of us the universe is deeply and sharply and completely divided into for example in my case, me, on one side, and everything else, on the other. This for each of us exhaustively defines the whole universe .... The whole universe. Self and Other' (90). Rick replies that it 'sounds uncontroversial' (90) to confirm the unquestionable truth of this distinction. Consequently, Bombardini explains that this law is not only ontological but also epistemological: it is 'not only that each of our universes has this feature, but that we are by nature without exception *aware* of the fact that the universe is so divided, into Self, on one hand, and Other, on the other. Exhaustively divided. It's part of our consciousness' (90).

In other words the universe is divided into self and other, and we are aware that it is so. This awareness guides human life: we act according to our knowledge that we are selves among not-selves. This is why Bombardini's ontological distinction is also epistemological and, ultimately, ethical. He explicitly states that it presents itself as a '*pre*scriptive axiom' (90, emphasis original), as a responsibility, as a terror of the inner life: 'the undoubtedly equally true and inarguable fact that we each ought to desire our own universe to be as *full* as possible, that the Great Horror consists in an empty, rattling personal universe, one where one finds oneself with Self, on one hand, and vast empty lonely spaces before Others begin to enter the picture at all, on the other. A non-full universe. Loneliness' (90). The universe is exclusively divided into self and other, and this is why loneliness presents itself as the Great Horror of emptiness. We want our universe to be full, and so loneliness terrifies us. A lack of self or of other creates a void in the fabric of our universe, and loneliness is the name we attribute to this horrifying emptiness.

This is why, for Wallace and Lasch, we need both individuality and community to fill the universe with the right balance of self and other. But Bombardini thinks differently, and therefore makes a mistake similar to that of Steeply, Marathe, and Schtitt. That is, he sees only the two pathological extremes as viable options. He thinks that, on the one hand, we can face the horror of loneliness by trying 'to have as much other around as possible' (90) – or, rather, by becoming a desirable *object* (this is the illusory solution of narcissism) – and, on the other hand, that we can choose the opposing path, absolute self-sufficiency. Bombardini tried the first option but failed: he tried to fill the universe with other but was rejected. Therefore he now chooses the other option, the option of absolute self-sufficiency: 'Rather than diminishing Self to entice Other to fill our universe, we may also of course obviously choose to fill the universe with *Self* ... . An autonomously full universe ... . Yes. I plan to grow to infinite size ... . And tonight Project Total Yang begins' (91).

This condemns him to suffering. But the origin of his suffering is not due to this final solipsistic choice but to his original interpretation of the distinction between self and other as entailing only two possible extreme solutions. Bombardini's final solipsistic choice is a necessary consequence of his earlier narcissistic dependence. In Wallace's work, to have the meaning of one's life depend upon the other is itself a form of narcissism-solipsism that impedes true human communion. When Bombardini despairs because his wife leaves, he demonstrates his narcissistic dependence upon the other and thus also, fundamentally, his mistaken interpretation of the ethical distinction between self and other.

Wallace makes representation of this problem absolutely central to *The Broom of the System* by constructing the relationship between Rick and Lenore as pathological for exactly the same reasons. That Rick feels like he cannot live without Lenore is evidence not of his love for her but of his narcissistic dependence on what he constantly calls 'the Object' (60) of his desire. His narcissistic dependence on Lenore is why he is not 'helping her', nor 'concerned with her needs', nor 'engaged in the sort of discriminating, mature love that focuses primary attention on the needs and interests of the beloved' (342).

Thus, for Wallace, the choice between self-dependence and self-sufficiency is not a choice at all. Both paths lead to solipsism, loneliness, and despair. One must confront both the terrors of the inner life and the need for community. Lasch expressed this by saying that one must strive for 'a creative tension between separation and union, individuation and dependence (Lasch, 1984: 177). For both authors, this is the only way to live a free, non-despairing life.

Both Wallace and Lasch thus consider this ethical principle to be in alignment with the fundamental truth of reality; that is, they think that this prescriptive axiom follows from the truth of epistemology and ontology. For them this means that one must strive to find the balance between the truth of the self (individual responsibility) and the truth of the other (the need to give oneself away), because their coexistence is itself the fundamental truth of human nature.

As we have seen, there are profound sociological, literary, and philosophical alignments between Wallace and Lasch. The extent and profundity of these convergences is evidence of a significant alliance between them. Recognizing this enriches our understanding of the cultural context within which Wallace's work arose and clarifies some implications of his sociological, literary, and philosophical arguments. In fact the alignment is so significant that it strongly suggests the possibility of Lasch's direct influence on Wallace. Yet this has not been the focus of this chapter. Not only because it is impossible to know how conscious Wallace was of this influence or whether he even recognized it but also because, even if Wallace's annotations in his HRC copy of *The Culture of Narcissism* always concern relevant overlaps, they also stop pretty early in the text (around page 40) – suggesting that he may have abandoned at least this copy of Lasch's work. Finally, many ideas that Wallace shares with Lasch may have simply been 'in the air' during the period: alignments and echoes cannot *prove* influence.

What is more certain is that *The Culture of Narcissism* and Wallace's oeuvre exhibit exceptional overlaps with regard to a multitude of ideas, concepts, and opinions, and they even frequently present these points through the same logical arguments. This is far more important than the problem of influence, and the comparative analysis in this chapter suggests that the alignment between Wallace and Lasch runs much wider and deeper than was previously noticed.

Of course there are limitations and divergences to acknowledge. The most important of which is that there *are* disagreements between Wallace and Lasch, and most of them have to do with the fact that Lasch was much more conservative and political than Wallace. Many have read a certain kind of conservatism in Lasch's works and, even though one may argue that those readings mischaracterized him, it is a fact that his works allow for such readings while Wallace's do not. In addition, nothing speaks louder of the differences between

Wallace and Lasch than their divergent career paths. There are reasons that led Lasch to be a historian-sociologist and Wallace to choose to be a novelist—the most important being that Lasch wanted to zero in on the wider socio-historical level, while Wallace always saw the individual existential level as primary and accordingly chose fiction writing as his art.

Yet these differences do not detract from the manifest similarities in their orientations, and divergences between socio-historical and fictional outlooks are largely a matter of point of view. To notice the alignment between Wallace and Lasch therefore can help us enhance our understanding of Wallace's relationship with past thinkers, and it especially reminds us of how much – in perfect coherence with his dialogic philosophy – Wallace allowed himself to be influenced by the work of other intellectuals. This recognition should moreover move us to acknowledge certain aspects of Wallace's work that we sometimes run the risk of overlooking: above all, the fact that Wallace's call to commit to the other was never meant to overshadow his belief in the primacy of individuality.

Notes

1 Wallace underlines at length the passage from which this quote is taken, from 'they fail to explore'… to 'deteriorating relations between men and women' (Lasch, 1979: 33).
2 This is why Wallace underlines this passage in *The Culture of Narcissism*: 'every society reproduces its culture – its norms, its underlying assumptions, its modes of organizing experience – in the individual, in the form of personality' (Lasch, 1979: 34).
3 Relatedly Wallace annotated this passage in *The Culture of Narcissism*: 'useful, creative [literary] work … provides the narcissist … with the best hope of transcending his predicament' (Lasch, 1979: 17). Here Lasch anticipates Wallace's belief in literature's obligation to provide individuals with the means to overcome their existential predicament.
4 The logic of Wallace's criticism of metafiction is perhaps the most-studied aspect of his work. I thus will not delve into it here. See Adam Kelly's seminal 'David Foster Wallace and the New Sincerity in American Fiction' (2010) as a point of entry into the matter.
5 Here I am citing a wide range of Wallace's work to highlight that Wallace made this argument *throughout his career*. This prevents me, however,

from having space to analyse any one text in depth. I am also asserting that Wallace's fiction 'makes arguments'. This position is justified – if by nothing else – by the fact that Wallace himself thought of fiction as argumentative: see, for example, 'The Empty Plenum' (1990), where he writes that 'Mr. T. Pynchon ... argues in *Gravity's Rainbow* for why the paranoid delusion of complete & malevolent connection, wacko & unpleasant though it be, is preferable at least to its opposite – the conviction that *nothing* is connected to *anything* else & that *nothing* has *anything* intrinsically to do with *you*' (Wallace, 2012: 88).

6 Hence why Wallace underlines this sentence in *The Culture of Narcissism*: 'the first thing to be done is to cease our hostility to the past' (Lasch, 1979: 9).
7 On Wallace's existentialism see Hirt (2008), Smith (2009), Ryerson (2011), Den Dulk (2015), and Thompson (2016).
8 On the extent of Sartre's influence on Wallace see Den Dulk (2015) and Pitari (2020).

References

Bateson, G. (1972). *Steps toward an Ecology of Mind*. San Francisco CA: Chandler.
Berman, M. (1981). *The Reenchantment of the World*. Ithaca NY: Cornell University Press.
Boswell, M. (2003). *Understanding David Foster Wallace*. Columbia SC: University of South Carolina Press.
Den Dulk, A. (2015). *Existentialist Engagement in Wallace, Eggers and Foer: A Philosophical Analysis of Contemporary American Literature*. London and New York NY: Bloomsbury.
Dudar, H. (2012). 'A Whiz Kid and His Wacky First Novel', 8–10. In Stephen J. Burn, ed., *Conversations with David Foster Wallace*. Jackson MS: University Press of Mississippi.
Hering, D. (2016). *David Foster Wallace: Fiction and Form*. London and New York NY: Bloomsbury.
Hirt, S. (2008). *The Iron Bars of Freedom: David Foster Wallace and the Postmodern Self*. Stuttgart and Hannover: Ibidem-Verlag Press.
Holland, M. K. (2013). *Succeeding Postmodernism: Language and Humanism in Contemporary American Literature*. London and New York NY: Bloomsbury.
Hyde, L. (1988). *Alcohol and Poetry: John Berryman and the Booze Talking*. Dallas TX: Dallas Institute of Humanities & Culture.

Kelly, A. (2010). 'David Foster Wallace and the New Sincerity in American Fiction', 131–46. In David Hering, ed., *Consider David Foster Wallace: Critical Essays*. Austin TX: Sideshow Media Group Press.

Kennedy, H. and G. Polk (2012). 'Looking for a Garde of Which to Be Avant: An Interview with David Foster Wallace', 11–20. In Stephen J. Burn, ed., *Conversations with David Foster Wallace*. Jackson MS: University Press of Mississippi.

Lasch, C. (1979). *The Culture of Narcissism: American Life in an Age of Diminishing Expectations*. New York NY: W. W. Norton.

Lasch, C. (1984). *The Minimal Self: Psychic Survival in Troubled Times*. New York NY: W. W. Norton.

Lipsky, D. (2010). *Although Of Course You End Up Becoming Yourself: A Road Trip with David Foster Wallace*. New York NY: Broadway Books.

Marin, P. (1975). 'The New Narcissism', *Harper's Magazine*. October.

McCaffery, L. (2012). 'An Expanded Interview with David Foster Wallace', 21–57. In Stephen J. Burn (ed.), *Conversations with David Foster Wallace*. Jackson MS: University Press of Mississippi.

O'Brien, J. (2012). 'Conversation with David Foster Wallace and Richard Powers', 110–20. In Stephen J. Burn, ed., *Conversations with David Foster Wallace*. Jackson MS: University Press of Mississippi.

Pitari, P. (2020). 'The Influence of Sartre's "What Is Literature?" on David Foster Wallace's Literary Project', in *Critique*, 61:4, 423–39.

Ryerson, J. (2011). 'Introduction'. In David Foster Wallace. *Fate, Time, and Language: An Essay on Free Will*. New York NY: Columbia University Press.

Sheehy, G. (1976). *Passages: Predictable Crises of Adult Life*. New York NY: Dutton.

Smith, Z. (2009). *Changing My Mind: Occasional Essays*. London: Hamish Hamilton.

Thompson, L. (2016). *Global Wallace: David Foster Wallace and World Literature*. London and New York NY: Bloomsbury.

Wallace, D. Foster. (1989). *Girl with Curious Hair*. London: Abacus.

Wallace, D. Foster. (1996a). *Infinite Jest*. London: Abacus.

Wallace, D. Foster. (1997a). *The Broom of the System*. London: Abacus.

Wallace, D. Foster. (1997b). *A Supposedly Fun Thing I'll Never Do Again*. London: Abacus.

Wallace, D. Foster. (2000). *Brief Interviews with Hideous Men*. New York NY: Back Bay Books.

Wallace, D. Foster. (2004). *Oblivion: Stories*. London: Abacus.

Wallace, D. Foster. (2005). *Consider the Lobster and Other Essays*. New York NY: Little Brown.

Wallace, D. Foster. (2009). *This Is Water: Some Thoughts, Delivered on a Significant Occasion, about Living a Compassionate Life.* New York NY: Little, Brown, 2009.
Wallace, D. Foster (2011). *The Pale King.* London: Penguin.
Wallace, D. Foster (2012). *Both Flesh and Not: Essays.* London: Penguin.

Internet sources

Wallace, D. Foster. (11 April 1996b). 'Bookworm: David Foster Wallace: *Infinite Jest*', hosted by Michael Silverblatt. KCRW. www.kcrw.com/culture/shows/bookworm/david-foster-wallace-infinite-jest (accessed 17 March 2021).

Wallace, D. Foster. (2003). 'Interview on ZDF'. youtube.com/watch?v=iGLzWdT7vGc (accessed 17 March 2021).

PART II

Consciousness, self, and others

5

'What all she'd so painfully learned said about her': a comparative reading of David Foster Wallace's 'The Depressed Person' and Fyodor Dostoevsky's *Notes from Underground*

Allard den Dulk

This chapter offers a comparative reading of David Foster Wallace's short story 'The Depressed Person' (1998/1999) and Fyodor Dostoevsky's novella *Notes from Underground* (1864) partly based on materials from the Wallace archive. Wallace expressed his admiration of Dostoevsky at length in his 1996 review of Joseph Frank's biography of the Russian novelist (2005). From this review we can identify two main aspects of Dostoevsky's work that Wallace admired and took as inspiration for his own: namely, Dostoevsky's cultural critique and his ability to transform such critical-theoretical ideas into fiction. Dostoevsky constituted an important example for Wallace that some philosophical problems are best approached through literature. In the work of both authors philosophy and literature operate as partly overlapping activities. In this sense Wallace's review of Frank's biography can be read as an artistic manifesto for Wallace's own fiction: whereas in previous writings, as D. T. Max notes, Wallace 'had mostly diagnosed a disease', in the review 'he was [now] giving a model for the cure' (2012: 209). Despite such affinities between Wallace and Dostoevsky, however, connections in their fiction have so far remained under-researched.[1]

To begin, it is worth noting that Wallace worked on his Dostoevsky article throughout 1995, including during his cruise experience that spring. The essay resulting from this cruise was published in January

1996 (around the same time that *Infinite Jest* came out) and bears clear traces of Wallace's immersion in Dostoevsky, especially in its engagement with themes like despair, self-disgust, and the need for real community. His review of the Frank biography came out in April 1996. 'The Depressed Person' seems to have been conceived the following year.[2] Yet though this chapter is interested in Dostoevsky's influence on Wallace, it does not depend on it: while anchored in careful attention to the texts and related archival materials, the readings offered below are inherently speculative.

So far most critics have interpreted 'The Depressed Person' as expressing a supposedly inevitable failure of language and communication (e.g., Boswell, 2003; Holland, 2013; Hayes-Brady, 2016). I will argue against such readings through a comparative close reading of the story with Dostoevsky's *Notes*, tracing shared themes, motifs, and formal traits. I will contend that 'The Depressed Person' and *Notes* offer a similar cultural critique and approach to casting critical-philosophical ideas into fiction by showing that both texts portray their protagonists as a type, an embodiment of the tendencies of their respective cultural formations. These tendencies foster hyperconsciousness, scepticism, and spite in the characters, leading both to distrust communication and the possibility of successfully explaining themselves – a view scholars have mistakenly interpreted as expressed by Wallace's story as a whole. I will argue that 'The Depressed Person' tempts the reader to replicate the protagonist's views in this regard, but that both fictions are in fact aimed at facilitating the possible realization of communication and empathy in the reader.

Failure of language?

Most scholars have concluded that 'The Depressed Person', like the rest of the collection *Brief Interviews with Hideous Men* (1999) in which it is contained, confirms a (supposedly inescapable) failure of language and communication. Mary K. Holland writes that the story 'asks, rather than elucidates, how we are to escape narcissism, all through language' and concludes that, like the rest of the collection, the story 'seems to imply that it (and we) cannot escape the suffocating and distorting conditions of language', since we are 'trapped' in a 'discursive loop' thanks to what Holland calls 'always-elusive poststructural language' (2013: 117, 126, 112). Similarly, according to Clare Hayes-Brady, 'The Depressed Person' offers an instance of 'total failure [of communication]', in which there is 'no room for the reader', a 'deadening logorrhea' that is the 'endgame of late postmodernist literature' (2016: 4, 135). Other scholars, such as Marshall Boswell and Christoforos Diakoulakis, have drawn similar conclusions (Boswell, 2003: 207; Diakoulakis, 2010).[3]

I disagree with such interpretations. What does it mean to say that language or communication fails in Wallace's story? As I have discussed elsewhere, such claims seem to suggest that an utterance is unable to refer, to accurately describe something, or to convey that something to somebody else, because, according to a 'poststructural' view, such references and descriptions are always partly ambiguous, incomplete, and thus unsuccessful (Den Dulk, 2015: 90–7, 132–45). This 'failure' of language and communication is what 'The Depressed Person' is taken to dramatize. What seems true is that the story's protagonist is gripped by the conviction that she cannot accurately describe herself and communicate what she feels to the other. But does that mean she is right? Can the story as a whole be said to confirm this view? Several scholars have established that Wallace's writing was influenced by, and can be read fruitfully in light of, the later Wittgenstein's view of language (e.g., Boswell, 2003: Den Dulk, 2015; Horn, 2014; Ramal, 2014). Contrary to, for example, Derridean deconstruction – which maintains that language is driven by the attempt to refer but necessarily fails to do so fully successfully – Wittgenstein shows that this idea of a necessary (failed) connection between language and world or thought is an illusion resulting from an over-reflective misperception of how words are actually used and is actually irrelevant for the meaningful functioning of language (cf. Den Dulk, 2015: 138–45). This means that the depressed person's self-absorption and scepticism with regard to language do not necessarily block meaningful expression and communication, since her story participates in a communal language and may lead to understanding and empathy in the reader. This strand in Wallace's writing can be connected to wider debates in literary studies about language and reading, particularly the work of scholars like Rita Felski and Toril Moi. Felski describes reading as an encounter in which '[l]anguage is not always and only a symbol of alienation and division' but also serves as a source 'mutual experiences of meaning' (2008: 31–32). Moi writes that the 'point of literature' is to 'overcome separation' (2009: 193).[4] She points out that 'texts are actions and expressions' which *'place a claim on others'* and proposes thinking of 'reading as a practice of acknowledgment' – not as a 'particular mental content' but as 'something we *do'*, 'a *response'*, in which we 'reveal [ourselves]' and 'picture our relationship to the other' (2017: 196, 207).

Outlining these theoretical debates on the philosophy of language in relation to Wallace's work and practices of reading in the humanities more generally lies beyond the scope of this chapter. Instead, I will proceed offering a comparative reading of Wallace's 'The Depressed Person' and Dostoevsky's *Notes*, first showing that the view that language and communication are somehow doomed to fail is, in fact, part of – and conducive to the exacerbation of – the narcissism of these texts' protagonists and then foregrounding how both texts clearly establish a space beyond this trap.

Wallace and Dostoevsky

There seem to have been two main aspects of Dostoevsky's work that inspired Wallace: firstly, Dostoevsky's analysis of the societal problems of his time and exploration of alternatives; secondly, Dostoevsky's ability to cast these theoretical ideas into fiction and still create stories and characters that are real, human, and lifelike. These aspects indicate an affinity in how Dostoevsky and Wallace saw the relation between philosophy and literature: their exploration of philosophical themes, rather than being conceptual or theoretical, is driven by a clear desire to express – and thereby allow the reader to experience – some of the most existentially urgent and painful aspects of human existence.

To take up the first aspect of inspiration: Dostoevsky's interpretation of his cultural context strongly influenced Wallace's understanding of his own culture, in terms of diagnosis as well as cure. In his review of Frank's Dostoevsky biography Wallace contends that Dostoevsky's novels are 'important to us as readers in 1996 America' (2005: 261) because of how Dostoevsky's critique of nihilism encourages us to consider in what ways we might also be 'under our own type of Nihilist spell' (271). In working on the review Wallace seems to have been especially struck by such similarities, scribbling remarks like 'Link to 1990s' and 'same conflict today' in the margins of the biography (Wallace, *Stir*, HRC: 333; *Miraculous*, HRC: 56), and commenting in his notes: 'striking parallel w/ present', and 'none of 1990s is new. The selfishness, loneliness, purposelessness – the fear, the loss of belief, the materialism' (Wallace, container 4.12, HRC). What we see in these comments is Wallace's identification of parallels between what Dostoevsky considered the main philosophical problems of mid- to late-nineteenth century Russia and his responses to them and Wallace's own time and the response to it he might offer in his work.

As to the second aspect: Wallace admired perhaps even more what he saw as Dostoevsky's ability to convert these philosophical analyses into fiction that is human and alive: 'theoretical agenda w/ living characters', Wallace wrote in his notes (Wallace, container 4.12, HRC). His review elaborates this observation by explicitly holding up Dostoevsky as a 'model' for writing 'morally passionate, passionately moral fiction' that is 'also ingenious and radiantly human fiction' (2005: 274). These observations about Dostoevsky are expressive of ideas that seem to underlie Wallace's own work: namely, that philosophy and literature are partly overlapping activities and that some philosophical problems are best approached through literature. I have already elaborated on these ideas elsewhere and will not re-hash them here, but Wallace's explicit praise of these aspects of Dostoevsky's work further confirms such conclusions (cf. Den Dulk, 2015: 154–60, 261–4). Moreover, Wallace's comments help us better understand his specific affinity with existentialism – and with Dostoevsky as an existentialist author – as part of a larger inquiry into human experience that blends philosophical and literary approaches.

As Simone de Beauvoir explains in her essay 'Literature and Metaphysics' (1946) regarding the possibility of 'philosophical literature': because of its emphasis on subjectivity and ambiguity as the 'essence' of human existence, existentialism sees literature as providing a legitimate mode of philosophical inquiry into 'metaphysical experience' – which Beauvoir defines as the individual 'placed in one's totality before the totality of the world' – because it seeks to explore experience in its 'singular and temporal form' without attempting to reduce it to a 'universal meaning in an abstract language' (2004: 273, 274). Beauvoir explains that 'it is not a matter of exploiting on a literary plane truths established beforehand on the philosophical plane, but, rather, of manifesting an aspect of metaphysical experience that cannot otherwise be manifested' (275). In a formulation strikingly similar to Wallace, Beauvoir describes Dostoevsky as a prime example of existentialist literature as 'living discovery' (271).[5]

Diagnosis of a type

Wallace seems to have been especially struck by the idea and potential of the underground man as a character who is explicitly presented as a type – that is, as a figure embodying certain cultural phenomena. In his copy of *Notes*, Wallace underlined the following passage from the footnote on the first page of Dostoevsky's novella: 'it is clear that such persons as the writer of these notes not only may, but positively must, exist in our society, when we consider the circumstances in the midst of which our society is formed' (Wallace, *Notes*, HRC: 13). In Frank's biography Wallace underlined the passage addressing this footnote: 'The underground man *must* exist as a type because he is the inevitable product of such a cultural formation' (Wallace, *Stir*, HRC: 314).

This notion of a main character embodying a 'necessary' type clearly applies to 'The Depressed Person': because of its title and eponymous, nameless main character, the story demands to be read not just as a portrayal of deep psychological despair but as the diagnosis of a type that is bound up with our specific time. Also note the similar nameless generality of the descriptors used to identify these two protagonists: '*the* underground man', '*the* depressed person'. These names make clear that these characters function partly as 'parodic caricature' (Wallace, 2005: 261 n5), to use Wallace's own description of the underground man – a characterization he again gleaned from Frank, underlining the following passage in the biography: '[the underground man] is, in short, conceived as a parodistic persona, whose life exemplifies the tragic-comic impasses resulting from the effects of such [European] influences on the Russian national psyche' (Wallace, *Stir*, HRC: 314). In other words he is a character who embodies the effects of a certain cultural formation.

Relatedly, several early typescript drafts of 'The Depressed Person' carry the title 'Provenience (Or, A Depressed Person)'. The term 'provenience' refers to source or origin, which might be connected to the source of the depressed person's pain or to a more general origin story – that is, a description of the tendencies of a cultural period and its effects, in this case highly self-reflective thinking that effectively takes on the form of a disorder. This earlier title speaks of '*a*' rather than 'the' depressed person, signalling that the person portrayed might be seen as an example or illustration through whom this 'provenience' is traced. In the first handwritten draft Wallace switches from 'a' (crossing it out) to 'the' ('Very Depressed Person'), then back to 'a' in the subtitle of the above-mentioned version, before later deciding on 'the' for the published story (Wallace, container 27.6, HRC). The difference between 'a' and 'the' depressed person is that 'the', as suggested above, can be seen to signal the portrayal of a type as opposed to an individual person who serves as a specific example.

Wallace praises Dostoevsky for his ability to combine precisely such a 'theoretical agenda' – in this case, the necessary existence of a 'moral-psychological' and 'social-ideological' type (Frank, 1986: 314) – with 'living characters'. In preparing for the Frank review, Wallace identifies *Notes* as a prime example of this quality he so admired in Dostoevsky: 'The often cerebral and parodistic function of characters – underground man, Prince Mishkin – is obscured and overwhelmed "by the immense vitality of their artistic embodiment"' (Wallace, container 4.12, HRC).[6] The same holds for 'The Depressed Person': despite – and, in the end, partly through – its purposely distanced and repetitive narration, the story offers a gripping, painful portrayal of the main character's tormented existence.

This brings us to a crucial question about 'The Depressed Person': how should we understand this portrayal that seems to critique – and, in its parodic exaggeration, perhaps even make fun of – its main character for her illness, depression? Most scholars have tried to solve this problem by following Boswell in his claim that the story's character is not truly suffering from depression but rather is actually a narcissist who has 'mistakenly, and self-aggrandizingly, diagnosed [her narcissism] as depression' (2003: 205; cf. Holland, 2003: 116;

Max, 2012: 241; Redgate, 2019: 96). I think this interpretation is unsatisfactory.[7] In my opinion the story does not propose a mutually exclusive decision between depression or narcissism.[8]

It has been well established that depression is a major theme throughout Wallace's entire oeuvre – a theme approached in many different ways in Wallace scholarship. Rob Mayo offers the most insightful and comprehensive study of Wallace's portrayal of 'dysphoria' (including loneliness, anxiety, boredom, and depression) as a 'mood' or emotion that is 'consciously and cognitively assessed' (2021: 5). Jamie Redgate insightfully proposes that Wallace imagines depression as a separation between the self and a foreign 'malign force which affects his characters' souls as fire would burn their bodies' (2019: 113). Some critics have focused primarily on Wallace's depiction of therapy culture: Catherine Toal takes *Infinite Jest* to make 'non-clinical depression a learned affect, a subjection to a rigid regime of instruction' (2003: 319). According to Kiki Benzon, Wallace's work, including 'The Depressed Person', portrays how the 'fundamentally social character of depression' is structurally 'evaded' and 'overlooked' (2006: 175). And others, like Jon Baskin, regard Wallace's descriptions of depression as 'therapeutic', which for Baskin refers to the 'mode of philosophy Wallace privileges' in his work: rather than 'simply describe and diagnose pain', or provide a theoretical explanation for it, Wallace's writing wants to 'treat' it by addressing the 'individual reader and the form of life that has produced that reader's habits of mind' (2019: 4, 12–13). These interpretations are highly relevant to my approach to 'The Depressed Person': I also take its protagonist to be in the grip of a hyperconscious mood triggered by social-cultural factors that produces a self-alienating split. My approach is perhaps closest to Baskin's, in that I am most interested in the type of thinking, and its existential implications, that the story may be seen to describe and, ultimately, try to 'treat' in its reader.

As mentioned above, the depressed person is a type and, as such, embodies aspects of our contemporary cultural formation. She is portrayed, above all, as excessively self-conscious, to the extent of experiencing meaninglessness and paralysis. This shows, on the one hand, that these tendencies – which do not lead to depression for everyone – are partly narcissistic, and that, on the other hand, if they do lead to depression, these tendencies none the less bear (and are experienced as having) narcissistic aspects. Both of these qualities contribute to the self-loathing that is part of depression: am I not merely a narcissist?

Here, again, comparison with the underground man as a type is illuminating. Wallace marks the passage in Frank's biography in which Dostoevsky's 'use of satirical exaggeration and parodistic caricature' is described as 'ideological eschatology'. The term captures, and identifies as a method, Dostoevsky's characterization of the underground man as carrying 'the logical presuppositions and possibilities' of the ideas of his time to their 'consistent conclusion' (Wallace, *Stir*, HRC: 345). Similarly, we might say that the depressed person as a type embodies a consistent thinking-through of aspects of our contemporary cultural formation that lead to depression, including that culture's narcissistic aspects. Instead of regarding her narcissism as somehow the only 'real' cause of her pain, it would be more accurate to say that narcissistic aspects contribute to or exacerbate her pain as part of her depression. In the depressed person, we can recognize tendencies of our cultural context and ourselves and see how these can lead to deep suffering. Although, as I will argue later, the story purposefully tempts us to judge the depressed person as 'merely' narcissistic, such a judgement entails failing to recognize our kinship to her and denying the reality of her pain – as well as the appeal to our concern implied therein (thus confirming her scepticism of language).

Wallace writes that the power of Dostoevsky's work, and of *Notes* specifically, lies in its 'admixture of the universal and the particular'. That is, on one hand, the novella and its protagonist are 'impossible really to understand without some knowledge of the intellectual climate of Russia in the 1860s'. On the other hand, the underground man's traits are recognizable to all of us: 'we can all see parts of ourselves' in him, Wallace writes (2005: 256). As we have seen, the depressed person offers a similar admixture of general and particular, bearing some features through time and others that are firmly rooted in her own historical period. In this regard the traits Wallace identifies in the underground man could also serve to accurately describe the depressed person: namely, a combination of self-importance and self-contempt, of rage and cowardice, of fervour and a paralysed inability to act (256). Furthermore, in both protagonists these traits are described as a form of illness. Taking a look at the roots and manifestations of these two characters' illnesses will show how the close affinities between Dostoevsky's novella and Wallace's text can further guide our reading of the latter.

Illness: hyperconsciousness and scepticism

In the opening sentence of *Notes* the underground man states: 'I am a sick man ... I am a wicked man' (Dostoevsky, 2004: 5). Part 1 of the novella is devoted to the underground man's description of his disease. He suffers from a 'heightened consciousness' that imprisons him in an 'inertia' of spiteful, 'wicked' thoughts (10). In his copy Wallace marks the following passage: 'I swear, gentlemen, that to be too conscious is an illness – a real thoroughgoing illness' (Wallace, *Notes*, HRC: 16). On the same page Wallace also marks a passage in which the underground man links this sickness to the cultural formation of which he is part, describing hyperconsciousness as the 'lot of a cultivated man of our unhappy nineteenth century' (16). The underground man's being overly conscious follows from his context, his education, his time and place. He cannot *not* be hyper-aware: it all 'occurs according to the normal and basic laws of heightened consciousness'; and what 'follows directly from these laws' is 'inertia', and 'consequently there is not only nothing you can do to change yourself, but there is simply nothing to do at all' (Dostoevsky, 2004: 10). In his notes for the Frank review Wallace expressed agreement with Dostoevsky's analysis of hyperreflexivity in his portrayal of the underground man: '<u>Vital</u>. Paralysis of hyperconsciousness'; 'Hyperc makes life meaningless'. Moreover, Wallace signals the need to extrapolate Dostoevsky's analysis to our contemporary cultural context: 'Today, when ... culture necessitate[s] so many more choices, so many more <u>actions</u> – Dost's exploration even more vital' (Wallace, container 4.12, HRC).

Wallace's fictions, like Dostoevsky's, are famously crowded with characters who suffer from the life-undermining consequences of their hyperreflexivity, but 'The Depressed Person' displays the most direct parallels with the underground man's condition. Like the opening sentence of Dostoevsky's novella, Wallace's story starts by stating its protagonist's illness: 'The depressed person was in terrible and unceasing emotional pain, and the impossibility of sharing or articulating this pain was in itself a component of the pain and a contributing factor in its essential horror' (1999: 31). Throughout the story the depressed person constantly scrutinizes her thoughts, feelings, *and* the attempts to formulate them – all of which seem insufficient to her and to impede conclusions and actions (as none can be established as superior to others), thus making her life meaningless.

An important difference between the narrations of the texts might seem to be that *Notes* is narrated in first person by the underground man (the text represents his 'Notes'), while 'The Depressed Person' is formally narrated in the third person. However, I propose that we should see the third-person narration of Wallace's text as his extrapolation of hyperconsciousness and its consequences: the narrative perspective represents the complete self-objectification (as if in third person) of the depressed person's self-narration, the result of the constant conscious observation of the only object that interests the depressed person – herself.[9] In line with Jean-Paul Sartre's analysis of reflection as the bad-faith attempt to treat oneself as a thing – which tries to make one's consciousness opaque instead of a translucent awareness of one's freedom (2010: 91) – the depressed person, watching herself as if from the outside as an object, can come to seem strange and inaccessible to herself.

The self-objectification of self-consciousness and its destructive consequences are reflected in the narration of *Notes* and 'The Depressed Person' by a similar contradiction. On the one hand, both characters can be said to prefer distanced, clinical observation: the underground man says he adheres to the scientific rationality of his time, which he in fact carries through to its extremes; and the narration of 'The Depressed Person' is characterized by moments of absurd precision (recurring, seemingly unnecessary clarification of referents, such as 'i.e. the depressed person' and 'i.e. the therapist') and clinical observation of the movements of her therapist's hands. On the other hand, the narration of both stories follows the digressions of self-consciousness of both characters: the underground man turns out to be a chaotic and highly excitable narrator, and his text is riddled with ellipses and exclamation marks; the depressed person's narration is increasingly interrupted by digressive footnotes, which, at a certain point, even become the site of the story's primary narration. As Boswell writes: 'the footnotes [dramatize] the layered nature of the woman's obsessive self-absorption, in which thoughts have tangents that themselves become winding thought helixes running parallel to the first-order line of consciousness' (2003: 204–5).

For Dostoevsky an important factor within the cultural formation of his time fuelling excessive self-consciousness was the ideology of rational egoism. The underground man's sickness is rooted in how he follows this ideology through to its logical, nihilist consequences. Rational egoism frames societal harmony and happiness in terms of individuals acting in accordance with the supposedly rational, natural laws of self-interest (Frank, 1986: 311–15). However, for the underground man, affirming this position leads to a spiralling of self-consciousness, as he wonders about the rational, egoistic response to things while also realizing that all behaviour is in fact determined by natural laws. The underground man describes – in a passage that Wallace again underlines – that all possible reasons for action therefore 'evaporate', 'the object flies off into air', and the underground man finds himself locked in 'inertia' (Wallace, *Stir*, HRC: 319).

In his review Wallace writes that 'our own [culture's]' equivalent of this 'Nihilist spell' is in fact one of 'congenital skepticism' (Wallace, 2005: 271 n28, 272). In 'The Depressed Person' hyperconsciousness and scepticism constantly feed into each other. For example the depressed person dwells at length on what might be seen as possible causes of her pain (such as her childhood insecurity about her 'snoutish pug nose' and her divorced parents' battle over her orthodonture costs), only then to dismiss such attribution as 'demeaning and pathetic'. Similarly she sees her interactions with her therapist as effectively buying an obligation-free friendship and conceives of her Support System as herself leaning heavily on others without giving anything back (Wallace, 1999: 32, 33). The depressed person's constant, self-critical scrutiny of such aspects only contributes to the toxic continuation and aggravation of her feelings and behaviours, to the point of absurdity – so that, even when her therapist dies and her most important Support System friend is diagnosed with cancer, the depressed person can only reflect on the impact of these events on her own 'emotional pain' (38).

Above all, the depressed person's sceptical hyperconsciousness is embodied in her assertion that she is unable to describe 'what the depression made her *feel like*' (49 n5). The depressed person invokes terms like 'agony' and 'despair' but immediately qualifies such terms as 'melodramatic' and 'minimizing' (51–2 n6). This attempt to describe her pain conceptually – only to sceptically dismiss concepts as, by definition, incapable of capturing that pain – sets up the depressed person's loop of hyperreflection. And it also shows the narcissism inherent to this process, as this endless, self-conscious doubt distracts her from the fact that, meanwhile, she has in fact been able to communicate her feelings (shame, guilt, self-hatred) throughout.

As noted above, I disagree with the prevailing interpretation of 'The Depressed Person' as confirming a supposed, inevitable failure of language. Narcissism and the workings of language itself do not impede the depressed person's self-description. Rather, that she convinces herself that language is incapable of expressing her inner life is an example of her narcissism. But even while describing this conviction, she in fact successfully communicates something about her suffering. We should not mistake a narcissistic view that language is bound to fail as proof that language does indeed fail. The following passage from Wallace's cruise essay 'A Supposedly Fun Thing I'll Never Do Again' – which he wrote in the same period as the Frank review, and a year before starting 'The Depressed Person' – can be read as an explanation, 'before the fact', of this aspect of the story that confirms the pain and difficulty of the expression of depression (through terms such as agony and despair) but also that it can be expressed: 'The word's overused and banalified now, *despair*, but it's a serious word, and I'm using it seriously. ... [It's] like wanting to die in order to escape the unbearable feeling of becoming aware that I'm small and weak and selfish and going, without doubt, to die' (Wallace, 1997: 261).

Illness: wickedness

We might experience an obstacle other than language, however, in our understanding of the depressed person: an aspect reminiscent of the underground man, wickedness. In the opening sentence of Dostoevsky's novella the statement 'I'm a sick man' is followed by 'I am a wicked man'. While both the depressed person and the underground man are in deep despair, there also seems to be – to use formulations from *Notes* – something 'crafty', a paradoxical 'pleasure', in their expression of (that is, in their 'moaning' about) their pain (Dostoevsky, 2004: 15). The underground man describes this pleasure via the example of not going to the dentist to get a toothache treated and moaning as a result, with Wallace marking the following passage: 'but they are not candid moans, they are malignant moans, and the malignancy is the whole point. The enjoyment of the sufferer finds expression in those moans' (Wallace, *Notes*, HRC: 22). This is one example of what the underground man calls his 'spitefulness' or 'wickedness': due to his heightened consciousness, he is filled with self-loathing about his inertia. At the same time this heightened consciousness – his awareness of the full implications of the beliefs of his time – gives the underground man a feeling of superiority. As such he turns the humiliation of his suffering into a wicked, paradoxical enjoyment. With regard to the toothache the underground man 'knows that his moans will be of no use to him; he knows better than anyone that he is only straining and irritating himself and others in vain' (Dostoevsky, 2004: 16). These others are needed to further exacerbate his humiliation. Wallace underlines the underground man's conclusion: 'the enjoyment was just from the too intense consciousness of one's own degradation' (Wallace, *Notes*, HRC: 17).

The depressed person also seems to use her suffering manipulatively vis-à-vis her therapist and the members of her Support System, in order to deepen her own humiliation – urging others to tell her how loathsome she is – but also to somehow establish her superiority over them – constantly underscoring her own complete awareness and honesty, while questioning that of her friends.[10] We can see this, for example, when the depressed person says to her best Support System friend that she '[wished to hear] [her] brutally honest opinion of her as a person, the potentially negative and judging and hurtful parts': this 'felt to her ... like an almost literal matter of life and death' (Wallace, 1999: 55). In this passage the depressed person tries to shame the friend into admitting her 'potentially negative and judging and hurtful' opinions about the depressed person. And by presenting this, manipulatively, as an 'almost literal matter of life and death', the depressed person forces the friend to give in to her demand, thus asserting power to increase her self-loathing.

In light of this comparison with the underground man's wickedness, it is interesting to note that one of Wallace's later typescript drafts carries the title 'THE DEVIL'. At the top of page 11 of the typescript in question, Wallace writes (in double quote marks) 'demonize', without a clear connection to or suggestion for insertion into a specific passage (Wallace, container 27.6, HRC). In the absence of such indications we might say that the story – and, given her possible disguised self-narration, perhaps its protagonist – demonizes her(self). This might be understood in several, layered ways.

First of all, the story describes the depressed person's process of slipping deeper into wickedness. The last paragraph (on page 12) of the typescript in question offers a summary of the intended conclusion, ending in the depressed person's questions about how to describe herself – similar to the questions that conclude the published versions of the story – and these are then explicitly connected back to the title of this draft. The last line reads: 'Depressed person worries her self-concern after death means she is not a good person; what could the word be for somebody who couldn't feel anything for another; what would the word be? "What did that make her?" (title: THE DEVIL?)' (Wallace, container 27.6, HRC). These references to 'demonize' and 'the devil' – with the final question, 'What did that make her?' apparently being answered by this draft's provisional title – suggest explicitly (perhaps too much so, which might be why Wallace abandoned the title after this draft) that the depressed person's behaviour is wicked, that she is not just suffering from an affliction but somebody who, while suffering, also takes pleasure in it. Which is to say, she employs her suffering to inflict suffering on others and somehow empower herself.

Moreover, 'demonize' refers not just to the content but also to the effect of the text: it demonizes the depressed person. Maybe Wallace foresaw some of the early critiques of the story, which saw it as a harsh indictment of someone suffering from a disease. But, more interestingly, the text's demonizing effect can be seen as a strategy, namely to *tempt* – which is after all the purpose of the demonic – the reader to understand the depressed person in a certain, negative way. As argued above, I disagree with readings that deny the protagonist is truly suffering from depression: it is not that the depressed person is actually suffering from narcissism instead of from depression but that depression entails narcissistic tendencies; the former interpretation ('it is just narcissism') is part of the depressed person's own feelings of self-loathing. The story's demonizing strategy means that a variant of this dynamic portrayed in the story also becomes a potential *effect* of the story: in its unrelenting focus on the depressed person's self-absorbed and self-pitying thoughts, the story tempts readers to dismiss the depressed person as merely annoying and spoiled, and thereby – like the depressed person – to close themselves off from the other, from the depressed person. In other words I am not claiming the character is not annoying and spoiled; she is clearly meant to create a conflicted response in readers. But what the story and its 'demonizing' strategy show us is that it is precisely the depressed person's own – demonic – dynamic of critical dismissal that we should avoid; by replicating it, we perpetuate the problem and overlook the alternative response the story is capable of disclosing.

This layered dynamic is highly similar to the underground man's self-dismissal and exacerbation of his humiliation. In a passage marked by Wallace the underground man describes his 'wicked' strategy as follows: 'the luckless mouse succeeds in creating around it so many other nastinesses in the form of doubts and questions, adds to the one question so many unsettled questions that there inevitably works up around it a sort of fatal brew, a stinking mess, made up of its doubts, emotions, and of the contempt spat upon it' (Wallace, *Notes*, HRC: 19–20). The depressed person can also be said to create a 'fatal brew' of constant, self-absorbed questioning and self-dismissal that invites contempt, the crown of her humiliation.

This analysis can be extended to include the question of gender. 'The Depressed Person' is the only story in *Brief Interviews* that has a woman as its sole protagonist. In my opinion the choice of a female character serves the story's strategy of demonizing and temptation: it ties the potential dismissal of the depressed person as a mere narcissist to misogynist ideas about women as 'spoiled', 'needy', and 'whining' – ideas that are voiced by some of the hideous men throughout the rest of the collection (and that might also be present in readers). Again the critical purpose here is to tempt us to judge in line with such ideas by dismissing the depressed person as a 'whiny' woman, and thereby, unobservedly, to align ourselves with – or even revealing ourselves to be like – those hideous men. What is striking in this respect, given the attention to gender issues in Wallace scholarship, is that the female protagonist of 'The Depressed Person' is indeed commonly dismissed as a self-pitying narcissist, while several scholars have, for example, tried to redeem the male, sexually predatorial interviewee in 'B.I. #20' (also from *Brief Interviews*) as a man trapped in the failures of language and the impossibility of reaching the other (e.g. Diakoulakis, 2010; McAdams, 2015).

We can take the above interpretation one step further and identify a 'hideous' narrator within the story, to whom we can ascribe the intention of demonizing the depressed person; and this interpretation can be combined with my above suggestion that the third-person narration is in fact the depressed person's objectified self-narration. What is relevant to note is that throughout the rest of *Brief Interviews* Wallace uses single quotation marks to render direct speech and quotations – see, for example, the rendering of the interviewees' responses in single quotations in the different 'Brief Interviews' or the single quotation marks used in 'Death Is Not the End' to scare quote (1999). In Wallace's punctuation, from *Infinite Jest* (1996) onward, double quotation marks are used within an enunciation, while 'The Depressed Person' consistently uses double quotation marks for scare quotes and renderings of direct speech. This suggests that the story is in fact someone speaking, i.e., that 'The Depressed Person' as a whole is a direct-speech utterance, but with the enclosing single quotation marks removed or placed beyond the frame of the story. Note that Wallace already uses double quotation marks in the first, two-page handwritten draft of the story, and this choice thus seems fundamental to the form of 'The Depressed Person'. It prompts the question: who, then, is speaking? In this light it seems significant that, at the top of one of the pages of another handwritten draft, Wallace writes (in single quotation marks) '"Brief Interviews with Hideous Men"?', signalling already in the draft stage that he regards 'The Depressed Person' as potentially part of these hideous men narratives (Wallace, container 27.6, HRC).

One fruitful way of hypothesizing this connection is to see the story as an utterance by a hideous man. The story's demonic strategy can then be ascribed to this narrator, who recounts the self-absorbed suffering of a depressed woman in a cold, clinical way so as to tempt the reader to dismiss her as 'spoiled' and 'whiny' – making the narrator a typical 'postmodern' misogynist, cunningly exploiting his awareness of different (including therapeutic) discourses, like the other hideous men in *Brief Interviews*. This interpretation can be combined with the earlier suggestion that the story's third-person narration is the depressed person's completely objectified self-narration: that is, this hideous narrator is in fact the depressed person herself who, out of self-loathing and convinced of the failure of communication, tempts the reader to dismiss her – thereby displaying a manipulativeness and internalized misogyny that makes the depressed person one of the hideous men.

Now it is important to emphasize that these aspects of the depressed person's wickedness – her self-loathing and manipulation, bundled together specifically to try to get the reader to dismiss her as a narcissist – do not deny the reality of the depressed person's pain: she genuinely suffers from horrible torment, like the underground man. Even though their misery is deepened by their own narcissistic vanity, which wants to draw a paradoxical pleasure or strength from the depths of their humiliation, both texts may facilitate acknowledgement – which these characters themselves cannot muster – of their characters' true despair.

Empathy

The endings of 'The Depressed Person' and Part 1 of *Notes* might be seen to point to an alternative; namely, a leap of faith, in the form of a manifestation of empathy. Towards the end of Part 1 of *Notes*, in the passage on the 'second crystal palace', the underground man implies that, if he were shown some faith-based, meaningful connection to something beyond himself, he would devote himself to it: 'seduce me with something else, give me a different ideal. ... [Let it even be] that by the laws of nature it should not even be, and that I've invented it only as a result of my own stupidity, as a result of certain old nonrational habits of our generation' (Dostoevsky, 2004: 34).[11] Here, through his protagonist, Dostoevsky hints that the problems of his time can be countered only by a recovery of faith and passion, which for Dostoevsky are always social, always involve the other – virtues regarded as outdated and irrational by the rational intellectuals he is criticizing.

This is similar to how Wallace presents his ideas for the moral, 'human' fiction needed for his own time and the likely response to those ideas. Wallace famously writes that the 'next real literary "rebels" in this country' might be those who 'dare somehow to back away from ironic watching' and deal with 'plain old untrendy human troubles and emotions in U.S. life with reverence and conviction'; they 'would be outdated, of course, before they even started. Dead on the page. ... Backward, quaint, naïve, anachronistic' (1997: 81). And in his review of Frank's biography Wallace connects this alternative to Dostoevsky, who 'appears to possess degrees of passion, conviction, and engagement with deep moral issues that we – here, today – cannot or do not permit ourselves', 'seem[ing] to require of our art an ironic distance from deep convictions or desperate questions' (2005: 271). Taking up the idea that Wallace looks to Dostoevsky as a guide not just for 'diagnos[ing] a disease' but also for 'giving a model for the cure' (Max, 2012: 209), we can see how 'The Depressed Person', like *Notes*, advocates for and aims to generate in readers a trust in communication and empathy that runs counter to the dismissal thereof by its own main character.

'The Depressed Person' ends with a long plea by its protagonist, punctuated by questions, about how to describe and understand herself – 'what all she'd so painfully learned said about her?' reads the question that concludes the story (Wallace, 1999: 58). This final passage places the reader in the position of a Support Friend to the depressed person. The long, winding plea and its repeated questions signal the depressed person's inability to believe she is heard and understood, to actually give herself over to the other. Thus the reader becomes the site of faith, of the willingness to feel the feelings of the depressed person, as her questions, and thereby the story, end. As Elliott Morsia notes, in the conception history of the story the addition of the depressed person's conversations with others, especially the questions at the end, signify a switch from a mostly 'monological' story – a description of the depressed person's suffering but without reference to discussions of this with others – to a 'dialogical' one, with the introduction of therapists and friends as interlocutors standing in for the reader: 'These new characters become external reference points', 'explaining *who* the depressed person recounts her examples of painful circumstances *to*' (2015: 92). The story's final question, Morsia writes, 'leaves the text open': 'in a sense, the text becomes an extended question posed to the reader' (93). Boswell similarly states – about *Brief Interviews* in general, but especially relevant to 'The Depressed Person' – that 'here the reader breaks *into* the story and interacts directly with the characters, who are themselves hiding behind their own walls of self-conscious deception' (2003: 188–189). Even though the depressed person partly undermines her own professed desire to communicate by her seeming unwillingness or inability to stop asking questions at the end of the story – convinced that she will never be understood anyway – these questions (directed, via the Support Friend, to the reader) introduce space for communication and the possibility of our empathetic understanding into the story.

The depressed person's inability to believe in successful communication finds its equivalent in *Notes*, for example, in a passage marked by Wallace, in which the underground man comments on his own writing and lack of audience: 'It is a form, an empty form – I shall never have readers. I have made this plain already' – to which Wallace adds in the margins 'To whom?' (Wallace, *Notes*, HRC: 41). Obviously, the underground man has a reader in us at that moment, and what has become plain to us is that these notes are not an empty form but a multi-layered expression of suffering.

We can connect the inability of these characters to trust the connection with the other back to Dostoevsky's relation of philosophy and literature as a possible model for Wallace's writing. In the run-up to his discussion of *Notes*, Frank situates his discussion of the novella in light of Dostoevsky's use of the phrase 'true philosophy' (1986: 306). Wallace identifies this section and writes 'USE' in the margin in relation to it (Wallace, container 4.12, HRC). Obviously he specifically means in his review but – given that the piece is above all a manifesto on Wallace's understanding, via Dostoevsky, of why and how to write literature – it also applies to Wallace wanting to use these ideas in his own fiction.

Dostoevsky regards 'true philosophy' as the attempt to convey – in his case, through fiction – the conflict between the 'law of personality' (life, suffering on earth) and the 'law of Christ'. The law of personality (or Ego) is impossible to overcome during earthly life, so the Christian law as it applies to existence is in fact a 'law of *striving toward* the ideal' of love and other-directedness (Frank, 1986: 306–309). Dostoevsky saw his writing, specifically *Notes*, as the staging of this striving: to portray the inability of the main character, in the singularity of his existence – which at the same time represents general cultural features – to take up this ideal of empathy but, at the same time, to facilitate the reader's ability to do so through the portrayal of a character who is almost unbearably vain – and thus might repulse our attention – but also genuinely deeply suffering. This is similar to the dynamic described above in 'The Depressed Person'. As Boswell writes, 'Wallace wants to test the boundaries of our willingness to "empathize"': we are tempted to dismiss the depressed person as vain, spoiled, and self-pitying; and because she does 'not engage in dialogue, properly speaking', the reader's empathy 'must be pure, since it cannot be returned by these characters' (2003: 189). Wallace's story is truly philosophical in that it provides a human encounter with certain effects of our cultural formation as well as the response it requires. The latter is fully realized not within the story (to be passively received by the reader) but through the reader's experience of and response to the story – to use Beauvoir's expression: as a 'living discovery'.

The fictions of Wallace and other existentialist writers, including Dostoevsky, have often been critiqued as, in the end, failing to portray the virtues – such as empathy – that these authors profess about their work and the world. I think this critique is inaccurate. Rather, what the works in question can be said to do is prompt readers to become aware of their own roles in – and the processes of reading that lead to – conclusions of empathy or a *lack* thereof. So, while 'The Depressed Person' makes us see its main character's desire to overcome her emotional pain as outweighed by her self-obsessive perpetuation of it, the potential role the story presents readers is not one of discerning flaws and drawing conclusions – although we can of course decide to limit ourselves to this. Rather we are positioned to embody the virtues implied as necessary by the story – namely, attention and empathy – having read and felt what the depressed person thought she was unable to express.

Notes

I am grateful for the support of the Frederic D. Weinstein Memorial Fellowship at the Harry Ransom Center (University of Texas at Austin), which made possible an important part of the research underlying this chapter.
1 The connection between Wallace and Dostoevsky is addressed in Timothy Jacobs's *The Eschatological Imagination* (2003) and Lucas Thompson's *Global Wallace* (2017). However, these studies offer little comparative close reading: Jacobs is focused on how Wallace's *Infinite Jest* and

Dostoevsky's *The Brothers Karamazov* share a similar overall eschatology; Thompson does identify more detailed connections to Dostoevsky throughout Wallace's work, but this does not lead – understandably, because of the broad scope of Thompson's study – to a sustained comparative interpretation of how such connections might guide our understanding of specific Wallace texts.

2 The HRC folder of handwritten drafts and typescripts of the story is dated June–October 1997 (HRC, 27.6).
3 Holland does conclude that, as a collection, *Brief Interviews* offers a few 'discrete moments, in which the reader can understand, even participate in, acts of empathy', but it is unclear how this caveat coexists with the repeated claim that 'the collection … [and we] cannot escape the suffocating and distorting conditions of language' (126–7).
4 Cf. Wallace's own, well-known description of the purpose of reading literature: 'I feel human and unalone and that I'm in a deep, significant conversation with another consciousness in fiction and poetry in a way that I don't with other art' (Miller, 2012: 62).
5 This approach to philosophy and literature is very much connected to the previous section's discussion of the supposed failure of language. Partly on the basis of Beauvoir's philosophy, Moi writes that 'the work of reading' – as an intersubjective 'practice of acknowledgment' – is 'akin to the work of philosophy': namely, a 'self-examination' in which the reader participates, 'stopping, pausing, paying attention and looking more closely'. As such, according to Moi, the 'work' of literature is 'not "outside" philosophy but "essential" to it' (2017: 182, 196; 2011: 129).
6 The last part of this passage is a quotation from Frank that Wallace underlined in the biography (Wallace, *Stir*, HRC: 315).
7 It is worth noting that Kate Gompert – perhaps *Infinite Jest*'s most severely depressed character – displays narcissistic features very similar to those of the depressed person, but this has not led scholars to doubt Kate's depression.
8 My reading is perhaps closest to Rob Mayo's take on the matter, which 'support[s] Boswell's assessment of the story as a portrait of narcissism instead of depression', but 'diverges from Boswell's in identifying the story's ultimate ambiguity which … directs the story's reader to "decide" between empathetic or pessimistic readings' (2021: 91).
9 I am grateful to Liza Kardami for first suggesting this interpretation to me.
10 Note the potential connection between the underground man's toothache and the depressed person's account of suffering her parents' fight over her orthodonture.

11 Part 2 of *Notes* can be said to describe the underground man's confrontation with the actuality of such an ideal.

References

Baskin, J. (2019). *Ordinary Unhappiness: The Therapeutic Fiction of David Foster Wallace*. Stanford CA: Stanford University Press.

Beauvoir, S. de (2004). 'Literature and Metaphysics', 269–77. In *Philosophical Writings*, ed. Margaret A. Simons, trans. Veronique Zaytzeff and Frederick M. Morrison. Urbana and Chicago IL: University of Illinois Press.

Benzon, K. (2006). *A Poetics of Chaos: Schizoanalysis and Postmodern American Fiction*. PhD Diss., University College London.

Boswell, M. (2003). *Understanding David Foster Wallace*. Columbia SC: University of South Carolina Press.

Den Dulk, A. (2015). *Existentialist Engagement in Wallace, Eggers and Foer. A Philosophical Analysis of Contemporary American Literature*. New York NY: Bloomsbury.

Diakoulakis, C. (2010). '"Quote Unquote Love … A Type of Scotopia": David Foster Wallace's *Brief Interviews with Hideous Men*', 147–55. In David Hering, ed., *Consider David Foster Wallace: Critical Essays*. Austin TX: Sideshow Media Group Press.

Dostoevsky, F. (2004). *Notes from Underground*, trans. Richard Pevear and Larissa Volkhonsky. London: Everyman's Library.

Felski, R. (2008). *Uses of Literature*. Oxford: Blackwell.

Frank, J. (1986). *Dostoevsky: The Stir of Liberation, 1860–1865*. Princeton NJ: Princeton University Press.

Hayes-Brady, C. (2016). *The Unspeakable Failures of David Foster Wallace: Language, Identity, and Resistance*. New York NY: Bloomsbury.

Holland, M. K. (2013). 'Mediated Immediacy in *Brief Interviews with Hideous Men*', 107–30. In Marshall Boswell and Stephen J. Burn, eds, *A Companion to David Foster Wallace Studies*. New York NY: Palgrave Macmillan.

Horn, P. (2014). 'Does Language Fail Us? Wallace's Struggle with Solipsism', 245–70. In Robert K. Bolger and Scott Korb, eds, *Gesturing Toward Reality: David Foster Wallace and Philosophy*. London and New York NY: Bloomsbury.

Max, D. T. (2012). *Every Love Story Is a Ghost Story. A Life of David Foster Wallace*. New York NY: Viking.

Mayo, R. (2021). *Depression and Dysphoria in the Fiction of David Foster Wallace*. New York NY: Routledge.

Miller, L. (2012). 'The Salon Interview', 58–65. In Stephen J. Burn, ed., *Conversations with David Foster Wallace*. Jackson MS: University Press of Mississippi.

Moi, T. (2009). 'What Can Literature Do? Simone de Beauvoir as a Literary Theorist', in *PMLA* 124:1, 189–98.

Moi, T. (2011). 'The Adventure of Reading: Literature and Philosophy, Cavell and Beauvoir', in *Literature & Theology* 25:2, 125–40.

Moi, T. (2017). *Revolution of the Ordinary: Literary Studies after Wittgenstein, Austin, and Cavell*. Chicago IL: University of Chicago Press.

Morsia, E. (2015). 'The Composition of "The Depressed Person"', in *Textual Cultures* 9:2, 79–99.

Ramal, R. (2014). 'Beyond Philosophy: David Foster Wallace on Literature, Wittgenstein, and the Dangers of Theorizing', 177–98. In Robert K. Bolger and Scott Korb, eds, *Gesturing Toward Reality: David Foster Wallace and Philosophy*. London and New York NY: Bloomsbury.

Redgate, J. (2019). *Wallace and I. Cognition, Consciousness, and Dualism in David Foster Wallace's Fiction*. New York NY: Routledge.

Sartre, J. P. (2010). *Being and Nothingness. An Essay on Phenomenological Ontology*, trans. Hazel E. Barnes. London: Routledge.

Thompson, L. (2017). *Global Wallace: David Foster Wallace and World Literature*. London and New York NY: Bloomsbury.

Toal, C. (2003). 'Corrections: Contemporary American Melancholy', in *Journal of European Studies* 33:3–4, 305–22.

Wallace, D. Foster. (1997). *A Supposedly Fun Thing I'll Never Do Again: Essays and Arguments*. New York NY: Back Bay Books.

Wallace, D. Foster. (1999). *Brief Interviews with Hideous Men*. Boston MA: Little, Brown and Company.

Wallace, D. Foster. (2005). 'Joseph Frank's *Dostoevsky*', 255–74. In *Consider the Lobster and Other Essays*. New York NY: Little, Brown & Company.

Archival resources

Wallace, D. Foster. (undated). Annotations in: Fyodor Dostoevsky, 'Notes from Underground', in *Classics of Modern Fiction*, edited by Irving Howe, David Foster Wallace Collection, Harry Ransom Center, The University of Austin (TX). [abbreviated as: Wallace, *Notes*, HRC]

Wallace, D. Foster. (undated). Annotations in: Joseph Frank, *Dostoevsky: The Stir of Liberation, 1860–1865*, David Foster Wallace Collection, Harry Ransom Center, The University of Austin (TX). [abbreviated as: Wallace, *Stir*, HRC].

Wallace, D. Foster. (undated). Annotations in: Joseph Frank, *Dostoevsky: The Miraculous Years, 1865–1871*, David Foster Wallace Collection,

Harry Ransom Center, The University of Austin (TX). [abbreviated as: Wallace, *Miraculous*, HRC].

Wallace, D. Foster. (undated). 'The Depressed Person', *Handwritten and Typed Drafts*, David Foster Wallace Papers, container 27.6–7, Harry Ransom Center, The University of Austin (TX).

Wallace, D. Foster. (undated). 'Joseph Frank's *Dostoevsky*', *Handwritten and Typescript Drafts*, Research Materials, David Foster Wallace Papers, container 4.12, Harry Ransom Center, The University of Austin (TX).

Internet sources

McAdams, J. (2015). 'The Violence of Rhetoric and David Foster Wallace's Hideous Men', in *Kritikos: An International and Interdisciplinary Journal of Postmodern Cultural Sound, Text and Image* 12:2. https://intertheory.org/mcadams.htm (accessed 1 July 2021).

6

Infinite Jest's 'trinity of You and I into We': Wallace's 'click' between Joyce's literary consubstantiality and Wittgenstein's family resemblance

Dominik Steinhilber

As Wallace explained to Larry McCaffery, what once intrigued him about philosophy and later literature was 'chasing a special sort of buzz, a special moment that comes sometimes', which he likened to the experience of a proof-completion, adding that this 'click' is inherently 'aesthetic in nature' (McCaffery, 2012: 34–5). While philosophy and literature work according to different rules and thus 'click' differently, Wallace's chase after the aesthetic 'click' in literature is nevertheless based in nuanced philosophical inquiries. To Wallace the 'click' lies in a coming together of form and content (34). The literary does not only allow Wallace to negotiate philosophical positions dialogically and to transpose the generalist stance of philosophy into the particularities of experience, but art also allows and calls for actualizing the dialogic, ethical aesthetics Wallace argues for into the lived reality outside the text. Wallace's cross of philosophy and literature is therefore different from simply narrativizing philosophy. For Wallace art must not only outline how the stimulation of communication can serve to counter solipsistic estrangement – a question at the core of Wallace's philosophical and literary engagement with a solipsistic generalized cultural irony – but must itself become this kind of communication that it (philosophically) argues for.

Wallace's creative cross-fertilizations between philosophy and literature become particularly apparent in how his novel *Infinite*

Jest treats the aesthetic of the trinity in Joyce's *Ulysses* alongside Wittgenstein's ordinary language philosophy. In *Infinite Jest* Joyce's literary and secularized use of the theological concept of consubstantiality, the mystery of the three persons of the trinity all being the one true God, is set in dialogue with the later Wittgenstein's public language-game philosophy. As will be shown, Wallace proposes this combinatory approach as a therapy for the mode of solipsistic, endless deconstruction which he sees as having become engrained in American culture. In *Infinite Jest* this culture-wide privacy is portrayed as detrimental to the family bond, producing failures of communication and an instable, continually deferred selfhood. The Wittgensteinian philosophy of language is viewed as a countermeasure to the post-structuralist positions Wallace depicts as producing such a solipsistic illusion of complete autonomy. However, as much as Wallace is trying to move beyond postmodernist and post-structuralist positions, he none the less exhibits an awareness of being inextricably tied up in its context and thus of necessarily having to write from within it. Therefore, although Wallace appears to champion goals closely related to those of Joyce's modernism in *Ulysses*, he also cannot leave behind postmodernist objections to modernism as groundless. Hence, while *Ulysses* could heal its solipsistic familial dysfunctions through reference to a shared human substance, these substances become deeply problematic in *Infinite Jest*. Instead, *Infinite Jest* reformulates Joyce's consubstantial family as a Wittgensteinian family resemblance and proposes the 'stimulation of conversation' (Ewijk, 2009: 136) through public-language games, which calls for an awareness of the dialogic other as subject in its own right, as a form of therapy for postmodern solipsism.

Wallace, however, does not simply update Joyce's trinity via Wittgenstein, nor does he rethink Wittgenstein philosophically. Instead, to Wallace literature serves as a way to communicate 'the consequences, for persons, of the *practice of theory*' (Wallace, 2012: 78). In *Infinite Jest* the aesthetics of *Ulysses* and the philosophy of the later Wittgenstein enter a creative cross-fertilization. This merging allows Wallace not only to (re-)conceptualize Joyce's trinity in Wittgensteinian terms but also to deploy said pattern to put the theoretical into practical, reintegrative action. By recasting Wittgenstein's public-language games within Joyce's trinitarian aesthetic, not only does Wallace propose a way of viewing literary communication that is different from the poststructuralism he agonistically rejects but this aesthetic turn gives Wallace's argument an ethical reality outside the text. As will be shown, this cross-fertilization between Joyce and Wittgenstein allows the novel to reinstall authorship as a meaningful category necessary for ethical communication in literature: by describing (literary) communication within a language of belief, the resacralized author can reappear as a distinct yet effaced presence within a trinity. The reader as part of this communicative trinity is thereby given another subject to converse with, producing meaning in a public-language game between author, reader, and text. The reader can thereby enter a mode of interacting with the world wholly distinct from the self-centred, endless deconstruction that causes such estrangement and isolation in the novel and in American culture as Wallace sees it. Wallace thus radicalizes the Joycean consubstantial aesthetic that seeks to make the author common with the regular world by mobilizing Wittgenstein, turning it into a communication between author and reader. At the same time, whereas (Wittgenstein's) philosophy can explain, question, and illuminate intellectually, Wallace's use of (Joyce's) literariness can turn philosophy into lived experience.

To investigate this reciprocal cross-fertilization, this chapter first will briefly introduce the connection between Wallace and Joyce as well as Joyce's use of the concept of consubstantiality in *Ulysses* before turning to the familial dysfunctions and issues of communication in *Infinite Jest* and analysing them in light of Joycean consubstantiality. While in *Ulysses* reference to shared substances serves to repair characters' alienation and end their solipsism, in *Infinite Jest* this same position results in what the later Wittgenstein would call a private language use that critically debars interpersonal connection and self-knowledge. Despite the apparent failings of the Joycean consubstantiality in Wallace's novel, *Infinite Jest*, as will be shown, recuperates the Ulyssean figure of the trinity by reconstituting it as a Wittgensteinian public-language game between co-equal subjects. By actualizing the Wittgensteinian theory of meaning as communal use through the literary aesthetics of *Ulysses*, *Infinite Jest* attempts to foster an alternative way of approaching the novel and the world that does not end in the infinite regress of self-reflective deconstruction. Art, as will be finally shown, is for Wallace the act of putting the theoretical and philosophical into practical action.

Consubstantiality

As Wallace remarked in a letter to Steven Moore, James Joyce represents a central touchstone for his writing (qtd in Thompson, 2017: 44). Wallace's *Infinite Jest* and Joyce's *Ulysses* in particular are closely linked: as Stephen Burn notes, *Infinite Jest* 'seems calculated to highlight ... extensive parallels to *Ulysses*' (Burn, 2012: 25). From the use of uniquely Joycean vocabulary such as 'scrotumtightening' (Joyce, 2008: 5) and a pronounced interest in metempsychosis to the appearance of an alcoholic paternal author-figure called James Orin Incandenza, abbreviated in the novel as JOI(yce), close connections between *Ulysses* and *Infinite Jest* abound. In addition to such a long list of overlaps, Wallace's novel furthermore appropriates certain patterns used in *Ulysses* to re-establish meaning and order in a fragmented modernity, transforming them to make them suitable to addressing the issue of postmodern solipsism.[1]

One of these patterns that recurs in *Infinite Jest* is Joyce's secularized use of the Christian notion of consubstantiality. Joyce's *Ulysses* re-establishes order and community by placing its estranged protagonists within a secularized trinity of shared human substance. The biological family can no longer serve as a meaningful social unit in *Ulysses*. The novel's protagonists Stephen Dedalus and Leopold Bloom enter the novel plagued by familial dysfunction. Stephen, a half-orphan who alienated his mother on her deathbed and is equally estranged from his living father, cannot mobilize the family as a source of meaning and order. Unable to form interpersonal relationships, Stephen is 'lonely' (Joyce, 2008: 48) and uncreative. His solipsism isolates him from any human relation from which meaning – and artistic creativity – could be derived (Heusel, 1983: 137). It is only through acceptance of basic communion with humanity that Stephen can leave the novel as a complete and creative artist ready to approach the modern world. Bloom similarly suffers under the modern erosion of the family. Grieving the early death of his son and unable to make peace with his dead father, Bloom struggles to find his place – both in his relationship with his wife Molly and in the world. In *Ulysses* the modern individual is orphaned in a fragmented and alienating world. To counteract this solipsism *Ulysses* envisions 'a family refounded on the idea of consubstantial (generic) as opposed to accidental (genetic) relatedness' (Vogel, 1965: 109).

At the end of the novel, community and meaning are created through the acceptance of a shared human substance – a human trinity completed by Molly, as the novel's (holy) ghost, 'through absence' (Joyce, 2008: 180). Stephen finds his consubstantial father in Bloom, and Bloom, in turn, can accept Stephen as his 'son' and make peace with the problems in his traditional family. As Daniel Shea notes, an aestheticized Catholic theology serves as 'the underlying philosophy of literary creation' (Shea, 2006: 29) in Joyce's writing. Joyce generates his aesthetic from the trinity by positioning himself as the God and creator of *Ulysses*, while the novel, his Son-like offspring, manifests his inspiration: the Holy Spirit of Joyce's aesthetic trinity. As the novel outlines through the character of Stephen Dedalus, to make the modern world accessible to literature and invest it with meaningful significance, this Joycean Author-God must become consubstantial with the everyday world – that is engage with lived, unadorned experience and take part in everyday life.

Isolation and familial dysfunction in *Infinite Jest*

Familial dysfunction and solipsism are central thematic concerns of *Infinite Jest* as well. The family and its failures to sustain reciprocal interconnectedness constitute a microcosm of *Infinite Jest*'s culture of solipsistic autonomy. As Mary Holland observes, in *Infinite Jest*, 'at the core of this disease of solipsism lies the destruction of the family bond' (Holland, 2014: 82). However, whereas in *Ulysses* philosophical substances serve to repair the family and establish meaning and order, in *Infinite Jest* pharmacological (yet, as we will see, ultimately also philosophical) substances appear to be the very cause of familial dysfunctions and the solipsism they produce. Indeed, the history of the novel's highly dysfunctional Incandenza family is marked by (pharmacological) substance abuse and drastic failures of communication – as I will argue, a form of private language use that can be viewed as a kind of 'abuse' of the philosophical notion of substance in language – producing a toxic, vicious circle. James Orin Incandenza's father is an alcoholic whose narcissism undermines all attempts at communicating with his son. JOI, in turn, also develops a dependence on alcohol and similarly struggles to reach out to his own son, whom he perceives as 'mute' (Wallace, 2006: 31) and unresponsive. Finally Hal inherits his father's and grandfather's interpersonal problems and predisposition for substance addiction: he is a heavy user of marijuana who is struck with an 'odd blankness about his family' (517). Since the 'dry sticky salivaless sounds' that are also a side-effect of his marijuana use are reportedly 'death to a good conversation' (27), substance abuse is closely linked to the failures of communication that run through the Incandenza family.

In fact the abuse of *pharmacological* substances in the novel is related to a more general, philosophical attitude that prevents communication and can be read as a dependence on *philosophical* substances. Pharmacological substance abuse can thus be seen as an objective correlative to the abuse of the philosophical *notion* of substances, i.e., a position that pares the meaning of a proposition down to an irreducible core, essential fact, or substance. This twofold substance abuse results in loss of the family bond, failures of communication, and ultimately solipsism. It is this dependence on (philosophical) substances that ultimately defines all the novel's solipsistic characters, drug addicted or not, and which produces a state of general isolation from both the other and one's self.

Hal can therefore be seen as not only abusing pharmacological substances but also heavily dependent on the *philosophical* notion of substances. While Hal is capable of conceiving, for instance, of all blue objects in his uncle's room as part of 'the blue *family*' (508–9; emphasis added), he paradoxically struggles to 'think about members of his immediate family as standing in relation to himself' (516). Given the ridiculousness of Hal referring to a list of blue objects as part of a 'blue family' simply because they share one substantial feature, the colour blue, yet failing to relate to his actual family as such, Joyce's redemptive notion of consubstantiality no longer seems to hold in *Infinite Jest*. Stephen Dedalus was able to repair his solipsistic estrangement through recognition of a shared substance, a family. In *Infinite Jest*, on the other hand, substances are at the heart of the existential challenge of the postmodern solipsism the novel depicts. Hal's notion of families as sharing one substantial feature does not repair his connection to the other Incandenzas but instead results only in the formation of absurd and meaningless categories. Conversely, Hal's reliance on substances, in both the pharmacological and the figuratively philosophical sense, is shown to isolate him from his next of kin.

Hal's failure to make sense of and connect to his family appears as a symptom of his disregard for what Wittgenstein would call 'family resemblance'. To Wittgenstein the observable heterogeneity of meaning in language can never be pared down to any irreducible substance or core fact. The meaningful usages of a proposition do not share one essential, defining feature – an objective fact which is mirrored in language. Instead, for Wittgenstein meaningful usages of language branch out depending on the specific context, or language game, in which they are used. Wittgenstein conceives of these language games as connected by what he calls 'family resemblances' – a 'complicated network of similarities overlapping and criss-crossing: sometimes overall similarities, sometimes similarities of detail' (Wittgenstein, 1986: §66) – but never one, defining characteristic. In its characters' failures to connect to the biological family, *Infinite Jest* appears to reify the philosophical position against which the later Wittgenstein argues. The novel thereby stages the solipsism that befalls its society as product of a culture-wide private language uşe: the illusion of autonomous meaning-making in language; a false autonomy precluding meaningful, reciprocal communication or (self-)knowledge that is most overtly portrayed in the novel through destruction of the familial bond.

The later Wittgenstein questions whether meaning in language can be coherently conceived as a substance and, therefore, whether meaning is a speaker's privately defined secret. Such a position is outlined in the early Wittgenstein's *Tractatus*, which conceives of propositions in language and the world as standing in a mimetic word–object relation. As the 'totality of propositions' (Wittgenstein, 2001: 4.001), language makes statements about the world as the 'totality of facts, not of things' (Wittgenstein, 2001: 1.1). Grammar and world thus correspond to one another by sharing the same 'logical pattern' (Wittgenstein, 2001: 4.014), with propositions serving as a kind of picture of facts. However, as Van Ewijk summarizes, '[s]ince we can only know or speak of those pictures, we are in fact divided from the external world' (Ewijk, 2009: 135). Taken to its logical conclusion, the vision of language in the *Tractatus* results in solipsism: independent and subjectless, the world it posits is shaped by a perceiving subject whose perception is inevitably linguistic, since '[a] logical picture of facts is a thought' (Wittgenstein, 2001: 3). The individual is thereby isolated from reality, as they appear to privately define meaning and thus to create the world without access to an exterior position.

Wittgenstein's *Philosophical Investigations*, on the other hand, describe language and meaning as a communal activity and thus reject the atomistic view of language advanced in the *Tractatus* as an incoherent private language use. Rather than viewing words as having an inherent meaning, i.e., as representation of an atomic fact, the later Wittgenstein states that a word's meaning is how it is used in language according to a given community's rules and conventions (Wittgenstein, 1986: §10). A proposition is thus meaningful not if it reflects a substance and refers to a fact in the world but if it is used in accordance with a community's rules and conventions. This conception of language as a socially conditioned, practical activity renders the notion of metaphysical substance irrelevant to linguistic meaningfulness (Hacker, 1990: 25). Hence, speaking of the self does not indicate reference to something that only oneself has (private) access to but rather situates (the meaning of) selfhood as always a product of the communal use of language.

In the novel's literalizing of philosophical vocabulary, private language use as something which cannot conceive of family resemblances results in a solipsism that destroys the literal family bond. Substances, in both metaphorically interrelated senses, disrupt reciprocal interconnection in the novel – creating failures of sincere communication and alienating Hal from his family. Hal hence 'likes to get high in secret, but a bigger secret is that he's as attached to the secrecy as he is to getting high' (Wallace, 2006: 49). Importantly, Hal's secrecy is not motivated 'by fear per se, fear of discovery' (54). Indeed, his secrecy is not merely an American youth's precaution against getting caught using illegal drugs. Rather, Hal's privacy when consuming substances literalizes Wittgensteinian private language use: his use of marijuana produces a detached, hyper-self-reflexive 'marijuana-type thinking' (136) that obfuscates the other as a subject in conversation. Instead, the substance abuser attempts to derive meaning from his own private definitions. In his individuating secrecy Hal hence paradoxically 'knows [a number of friends] all know [he] gets regularly covertly high' (50). Privacy as reliance on philosophical substances from which all meaning in language is supposed to be derived – represented most overtly in a dependence on pharmacological substances – thus results in the disruption of familial connections and exemplifies the overall interpersonal isolation of society in the novel.

In *Infinite Jest*, Hal's function as a private language user also becomes apparent in his characterization as a 'lexical prodigy' (30) who learns dictionary definitions by heart (cf. 26, 97, 745, 899, 900, 1011). The memorized dictionary, in referring a word to a set of definitions, serves – and here Wallace is almost 'quoting' examples from the *Philosophical Investigations* (Wittgenstein, 1986: §265) – as an analogy for the private language user's atomistic view of language. Rather than viewing meaning as based in communal usage, and thus as heterogeneous and changing, a private language user would conceive of an ideal language as a kind of (prescriptive) dictionary or table: propositions in language, causally unconnected (Wittgenstein, 2001: 1.21), correspond to facts, all-encompassing, substantial definitions. Instead of viewing the dictionary as a reflection of communal usage, Hal learns it by heart as if it were a table of an ideal language. Although Hal's great 'mnemonic' (Wallace, 2006: 30) ability allows him to remain fairly operational, being able to more accurately remember his dictionary definitions than others does not save him from the solipsism and infinite regress of (self-)justification that results from his word–object illusion. Physiological memory-traces, regardless how great or small the speaker's memory, are irrelevant to the functioning of language (Malcolm, 1989: 195). Even with a perfect memory like Hal's, language cannot be reduced to stable definitions but is a form of behaviour that occurs in, and constantly shifts depending on, the public language game in which it is used.

As a private language user, Hal thus knows 'way less about why he feels certain ways about the objects and pursuits he's devoted to than he does about the objects and pursuits themselves' (Wallace, 2006: 54). Since his atomistic lexical inventory lacks all causal connection, Hal does not view his own behaviour but can only speak of his interiority as an object to be defined. As Den Dulk notes, however, real self-knowledge is, according to Wittgenstein, only possible through 'connection to the world, a community of meaning' (2015: 148). Private language user Hal is able to learn, remember, and apply more definitions than others – yet he remains internally 'empty' (Wallace, 2006: 694). Viewing not only the other but also his own self as a kind of object he solipsistically defines in his private language, Hal grows to feel 'robotic' (694). Hal is only able to apprehend and reproduce interiority as atomistic 'variables in rarified equations' (694). He cannot conceive of them as meaningful actions involving a community. For the detached solipsist '*happiness, joie de vivre, preference, love* – are stripped to their skeletons and reduced to abstract ideas' that cannot be put into the 'full and fleshy' (693) practical action that alone gives them meaning. For the lexical prodigy who reduces everything to (ironic) abstraction and defines meaning privately through a (semi-)solipsistic exclusion of the other as subject, meaningful selfhood that emerges from communal interplay is impossible.

Private language use in *Infinite Jest* thus creates a hermetically closed, self-centred system of what Boswell refers to as 'the solipsism of the logocentric thinker' (2003: 53). Family (resemblance) is lost as a source of meaning and interconnection. Not only does this 'illusion of autonomy poison ... family relations, creating failures of communication so extreme they become tragic' (Hayles, 1999: 689) but these failures of communication also prevent the formation of stable and meaningful selfhood. The existential 'loneliness' (Wallace, 2006: 202) that befalls *Infinite Jest*'s private language users is therefore decidedly 'not a function of solitude' (202). Rather the novel's substance abusers' 'radical abstracting of everything' (693) produces a solipsistic view of the world, with the individual – as the sole, linguistic, creator of its world – at its elevated, yet 'empty' (694) and 'lonely' (694) centre. Hal's 'secrecy' and resulting solipsism occur despite his being surrounded by others. He isolates himself through an understanding of language as deducible to the 'denotation[s]' (693) of lexical definitions rather than their usage or function, their 'connotation[s]' (693) within a community. Constructing the world, privately, from his own language, the private language user views other and self as definable and object-like. Meaningful interaction, and thus the possibility of meaningfully speaking of selfhood, is possible, however, only within the rule-based reciprocity between subjects outlined in Wittgenstein's public language games.

Only capable of conceiving of connection as based in shared substance, Hal is incapable of meaningfully relating to others.[2] There is no substantial connection apparent in his family. Hal is 'the only extant Incandenza who looks in any way ethnic' (Wallace, 2006: 101) and is thus completely unlike his brother Orin, who 'got the

Moms's Anglo-Nordo-Canadian phenotype' (101), whereas his 'next-oldest brother Mario doesn't seem to resemble much of anyone they know' (101). Significantly, Hal's private language use denies him identification with his father, the only other family member who also 'looked ethnic' (101) but 'isn't extant' (101). The fact of his father's death appears to dismiss JOI for Hal as a source of meaningful family connection. This is because, in the solipsist's language, the deceased JOI must appear as a word without referent in the world – and therefore as meaningless (Wittgenstein, 1986: §39–43, §55). Since '[t]he world is all that is the case' (Wittgenstein, 2001: 1), and language is the 'totality of propositions' (Wittgenstein, 2001: 4.001) about these facts, JOI is disqualified as a meaningful connector: nothing in the world corresponds to the name 'JOI' after his death.

This incapacity to relate to the family also affects the establishment of stable subjects. As Boswell remarks, by giving JOI the moniker 'Himself', 'Wallace can connect the unknowable other (in this case Hal's elusive father) with Hal's own interior self, his own subjectivity. Not only are the interiors of others hidden from us, but our own interiors are hidden as well. Hal knows neither himself nor Himself' (2003: 151). As much as 'JOI' – and 'Himself' – remains meaningless (to Hal) as it is a word without referent in the world, so is Hal incapable of forming a self he can only ever privately define as an object which others do not have access to and which therefore cannot appear meaningfully in a public language game.

To overcome this isolation from the other and from his own self (H/himself), Hal would have to give up his insistence on (the failure of) referentiality and recognize family resemblances, i.e., let go of his demand for ontological autonomy. As will be shown, this is also what the novel demands of its reader: to end the culture of endless deconstruction, a reader must become aware of the novel's 'father', Wallace, having a communicative presence that does not necessitate referentiality. As we will see in the following two sections, it is here that Joyce's trinity – as an aesthetic in which the author assumes an engaged connectedness with the world – and Wittgenstein's family resemblances – as the foundation of meaningful, reciprocal, and 'substance-free' communication – come together. Although *Infinite Jest* rejects Joyce's use of substances, Wallace, too, ultimately aims towards a recognition of the author's

Father-like engagement with the world as a remedy for solipsism and meaninglessness.

A 'trinity of you and I into we': the ironist's solipsism and the Joyce of Wittgenstein

Privacy's disruption and constant deferral of selfhood in an alienation from familial and communal bonds – essentially solipsistic rejection of the communicative other's selfhood and total otherness (Ewijk, 2009: 138) – are also apparent in *Infinite Jest*'s depiction of Hal's brother, Orin. The private language user's (semi-)solipsist constructivism absorbs the other as the individual's creation into the self. Orin is exemplary of the postmodern, self-reflexive solipsism that *Infinite Jest* criticizes. He views 'truth as *constructed*' (Wallace, 2006: 1048) and uses ironic pick-up lines such as 'Tell me what sort of man you prefer, and then I'll affect the demeanor of that man' (1048) – a strategy likened to postmodernist metafiction (Boswell, 2003: 153) – to manipulate an endless number of women into sexual intercourse. A natural ironist, Orin subscribes to the postmodernist equation of representation with reality, treating language and world as if they ran parallel to one another. Wallace sees atomist private language use and generalized irony as the postmodernist language that contemporary America has absorbed; they appear to Wallace as ultimately 'just the inverse of the same delusion' (Wallace, 2006: 694), two sides of the same solipsistic coin. They both are forms of (philosophical) substance abuse. As Den Dulk explains, both atomism and post-structuralism rely on (the illusion of) a link between language and reality. Although rejecting metaphysical substances as illusory, deconstruction thus maintains 'that the illusion of metaphysical essences is inevitable and indispensable to the functioning of language' (2015: 136). Language acquires – or, in post-structuralism, perpetually fails to acquire and defers – meaning 'by referring (or trying to refer) to something outside of itself' (138). This deferral of meaning leaves the individual in perpetual want: their existential attitude of generalized irony cannot afford them with stable meaning, including meaningful selfhood, but leaves them to an infinite regress of self-justification.

Orin's sexual escapades, clearly presented as a result of his alienation from his family, highlight the problem of meaning and selfhood in the existentially ironic culture of *Infinite Jest*. Tellingly, Orin refers to the women he objectifies as 'Subjects'. Boswell thus notes that Orin 'seems to accept the object-like nature of subjectivity' (2003: 152). A private language user like Orin not only treats others as objects against which to define himself (rather than as other subjects in their own right) but in turn also understands the subject, his self, as a kind of object. Orin's 'sexual mode' (Wallace, 2006: 566) thus represents a deeply self-centred communication. To justify his selfhood Orin seeks to reduce others (and himself) to products of his own, private linguistic creations. During sexual intercourse, Orin hence attempts to assimilate his other into himself until there is 'inside her a vividness vacuumed of all but his name', as he seeks to become 'both offense and defense' (566). The other, perceived as Orin's private linguistic construct, is treated as an object to be absorbed into the self in a struggle for autonomy (Ewijk, 2009: 138). The objectifying one-sidedness of this approach to selfhood leaves no room for intersubjective, reciprocal interaction.

Clearly this is in no way a form of meaningful intercourse.[3] Orin's hostile, private self-definition against other objects can never produce a stable self since it excludes the other from being a subject distinct from him. However, only communication with such an other could possibly provide him with a means of meaningfully speaking of, and thus occurring as, a subject. Accordingly, Orin's private attempts at self-justification demand an endless number of objects totalized into his selfhood without there ever being an end to this projection of reference. Once again, as for Hal (self-)objectification through private ostensive definition cannot establish meaningful self-knowledge and instead leads into an infinite regress. Real self-knowledge is impossible if one treats the other and one's self as objects to be privately defined.

Notably, interrupting the description of Orin's solipsistic intercourse with his 'Subject', the narrator adds in a parenthesis indicating conceptual distance from the scene:

> This is why, maybe, one Subject is never enough, why hand after hand must descend to pull him back from the endless fall. For were there for him just one, now, special and only, the One would be not he or she but what was between them, the obliterating trinity of You and I into We. Orin felt that once and has never recovered, and will never again. (566–7)

Orin's self-centred approach is juxtaposed with a more reciprocal, intersubjective conception of communication as a 'trinity of You and I into We' (567). Orin's pursued 'One', represented by the letter 'O.' (566) – for 'Orin' and the 'Other' – suggests a view of the subject as object absorbing the other, thereby eradicating its otherness. In contrast, the 'One' envisioned by the parenthetical comment displays a communal approach to selfhood shaped as a trinity. As in Wittgenstein's philosophy, meaning – and thus also the possibility of self-knowledge – emerges from the reciprocal interaction between self and other, the community of 'We'. Boswell too sees in *Infinite Jest* an affirmation of 'Wittgenstein's communitarian model of signification as the solution to Orin's relativistic nightmare of perpetual displacement and interior absence' (2003: 154). However, although Boswell's association of 'the obliterating trinity of You and I into We' with 'the communitarian model of meaning proposed in the *Philosophical Investigations*' (155) is sound, Boswell strangely fails to remark on the specifically *trinitarian* aspect of the model proposed – a notion completely absent from Wittgenstein's philosophy.

This trinitarian conception can be linked back to the use of consubstantiality in *Ulysses*. *Ulysses* achieves stable meaning and community through the creation of a secular trinity. Thus, the scene in the 'Ithaca' chapter in which Stephen and Bloom urinate, or we(e), in Bloom's garden – seeing each other in 'theirhisnothis fellowfaces' (Joyce, 2008: 655) – is widely regarded as the novel's climax, an atonement (or at-one-ment) of Father and Son (Heusel, 1983: 138). This trinity, completed by Molly as Ghost through absence, is also represented in a typographical metaphor. In their urinating communion, the trajectory of Bloom's urination forms 'the bifurcated penultimate alphabetical letter' (655), while Stephen's stream, with greater 'vescical pressure' (655), is 'more sibilant' (655) – sibilant denoting sounds such as [s] or [z]. Bloom and Stephen thus produce 'Y' and 'S', foreshadowing Molly's final 'Yes' (732): as in the trinitarian 'ghoststory' (25) of *Hamlet* that Stephen tells in *Ulysses* – when he argues for Shakespeare's authorial presence in the play as a ghost 'through absence' (180) – Molly Bloom, present through absence, can be inferred to supply the missing 'E'. Their male, urinating 'yes' therefore mirrors the feminine 'yes' of the urinating and menstruating Molly that closes the novel. *Infinite Jest* echoes this concluding trinitarian 'yes' in its own, Wittgensteinian trinity. 'The One' – stable and individuated selfhood in a public language game (O) – results from the communicative interaction of 'You' (U) and 'I' (I), forming 'We' (OUI), the French affirmative that is homophonous to the English 'we' and a literal echo of Joyce's consubstantiality in 'wee'. *Infinite Jest* thus recasts Joyce's consubstantiality in Wittgensteinian terms. The we(e)ing 'YES' of Joyce, consolidating meaning and order through a human trinity,[4] is reproduced in another language (-game), French and/or late Wittgenstein's philosophy, to the same or similar effect.

In the name of the author, the reader, and the holy text: literary communication after the death of the author

As in Joyce's novel, *Infinite Jest*'s (Wittgensteinian) trinity not only functions in the story-world but is also applied at the metalevel of text, where it serves to reconceptualize the relation of author, reader, and text by recovering the novel from a solipsistic deconstruction – in which the reader functions as the sole centre of meaning – and refashioning it as a therapeutic public language game. To this effect the novel proposes a trinitarian constellation of author, reader, and text and 'resurrects' the author declared dead by post-structuralists. With 'The Death of the Author', Roland Barthes sought to desacralize the image of the author as an interpretative category. This 'deicide' allows the reader the freedom to reject deciphering an author's 'single "theological" meaning' and instead view the text as 'a multi-dimensional space in which a variety of writings, none of them original, blend and clash' (Barthes, 1977: 146). Wallace's use of the Joycean trinity explicitly plays upon Barthes's vocabulary of the dead 'Author-God' (Barthes, 1977: 146). By referencing Joyce's trinity in its reconceptualization of literary meaning as product of a public language game, *Infinite Jest* resurrects the dead author. This resurrection and resacralization, however, does not entail repudiation of post-structuralism's decentring of the author as ultimate interpretative authority or regression to an intention-based reading. As Hering shows, Wallace's fiction is concerned with moving from a monologic to a dialogic conception of the author (2016: 34). Rather than calling for a return to biographical reading, *Infinite Jest* re-establishes the author as effaced and unbiographical but present, serving as a communicative partner in an ethical, reciprocal interaction – an other without whom the reader would only indulge in solipsizing self-reflection. The historical writer is irrelevant in this structure since the assumption of an Author-God does not necessitate referential fixity for communication to function. Just as JOI's death leaves his name a word without referent yet does not make it meaningless, the death of the (historical) author does not cause the concept of authorship to disappear. As exemplified by the return of the novel's auteur-figure James Orin Incandenza as a wraith towards the end of the novel, the author is 'dead' but returns – not as a living, historical, but as a 'ghostly', dialogic author.[5]

The 'ghostliness', as Hering calls it, of the author's return in *Infinite Jest* should be seen not as a complete renunciation or reversal of Barthes's claim but as a dialogic revaluation of it. The author remains dead: effaced and stripped of interpretative omnipotence. At the same time, however, viewed through later Wittgenstein's philosophy, the author is allowed to resurface as a communicative other necessary for ethical communication alongside reader and text. Wallace's use of Joyce's trinity thus can be seen as a comment on Barthes's language, whereby the philosophical is addressed aesthetically and thereby put into ethical practice. By locating the author in a literary trinity producing meaning as a public language game, *Infinite Jest* performs a self-conscious resacralization of the author – a reinstalment of Barthes's decried 'Author-God' as dialogic and effaced yet present. This gives the reader someone to converse with in a public language game while nevertheless affording agency and authority to the reader. In this trinitarian reconceptualization author, reader, and text appear as co-equal persons producing philosophically stable if plural meaning through interaction.

Notably, *Infinite Jest* not only *proposes* this therapeutic reconfiguration of literary communication philosophically; its aesthetic components also *actualize* Wallace's philosophical inquiry in the reader's lived experience. Hence, for example, the novel's infamous unwieldiness, its use of endnotes that make the reader page back and forth through the book, a move mirroring a game of tennis – one of the novel's primary metaphors for reintegrative public language games: such features remind the reader of the book's, her own, and, finally, the author's materiality and behaviour. In this sense, the book as object can be recognized as a manifestation of the author's reasoning, yet not be equated to it.

Instead, *Infinite Jest* draws attention to the family resemblance among author, reader, and text as they operate as reciprocal actors in the production of meaning. Hence, for example, the novel's opening 'I am in here' (Wallace, 2006: 3) affords a 'trinitarian' identification of text, reader, and author: with Hal narrating the section and thus 'speaking' these words, on the most basic level, he as a character in the text is 'in here', producing meaningful language. Furthermore, however, similarly to the ghostwords projected into Gately's mind at the end of the novel, this first-person narration also draws the reader 'in here', as she too produces meaning through the act of reading; an immersed reader, i.e., one who does not compulsively reflect on language and is instead drawn into the book, will hear 'I am in here' in her own mind while reading. The book is thus drawn into the reader as its words take place in her mind. Through this reciprocity the reader too becomes a Godlike creator of meaning. As Hal remarks, 'transcendence is absorption' (12): to transcend (become 'Godlike' and move beyond the infinite cycles of self-reflective deconstruction), one has to immerse oneself naively in the narrative and *believe* in the unprovable, yet common-sense, possibility of communication.[6]

Finally the author also announces his presence 'in here', resembling the various attempts at communication staged throughout the novel – most importantly that of its principal ghost-auteur, JOI. David Foster Wallace, like Hal, 'transcends the mechanics' (12). Although he is not a body to which the reader can refer, the author is nevertheless 'in here' – yet, like Hal in the opening sequence, unable to respond directly to his interrogator, the reader. Wallace, in the opening of the novel, can only communicate with the reader through Hal. Hal and Wallace alike must therefore 'trust Uncle Charles' (17) – and the name of Hal's uncle, who speaks for him during the scene, subtly references both the familial connections the novel seeks to repair and Joyce's mode of free indirect discourse, which Hugh Kenner famously termed the 'Uncle Charles Principle'. Just as the Uncle Charles Principle in Joyce's writing allows for a character's language to shine through third-person narration (Kenner, 1979: 18), Wallace's aesthetics, reinterpreting Joyce's model into a form of 'meta-nonfiction' (Konstantinou, 2012: 98), continuously point not inward but outward, towards an authorial presence behind and beyond the text – an authorial 'I' refracted through the 'I' of the first-person narrator, Hal. As in Joyce's stylistics, there is another presence to be discovered behind the words read –in *Infinite Jest*'s case one outside the text.

It is this authorial presence that saves the process of reading *Infinite Jest* from devolving into the kind of self-conscious, private activity the novel rejects – not despite of the fact that but *because* it lacks any referent in the world. Drawing on Joyce's aestheticization of the trinity into a secular model for the author's oneness (as the work's God and Creator) with the everyday reality of his work, this identification is conceptualized as an act of belief.[7] While the novel's stylistics and themes thus point towards an extratextual reality that author and reader share, this recognition of David Foster Wallace as a meaningful name without referent is ultimately left to be the reader's own leap of faith. If the reader is to escape from her self-centred practices of reading into a reintegrative literary public language game with the authorial other, she must, like Gately speaking to the wraith, 'stop trying to figure it out and just capitalize on its presence' (Wallace, 2006: 830). In this way the reader can recognize the author – stripped of his interpretative omnipotence and unreferential, yet like a ghost 'in here' with her none the less – as a dialogic other with whom she can enter a meaningful form of communication. Redemption from solipsistic self-consciousness requires reader, author, and text equally to relinquish their autonomy, i.e., their conceptual claim to authoritative primacy, act as a trinity, and thereby enter into dialogue as co-equal partners.

The 'click' of art: 'only artists can transfigure'

Literature can do things that conventional, 'sound' philosophy cannot. Art and philosophy, to use Wallace's vocabulary, 'click' differently. Connections in the language game of literature are aesthetic at heart: an aesthetic connection does not rely on logic and causality but rather on association – their 'sound' – to work. Philosophical language, on the other hand, primarily relies on logical arguments for 'soundness'. Furthermore, while philosophy can theorize, question, and, perhaps, give advice, art for Wallace can become the *'practice of theory'* (Wallace, 2012: 78). This practicality of art can also be seen in the way Wallace cross-fertilizes Joyce's literary trinity with Wittgenstein's philosophy, not only to argue against post-structuralist and postmodernist positions, as a philosopher would, but to actualize his argument for public language games into lived experience through literature. In a climate of 'intellectualization and aestheticizing of principles and values' (Miller, 2012: 60) such as that of Wallace's world, aesthetics – not only the aesthetics of literary representation but also the aesthetics of living in and viewing the world philosophically – gain an ethical quality. Through this aestheticization of philosophy, philosophical positions are not only narratively illustrated but they transfigure into a space of ethical dimension that allows for their new and creative application to life. Wallace's conceptual focus on an aesthetics that entails ethics allows him to meaningfully employ the Joycean trinity, reinterpreted through Wittgenstein's philosophy, as a countermeasure against the post-structuralist practices of self-centred reading. Wallace thus mobilizes Joyce's literary trinity as a direct, reified response to Barthes's *language* of deicide in 'The Death of the Author'. As becomes most apparent in Wallace's manifold reifications of philosophical concepts, rather than simply providing a philosophically sound counterargument, he sets one 'religious' image – that of literary communication as a trinity – against another, Barthes's dead Author-God. The aesthetic and literary in Wallace's art are always tied up with the ethical and philosophical: both functions operate in a field of betweenness that neither dissolves the one into the other nor arranges them into a hierarchy of core and decoration.

Wallace's art allows his philosophical inquiry to become actualized in the reader's own lived experience. While, as Wallace remarks in an early essay, '[e]ntertainers can divert and engage and maybe even console', and philosophers may critique and propose new ways of thinking, 'only artists can transfigure' (Wallace, 2012: 53). This transfiguration which art, in its cross-fertilization between the aesthetic and philosophical, alone is capable of becomes particularly apparent in the way *Infinite Jest* employs Joyce and Wittgenstein to transfigure (i.e., lift to 'divine' status) author, text, and reader – and thereby to transcend the textual bounds of the novel by allowing its philosophical argument to take practical shape in the real world outside the text. Thus *Infinite Jest* not only reinterprets Joyce's consubstantiality through Wittgenstein but also enhances Wittgenstein's philosophy with Joyce's figure of the trinity. The trinity allows *Infinite Jest* to re-evaluate, through aesthetic means, the post-structuralist rejection of authorship in a reintegrative and meaningful fashion by conceptualizing the production of meaning-making as part of a communal language game unfolding among author, reader, and text. Wallace thereby offers something more than just literature interlaced with philosophical themes: in seeking the literary 'Click', he develops a philosophical inquiry that becomes actualized in the reader's own, lived experience.

Notes

1 See for instance Michael O'Connell's '"Morally Passionate, Passionately Moral": David Foster Wallace and Modernism', Jeffrey Staiger's '"Turning a Man's Life Right Around": Wallace's Rehabilitation of Frederick Exley in *Infinite Jest*', or my own 'Modernist Aims with Postmodern Means: Joycean Parallax and the Doppler Effect in Wallace's *Infinite Jest*' in issue 3 of *The Journal of David Foster Wallace Studies*. In fact, whereas *Ulysses* ends with Stephen Dedalus leaving the novel to become an artist equipped with a 'jew's-harp' (657) that emblemizes the novel's newfound aesthetic, a young Hal in *Infinite Jest* states he is 'just starting on *jew's-harp*' (30). *Infinite Jest*, it appears, seeks to continue the Joycean project into a time after postmodernism.
2 If Hal were able to conceive of relationality in a Wittgensteinian manner, he could discover a family resemblance in his family: e.g. Orin's insectophobia reappearing in JOI's and his father's arachnophobia; Hal answering the phone with the sound 'Mmmyellow' (Wallace, 2006: 32), since '[a]nother way fathers impact sons is that sons ... invariably answer the telephone with the same locutions and intonations as their fathers' (32); or Hal's dental problems as 'Himself's legacy' (1010) – to name but a few.
3 The pun on sexual/communicative intercourse is certainly intended here. Indeed, Wallace likens literary communication to sexual intimacy, whereas 'trash fiction' (Wallace, 2012: 53), i.e. literature that panders to a reader's (ironic) needs without demanding any intellectual reciprocity, is strikingly similar to Orin's behaviour.
4 Cf. Vincent J. Chang's '"Goddinpotty": James Joyce and the Language of Excrement', Michael Lavers's '"To No End Gathered": Poetry and Urination in Joyce's *Ulysses*', and Bernard Benstock's 'Who P's in U?' for an investigation of the connection between God, creative power, and excrement in Joyce's writing – a connection Wallace appears to mirror

by repeatedly linking excrement to 'almost religious' (103) experience and sobriety, i.e., abstinence from substance abuse. In *Infinite Jest*, for instance, urine is mentioned only in reference to drug tests. In this sense the excremental is a language of the body that, though most private, remains universal to all and communicable.

5 The novel's use of 'wraith' (Wallace, 2006: 829) is significant. As the *Oxford English Dictionary* states, itself a central intertext to *Infinite Jest*, a wraith is '[a] ghost or ghostlike image of someone, especially one seen shortly before or after their death' (*OED*, 1989: 'wraith') and thus largely equivalent to the more common 'ghost'. However, unlike the *OED*'s 'ghost' entry, the etymology of 'wraith' is said to be 'of unknown origin' (*OED*, 1989: 'wraith'). Like the wraith's authorial properties, the word 'wraith' itself cannot be traced back to a definite, historical source. The intertextual reference to the dictionary thereby also turns from a prescriptive instrument as which Hal's private language use employed it into a description of the ever-changing communal use of a word in public language games. By stylizing the wraith as an 'accretion of authorial characteristics' (Hering, 2016: 167) that, however, cannot be traced back to a definite, historical origin, *Infinite Jest* can heed Barthes and still employ an (authorial) other necessary for ethical communication.

6 Also see Adam Kelly, Chapter 1 above, whose investigation of (new) sincerity, readerly absorption, and Hegel's *Geist* speaks clearly to my chapter.

7 In playing into this religious *aesthetic*, the use of Joyce's trinity in *Infinite Jest* fulfils a function that goes beyond other tripartite *theoretical* models of literary communication, such as for example Jakobson's scheme.

References

Barthes, R. (1977). 'The Death of the Author', 142–8. In Barthes, *Image, Music, Text*. ed. Stephen Heath. London: Fontana.

Boswell, M. (2003). *Understanding David Foster Wallace*. Columbia SC: University of South Carolina Press.

Burn, S. J. (2012). *David Foster Wallace's Infinite Jest: A Reader's Guide*, 2nd edition. London and New York NY: Bloomsbury.

Den Dulk, A. (2015). *Existentialist Engagement in Wallace, Eggers and Foer: A Philosophical Analysis of Contemporary American Literature*. London and New York NY: Bloomsbury.

Ewijk, P. van. (2009). '"I" and the "Other": The Relevance of Wittgenstein, Buber and Levinas for an Understanding of AA's Recovery Program in

David Foster Wallace's *Infinite Jest*, in *English Text Construction* 2:1, 132–45.
Hacker, P. M. S. (1990). *Wittgenstein Meaning and Mind*. Oxford: Basil Blackwell.
Hayles, N. K. (1999). 'The Illusion of Autonomy and the Fact of Recursivity: Virtual Ecologies, Entertainment, and *Infinite Jest*', in *New Literary History* 30:3, 675–97.
Hering, D. (2016). *David Foster Wallace Fiction and Form*. London and New York NY: Bloomsbury.
Heusel, B. S. (1983). 'Parallax as a Metaphor for the Structure of Ulysses', in *Studies in the Novel* 15, 135–46.
Holland, M. K. (2014). *Succeeding Postmodernism: Language and Humanism in Contemporary Literature*. London and New York NY: Bloomsbury.
Joyce, J. (2008). *Ulysses*, ed. J. Johnson. Oxford: Oxford University Press.
Kenner, H. (1979). *Joyce's Voices*. Berkeley CA: University of California Press.
Konstantinou, L. (2012). 'No Bull: David Foster Wallace and Postironic Belief', 83–112. In Samuel Cohen and Lee Konstantinou, eds, *The Legacy of David Foster Wallace*. Iowa City IA: University of Iowa Press.
Malcolm, N. (1989). *Nothing Is Hidden: Wittgenstein's Criticism of His Early Thought*. Oxford: Blackwell.
McCaffery, L. (2012). 'An Expanded Interview with David Foster Wallace', 21–57. In Stephen J. Burn (ed.), *Conversations with David Foster Wallace*. Jackson MS: University Press of Mississippi.
Miller, L. (2012). 'Interview with David Foster Wallace', 58–65. In Stephen J. Burn, ed., *Conversations with David Foster Wallace*. Jackson MS: University Press of Mississippi.
The Oxford English Dictionary. (1989). 2nd ed. Oxford: Clarendon Press.
Shea, D. M. (2006). *James Joyce and the Mythology of Modernism*. Stuttgart: Ibidem Press.
Thompson, L. (2017). *Global Wallace: David Foster Wallace and World Literature*. London and New York NY: Bloomsbury.
Vogel, J. (1965). 'The Consubstantial Family of Stephen Dedalus', in *James Joyce Quarterly* 2:2, 109–32.
Wallace, D. Foster. (2006). *Infinite Jest*, 10th anniversary edition. New York NY: Back Bay Books.
Wallace, D. Foster. (2012). *Both Flesh and Not: Essays*. New York NY: Back Bay Books.
Wittgenstein, L. (1986). *Philosophical Investigations*, trans. G. E. M. Anscombe. Oxford: Basil Blackwell.
Wittgenstein, L. (2001). *Tractatus Logico-Philosophicus*, trans. D. F. Pears and B. F. McGuinness. London and New York: Routledge.

7

Solipsism, loneliness, alienation: David Foster Wallace as interpreter of Wittgenstein

Guido Baggio

> The pleasure I take in my thoughts is pleasure in my own strange life. Is this joi de vivre?
>
> Wittgenstein, 1998: 20

According to David Foster Wallace, one of Ludwig Wittgenstein's main concerns during the years between publication of the *Tractatus Logico-Philosophicus* and the *Philosophical Investigations* was the inability of atomistic language to face the question of the 'meaning of life'.[1] The idea that language mirrors the world and must do so in the clearest and most exact manner possible brings with it the idea of a world metaphysically composed of facts that have no intrinsic connection with other facts or with us. In other words, according to Wallace, the *Tractatus* led directly to solipsism, as he explicitly stated in his essay 'The Empty Plenum' as well as in his interview with Larry McCaffery.

The impossibility of a logical connection between the will and the world led Wittgenstein to move beyond the *Tractatus* in attempt to overcome the existential drama that would have resulted from a notion of life that carried metaphysical solipsism to its logical conclusion. Even though Wittgenstein eventually overcame this solipsism in his therapeutic philosophical work undertaken in the twenty years following the *Tractatus*, by pointing to language as something public Wallace writes that he in fact highlighted a far more serious risk: he removed any possibility of contact with the outside world, alienating us in language instead of in our minds. In other words, Wallace finds Wittgenstein's argument that inner thoughts can be legitimised only within the framework of a pre-established and shared public dimension of language to have brought to light a much more serious limitation: our dependence on language and therefore also on the misunderstandings and paradoxes of meaning that occur within language. This means that Wittgenstein eliminated solipsism but not the threat of existential drama related to it. In Wallace's words we are, nevertheless, 'still stuck with the idea that there is this world of referents out there that we can never really join or know because we're stuck in here, in language, even if we're at least all in here together' (McCaffery, 2012: 44).

This interpretation of Wittgenstein's thought is strongly influenced by the way Wallace considered his own relationship with the world and with writing. It does not seem unrealistic to trace an analogy between Wallace's involvement in the search for answers to 'really deep' questions and Wittgenstein's commitment to disentangling linguistic misunderstandings in their possible answers, especially in regards to ethics. As Ardovino, Den Dulk, and Masiero argue in the Introduction above, Wallace's fiction 'turns philosophy into a first-person, fully embodied matter' (p. 8), highlighting, I would add, the personal existential drama behind philosophical issues.

Although standard critical interpretation takes for granted that Wallace mostly managed to solve the problem of solipsism, thanks in part to his mobilization of Wittgenstein, I maintain that Wallace does not overcome the risk posed by its consequences. My aim in what follows is therefore threefold. Firstly, I argue that Wallace's interest in the solipsistic position of the *Tractatus* and its pathological dramatization in Markson's *Wittgenstein's Mistress* is conditioned by a concern that is at once deep and existential, emphasising the close link between the reflective and ethical dimensions that, like Wittgenstein, Wallace experienced personally and interlaced in his narrative work. To do this I will refer to both his review of Markson's novel and the short story 'Suicide as a Sort of Present'. Secondly, I maintain that, according to Wallace's reading of Wittgenstein, the 'discovery' that language is something public articulated in the *Philosophical Investigations* did not eliminate the risk of solipsism. On the contrary Wallace understood it to eliminate the possibility of contact with the outside world and leave us trapped in language, rather than in our private thoughts. This idea of language as both a 'cage' and a boundary between subject and world can be clearly discerned in Wallace's first novel, *The Broom of the System*. Thirdly, I highlight the close connection in Wallace's narrative work between solipsism as a metaphysical position and loneliness and alienation as existential drama. To do so I will draw from some passages of *Infinite Jest*.

Language and solitude

Wallace explains his reading of Wittgenstein's *Tractatus* in his review of David Markson's *Wittgenstein's Mistress*. According to Wallace, Markson's novel describes (or, rather, shows) what it would be like to live in a world in which the consequences of the metaphysical solipsism outlined in the *Tractatus* are played out as an existential drama applied to a flesh and blood (if fictional) life in which 'cold formal beauty' embraces passion, 'cerebration & emotion, abstraction & lived life, transcendent truth-seeking & daily schlepping' show their inseparable connection – things which 'in our happy epoch of technical occlusion and entertainment-marketing seem increasingly consummatable only in the imagination' (Wallace, 2012: 74). The novel, explicitly inspired in terms of both content and style by Wittgenstein's *Tractatus*, develops via a succession of short propositions (albeit without the ascending order of decimals) that reflect the unravelling of Kate's stream of consciousness. One of the main characteristics of her monadic narration is repetition, which reflects the recursiveness of language and the obsessive return of thought to itself. Sentences and paragraphs are repeated throughout the novel, just as the same entities, people, and places are mentioned over and over again.[2] Repetition, recursiveness, and obsession become part of a linguistic flow that defies the limits of meaning and succeeds in showing what a solipsistic life would be like, or, rather, offers a window into a *Tractatus*-like world. Kate's thinking is all-encompassing, tragically all-pervasive; her world is the whole world. Through the act of writing she identifies and represents this world: only the words she writes are safe for her. In fact Kate's monopoly on words prevents readers from knowing whether the text is the account of a madwoman or of someone who is truly alone in the world of the novel. Indeed, although Kate's words reflect a lucid disenchantment with the possibility of anyone else reading her notes, she exists exclusively in the act of her own writing. Yet it is precisely Kate's attitude, which makes us doubt her madness that reveals the close entwinement of solipsism and alienation. If we assume, as Kate does, that life and thought are inseparable, then considering one's own thought as the totality of the world and the sign as that which represents this totality inevitably leads to 'existential skepticism' towards everything outside of one's thought and to a sense of total alienation in one's existence.

Starting from an analysis of the monadic protagonist of Markson's novel, the dramatized alter ego of the troubled Viennese philosopher, Wallace comes to see the linguistic solipsism sustained in the *Tractatus* as an expression of the alienation of the individual with philosophical roots in Descartes's radical scepticism and which finds its roots in Kant's attempt to answer the question of what the world must be like for language to be possible. In fact the idea that language has the function of reflecting/representing the world and that it must do so through the clearest and most precise language available produces an image of the world as composed metaphysically only and entirely of facts with no intrinsic relation among between them – a world in which '*nothing* is connected to *anything* else & that *nothing* has *anything* intrinsically to do with you' (Wallace, 2012: 88). This 'marriage' shows what taking one's own thought as the totality of the world actually means.

Reviewing Markson's novel offers Wallace the possibility of elaborating an interpretation of Wittgenstein's thought that interweaves theoretical reflections with a psychological portrait of the author of the *Tractatus*. According to Wallace, Wittgenstein's life constitutes the paradigmatic extreme form of modern alienation, since he denied his body and starved his senses but not to feed his spirit (like a monk). Rather, through his philosophical writings he denied himself and the things that were most important to him.[3]

Wallace starts from the philosophical notion of solipsism expressed in the *Tractatus* and eventually interprets it in a more pathological sense as alienation and existential loneliness. His interpretation of Wittgenstein's solipsism as an expression of human alienation moves beyond the boundaries of theoretical reflection to embody a human condition that seeks no philosophical refutation but rather calls for what Schopenhauer would term care.[4] Such an interpretation is certainly questionable in purely theoretical terms. It runs the risk of reducing Wittgenstein's work to his mental disorders, to his sociopathy. The reader is likely to see him, in short, as a character in a fictional biography (*à la* Thomas Bernhardt). However, as William James (1975) noted, the temperamental inclinations of authors necessarily condition the way they see the world, and therefore how they do philosophy. This is particularly true for philosophers like Wittgenstein, in whose works it is hard not to glimpse biographical traces that make them even more complex and fascinating.[5] In this sense Wallace's reading of Wittgenstein does not seem so off base.[6]

Indeed, from this blurring of the boundaries between philosophical argumentation, existential narrative, and pathological drift, it is possible to better understand the reason for Wallace's interest in dramatization of the solipsism found in the *Tractatus*. In his review of Markson's novel, Wallace's interpretation of Wittgenstein is conditioned by deep existential concern that emphasises the close link between thought and life. Sympathetic to Wittgenstein and his alter ego Kate, Wallace highlights how Markson gives literary expression to a solitary temperament that tends to consider its own thought as the entire world. This is evident if one relates Wallace's words to the difficulty he experienced in writing his review of Markson's novel. Barely a month after arriving at Granada House, he wrote to Steven Moore, managing editor of the *Review of Contemporary Fiction* at the time: 'I think part of why WM is so hard for me right now is that I'm feeling very Kate-ish' (Max, 2012: 142).

The intimate connection between radical scepticism and solipsism, existential alienation, and responsibility to the world runs through all of Wallace's narrative work.[7] In particular the existential drama of perceiving responsibility for the world as an unsustainable burden is depicted well by the image of a mother's responsibility for her child that Wallace employs in his review of Markson's novel to describe the existential drama of solipsism and which we also find on numerous occasions in his short stories and novels.[8] As he argues in the review,

> it's easy to see how radical skepticism ... yields at once omnipotence and moral oppression. If the World is entirely a function of Facts

that not only reside in but *hail from* one's own head, one is just as Responsible for that world as is a mother for her child, or herself. This seems straightforward. (Wallace, 2012: 99, original emphasis)

Such an image highlights how Wallace perceived the risk of being unable to relate to the world outside of one's own head.[9] This is evident in some of his short stories, with 'Suicide as a Sort of Present' being a paradigmatic case. There Wallace stages the ultimate consequence of the embodied nature of solipsism experienced as responsibility towards the individual and the world through the spectacle of the psycho-pathological degeneration of a subject unable to escape her own ego. The story describes a mother who feels a burden of responsibility for all the evil in the world and the consequences of this self-destructive weight. Wallace depicts the degeneration of a toxic relationship between mother and child that arises from the mother's awareness of the inner conflict between her role as a mother who *must* love her child and her hatred for him as an individual distinct from herself (Wallace, 2009: 351). What is extreme is the discrepancy between what occurs in her interior world and what is seen from an 'objective perspective', as Wallace defines it. Responsibility becomes a defective projection of responsibility for the world and for her child (see Wallace, 2009: 351).

The absurd relationship that Wallace describes, the way he sets up his analysis of the 'dark side' of alienation, invokes loneliness as an existential drama that finds expression, on the one hand, in our inability to recognize our need of others without objectifying them, and on the other, in amplification of the problem of communication.[10]

Our inability to establish a sincere relationship with another person – a relationship in which both parties can experience real communication able to overcome the risk of solipsism or solitude – compels Wallace to tackle questions related to the problems of the objectification of the other and of being objectified by them.[11] Thus, the mother in 'Suicide as a Sort of Present' also proves unable to express her feelings, thoughts, desires, or subconscious fears, since she is not able to open herself to the other, and this inability is rooted in her fear that the other might really see how she is 'inside'. Interestingly Wittgenstein similarly maintains that 'hate between human beings comes from our cutting ourselves off from each other. Because we don't want anyone else to see inside us, since it's not a pretty sight in there' (Wittgenstein, 1998: 52).

The Broom of the System: a solution to the risk of solipsism?

Is there a way out of solipsism? Wallace considers Wittgenstein's overcoming of the *Tractatus* the result of a course of therapeutic treatment that he accomplished through philosophy. After arriving at the risk of solipsism, Wittgenstein became more open to affirming the public nature of language, considered it no longer the representation of the world but an instrument – and, therefore, no longer a limitation. In other words, according to Wallace, after the *Tractatus* Wittgenstein turns his attention to the possibilities afforded by the use of language. He has made peace, so to speak, with its limits and his own limits and highlights the potentialities. According to this development in his thinking, language cannot represent, mirror, or assert, but it can show, indicate, and describe. Language is not the world. Rather it describes the world through words that serve as tools to interact with it. This very idea of language, Wallace argues, depends upon a community of communication, which constitutes the most powerful attack on the coherence of scepticism and solipsism (Wallace, 2012: 109). In fact in the *Investigations* Wittgenstein argued against a referential theory of language in which the meaning of words would be sought in their function within the given public context in which they are used instead of in a mental process. In this sense language is not solely an affair of the individual soul; its laws would not have even the slightest meaning if read exclusively in terms of the experience of the individual. If language is public, hence metaphysical, the ego's private language is inconsistent.[12] In other words for Wittgenstein philosophy was a cure for solipsism (and perhaps an alternative to the 'madhouse') – or at least seems to be. For Wallace Wittgenstein's *Investigations* was 'the single most comprehensive and beautiful argument against solipsism that's ever been made' (McCaffery, 2012: 44).

However, Wallace also believes that Wittgenstein's evolution, that is, his 'discovery' that language is something public, does not help us eliminate the risk of solipsism. In fact he considered Wittgenstein to have eliminated any possibility of contact with the outside world, leaving us trapped in language rather than in our private thoughts: 'unfortunately we're still stuck with the idea that there is this world of referents out there that we can never really join or know because we're stuck in here, in language, even if we're at least all in here together' (McCaffery, 2012: 44). In other words Wittgenstein eradicated solipsism but not the risk of it. For Wallace this resulted in a new drama of being trapped in language, unable to escape it, and needing to overcome the related risk of being unable to understand the world, ourselves, and others.[13] The risk of solipsism thus concerns something broader and perhaps even more vital than solipsism itself: the idea that there is a world of referents out there that we can never really reach or know. Even more importantly, others are part of that world – so, despite the publicness of language, we can no longer reach others, and they cannot reach us, because we are all potential victims of the misunderstandings and paradoxes of meaning that occur within language. For Wallace

> This was Wittgenstein's double bind: you can either treat language as an infinitely small dense dot, or you let it become the world – the exterior and everything in it. The former banishes you from the Garden. The latter seems more promising. If the world is itself a linguistic construct, there's nothing 'outside' language for language to have to picture or refer to. This lets you avoid solipsism, but it leads right to the postmodern, poststructural dilemma of having to deny yourself an existence independent of language. (McCaffery, 2012: 45)

In his first novel, *The Broom of the System*, Wallace addresses both these perspectives through the related issue of the subjectivation and autonomy of the self. Although, according to some readers, the novel depicts the overcoming of the metaphysical problem of solipsism through presentation of the anti-solipsistic perspective of the *Philosophical Investigations*,[14] I would contend that Wallace actually takes up the two Wittgensteinian positions in this work, showing how in both cases the impossibility of overcoming the threshold of language fosters the risk of ego alienation, whether through solipsism or through immersion in language. To face the limit that language poses, there are in fact, according to Wallace, two possibilities: either the linguistic subject expands infinitely to include the surrounding world (*Tractatus*) or it suffers through language as the only means of truly existing (*Philosophical Investigations*).

Both possibilities highlight the pathological, alienating tendency of the subject.

The former is dramatized in the character of the extremely wealthy and rotund Norman Bombardini, owner of the Bombardini Company. Norman represents the expansion of the linguistic subject to include the whole world as a way of overcoming the conflict and insurmountable limit between subject and world. In fact Bombardini's aim is to swallow up everything outside of him: to grow infinitely in size until 'in the universe there is no room for anyone else' (Wallace, 2004: 146), or rather, the microcosm that he is becomes co-extensive with the macrocosm and his limit is literally the limit of his world. Bombardini's point of view, a Pantagruel-like and paroxysmal version of the 'I Am My World' of the *Tractatus*, inverts the Weight Watchers' weight loss programme. On the one hand, Weight Watchers presents itself as a 'warrior in the great war against loneliness' (Wallace, 2004: 145), offering everyone the chance to relate to the world and be surrounded by as much 'Other' as possible through a minimization of the self and maximal expansion of the Other. On the other hand, Norman's intention is to develop infinitely in order to reach immeasurable dimensions and leave room for nothing else. However, no matter how much the ego extends to include the macrocosm and all that it contains, total identity between the two through subtraction and absolute reduction of one of the two terms proves impracticable in reality.

While Norman Bombardini is paradigmatic of the 'Tractatus*ized*' version of an 'I–other' relationship in which the 'I' stands as the absolute referent of external reality, Lenore Beadsman's life instead represents our impotence with respect to the cage of language and the drama of an existence dependent on the 'other' whose only solution seems to be reduction to an 'infinitely small and dense' dot. Lenore, in fact, exemplifies a reversal with respect to the I–other relationship of the *Tractatus*: here the other is given through language, which, in so far as it precedes the self, is a constitutive condition of its subjectivation. Lenore has been convinced by her great-grandmother – a former student of Wittgenstein whose character is inspired by Alice Ambrose, to whom Wittgenstein dictated the *Brown Book* in 1934–35 – that language exists but nothing beyond it does. Lenore is then convinced to coincide herself with what people tell her through language. She lives this inner conflict on the one hand through assertion of her identity through language, or rather, the existential importance of words – which leads her to speak about the living drama of the performativity of words (Wallace, 2004: 433–4) – and, on the other hand, through the multiple identities that derive from people's various definitions of her (Wallace, 2004: 383). The fact that Lenore is completely subject to a power not in her own hands but in those of others who can name her into existence mirrors the Cartesian *Cogito ergo sum*: you are spoken about, therefore you exist. LaVache's explanation of Lenore's problem exemplifies this point:

> Lenore has you believing ... that you're only real insofar as you're told about, so that to the extent that you're real you're controlled, and thus not in control, so that you're more like a sort of character than a person, really – and of course Lenore would say the two are the same, now, wouldn't she? (Wallace, 2004: 383)

LaVache makes explicit the dynamic of objectification in the novel, in which the characters that have to do with Lenore mask a monological and solipsistically dominant approach that hides behind an apparently dialogical attitude.[15] Dr Curtis's scenes with Lenore and Rick Vigorous, for instance, are monological. Indeed, Dr Curtis sums up everything they say in a performance of hermeneutic theory that symbolizes the patients' imaginary identifications through the act of speech, using the structural ambivalence of language to manipulate them. Even more paradigmatic is Rick Vigorous: through his desire to absorb and possess Lenore, Rick's voice develops through a narrative that evokes epistemological solipsism (he is precluded from ontological solipsism by his obsession with Lenore) and involves the conviction that, even though others exist, one can never have access to their inner states. Associated to this epistemological solipsism is Rick's monological discourse regarding his physical impairment – the reduced size of his penis – which prevents him from having satisfactory penetrative relations with Lenore, so that any sexual attempt will never lead to true union between them.[16] As Mayo notes (2020), while Rick's deformity is often used as a comic element in the story, it is also a clear symbol of Wallace's concern with finding a way to eliminate the emotional pain of loneliness, which expresses nostalgia for something that is actually already there, through interpersonal connection and romance. Just as one can be lonely without being alone, one can desire something that one already possesses. Thus, although Lenore is already his girlfriend, Rick's desire for union expresses an appeal for recognition, the meaning of which is rooted in the possibility of being accepted and loved completely by Lenore. Rick's desperate desire to hear Lenore say 'I love you', and Lenore's refusal to respond to Rick's desire, highlight the performative and subjugating character of language. The expression 'I love you' is in fact performative in two opposite senses: for Rick it is a means of coping with his insecurity and satisfying his request for recognition and love, and thus of being able to possess the desired object; for Lenore the expression realises the other's desire to nail her 'like a butterfly on a board' (Wallace, 2004: 436). These are two different ways of highlighting the performative value of the dominance of language. Under the illusion of being able to overcome his epistemological solipsism, Rick uses language to define Lenore in relation to the impossibility of satisfying his desire for union, projecting his own image on to her and refusing any dialogical exchange. This move is the only one Rick can make precisely because Lenore, on the other hand, recognizes the risk of Rick's language and tries to oppose its dominance by evading it and trying to defuse her phallus-logo-centric obsession:

> You want to know what I really definitely don't love? I don't love this sick obsession with measuring, and demanding that things be said, and pinning, and having, and telling. It's all one big boiling spasm that makes me more than a little ill, not to mention depressed. (Wallace, 2004: 439)

Language is thus the only condition of possibility for the process of subjectification, and solipsism is located in the perspective of the other who is the condition of possibility for the subject's existence: there is no self without the other who narrates it. The trauma experienced by Lenore is therefore the 'trauma of language', which provides the conditions for her emergence as a subject through definition of her in the web of language. The two apparently viable solutions to eschewing solipsism both seem to condemn her to alienation: on the one hand, silence is the ultimate subtraction from the other; on the other hand, it is the acceptance of the sole reality of narrative and self-narrative, namely the fiction of writing. Wallace seems to take the first path: Lenore's silence at the end of the novel seems to be the only way out from the anguished need of others to keep her under control, in the domain of their own narration of her. Silence seems here to be the only safe haven from the pitfalls and deceptions, misunderstandings and misinterpretations, of language. However, in my opinion, this turns out to be an illusory solution. Rather, silence is an arrogant move that, through negation, makes explicit and confirms the very thing from which the subject seeks to escape: language.[17]

Solipsism and loneliness in *Infinite Jest*

Most critics agree that *Infinite Jest* and Wallace's later works overcome the solipsism that he failed to avoid in his early works.[18] Boswell (2003: 154–5), for instance, maintains that at some points in *Infinite Jest* Wallace affirms Wittgenstein's communitarian model of signification as the solution to the nightmare of interior absence. In particular Boswell interprets Orin Incandenza's sense of emptiness as an ontological error. According to Boswell, Orin can overcome ontological error through the communal dimension of meaning, the possibility of which is rooted precisely in the perception of uniqueness he was able to experience in the past. In support of this thesis Boswell mentions a parenthetical passage close to the one in which Wallace describes Orin's lovemaking techniques:

> (This is why, maybe, one Subject is never enough, why hand after hand must descend to pull him back from the endless fall. For were there for him just one, now, special and only, the One would be not he or she but what was between them, the obliterating trinity of You and I into We. Orin felt that once and has never recovered, and will never again.) (Wallace, 2006: 566–7)

Boswell mobilizes a Wittgensteinian reading of the concept of 'meaning as use' to argue that the meaning of Orin's interiority cannot be found in others or in the self but in the 'obliterating trinity of You and I in the We'. However, I would argue that Orin's sexual addiction can also be interpreted as the expression of a relational incapacity, in the sense that his need for a complete fusion of identities is limited to an exclusively momentary search for unity – but not as the result of a search for love, since love 'kills what needs it' (Wallace, 2006: 566). Rather, it is the result of a *hope* of possession: 'the need to be assured that for a moment he *has* her, now has *won* her as if from someone or something else, something other than he, but that he *has* her and is what she sees and all she sees ... nothing but this one second's love of her, *of*–her'. And this one second's love of her, in which 'he is the One' to her, is the only way Orin has not to 'dissolve into worse than nothing' (Wallace, 2006: 566). Yet precisely because this experience is only momentary and never sufficient, Orin continues to search for that unity through possession of the women he seduces without ever achieving it. It is precisely because love has killed him once that he is now afraid of losing himself again and the desire to *have* the Other, that is to swallow the other into his own ego, is greater than his desire to lose himself in unity.

Orin's brother Hal also exemplifies 'the inability to escape the damage of the cycles of addiction and solipsism created by the cultures of his nation and family' (Holland, 2018: 136).[19] In *Infinite Jest* the feeling of estrangement that Hal Incandenza experiences in his relationship with his mother is an expression of this sort of alienation and loneliness (Wallace, 2006: 693–4). Referring to the tennis school, Hal wonders how 136 people so deeply alone could be trapped together, a problem that one of them (Arslanian) diagnoses with the terms 'alienation' and 'solipsism', though he defines it in emotional terms: 'In a nutshell, what we're talking about here is loneliness' (Wallace, 2006: 113). This concludes a conversation about the meaning of competition and suffering and how it is possible in an individual sport such as tennis to establish sincere friendship. In this passage Wallace uses terms like individualism, loneliness, and alienation as synonyms for solipsism, thus making explicit their common existential matrix. Wallace considers the viewpoints of completely isolated subjects unable to escape from their egos, thus highlighting the need to refer to their self-narratives as part of a broader narrative structure that points out the contradictions and paradoxes of existence. The fear of isolation thus struggles against the risk of the inner emptiness, so that any contact with reality is experienced as a terrible danger by the subject.

Although in his 2005 'Authority and American Usage' Wallace argued that the idea of a private language, like most of the other solipsistic brainstorms with which he was afflicted, was false, the threat of solipsism accompanied him in all of his writing, and he actually experienced this threat as an existential drama.[20] Though he sought to overcome it through the communion, that hope did not win out over solipsism. The latter, in its existential declination of loneliness and alienation, prevailed.

What makes Wallace's writing particularly apt for describing the borderline aspects of human relations is its continuous tension between the need for authentic relationships and the solipsistic and alienating tendencies of individuals. Through fiction Wallace reveals the close link between the existential drama of alienation and the idea of responsibility for the world, understood as the responsibility of a mother for her child. His works offer various levels of understanding of this tension, passing from the pure aesthetic enjoyment that one feels in following the vortices of a bizarre thought as it reaches down into the innermost folds of the human soul to a sort of mental agitation caused by existential questions about the meaning of life, of suffering, and what they might mean, and about how it might be possible to have sincere relationships with others.[21] Yet what makes Wallace's writing so impressive is the perception it gives that he is trying to exceed the limits of the idea that 'I am my world'. In this sense it is not difficult to find an analogy between Wallace's involvement in the search for answers to 'very deep' questions and Wittgenstein's commitment to clearing up linguistic misunderstandings regarding possible answers to ethical issues.

Notes

1 For documentation on Wallace's interest on Wittgenstein see, among other texts, Max (2012: ch. 2); Nadel (2012); Ryerson (2010); Horn (2014); Ramal (2014); Den Dulk (2015; 2019).
2 On the recursiveness of Kate's thought cf. Kelleher and Keane (2017). For a more extensive survey of Markson's work see Palleau-Papin (2007).
3 See Wallace (2012: 96). For a similar reading of Wittgenstein's *Tractatus* see Gellner (1999).
4 On Schopenhauer's influence on Wittgenstein's thought see Anscombe (1959) and Morris Engel (1969).

5 Among the authors who criticize Wallace's interpretation of Wittgenstein's thought are Ramal (2014: 190n) and Horn (2014). According to Horn, Wallace neglects 'Wittgenstein's emphasis (both early and late) that ... he is not offering an argument, a doctrine, or a theory against solipsism' (Horn, 2014: 246) and 'the later Wittgenstein's attempts to show us that cogent language is not limited to object language' (247).
6 See Engelmann (1968: 19–20); Pitcher (1964: 10); (Monk 1990: 126; 146). See also Bartley III (1974); Antiseri (1978); Parak (1969); Leavis (1984); Heller (1978).
7 Boddy (2013: 41) points out that the words *solipsism* and *loneliness* often function as simple synonyms in Wallace. Mayo (2020) distinguishes between 'instances of situational loneliness, whereby the subject is literally alone and experiences their want for the company as a dysphoric feeling, and inherent loneliness, which is essential to the condition of subjectivity' (Mayo, 2020: 69).
8 I cannot delve into this theme here, but it would suffice to think of the strained mother–son relationships between Avril and her sons Orin and Hal in *Infinite Jest* or about the role of Mother Death played by Joelle Van Dyne in Jim Incandenza's film. In addition some stories in *Brief Interviews with Hideous Men* discuss the mother–son relationship.
9 According to Bennett (2014: 166), 'the head is undoubtedly the problem for David Foster Wallace', and this 'problem' is closely related to the more fundamental issue of suicide, as it is thematized in his various novels and short stories.
10 See, on this point, the interesting and still relevant analysis by Lasch (1979). On Wallace and Lasch see Holland (2006).
11 See Wallace (2009a: 82).
12 Wittgenstein develops the well-known argument against private language in 1998: §§243–71. He invites us to imagine a private language according to which the meanings of linguistic signs are made up of the lived experiences of a subject and by definition are not shared by any other subject. However, according to Wittgenstein (2009: §258), no matter how much one tries to imprint a certain sensation on one's mind by connecting it to a sign, this sort of inner 'ceremony' cannot guarantee that one will correctly remember that connection in the future: there is no criterion for correct coherence in the absence of intersubjective exchange. Consequently, we must admit that private language is not a language game and that its signs have no use that can be called meaning. Even proposing to use a sign, from now on, in a certain way (for example in relation to one's own sensation and its repetition) is something that can only occur through public language (§263). On this point see Wallace (2006: 87–8). Among the many essays on Wittgenstein

Solipsism, loneliness, alienation 175

and private language I will mention only the well-known Kripke (1982) and more recent Mulhall (2007).

13 Also see Malcolm (2001: 58).
14 See Ryerson (2010: 28–9). James Ryerson, for instance, writes that just as Markson expressed the solipsism of the *Tractatus* though artistic creation, in this work Wallace wanted to express the anti-solipsistic perspective of *Philosophical Investigations*. I would argue, however, that Wallace instead highlights the paradoxes of narration, showing how language games do not deconstruct the barriers of language but simply emphasize their impassability. In other words he took the solipsism of the *Tractatus* to an extreme, showing how the *Investigations* are merely an extension of the *Tractatus* and not an attempt to resolve its philosophical problems. There is no solution to solipsism or non-communication. There is only *silence*: Lenore's silence at the end of the novel. Silence is her only escape from the narrowness of the Other that both Rick Vigorous (the inside) and the author (the outside) represent with their tales of her. This perspective is the only way to escape the cage of language – but it is not feasible, at least not in this world.
15 See Kelly (2012).
16 See Wallace (2004: 118). Rick Vigorous also evokes epistemological solipsism, namely the conviction that, while others may well exist, they can never be known in the way that only the self can know itself. Rick's physical condition, in fact, prevents him from having penetrative sex with Lenore; this means that any attempt at sex cannot involve a true union.
17 Perhaps this is also why Wallace later partly repudiated the cynical stance characterising the end of *The Broom of the System*. See Lipsky (2010: 91).
18 According to N. Katherine Hayles (1999), for instance, in *Infinite Jest* Wallace constructs an alternative to liberal individualism through two technologies of the self: elite tennis at Enfield Academy and AA, as represented by Don Gately's narrative. Both regimes outsource the collective will and recognize that individual actions have common consequences. Freudenthal (2010) argues that anti-interiority plays a central role in Don Gately's recovery, which is depicted as 'a compulsive, ritual, and physical investment in an entity outside of himself that may or may not exist' (Freudenthal, 2010: 192). In this regard the passages on AA in the novel do not simply replace free will with the 12 steps, but repeatedly emphasize that the process of rational thought makes one vulnerable to the usurpation of self-control by addiction. According to Den Dulk (2014), both Gately and Hal – though they struggle with excessive self-reflection, irony, and cynicism – 'undergo a development

from these problems toward an attitude of sincerity' (Den Dulk, 2014: 214).
19 Also see Holland (2006); Burn (2013).
20 On this point see also Bennett (2014: 71); Den Dulk (2015).
21 See in particular the essays gathered in Wallace, 2005 and 2009b.

References

Anscombe, G. E. M. (1959). *An Introduction to Wittgenstein's* Tractatus. New York NY: Harper & Row.
Antiseri, D. (1978). 'Introduzione a L. Wittgenstein'. In *Dizionario per le scuole elementari*. Rome: Armando.
Bartley III, W. W. (1974). 'Theory of Language and Philosophy of Science as Instruments of Educational Reform: Wittgenstein and Popper as Austrian Schoolteachers', 307–37. In Robert S. Cohen and Marx W. Wartofsky, eds, *Methodological and Historical Essays in the Natural and Social Sciences*. Boston Studies in the Philosophy of Science, XIV. Boston MA: D. Reidel.
Bennett, A. (2014). *Suicide Century: Literature and Suicide from James Joyce to David Foster Wallace*. Cambridge: Cambridge University Press.
Boddy, K. (2013). 'A Fiction of Response: *Girl with Curious Hair* in Context', 23–41. In Marshall Boswell and Stephen J. Burn, eds, *A Companion to David Foster Wallace Studies*. New York NY: Palgrave Macmillan.
Burn, S. (2013). '"Webs of nerves pulsing and firing": *Infinite Jest* and the Science of Mind', 59–85. In Marshall Boswell and Stephen J. Burn, eds, *A Companion to David Foster Wallace Studies*. New York NY: Palgrave Macmillan.
Den Dulk, A. (2014). 'Good Faith and Sincerity: Sartrean Virtues of Self-Becoming in David Foster Wallace's *Infinite Jest*', 199–220. In Robert K. Bolger and Scott Korb, eds, *Gesturing Toward Reality: David Foster Wallace and Philosophy*. London and New York NY: Bloomsbury.
Den Dulk, A. (2015). *Existentialist Engagement in Wallace, Eggers and Foer. A Philosophical Analysis of Contemporary American Literature*. London and New York NY: Bloomsbury.
Den Dulk, A. (2019). 'Wallace and Philosophy', 155–68. In Stephen J. Burn and Mary K. Holland, eds, *Approaches to Teaching the Works of David Foster Wallace*. New York NY: The Modern Language Association of America.
Engelmann, P. (1968). *Letters from Ludwig Wittgenstein with a Memoir*. Oxford: Blackwell.

Freudenthal, E. (2010). 'Anti-Interiority: Compulsiveness, Objectification, and Identity in *Infinite Jest*', in *New Literary History* 41:1, 191–211.
Gellner, E. (1999). *Language and Solitude. Wittgenstein, Malinowski and the Habsburg Dilemma.* Cambridge: Cambridge University Press.
Hayles, N. K. (1999). 'The Illusion of Autonomy and the Fact of Recursivity: Virtual Ecologies, Entertainment, and *Infinite Jest*', in *New Literary History* 30:3, 675–97.
Heller, E. (1978). 'Wittgenstein: Unphilosophical Notes', 317–32. In Kuan T. Fann, ed., *Ludwig Wittgenstein: The Man and His Philosophy*. New York NY: Humanities Press.
Holland, M. K. (2018). '*Infinite Jest*', 127–41. In Ralph Clare, ed., *The Cambridge Companion to David Foster Wallace*. Cambridge: Cambridge University Press.
Holland, M. K. (2006). '"The Art's Heart's Purpose": Braving the Narcissistic Loop of David Foster Wallace's *Infinite Jest*', in *Critique* 47:3, 218–42.
Horn, P. (2014). 'Does Language Fail Us? Wallace's Struggle with Solipsism', 245–70. In Robert Bolger and Scott Korb, eds, *Gesturing Toward Reality. David Foster Wallace and Philosophy*. London and New York NY: Bloomsbury.
James, W. (1975). *The Works of William James*, vol. 1. Cambridge MA: Harvard University Press.
Kelly, A. (2012). 'Development Through Dialogue: David Foster Wallace and the Novel of Ideas', in *Studies in the Novel* 44:3, 267–83.
Kripke, S. (1982). *Wittgenstein on Rules and Private Language. An Elementary Exposition.* Cambridge MA: Harvard University Press.
Lasch, C. (1979). *The Culture of Narcissism. American Life in an Age of Diminishing Expectations.* New York NY: W. W. Norton & Company.
Leavis, F. R. (1984). 'Memories of Wittgenstein', 50–67. In Rush Rhees, ed., *Recollections of Wittgenstein*. Oxford: Oxford University Press.
Lipsky, D. (2010). *Although of Course You End Up Becoming Yourself: A Road Trip with David Foster Wallace*. New York: Crown.
Malcolm, N. (2001). *Ludwig Wittgenstein. A Memoir*. Oxford: Clarendon Press.
Max, D. T. (2012). *Every Love Story Is a Ghost Story: A Life of David Foster Wallace*. New York NY and London: Viking Penguin.
Mayo, R. (2020). '"That's my sad, it's not your sad": Love, Loneliness, and Communication in *The Broom of the System* by David Foster Wallace', in *Critique* 61:1, 67–78.
McCaffery, L. (2012). 'An Expanded Interview with David Foster Wallace', 21–57. In Stephen J. Burn, ed., *Conversations with David Foster Wallace*. Jackson MS: University Press of Mississippi.

Monk, R. (1990). *Ludwig Wittgenstein: The Duty of Genius*. London: Jonathan Cape.
Morris Engel, S. (1969). 'Schopenhauer's Impact on Wittgenstein', in *Journal of the History of Philosophy* 3:7, 285–302.
Mulhall, S. (2007). *Wittgenstein's Private Language. Grammar, Nonsense, and Imagination in* Philosophical Investigations, *§§243–315*. Oxford: Oxford University Press.
Nadel, I. B. (2012). 'Consider the Footnote', 218–40. In Samuel Cohen and Lee Konstantinou, eds, *The Legacy of David Foster Wallace*. Iowa City IA: University of Iowa Press.
Palleau-Papin, F. (2007). *Ceci n'est pas une tragédie: L'écriture de David Markson*. Lyon: ENS Éditions.
Parak, F. (1969). *Am anderen Ufer*. Vienna: Europäischer Verlag.
Pitcher, G. (1964). *The Philosophy of Wittgenstein*. Englewood: Prentice Hall.
Ramal, R. (2014). 'Beyond Philosophy: David Foster Wallace on Literature, Wittgenstein, and the Dangers of Theorizing', 177–98. In Robert K. Bolger and Scott Korb, eds, *Gesturing Toward Reality. David Foster Wallace and Philosophy*. London and New York NY: Bloomsbury.
Ryerson, J. (2010). 'Introduction'. In David Foster Wallace, *Fate, Time, and Language: An Essay on Free Will*. New York NY: Columbia University Press.
Wallace, D. Foster. (2004). *The Broom of the System*. New York NY: Viking Penguin.
Wallace, D. Foster. (2005). *Consider the Lobster and Other Essays*. New York, NY: Little Brown.
Wallace, D. Foster. (2006). *Infinite Jest*. New York NY: Little, Brown.
Wallace, D. Foster. (2009). *Brief Interviews with Hideous Men*. New York NY: Little, Brown.
Wallace, D. Foster. (2012). *Both Flesh and Not: Essays*. London: Penguin Books.
Wittgenstein, L. (1998). *Culture and Value: A Selection from the Posthumous Remains*, ed. G. H. von Wright. Oxford: Blackwell.
Wittgenstein, L. (2009). *Philosophical Investigations*, 4, ed. and trans. P. M. S. Hacker and Joachim Schulte. Oxford: Wiley-Blackwell.

Internet sources

Kelleher, C. and M. T. Keane. (2017). 'Plotting Markson's "Mistress"'. In *Proceedings of the Joint SIGHUM Workshop on Computational Linguistics for Cultural Heritage, Social Sciences, Humanities and Literature.*

Association for Computational Linguistics. https://aclanthology.info/papers/W17–2205/w17–2205 (accessed 21 December 2021).

Monk, R. (22 May 2020). 'Wittgenstein's Self-Isolation', in *Standpoint*. https://standpointmag.co.uk/issues/may-june-2020/wittgensteins-self-isolation/ (accessed 21 December 2021).

8

'This is just my opinion': modelling a public sphere in *The Pale King*

Daniel South

Political pollution

In a 2003 interview for *The Believer* David Foster Wallace identifies something of a double bind for the politically minded author: 'the reason why doing political writing is so hard right now is probably also the reason why more young ... fiction writers ought to be doing it. As of 2003, the *rhetoric* of the enterprise is fucked' (Wallace, 2003). The problem faced by political writing, Wallace argues, is both a symptom and cause of a broader problem concerning all forms of contemporary American political discourse: '95 percent of political commentary, whether spoken or written, is now polluted by the very politics it's supposed to be about. Meaning it's become totally ideological and reductive ... . Opposing viewpoints are not just incorrect but contemptible, corrupt, evil'. In this interview Wallace expands on the themes of his essay on John McCain's 2000 presidential campaign, lamenting how 'there's no more complex, messy, community-wide argument (or "dialogue"); political discourse is now a formulaic matter of preaching to one's own choir and demonizing the opposition. Everything's relentlessly black-and-whitened.' Although he doesn't name it as such, Wallace is talking here about the public sphere – a subject he became increasingly focused on in the latter half of his career. In this chapter I will suggest that Wallace's interest in the concept is key to understanding the kind of political writing he produces in *The Pale King* (2011): a political-philosophical inquiry which serves to model priorities, values, and behaviours for readers' participation in the public sphere.

Given the centrality of the public sphere to my argument, it is worth briefly introducing the concept (for more, see Calhoun, 1992; Gripsrud et al., 2010: xxi–xxviii). The public sphere can be very broadly defined as the sphere in which private citizens come together to discuss publicly relevant issues. This need not be a physical space – in fact, the original German term from which we translate 'public sphere' is actually closer to 'publicness', a state of being or set of practices. The work of Jürgen Habermas looms large in any discussion of the topic, especially his seminal 1962 study *The Structural Transformation of the Public Sphere*. The concerns of Habermas's book usefully represent what remain to this day the three primary, overlapping elements of public sphere theory: its historical functioning, normative ideals, and contemporary manifestations. The story that Habermas tells focuses on a Western European history of bourgeois culture in the seventeenth and eighteenth centuries, the public sphere of which, he argues, depended upon the ability of citizens to make competing claims that would persuade others on the basis of rationality and argumentation alone. The public sphere of the mid-twentieth century was one in which this was no longer possible, he suggests, in part due to broadcast media's manipulation of the form of public debate. Habermas's story has been shown to be inadequate in several ways (not least in its historiographic and ideological neglect of counter-publics comprising women and working-class participants), but most work on the public sphere still operates as a response to Habermas in one way or another, whether contesting or affirming his account of its history and normative ideals.

In his essay 'Host' Wallace (2005) demonstrates his own awareness of the public sphere's historical foundations, noting how the faltering discourse of twenty-first-century politics finds an equivalent in the 'bilateral venom of Hamiltonian Federalists vs. Jeffersonian Democratic-Republicans c. 1800' (284). His essay mainly attends, however, to the particularities of the highly mediatised contemporary public sphere, specifically hyper-partisan news media. In a later piece, his introduction to the *Best American Essays of 2007*, Wallace (2013) in fact highlights the disconnect between notions of publicness in these different eras: 'Whatever our founders and framers thought of as a literate, informed citizenry can no longer exist', he wrote, 'at least not without a whole new modern degree of subcontracting and dependence packed into what we mean by "informed"' (314–15). For Wallace (2013) the literary essay might offer particular hope by functioning as 'a model for what free, informed adulthood might look like in the context of Total Noise' (315).

Wallace's invocation here of the idea that literature might provide a model for certain citizenship behaviours highlights the area of overlap between literature and philosophy that my chapter will focus on. The most recognizable kind of contribution that literature makes to the public sphere is an argumentative one – a contribution which can manifest in both content and form and can be either a straightforwardly presented contention about an issue or a point more complexly embedded in narrative. But another kind of contribution is just as important – the kind that inherently addresses the idea of the public sphere itself by modelling discursive norms, ideals, and practices (a phenomenon I term 'literary publicness' in South, 2019). Appositely, Wallace's apparent belief is that 'since fictionists or literary-type writers are supposed to have some special interest in empathy ... they might have some useful part to play in a political conversation that's having the problems ours is' (Wallace, 2003). Furthermore, the qualities that Wallace highlights in his *Believer* interview as absent from a dysfunctional public sphere – complexity, messiness, dialogue, nuance, the breaking of formulas – are frequently linked to literature in aesthetic theory. Amanda Anderson has noted, after caveats acknowledging 'the long and varied history of thinking on the aesthetic', that it 'involves a broad spectrum of values associated with complexity, difficulty, variousness, ambiguity, undecidability, hermeneutic open-endedness and threshold experiences' (Anderson, 2011: 253). In this chapter I will explore the qualities of publicness that Wallace models in *The Pale King* – in other words, how he uses literature to engage with political-philosophical questions about what values, norms, and practices should govern the public sphere. I will begin with reference to Robert Asen's work on the idea of a neoliberal public sphere to show how Wallace resists this contemporary reformulation. I will go on to argue that Wallace also looks to provide a method of resistance to informational abundance in the public sphere through the act of reading. By highlighting reading as a contingent process, Wallace frames literature as a form that can insist upon the value of the particular without valorizing the figure of the individual. I then perform a close reading of two sections of *The Pale King* to suggest that Wallace's model of publicness is less aligned with Habermas's vision than with a Bakhtinian conception of the public sphere.

Putting the I in public

Wallace's interest in neoliberalism is evident throughout *The Pale King*. In §19 of the novel, for example, several IRS employees engage in a debate about contemporary politics while stuck in an elevator. Their discussion takes in a wide range of issues, including civics, taxes, the American Revolution, individual responsibility, consumerism, and the upcoming 1980 presidential election (which Ronald Reagan would win in a landslide). Adam Kelly has highlighted how in this scene, 'in keeping with swathes of emerging scholarship on the era of "neoliberal" capitalism, Wallace places the key transitional moment to contemporary American society in and around 1980' (Kelly, 2014: 17). Many of the themes in the elevator discussion also play out in the novel's ongoing debate over the Spackman Initiative, a restructuring process which, 'distilled to its essence', concerns the question of 'whether and to what extent the IRS should be operated like a for-profit business' (Wallace, 2011: 85). Although fictional, the Initiative is grounded in historical shifts associated with Reagan's economic policies – it functions as Wallace's dramatization of the integration of a neoliberal rationality into liberal democratic institutions. This rationality goes beyond the constructions of institutions, however. Wendy Brown has summarized it as a rationality which 'disseminates the *model of the market* to all domains and activities – even where money is not an issue – and configures human beings exhaustively as market actors, always, only, and everywhere as *homo oeconomicus*' (Brown, 2015: 31). A number of Wallace scholars have attended to the author's interest in this characteristic of contemporary life and have read his work as both critical of, and prey to, neoliberal norms and values (Brooks, 2015; Konstantinou, 2016; Kelly, 2017). But one facet of Wallace's focus here remains relatively unexamined: how Wallace's attention to neoliberalism addresses (and attempts to resist) the ideology's effects on the public sphere.

The rise of a neoliberal dispensation has had particular impacts on the conception and operation of the public sphere. Robert Asen has identified three significant challenges that neoliberalism presents to the public sphere, challenges which in fact recur throughout *The Pale King* as thematic strands. The first challenge Asen highlights is to traditionally public-minded notions of subjectivity. He cites Hannah Arendt's work on the public sphere to outline how publicity helps to fashion subjects: 'individuals do not appear as discrete, ready-made actors prior to their interactions with others. Rather, interactions constitute the individual' (Asen, 2018: 173). By contrast 'neoliberal models of publics assert a view of the subject as an atomistic individual motivated by their own self-interest' (173). Throughout *The Pale King*, as Wallace details the effects of neoliberal governance on the IRS, he employs a strategy that looks to provide formal resistance to this atomizing view. To this end he includes snippets of stories from the lives of previously unknown or minor characters at unexpected moments in the narrative. For example, on the bus to an IRS facility, one character's mind wanders, and, as he remembers a high-school girlfriend, readers are given a brief insight into her life and the lives of their classmates:

> And without being conscious of any of the connections between the field that now passed … and the girl, he was thinking in a misdirected way of Cheryl Ann Higgs, now Cheryl Ann Standish and now a data-entry girl at American Twine and a divorced mother of two in a double-wide trailer her ex had apparently been arrested for trying to burn up … Danny something, his daddy died not much later, but he couldn't play Legion ball that summer because of it … and lost his scholarship and God knows what-all became of him. (Wallace, 2011: 51)

Similar interruptions recur sporadically throughout the novel and function as Wallace's reminders to readers of our intersubjective social condition, in contrast with the neoliberal vision of a society comprising atomized individuals. Even inanimate objects spark stories of the humans who have used them ('the corrugate trailer where it was said the man left his family and returned some time later with a gun and killed them all as they watched *Dragnet*', 55). Wallace concludes another paragraph by pivoting from the section's focus, Leonard Stecyk, to sketch one of his nameless classmate's experiences of the Vietnam War ('he had just stood up and told them to strip ordnance off the dead and form a defilade against the opposite side of the creek-bed, and everyone had obeyed', 424). Not only do these interruptions provide reminders of characters' intersubjective formations, they also allow the narrative to move from one character's interiority to another's and engage with multiple perspectives, as most conceptions of the public sphere would expect participants to do.

Leonard Stecyk is also key to Wallace's treatment of the second challenge that neoliberalism poses to the public sphere, namely the wholesale dismissal of public concerns. According to Asen, engagement with public life 'draws importantly on the promise of a public good', which 'refers to a practice of cultivating relationships with others that recognizes the mutual standing required to address shared concerns' (Asen, 2018: 173). This notion of public good is not tenable in a neoliberal model, as 'calls to advance a public good cannot produce efficacious action' precisely because 'they ask people to make decisions outside of their direct experiences' (173). §5 of *The Pale King* concerns the many good deeds of a ten-year-old Leonard Stecyk, whose selfless actions mount throughout the chapter in parodic escalation. He volunteers to help younger children cross the road, delivers Meals on Wheels at a home for the aged, gives his allowance to UNICEF, and, when he breaks his leg, donates his crutches to the paediatrics wing of a local hospital 'even before the minimum six weeks the doctor sternly prescribed' (Wallace, 2011: 31–2). Yet despite Stecyk's public-mindedness, 'everyone hates the boy' (34): parents swerve their cars towards him as he works on the crosswalk; the charity home's 'administrator lunges to bolt her office door' as he approaches (31); his teacher has a nervous breakdown and threatens to 'kill first the boy and then herself' (36). In §5 Wallace looks not only to characterize Stecyk but also to describe the world and institutions he exists in, which collectively find his public-mindedness repulsive. Those around him are, knowingly or not, expressing a neoliberal model of publicness, which identifies 'self-interest as a universal human motivation, ... and asserts a limited view of knowledge as direct experience as the sole basis for public engagement' (Asen, 2018: 173). Furthermore, this chapter is set in and around 1964, suggesting that Wallace recognizes how the roots of neoliberal thought were already taking hold well before the 1980s. A general suspicion of public mindedness that already existed in America was ripe for exploitation, he suggests – indeed, it *had* been exploited just two years earlier by Milton Friedman, who claimed in *Capitalism and Freedom* (1962) that, 'to the free man, the country is the collection of individuals who compose it, not something over and above them' (1–2).

This refusal to believe that forces beyond the decisive actions of individuals can affect society highlights the third and final problem that Asen claims neoliberalism poses for the public sphere. Much post-Habermasian work on the public sphere has been concerned with acknowledging how structural conditions limit the agency of subjects in public, whether due to the marginalization of certain identities or untenable norms and expectations. By contrast neoliberal publics discount these structural constraints, focusing instead on individuals' behaviours. Even as *The Pale King* perpetuates some of the more problematic elements of Wallace's writing regarding race and gender (Thompson, 2018; Araya, 2015), its interest in the links between agency and structures is undeniable. Stretches of the novel are spent detailing the minutiae of the US tax system, as readers are reminded of their existence within systems of governance that they lack the specialized knowledge to fully understand. The bureaucracy characterizing the day-to-day life of IRS employees is so all-encompassing that it is 'a parallel world, both connected to and independent of this one, operating under its own physics and imperatives of cause' (88). Wallace wants readers to remember that they are always implicated in systems and that their lives are beholden to the ripple effects of invisible structures: 'tiny movements' in one part of a system are 'transmitted through that system to become the gross kinetic charges … at the periphery' (88). Even if we experience our lives as *individuals within* a system, Wallace would not have his readers believe for a second that their agency is limitless.

These textual strategies remind readers to be mindful of their intersubjective social conditions, their attitudes towards public good, and their existence within complex systems. They coalesce in *The Pale King* to form an important part of Wallace's literary model for publicness, as he attempts to find, in the novel form, modes of resistance to neoliberalism's refiguring of the public sphere.[1] As the novel progresses, further threats to the public sphere emerge as themes, not least the threat of informational abundance. Wallace's response to this issue further highlights literature's public potential – this time through a focus on the process of reading, as I will now show.

Re: reading

The Pale King takes place in a world saturated with information, and the novel follows suit formally. Streams of data interrupt the narrative: §11 comprises a list of forty-two 'syndromes/symptoms associated with Examinations postings in excess of 36 months' (Wallace, 2011: 89), while §34 outlines the sixteen parts of the United States' alternative minimum tax formula for corporations (388). §38 consists of a recounting of problems with the IRS's 'integrated data system', complete with separately formatted words to indicate computer commands ('a BLOCK and RESET sub-subroutine', 416), while the lyrically written account of Toni Ware's childhood is interjected with a list of her address, height, weight, and 'Mother's Stated Occupations, 1966–1972 (from IRS Form 669-D …)' (62). Implicit within these interruptions is the question of whether, and why, the information provided is valuable or not. Wallace draws out this question more directly when he writes about Claude Sylvanshine, an IRS employee described as a *'fact psychic'* – a person who experiences 'sudden flashes of insight or awareness' into mundane, niche, and unverifiable information, such as 'how many people faced south-east to witness Guy Fawkes's hanging in 1606', or 'the number of frames in *Breathless*' (120–1). The information that Sylvanshine receives is less important than his experience of receiving it, however, as this experience reveals the way Wallace's other informational interruptions function for readers of *The Pale King*.

Through Sylvanshine, Wallace dramatizes the experience of online informational triage first described in his 1996 interview with David Lipsky: the 'completely overwhelming' feeling of 'four trillion bits coming at you' (Lipsky, 2010: 87). Sylvanshine is forced to confront life in terms of data – he is given no other option. For him pieces of information 'come out of nowhere, are inconvenient and discomfiting like all psychic irruptions' (Wallace, 2011: 120). He has no use for anything he intuits: 'perhaps one in every four thousand such facts is relevant or helpful' (122); others, like 'the number of blades of grass in the front lawn of one mailman's home', simply 'intrude, crash, rattle around' (121). 'Random Fact Intuition' afflicts Sylvanshine so much not just because of its relentlessness, then, but because he is unsure of what any of the information relates to and how he should relate to it (120). Wallace's interrupting data streams function in similar ways and draw attention to questions he thematizes elsewhere in the novel. In §24 Wallace again uses blades of grass as an example to explore these broader questions attending Sylvanshine's situation:

> There are vastly different kinds of truth, some of which are incompatible with one another. Example: A 100 percent accurate, comprehensive list of the exact size and shape of every blade of grass in my front lawn is 'true', but it is not a truth that anyone will have any interest in. What renders a truth meaningful, worthwhile, & c. is its relevance, which in turn requires extraordinary discernment and sensitivity to context, questions of value, and overall point – otherwise we might as well just be computers downloading raw data to one another. (261)

Whereas Jeffrey Severs suggests that, for Wallace, we are approaching a time when 'human decision making can no longer disentangle itself from computing's complexity' (Severs, 2017: 180), this section of the novel also seems to locate within literature the possibility of an alternative form of deciding what has value. In §24 the author-character David Wallace claims that he has 'no intention of inflicting on you a regurgitation of every last sensation and passing thought I happen to recall', as he is concerned with 'art here, not simply reproduction' (Wallace, 2011: 261). The author-character here aligns art with a kind of truth that is not solely mimetic, and he suggests that its ability to produce such truths sets it apart from the exhaustive data streams of technology. The 'truth' of Wallace's informational interruptions, then, lies precisely in how they relate to the rest of the novel; their 'relevance' is guaranteed by the reader's very questioning of whether or not the information is valuable. This is because, having established throughout *The Pale King* the dual problems of overwhelming information and a culturally prevalent inability to decide what is valuable – problems which produce a dysfunctional and dyspeptic public sphere – Wallace moves to position literature as a potential curative for these ills. He also recognizes, however, that precisely because the problem he has identified is an abundance of information, he cannot base his model of publicness solely on the activity of writing. Instead he must underwrite his textual strategies with a corresponding focus on a process of interpretation rather than creation: namely, the process of reading.

In one section of the novel, the author-character Wallace outlines his decision to write *The Pale King* in the way that he did, claiming that it is in fact 'substantially true and accurate ... and more like a memoir than any kind of made-up story' (69). Stephen J. Burn notes that 'amidst the calculated misdirection' of this section's false details about the real Wallace's life, the 'commentary on the author's past shades into a suggestive account of the novel's literary ancestors' (Burn, 2016: 450). The author recounts how his 'specific dream' as a young person 'was of becoming an immortally great fiction writer à la Gaddis or Anderson, Balzac or Perec, & c' (Wallace, 2011: 75). Burn convincingly argues that this list marks 'a richer entry point than it first seems in determining what distinguishes Wallace's generation from the first-generation postmodern novelists who mostly came to prominence in the 1960s' (Burn, 2016: 450), but it is also important to remember that the version of Wallace narrating this section is not the 'real' one. David Hering has suggested, in fact, that Wallace conceived of 'the "author" of *The Pale King*' as directly linked to his previous journalism and that the novel is framed as a narrative '"written" by Wallace's non-fiction persona, *not* by the "fiction writer"' (Hering, 2016: 144). Understanding Wallace as a character within the novel aligns his references to these novelists with *The Pale King*'s other mentions of books and writers, which are articulated with specific reference to the lives of its characters. So Anderson, Balzac, Perec, and Gaddis are framed as exemplary figures of individual genius that the author-character David Wallace aspired to emulate as a young adult. Later, Chris Fogle recalls a formative moment of taking drugs and '*reading Albert Camus's* The Fall *for the Literature of Alienation midterm*' (Wallace, 2011: 186). Another key figure, Toni Ware, moves from reading road signs in her itinerant youth, in order 'to know the facts of her own history and present', to a broader selection of fiction and non-fiction:

> The girl read stories about horses, bios, science, psychiatry, and *Popular Mechanics* when obtainable. She read history in a determined way. She read *My Struggle* and could not understand all the fuss. She read Weiss, Steinbeck, Keene, Laura Wilder (twice), and Lovecraft. She read halves of many torn and castoff things. (60)

In *The Pale King*, through scenes like those quoted above, Wallace draws attention to the process of individual reading – and thus to the contingency of meaning and importance of perspective. As Michael Warner notes in a critique of the Habermasian model of a rational-critical public sphere, 'the attribution of agency to publics works in most cases because of the direct transposition from private reading acts to the sovereignty of opinion' (Warner, 2005: 123). But even if Wallace's literary model of publicness sets great store by the idea that reading is a contingent process, and that readers will draw their own conclusions, he does not look to replicate an Enlightenment rationality wherein reading processes move through the discussion of opinions with the aim of establishing a single, convincing truth. Rather he recognizes, like Warner, that this idea of 'the unity of the public ... is ideological' and rests upon a misleading 'stylization of the reading act as transparent and replicable' (117). Wallace's writing clearly attempts to move away from such a stylization – for in *The Pale King* reading is never characterized thusly. Even when novels are referenced as shorthand for certain cultural values or ideas, the notion of their accuracy or stability as artefacts of signification is undermined. When one character mentions the rise of 'the corporation and the military-industrial complex' in the 1950s, for example, another makes a throwaway comment: 'The man in the gray flannel' (Wallace, 2011: 147). This reference to Sloan Wilson's *The Man in the Gray Flannel Suit*, however, is not taken up: 'What *is* gray flannel anyway?' another character asks (147). Later an IRS employee mentions Jack Kerouac's *Dharma Bums* in a list of iconic cultural works and events that defined the American 1960s, making numerous comments about how his interlocutors 'won't get some of it', as the artefacts' manifold meanings are 'impossible to describe' to those who were not 'alive in the late sixties' (428–9). Indeed *The Pale King*'s characters' experiences of books always depend upon their previous experiences in life – as when Toni Ware is said to have 'read a coverless *Red Badge* and knew by sheer feel that its author had never seen war' (60).

This attention to reader response is consistent with Wallace's past comments about reading. As early as his 1993 interview with Larry McCaffery, Wallace aligned his view with 'Barthian and Derridean post-structuralism', claiming to feel that 'once I'm done with the thing, I'm basically dead, and probably the text's dead; it becomes simply language, and language lives not just in but "through" the reader' (McCaffery, 2012: 40). This sentiment endured throughout Wallace's career, forming the foundations of his thinking about aesthetic value. Severs draws attention to the author's meditation on literary value in 'Deciderization 2007 – A Special Report', suggesting that the essay 'makes vivid Wallace's commitment to making this search for value a performative process for a reader – in fact, one in which differentiating one detail's importance from another's and being the "human doing the valuing" are, in effect, aesthetic value itself' (Severs, 2017: 173). The model of publicness that emerges throughout *The Pale King* casts this act of valuation as a political imperative and identifies reading as a radically contingent, democratically vital task. Indeed, in 'Deciderization' (a title that parodies George W. Bush's 2006 claim that he was 'the decider' in American politics), Wallace explicitly links the question of how to discern aesthetic value to a broader premise about the 'emergency' facing 'America as a polity and culture' (Wallace, 2013: 313), which manifests as a 'retreat to narrow arrogance, pre-formed positions, rigid filters, and the "moral clarity" of the immature' (316). For Wallace, as I quoted earlier, literature might offer hope by functioning 'as a model for what free, informed adulthood might look like in the context of Total Noise' (315).

Taking this suggestion seriously can help clarify Wallace's literary model for the public sphere. A Habermasian vision of truth depends upon instrumental discourse – for Habermas, as Ken Hirschkop puts it, 'claiming that something is true is claiming that one could, in an ideal situation, persuade others that it is the case through sheer force of argument alone' (Hirschkop, 1999: 206). The importance that Wallace places on being properly informed in 'Deciderization' and on individual reading in *The Pale King* suggests, however, that his literary publicness is closer to the work of Mikhail Bakhtin. For Bakhtin truth is 'formally unified not by the notion of the "better argument" but by virtue of the dialogical action – the taking of positions, the making of assertions, agreement and disagreement' (206). Bakhtin's vision of truth rests on the 'higher ethico-religious truth ... of our intersubjective condition' (207), a condition which, it could be argued, was the most enduring theme in Wallace's writing and which I have already shown is a central concern in *The Pale King*. It will be worth bearing Bakhtin in mind while attempting to unpack the further treatment of the public sphere in *The Pale King*, as Bakhtin's work plays a central role in understanding Wallace's perspective: both writers overlap especially in how they highlight the particularity of human experiences in their thinking about the public sphere. By focusing on the contingency of these experiences, Wallace can insist upon the value of the particular without valorizing neoliberal individualism, and, as I will now argue, is able to articulate his vision of a dialogic, agonistic public sphere.

Bakhtin's the future

The conversation in §19 that I highlighted earlier, especially the section's formal qualities, is key to understanding how Wallace models his literary publicness after Bakhtin. Kelly has traced Wallace's development as a writer across his novels with specific reference to scenes of dialogue. Applying Bakhtin's conception of monologic and dialogic notions of truth, Kelly suggests that Wallace's fiction increasingly moves towards dialogism, wherein forms of speech 'emphasize responsivity and open communication with others in the joint pursuit of truth' (Kelly, 2014: 6). Wallace's particular employment of dialogism 'rests in the anticipatory anxiety his characters feel when addressing others', so that when the process of speech 'becomes genuinely dialogic in Bakhtin's sense – when truth appears to be generated "between people" – something important has occurred in Wallace's ethical world: the means have become the ends' (7). If §19 – with its informed, rational, and considered arguments – can 'be read as Wallace's depiction of what an informed and open conversation about American political and intellectual history might look like' (15), however, it is not immediately obvious that Wallace's literary model of publicness is Bakhtinian in character (that is, founded on multiplicity, alterity, affect, and 'interhuman ... relations that are not simply cognitive or narrowly "rational"', Gardiner, 2004: 45). Rather, we might initially be tempted to align the conversation with a Habermasian view of public discourse.

In §19, DeWitt Glendenning's reminder that he is 'not a political scientist' evokes the ideal of popular inclusion, and his suggestion that 'the concrete reality of civic decline's consequences' are of utmost importance also endorses a Habermasian discursive model, since it focuses on tangible outcomes (Wallace, 2011: 137). So too does Nichols's comment that 'politics is about consensus' (149). Furthermore, several deferent phrases recur throughout the conversation, gesturing towards idealized civil discourse: 'that example makes it a lot easier to see your point' (141); 'let him finish' (146); 'this is just my opinion' (149). This dialogue is unattributed, echoing the Habermasian ideal that it should not matter who is delivering an argument, and the conversation avoids the kind of partisan positioning that Wallace laments in his essay 'Host'; Wallace 'is not particularly interested', Kelly notes, 'in dividing the positions of his characters into traditional liberal/conservative or left/right binaries' (Kelly, 2014: 15). Other passages in the novel can be understood as forms of Habermasian dialogue as well. One such scene takes place between two examiners, Meredith Rand and Shane Drinion. Rand is a 'legendarily attractive but not universally popular' examiner, while Drinion is described by colleagues as 'a total lump in terms of personality, possibly the dullest human being currently alive' (Wallace, 2011: 449–50). As Mary K. Holland notes, when Rand asks questions, Drinion 'responds to her perfectly logically, speaking of "true answers"' (Holland, 2016: 9) and engaging in critical reflection about his own positions. Could we think of Drinion as an ideal Habermasian subject, then? It is not just his habit of critical reflection that suggests so. Habermas's focus on rationality in his theorisation of the public sphere has been criticized for not paying due attention to 'the embodied experiences and activities of actual people in the context of their everyday lives' (Gardiner, 2004: 31). Gardiner suggests that 'there is a Habermasian subject, but it is a rather insubstantial entity, one marked by an interchangeable, "minimalist" body (mainly having to do with the human capacity for labour), subtended by a rational mind that engages in purposive dialogue and moral reflection' (31). Drinion himself is primarily defined through his capacity for labour, as a 'very solid … examiner' (Wallace, 2011: 450), one 'several orders of magnitude more effective than Rand' (460). Drinion's definition as a worker is linked directly to his ability to pay deep attention to whatever he is doing, a trait that manifests in this scene as a literal minimization of his body – at the start of the section, it is noted that 'he's there but in an unusual way; he becomes part of the table's environment, like the air or ambient light' (450). As the scene progresses, Drinion becomes literally weightless: at first his 'bottom is hovering very slightly ... above the seat of his wooden chair'; later 'no part of his bottom or back is touching the chair' (470–1).

Yet Drinion's presentation as a Habermasian subject is not without an implied critique from Wallace. Indeed, his conversation with Rand entails no actual communication. As Holland notes,

> the asexuality that allows Drinion to pay concerted, unself-conscious attention to the intimidatingly attractive Rand amounts to total disaffection rather than any kind of care. ... The result is that he is never in conversation, merely processing information according to his own interests ... and his utter self-containment short-circuits the communication cycle it seemingly enabled. (Holland, 2016: 9)

Drinion's disaffection can be taken as a critique of a Habermasian model in which, Stanley Aronowitz claims, 'the public sphere is always a *restricted* space', dependent upon 'the separation of knowledge from interest, manifested in the ability of the intellect to transcend the materiality of the body, including emotion' (Aronowitz, 1993: 91). Throughout the rest of *The Pale King*, as I have shown, Wallace actively asserts (as Aronowitz also claims of the public sphere) that 'all cultural formation is embodied and interested', with the attendant hope that such recognition means that the 'antidemocratic exclusions' mentioned above cannot continue (91–2). If Drinion's and Rand's conversation cannot evince the dialogic qualities of §19, this is partly because, where Drinion is an affectless drone in dialogue, the interlocutors of the elevator scene are resolutely not. Revisiting the elevator conversation with these affective qualities in mind, then, will reveal Wallace's literary publicness as far less Habermasian than Bakhtinian – which is to say, as interested in dialogue as an end in itself rather than as an instrumental means.

The dialogue of §19 is at times heated, and, at several points during the discussion, a character referred to as 'X' interjects with fair questions and commentary only to be threatened by one of his interlocutors: 'If you don't shut up I'm going to put you up on the roof of the elevator and you can stay there' (Wallace, 2011: 137); 'I'll throw you off this elevator, X, I swear to God I will' (139); 'let me throw him off, Mr. G., I'm pleading with you' (143). These comments draw attention to the personal relationships between these characters and their affective reactions to the rational points raised in conversation – as does the meandering nature of the topic. By the dialogue's conclusion, its instigator, DeWitt Glendenning, notes that 'we're now very very very far afield from what I started out trying to describe as my thinking about taxpayers' relation to the government' (149). This is in part due to Glendenning's attempt to strengthen his argument with an appeal to the personal (which itself stems from his own emotional reaction to the debate):

> 'I'm regretting this conversation more and more. It – you like movies?'
> 'You bet.'
> 'Are you kidding?'
> 'Nothing like cozying up on a rainy evening with a Betamax and a good film.' (139)

More than any of this, however, it is Nichols's contribution that foregrounds the importance of affect to Wallace's view of the public sphere. Nichols suggests that the story of 'civic decline' in America 'goes beyond politics' and is 'almost more a matter of metaphysics', or perhaps 'existential' (145). He ruminates on 'the individual US citizen's deep fear ... of our smallness, our insignificance and mortality', imagining both a future where he will not be remembered and a past whose inhabitants he knows nothing about (145). He links the avoidance of this fear that 'we're all less than a million breaths away from an oblivion more total than we can even bring ourselves to even try to imagine' with the 'manic US obsession with production' (145), suggesting that a person's 'terror of not really ever even existing makes them that much more susceptible to the ontological siren song of the corporate buy-to-stand-out-and-so-exist gestalt' (151). By placing Nichols's rumination on the vulnerability and irrationality of human affect within this particular dialogue, and by having him be carried away by a personalised tangent ('not only will I have passed away but it will be like I was never here, and people in 2104 or whatever will no more think of Stuart A. Nichols Jr'), Wallace considers how such affects play out in public discourse (145).

This is not simply humanistic pondering on Wallace's part: 'hundreds of empirical studies' have confirmed the existence of a phenomenon 'called the mortality salience hypothesis', which shows that fear of death 'can amplify nationalism and intensify bias against other groups' (Azarian, 2016). Clearly, there is a danger to ignoring the effects of affect in political life. As Chantal Mouffe has outlined, in an argument that runs in parallel with much of the elevator dialogue's, 'by privileging rationality, both the deliberative and the aggregative perspectives on the public sphere leave aside a central element which is the crucial role played by passions and affects in securing allegiance to democratic values' (Mouffe, 2000: 95). For Mouffe, a functioning democracy requires 'providing channels through which collective passions will be given ways to express themselves' (103). Her model of public discourse, which she names 'agonistic pluralism', involves identifying those with whom we debate as 'adversaries' rather than as 'enemies' – that is, as legitimate opponents in a public sphere underwritten by the shared ethico-political principles of liberty and equality. Mouffe concludes her vision by gesturing to the future: 'By warning us against the illusion that a fully achieved democracy could ever be instantiated, 'agonistic pluralism' forces us to keep the democratic contestation alive' (105). Appositely, in her monograph on Wallace, Clare Hayes-Brady argues that 'the persistent structural and stylistic resistance to closure that marks his work' in fact stems from 'a dogged and sometimes uneasy pluralism', one which 'emerges as a fundamentally political invocation of free will' (Hayes-Brady, 2016: 9). She suggests that an Aristotelian notion of perfectibility runs through all his work – a concept which conversely 'precludes the achievement of perfection, focusing instead on constant improvement' (30). In Hayes-Brady's reading,

> Wallace's Perfectionist resistance to ending, and the concomitant commitment to process are a fundamentally political series of actions, seeking to draw readers out of the search for finality, and toward a comfort with ambiguity that would allow for simultaneous conservative and liberal politics. (30)

In my reading of *The Pale King*, this recurrent element of Wallace's work aligns the author with Mouffe's vision of agonistic pluralism and points us to the ideal outcome of his form of literary publicness – which is to say, the novel's model is one with no final outcome at all but rather an ongoing debate along agonistic, pluralistic lines.

Wallace's literary publicness is a patchwork of ideas reflecting his consistent interest in the validity of multiple perspectives. His writing's resistance to finality echoes Mouffe's call for an endlessly renewing democratic project, aligning his literary publicness with agonistic ends. Following the Bakhtinian idea that dialogue necessarily expresses 'a wide range of moral, cognitive, aesthetic and affective qualities, designed to provoke active responses and express broader perspectives and world-views' (Gardiner, 2004: 36), I have shown how Wallace's literary publicness acknowledges the importance of affect and the contingency of individual identity. In *The Pale King*, Wallace situates reading as the central task of his literary publicness – in part because, as an activity, it captures this notion of contingent response. But he also hopes that focusing on reading will highlight the public sphere's need for shared points of reference in an era when it is overwhelmed by information. As Wallace outlines in his essay on conservative talk radio, 'Host', acknowledging the contingency of individual views must not simply lead to 'a kind of epistemic free-for-all in which "the truth" is wholly a matter of perspective and agenda' – while 'in some respects all this variety is probably good, productive of difference and dialogue and so on, ... it can also be confusing for the average citizen', and instantiate an inert public sphere (Wallace, 2005: 284). If 'it is increasingly hard to determine which sources to pay attention to and how exactly to distinguish real information from spin' (285), as Wallace claims, then his literary publicness might even highlight the need for a new, civically minded literary canon – if we are reading the same things, he seems to suggest, then at least we can argue about the same things. When we talk about our experiences of reading, we might think of ourselves as participating in the kind of recuperative discourse that Wallace's final novel sought to explore. Whether we succeed or not is a matter of perspective; this is just my opinion.

Note

1 Another major element of Wallace's attention to neoliberalism that remains unexamined in academic inquiries is how *The Pale King* associates this transitional moment in socio-economic thinking with an equally important transition in technological development. For more see South, 2019: 168–205.

References

Anderson, A. (2011). 'The Liberal Aesthetic', 249–62. In Jane Elliott and Derek Attridge, eds, *Theory after 'Theory'*. Abingdon: Routledge.

Araya, J. (2015). 'Why the Whiteness? Race in *The Pale King*', 238–51. In Philip Coleman, ed., *Critical Insights: David Foster Wallace*. Ipswich MA: Salem Press.

Aronowitz, S. (1993). 'Is a Democracy Possible? The Decline of the Public in American Debate', 75–92. In Bruce Robbins, ed., *The Phantom Public Sphere*. Minneapolis MN: University of Minnesota Press.

Asen, R. (2018). 'Introduction: Neoliberalism and the Public Sphere', in *Communication and the Public* 3:3, 171–5.

Brown, W. (2015). *Undoing the Demos: Neoliberalism's Stealth Revolution*. New York NY: Zone Books.

Burn, S. J. (2016). 'Second-Generation Postmoderns' 450–64. In Brian McHale and Len Platt, eds, *The Cambridge History of Postmodern Literature*. Cambridge: Cambridge University Press.

Calhoun, C. (1992). 'Introduction: Habermas and the Public Sphere', 1–50. In Craig Calhoun, ed., *Habermas and the Public Sphere*. Cambridge MA: The MIT Press.

Friedman, M. (1962). *Capitalism and Freedom*. Chicago IL: University of Chicago Press.

Gardiner, M. (2004). 'Wild Publics and Grotesque Symposiums: Habermas and Bakhtin on Dialogue, Everyday Life and the Public Sphere', in *Sociological Review* 52, 28–48.

Gripsrud, J., H. Moe, A. Molander, and G. Murdock, (2010). 'Editors' Introduction', xiii–xxviii. In Jostein Gripsrud, Hallvard Moe, Anders Molander and Graham Murdock, eds, *The Idea of the Public Sphere: A Reader*. Lanham MD: Lexington Books.

Hayes-Brady, C. (2016). *The Unspeakable Failures of David Foster Wallace: Language, Identity, and Resistance*. London and New York NY: Bloomsbury.

Hering, D. (2016). *David Foster Wallace: Fiction and Form*. London and New York NY: Bloomsbury.

Hirschkop, K. (1999). *Mikhail Bakhtin: An Aesthetic for Democracy*. Oxford: Oxford University Press.

Holland, M. K. (2017). '"By Hirsute Author": Gender and Communication in the Work and Study of David Foster Wallace', in *Critique* 58:1, 64–77.

Kelly, A. (2014). 'David Foster Wallace and the Novel of Ideas', 3–22. In Marshall Boswell, ed., *David Foster Wallace and 'The Long Thing': New Essays on the Novels*. London and New York NY: Bloomsbury.

Kelly, A. (2017). 'David Foster Wallace and New Sincerity Aesthetics: A Reply to Edward Jackson and Joel Nicholson-Roberts', in *Orbit: A Journal of American Literature* 5:2.
Konstantinou, L. (2016). *Cool Characters: Irony and American Fiction.* Cambridge MA: Harvard University Press.
Lipsky, D. (2010). *Although of Course You End Up Becoming Yourself: A Road Trip with David Foster Wallace.* New York NY: Broadway Books.
McCaffery, L. (2012). 'An Expanded Interview with David Foster Wallace', 21–57. In Stephen J. Burn, ed., *Conversations with David Foster Wallace.* Jackson MS: University Press of Mississippi.
Mouffe, C. (2000). *The Democratic Paradox.* London: Verso.
Severs, J. (2017). *David Foster Wallace's Balancing Books: Fictions of Value.* New York NY: Columbia University Press.
Thompson, L. (2018). 'Wallace and Race', 204–19. In Ralph Clare, ed., *The Cambridge Companion to David Foster Wallace.* Cambridge: Cambridge University Press.
Wallace, D. Foster. (2005). *Consider the Lobster and Other Essays.* London: Abacus.
Wallace, D. Foster. (2011). *The Pale King.* London: Penguin.
Wallace, D. Foster. (2013). *Both Flesh and Not: Essays.* London: Penguin.
Warner, M. (2005). *Publics and Counterpublics.* New York NY: Zone Books.

Internet sources

Azarian, B. (2016). 'How the Fear of Death Makes People More Right-Wing', *Aeon.* https://aeon.co/ideas/how-the-fear-of-death-makes-people-more-right-wing/ (accessed 30 December 2020).
Brooks, R. M. (2015). 'Conflict before Compromise: A Response to Rachel Greenwald Smith', *The Account: A Journal of Poetry, Prose and Thought* 4. http://theaccountmagazine.com/?article=forum-on-compromise-aesthetics (accessed 30 December 2020).
South, D. (2019). *Literature and the Public Sphere in the Internet Age.* PhD Diss., University of York. http://etheses.whiterose.ac.uk/24438/ (accessed 30 December 2020).
Wallace, D. Foster (2003). 'David Foster Wallace'. By Dave Eggers. *The Believer.* www.believermag.com/issues/200311/?read=interview_wallace (accessed 30 December 2020).

9

Pioneers of consciousness: hypothesis for a diptych

Lorenzo Marchese

Twin stories

Oblivion (2004) places at its centre the interrelated problem of negative experience – be it historical trauma in 'The Suffering Channel', shock in 'The Soul Is Not a Smithy', or psychological despair, such as in 'Good Old Neon' – and the traumatized or harmed subject's attempt to express his or her 'dynamics of consciousness' (Tracey, 2009: 177) through a shared language (Boswell, 2013: 151–69). This problem emerges in Wallace's late work, which is ever more ominous and meditative, less playful and friendly, and finds its emblematic presentation in the stories 'Incarnations of Burned Children' and 'Another Pioneer', which were written and published one shortly after the other ('Incarnations of Burned Children' first appeared in *Esquire* on 1 November 2000, 'Another Pioneer' in *Colorado Review* 28 in the summer of 2001). Moreover, as I will argue in this brief chapter, these stories – overlooked as a whole by critics in favour of better-known stories in the *Oblivion* collection, such as 'The Soul Is Not a Smithy' and 'Good Old Neon'[1] – should be read as two parts of a single narrative entity, for thematic and philosophical (so to say) reasons. In the first section of this chapter I will provide a short description of the plot and main topics treated in these two stories, with the aim of illustrating that they have so much in common, on a content level, that they might be considered an unstated narrative diptych. As I will point out, they are both exemplary illustrations of Wallace's narrative approach to analysis of the intermittent relation between self-consciousness and the limits of communicative language.[2] In addition they are especially conceptual works, which develop narratives very familiar to postmodern philosophical suggestions (Derrida) and pragmatist and post-analytic issues (I will focus mainly on some ideas from Nagel and Rorty). However, the author's way of confronting questions concerning the nature of consciousness and the limits of mutual understanding among humans does not reflect a strictly philosophical approach to the several issues raised. Instead Wallace leans towards dramatization, and his late narrative work constitutes a complex monument to ambiguity: the situations portrayed by Wallace in the two short stories examined do not represent definite solutions to long-standing issues and are not even pieces of a recognizable, original thought system. Through a juxtaposition of autobiographical elements and poetics Wallace's work may be defined as philosophical narrative rather than narrative philosophy (as it may appear at first sight): philosophy is (one of) the writer's means rather than his destination. I shall discuss this question briefly, without any pretence of giving a definitive answer, in the chapter's conclusion.

The first story is short (1,131 words long) and is made up of a small number of long sentences that describe a serious domestic incident involving an infant. Told primarily from the father's perspective, as the opening sentence indicates ('The Daddy was around the side of the house hanging a door for the tenant when he heard the child's scream and the Mommy's voice gone high between them', Wallace, 2004a: 114), the third-person-narrated story describes with galloping rhythm the various phases of the incident, using a dismayed tone that more than once crosses the line from pathos to poignancy:[3] the boiling water that, beyond the father's gaze, falls on the child; the father called to the rescue by the mother; the attempts to heal the burned skin; and the desperate, incessant, inexplicable screams of the infant. In the second half of 'Incarnations of Burned Children', when the parents take off their child's clothing, we understand the reason behind the infant's screaming: the boiling water entered the diaper, scalding the lower half of the child's body. The two adults, however, had not noticed until it was too late, after the damage was already irreversible:

> the diaper, which when they opened the towel and leaned their little boy back on the checkered cloth and unfastened the softened tabs and tried to remove it resisted slightly with new high cries and was hot, their baby's diaper burned their hand and they saw where the real water'd fallen and pooled and been burning their baby boy all this time while he screamed for them to help him and they hadn't, hadn't thought ... (115)

The tragic dimension of the story resides in this misunderstanding, which, over the course of three sentences, leads to the unravelling conclusion of the story. Once the extent of the damage caused by the boiling hot water is unveiled, the father brings the child to the hospital in a last attempt to save him. The impossibility of communication between the child and its parents is a synecdoche for the difficulty of establishing authentic human communication as a whole. This emphasis on incomprehension is underlined by the fact that the story is narrated mainly through the perspective of the father, who does not exactly understand how to help his son. Beyond the material cause of harm (the boiling water), it is the lack of understanding that sends the events hurtling toward catastrophe. The death of the child, a grotesque estrangement depicted in the story's final sentences, takes us far from the kitchen where the incident took place. Detaching itself from its body, the soul of the child, freed from life, transfigures reality into a childish drawing that masks, and exacerbates, the horror of his death:[4]

> though hours later what the Daddy most won't forgive is how badly he wanted a cigarette right then as they diapered the child as best as they could in gauze and two crossed handtowels and the Daddy lifted him like a newborn with his skull in one palm and ran him out to the clinic's ER with the tenant's door hanging open like that all day until the hinge gave but by then it was too late, when it wouldn't stop and they couldn't make it the child had learned to leave himself and watch the whole rest unfold from a point overhead, and whatever was lost never thenceforth mattered, and the child's body expanded and walked about and drew pay and lived its life untenanted, a thing among things, its self's soul so much vapor aloft, falling as rain and then rising, the sun up and down like a yoyo. (116)

'Another Pioneer' has seemingly little to do with 'Incarnations of Burned Children'. It is entirely different in terms of plot (the story of a child endowed with miraculous powers and born into a distant tribe), its length ('Another Pioneer', in its published version, takes up around twenty pages), and its style. Yet like 'Incarnations of Burned Children', 'Another Pioneer' is quite rich and extremely syntactically sophisticated. The terminology of the story, however, differs: in 'Another Pioneer' Wallace reaches greater heights of verbal sophistication, drawing extensively from philosophy, literary theory, and science. The way the story is presented differs, too: instead of a tale devoid of variation and told 'live' almost entirely through the perception of a single character (the father), in 'Another Pioneer' the multiplication of narrative levels through which we come to know the history of the boy-prodigy prevents the first-person narrator from focusing on the object of the story. This narrative perspective, originally clear, is slowly complicated as we read, turning the child's anecdote into something almost indecipherable. The basis of the story is in fact legend or myth – an incredible story, lying beyond the principle of reality. In the tradition of the mythological tale, the story's addressee has to suspend disbelief before reading; here instead the transcription, referred to us by an indirect witness, is inscribed in a register of postmodern scepticism that critically (de)composes the fable-like tale. In the *incipit*, the reader is presented with a story told orally, which the anonymous narrator, addressing an abstract audience of 'gentlemen', claims to have heard from a friend – who in turn had heard it during a flight (but the friend could not hear well and missed the entire first part).[5] Wallace breaks up the story of the boy-prodigy from the first few lines, inviting us to adopt a sceptical stance towards what we 'hear'. In the supernatural aspects of the story – as when we are told, in an aside, of the superhuman fasting of the child – the first-person narrator insists both on the conventional nature of the story that is told and that we need not suspend disbelief (as fiction normally requires): 'here evidently echoing the way certain medieval hagiographies depict their own extraordinarily high-powered, supernaturally advanced subjects as being capable of fasting for months and even years without discomfort' (Wallace, 2004a: 138–9).

What exactly are the author's intentions here? Not to play with us – the overall tone of 'Another Pioneer' is decidedly serious, as is its vaguely apocalyptic ending. The hyper-educated lexicon and convoluted phrasing do not reflect the playful aspect of Wallace's early stories (such as 'The Girl with Curious Hair', 1989). In a speech betraying a large amount of unaccountability, we are invited to doubt what we read, because of both its mythological elements and the sceptical attitude the narrator upholds towards the bizarre story he is overhearing. At the same time the abundance of variants and lacunae in the child's story marks the impossibility of capturing something true, undoubtable, in the parable of the pioneer. On a metanarrative plane there is something notable about a story so culturally shrewd and baroque: its accretion of references that makes the written page always mendacious. The reader is called upon to assume a critical posture, embrace the conviction that one cannot naively abandon oneself to the story – since that innocence, as the parable of the child proves (from pure and uncontaminated genius to guilty victim of his own monstrous self-consciousness), is not one of this world. Even though it is commonsensical to claim that a genuine correspondence between fiction and facts is not possible, Wallace seems to be taking this statement as his point of departure (which dates back at least to Plato's *Republic*, Book X). That literature offers no authentic knowledge of facts might imply that it can not tell us anything true about reality as a whole, along the lines of Derrida in 'The Double Session'.[6]

In 'Another Pioneer', to summarize, the fantasy-like frame does not lend an 'indubitable' tone to the tale. On the contrary the narration prevents the reader from giving a correct answer to a twofold question: 'Who is narrating this story?' and 'What is the point of view?' As though this were not enough, Wallace (de)composes the development of the story to render even more unreliable the 'multiplied' narrator of 'Another Pioneer'. If in the first part (defined as the original *exemplum*) the child is introduced along with his exceptional cognitive gifts, which make him a genius as well as a fundamental resource for his village, in the second part we are presented with three variations of the same story: 'Structurally, this scene apparently functions as both the climax of the protasis and the as it were engine of the narrative's rising action, because at just this point we are told that the original exemplum splits or diverges here into at least three main epitatic variants' (Wallace, 2004a: 126).

There are three possible versions (each one packed with subvariations), which should explain for what reason, in the third and last part (the 'catastasis', 130), the child's answers become enigmatic and doubting (133–6), as he no longer responds in the dependable, 'almost idiotic, cybernetically literal way' (131) of the beginning of the story, as well as why he ends up rebelling against the village that worships him like a demigod, becoming a menace to all, until he is abandoned and finally set on fire by his terrorized fellows. A fourth cause of the child's 'madness' is adduced right before the story's conclusion, in a sort of contrast with the three prior versions (138). In fact, the fourth version concerns the child's ineradicable doubt about his own imposture, when he himself, incited by an elder of the village, begins to suspect that he is not the genius everyone thinks he is: 'not half so complete as they believe' (138). This uncertainty regarding his own gifts, the self-questioning moment we find here, becomes the conceptual fulcrum of the story that follows 'Another Pioneer' in *Oblivion*, namely 'Good Old Neon', which begins with the famous declaration 'My whole life I've been a fraud. I'm not exaggerating' (141). Incidentally this may be a further piece of evidence for the overlooked thematic coherence of *Oblivion* as a short-story collection.

The finale of 'Another Pioneer' is presented without any narratological filter. We do not return to the beginning of the story, which had established the context of the first-person narration. Instead the scary intensification of the story brings us close to the dramatic undertones in 'Incarnations of Burned Children', as the frame-like introduction is set aside. The abandonment of the village is related univocally and without irony ('Because eventually they left. The village did. When the child failed to starve or leave the dais but merely continued to sit there atop it', 139); there are no longer discordant versions and, in the narrator's voice, we detect no echo effects coming from secondary voices. Through a turn of phrase we grasp an indication of the ultimately inaccessible conscience of the boy-prodigy ('In the humid quiet of dawn, however, the child could detect a difference in the center's dead stillness …', 139). The protagonist's death, as in 'Incarnations of Burned Children', is described with an umpteenth, unannounced change of perspective: not with the naive and vaguely nonsensical repetition of events suggested by the final infantile image ('the sun up and down like a yoyo'), but with a great scene of destruction – filtered through the gaze of another infant, which reinforces the overall darkness and solemnity of the story:

> until one keen-eyed child, hanging extrorse in its sling on a mother's back, saw blue hanging smoke in the dense fronds behind them, and low-caste stragglers, turning round at the long column's rear, could make out the red lace of a fire seen through many layers of trees' moving leaves, a great rapacious fire that grew and gained ground not matter how hard the high castes drove them. (140)

After this short, double synopsis, which already reveals some analogies and formal distances between the two stories examined, I will now try to deepen our reasoning on the diptych-like nature of the two texts. We start over from the beginning, actually from the title of 'Another Pioneer'. What does the word 'Another' refer to, if we have no news in the text of a first, earlier 'pioneer'? And that conjunctive adverb 'Nevertheless' with which 'Another Pioneer' opens, does it call back to a preceding discourse or is it only an *ex abrupto* beginning which starts in the middle of a dialogue? After all it occurs often in the collection, for example in 'Philosophy and the Mirror of Nature', 'Oblivion', and 'The Suffering Channel'. My hypothesis is that both the title and the *incipit* are connected to 'Incarnations of Burned Children', which in turn similarly speaks of 'Incarnations' and 'Burned Children' in the plural. It is not the most intuitive title, since there is only one burned child in the story – but what if the titles of 'Incarnations of Burned Children' and 'Another Pioneer' instituted a distant parallelism between two 'pioneer' children who resemble one another a great deal? Both are condemned to infantile muteness: the first because, being an infant, he does not yet speak; the second due to his autistic and impenetrable genius. Both are inaccessible, for similar reasons, to the understanding of others: the former dies because he is not able to tell his parents the cause of his physical pain; in the latter the child is relegated to being a miraculous creature and is so superior to his context that no one seems to understand him. Their trajectories are comparable, both ending with death by burning – a consequence of their linguistic solitude. The diptych thus narrates, according to this interpretation, the parallel destinies of these two 'burned children'. They employ different modalities of narration mimetically adapted to the character of each text: a simple, fast, linear, and anti-ironic style to communicate the urgency and universality of the domestic drama in 'Incarnations of Burned Children'; hyper-sophisticated, doubting, and reference-laden in 'Another Pioneer' to trace the cerebral and tortuous thinking of the brilliant protagonist and decompose the narrated actions into an exegesis that turns upon itself. Through such narration Wallace suggests that the two stories ultimately display an analogous subtext, because both depict extremes of infantile simplicity and superhuman intelligence that come together in a shared destiny of misunderstanding and idiocy: a scenario in which both burn because they are unable to communicate their own consciousness to others, who, in their turn, cannot figure out what these 'burned children' are experiencing and thinking.

Opaque minds

Solipsism, a leitmotif of this diptych, is a recurring topic in Wallace's artistic trajectory. In a well-known interview given in 1993, Wallace emphasizes the power that fiction has over ordinary communication:

> But there are a few books I have read that I've never been the same after, and I think all good writing somehow addresses the concern of and acts as an anodyne against loneliness. We're all terribly, terribly lonely. And there's a way, at least in prose fiction, that can allow you to be intimate with the world and with a mind and with characters that you just can't be in the real world. I don't know what you're thinking. I don't know that much about you as I don't know that much about my parents or my lover or my sister, but a piece of fiction that's really true allows you to be intimate with ... I don't want to say people, but it allows you to be intimate with a world that resembles our own in enough emotional particulars so that the way different things must feel is carried out with us into the real world. I think what I would like my stuff to do is make people less lonely. Or really to affect people. (Kennedy and Polk, 2012: 16)[7]

Fiction attempts to show the reader what occurs in other people's minds, creating a mechanism of empathic identification that attenuates the ineliminable existential solitude of our experience of reality. None of us *really* know what others think, but fiction creates the illusion that it is possible to do so with fictional characters – even if, naturally, this is only due to narrative artifice. When the 'transparency' of thought is a narratological effect by which created characters get interiority and we, the readers, can move effortlessly among their thoughts, we have so-called 'psycho-narration' (Cohn, 1978: 21–57): a form that, from the nineteenth century onward, has progressively imposed the novel as the privileged narrative genre for describing the intertwining of public events and inner life.

'Incarnations of Burned Children' and 'Another Pioneer' programmatically overturn the role of psycho-narration in fiction: the dramatic unfolding of events in these two stories hinges on the inaccessibility of the thoughts of others, which faithfully replicates the *real* impossibility of literally reading thoughts. In these two stories from *Oblivion* fiction does not depict a successful empathy among human beings. On the contrary the diptych stages the impossibility of genuine communication. In 'Another Pioneer' the inhabitants of the village do not actually know what the child thinks or whether he has the same way of thinking as they do; this diffidence is reciprocal, since the child finds them stubborn and engages them with questions that destroy their sanity (Wallace, 2004a: 135). The village inhabitants also ignore the reason behind the child's transition 'from messianic to monstrous' (136): they feel fear without understanding it. The inhabitants interpellate the child as an oracle, relying on him to resolve their doubts rather than learning how to confront them directly. It should be noted, after all, that the only question that addresses the child-prodigy *as a person* and requires some introspective effort is the final one, which concerns the issue of intellectual imposture and aims, not very subtly, to destroy him. Indeed, the aforementioned fourth version of the story (also called the 'catastasis of the first epitatic variant', 137) recounts that the village shaman unsettles the child by questioning his supposed natural genius: is the child really as wise as everyone thinks he is? What if, conversely, he is revered by the inhabitants of the village only because, in the shaman's words, 'they have exaggerated your gifts, have transformed you into something you know too well you are not?' (138). Upon closer look, this theme of incommunicability may also reflect an autobiographical matrix: the (self) destructive nature of genius in 'Another Pioneer' seems to a question that, thanks to the mediatic attention devoted to Wallace after *Infinite Jest* and his reception of the MacArthur Award in 1997, would become ever more pressing for the author from the second half of the 1990s on. It is also representative of the unbridgeable distance between the public and a writer who is put on a pedestal yet not approached as a true person.

In 'Incarnations of Burned Children', something analogous takes place with respect to the incommunicability of consciousness. The father truly does not know why the child is screaming: he intuits it in a confused way (realizes that it is due to the boiling water) but does not understand where the child feels physical pain (under his diaper), and for this reason his cures unwittingly aggravate his son's condition. Here the linguistic gap is tightly connected to the horizon of incomprehensibility. It is worth noting that in 'Incarnations of Burned Children' Wallace never allows the parents to truly speak to each other, apart from the few orders given to the mother by the father. The question with no answer that emerges in the story is slightly different from that of 'Another Pioneer': how can a being in his preverbal phase (the infant) make itself understood by someone possessing complex verbal language (the adult)?

This is hardly an isolated question in Wallace's oeuvre. In fact the child in 'Incarnations of Burned Children' is not the only creature who perishes by boiling hot water in his work. Another living being void of language comes to the same end: the lobster. In his reportage 'Consider the Lobster' Wallace, under the pretext of reporting on the 2003 Maine Lobster Festival, advances an argument concerning the ethical permissiveness of boiling animals alive. Four years after 'Incarnations of Burned Children' his argument departs from the same conceptual basis: pain is subjective, and we cannot know how much the lobster suffers when it is thrown into a pot of boiling water.

> Since pain is a totally subjective mental experience, we do not have direct access to anyone or anything's pain but our own; and even just the principles by which we can infer that other human beings experience pain and have a legitimate interest in not feeling pain involve hard-core philosophy – metaphysics, epistemology, value theory, ethics. The fact that even the most highly evolved nonhuman mammals can't use language to communicate with us about their subjective mental experience is only the first layer of additional complication in trying to extend our reasoning about pain and morality to animals. And everything gets progressively more abstract and convoluted as we move farther and farther out from the higher-type mammals into cattle and swine and dogs and cats and rodents, and then birds and fish, and finally invertebrate like lobsters. (Wallace, 2004b: 246)

As is common in Wallace's writing, his non-fiction treats a problem that is also confronted through fiction (the incommunicability of pain), yet in a different tone. The missed communication in 'Incarnations of Burned Children' takes the form of a panting, anxious story, devoid of theoretical frames and strategies of persuasion (its main aim is to strike the reader emotively). The discourse of 'Consider the Lobster', despite confronting the same basic theme, is instead friendly and reflexive, as befits the setting and journalistic conventions of the writing. Wallace's reportage does not present narrative situations but it does discard the occasion of the festival almost immediately, slipping instead into essayism – that is, into non-systematic, subjective problematization of a general question starting from a concrete cue,[8] with an almost persuasive inflection in how it presents the question. Wallace does not want to shock his readers: he prefers instead to lead them to reflect on the difference between 'pain as a purely neurological event' and 'actual suffering, which seems crucially to involve an emotional component, an awareness of pain as unpleasant, as something to fear / dislike / want to avoid' (251). To truly understand the suffering of those who do not share our language, Wallace proposes two ways forward: to close the question, after Descartes, by upholding that animal-machines are not capable of experiencing emotions comparable to those felt by humans;[9] or instead, as is suggested in the last part of the essay, to presume the lobster has the capacity to feel pain and, through an effort of empathic imagination not far from the one Wallace proposes with respect to fiction, to save the animal from pointless suffering (given that the lobster could be boiled dead and not alive, with no particular consequence for our palates). Here we see the author taking up a point made in Thomas Nagel's famous 1974 essay 'What Is It Like to Be a Bat?' which, from its very title, takes up the possibility of 'entering into' the head of another living being and poses this question by inserting the variable of 'consciousness' into the Cartesian mind–body dualism ('Without consciousness the mind–body problem would be much less interesting. With consciousness it seems hopeless', Nagel, 1974: 436). Nagel's reflections thus reaffirm the subjective character of experience: we cannot avail ourselves of the help of a shared, indisputable theory to know what it is like to be a bat. The subjective state of mind of an animal cannot be objectively expressed (and understood) by a human subject:

But fundamentally an organism has conscious mental states if and only if there is something that it is like to be that organism – something it is like for the organism. We may call this the subjective character of experience. It is not captured by any of the familiar, recently devised reductive analyses of the mental, for all of them are logically compatible with its absence. It is not analysable in terms of any explanatory system of functional states, or intentional states, since these could be ascribed to robots or automata that behaved like people though they experienced nothing. (Nagel, 1974: 436)

The provisional solution that Nagel offers, as philosopher, is quite distant from Wallace's. Nagel concludes at the end of his essay that we must confront the question of the distance between objective and subjective, in order to elaborate an 'objective phenomenology not dependent on empathy or the imagination' (Nagel, 1974: 449).[10] For Wallace an 'objective phenomenology' cannot be given, and empathy and imagination are the only possible ways to proceed.

In the collection *Oblivion*, and more generally in his fiction of the early 2000s preceding *The Pale King*, Wallace insists that identification and understanding are huge efforts – and often destined to fail in a world composed of myriad subjective, separate visions of reality and in which the 'contingency of language', to borrow a category from Rorty, a philosopher Wallace knew well,[11] is the only objective certainty.[12] The unbridgeable gaps left by these distant subjectivities is where Wallace's more pessimistic writing takes place and is certainly the terrain inhabited by the diptych, which sees language create gaps, seek to fill them, and speak of nothing else. It is precisely in this sense that the term 'pioneer' should be interpreted in both stories: the child protagonists can be defined as unwilling 'discoverers' of the tragic connection between the intrinsic fallibility of communication among human beings and the fate of ending up consumed by one's own indecipherable condition as a solitary individual. Pioneers forging unknown lands often end up dead or lost. Exploring dramatic ('Incarnations of Burned Children') or fantastical ('Another Pioneer') narrative hypotheses, Wallace allows us to discover in these stories the limits of empathy and identification, thus pushing us toward the limits of the potentialities of language – limits that not even fiction can overcome.

Narrative philosophy or philosophical narrative?

'Incarnations of Burned Children' and 'Another Pioneer' are both stories marked by a profound interest in philosophy (though one could certainly say the same about other stories in this collection and elsewhere). Wallace himself, as is well known, had a background in analytic philosophy and logic – disciplines that he gradually abandoned, at least partially, in favour of creative writing. If the conceptual power of 'Incarnations of Burned Children' is located in the diegetic implications of a text that is so brief and not essayistic, 'Another Pioneer' instead is organized as a de-structured *conte philosophique*, in which the tale of the child-prodigy serves as a form of philosophical education (even if, in keeping with the pessimism pervading the entire story, it is not clear what kind of lesson we should draw from these events). Fantastical or simply bizarre elements abound in Wallace's fiction, but 'Another Pioneer' is an isolated case in his oeuvre with respect to how it revisits Platonic myth in a postmodern register (Plato's *Phaedo*, which mournfully ends with the philosopher who is sent to martyrdom by his community). Philosophy is not only present in Wallace's language and arguments but is also represented by main characters in 'Another pioneer'. Yet despite these aspects, I contend, we should not consider Wallace a philosopher leaning towards narrative. In fact Wallace does not recur to allegories and narrative situations to offer us his own, original philosophical thoughts (as proper philosophers do: think again of Plato's myths, Voltaire's *Candide*, Putnam's 'brains in a vat'). On the contrary Wallace is a writer who often relies on the philosophical systems of others, drawing concepts and issues from several thinkers. His approach to philosophy is unorthodox and asystematic as he looks to various thinkers and recombines their ideas to offer a more accurate, very personal, problematic glimpse of the contemporary world.

In his famous interview with Larry McCaffery Wallace explains that 'Fiction is about what it is to be a fucking *human being*' (McCaffery, 2012: 26). This choice of an indeterminate article marks the difference in approach between the writer of fiction and the philosopher: the first recounts a *particular* human experience, without any pretence of elaborating general laws from the telling of stories and with the aim of instilling empathy, identification, and emotion in the readers; the second, even when drawing inspiration from their own contingent experience, speaks of '*the* human being' as a concept and universal subject. The first thus always turns towards his or her own particularity and interrogates it; the second seeks to punctuate it through the abstraction of concepts. The first generally does not offer solutions to philosophical problems, while the task of the second is generally to find new perspectives and original answers to theoretical, ethical, and aesthetic questions in regards to which most of us would not know how to orient ourselves. Situating fiction in relation to the single human and avoiding general laws and abstract, universal ideas – in accordance with the perspectives of analytic philosophy and neo-pragmatism (notably Rorty) – Wallace sided himself with fiction writers attempting to investigate the human being by going beyond philosophy. Hypothesizing a shift in philosophy's aims, Richard Rorty, the American philosopher and author of *Contingency, Irony, and Solidarity*, posited the novel as an expressive instrument for the refinement of sensibility and the redescription of the self and others vis-à-vis ethical ends. Wallace's aims as a writer, starting from the years he composed *Infinite Jest*, are quite close to those expressed by Rorty in this passage:

> In my utopia, human solidarity would be seen not as a fact to be recognized by clearing away 'prejudice' or burrowing down to previously hidden depths but, rather, as a goal to be achieved. It is to be achieved not by inquiry but by imagination, the imaginative ability to see strange people as fellow sufferers. Solidarity is not discovered by reflection but created. It is created by increasing our sensitivity to the particular details of the pain and humiliation of other, unfamiliar sorts of people. Such increased sensitivity makes it more difficult to marginalize people different from ourselves by thinking, 'They do not feel it as we would', or 'There must always be suffering, so why not let them suffer?' This process of coming to see other human beings as 'one of us' rather than as 'them' is a matter of detailed description of what unfamiliar people are like and of redescription of what we ourselves are like. This is a task not for theory but for genres such as ethnography, the journalist's report, the comic book, the docudrama, and, especially, the novel. (Rorty, 1989: XVI)

The writer–philosopher distinction is strongly present in Wallace. Even fiction marked by a distinctively philosophical inflection, such as that of Kafka and Dostoevsky, Wallace does not define as philosophy in the strict sense; while David Markson's experimental novel *Wittgenstein's Mistress*, which literally thematizes theories contained in Wittgenstein's *Philosophical Investigations* (1953), he speaks of as 'philosophical sci-fi' (Wallace, 2012: 85). Asked about this in September 2006 by the Russian journalist Ostap Karmodi, Wallace was clear about his allegiances:

> OK: Your stories are very philosophical and quite political too. Is there for you any big difference between a story and an essay?
> DFW: I don't know that I agree that my fiction is really all that political.
> OK: Philosophical at least.
> DFW: People are often surprised, I think I'm fundamentally a fairly traditional, conservative kind of writer. I tend to think of fiction as being mainly about characters and human beings and inner experience, whereas essays can be much more expository and didactic and more about subjects or ideas. If some people read my fiction and see it as fundamentally about philosophical ideas, what it probably means is that these are pieces where the characters are not as alive and interesting as I meant them to be. (Karmodi, 2011)

In conclusion, considering the two stories analysed here as philosophical writing would offer us only a weak understanding of Wallace's work: calling his work 'philosophy' would require identifying an original philosophical thought, an aim that was simply outside the purview of Wallace's intentions. Rather 'Incarnations of Burned Children' and 'Another Pioneer' invite us to draw from these stories *as such* and not in terms of a univocal, incontestable thesis of the author (as typically occurs in philosophy). There are characters with whom we can identify (the father in 'Incarnations of Burned Children', thanks to the perspective of the story) or that we can try to decipher (the child prodigy in 'Another Pioneer', with greater effort). The two stories rely on a recognizable philosophical background but do not propose innovative philosophical theses. Wallace aims to speak of a consciousness unable to express itself, but he does not offer an articulate, distinguishable argument about the problem, let alone a solution. Rather than transmit a 'message' or propose an answer for unsolved issues, the diptych draws us very close to the private, distorted worlds inhabited by the two 'pioneers' while preventing us from crossing the threshold of their consciousnesses. The unfathomable nature of these characters and the impossibility of extracting a moral from them discloses the real nature of this side of Wallace's work: rather than narrative philosophy, it might best be defined as philosophical narrative. As I have tried to demonstrate, Wallace's inspirations are well-known and quite recognizable (Derrida, Nagel, Rorty, among others). Wallace puts philosophy at the service of fiction and considers it one of the many tools that can be employed by a narrator: it is a device for inquiring into the world of the particular, helping create better understanding of 'what it is to be a fucking human being'. Finally, while the traditional purpose of philosophy is to provide answers to the great questions of life or teach us how to live better lives, Wallace's narrative goes in the exact opposite direction, destabilizing us, leaving readers scalded (on a metaphorical level, unlike the 'pioneers'). Whether this constitutes a failure of Wallace's moral-literary project or his aesthetic peak is an open question.

Notes

1 Even the best-known monograph dedicated to *Oblivion* pays scant attention to the two stories, limiting itself to a plot summary (Carlisle, 2013).
2 Hering also goes in a similar direction, noting concisely: 'The inscrutability or loathsomeness of children are common tropes in Wallace's later work. The injured baby in "Incarnations of Burned Children" suffers because he cannot make himself understood to his parents, while the child-seer in "Another Pioneer" inspires both devotion and rage' (Hering, 2018: 104).
3 Example: 'the Mommy over his shoulder invoking God until he sent her for towels and gauze if they had it, the Daddy moving quickly and well and his man's mind empty of everything but purpose, not yet aware of how smoothly he moved or that he'd ceased to hear the high screams because to hear them would freeze him and make impossible what had to be done to help his own child' (Wallace, 2004a: 114–15).
4 A negative interpretation (the child dying) seems preferable to a more open or positive ending, in that it is a more logical conclusion to the story's development: incident > fatal misunderstanding > death. Moreover, one should not forget that this scene explicitly echoes the modalities of another death in Wallace's work: the assassination of Lucien, as it is described in *Infinite Jest*, leads to a phantasmagorical exit from his

body that follows the scene in 'Incarnations of Burned Children' quite closely: 'Lucien finally dies, rather a while after he's quit shuddering like a clubbed muskie and seemed to them to die, as he finally sheds his body's suit, Lucien finds his gut and throat again and newly whole, clean and unimpeded, and is free, catapulted home over fans and the Convexity's glass palisades at desperate speeds, soaring north, sounding a bell-clear and nearly maternal alarmed call-to-arms in all the world's well-known tongues' (Wallace, 1996: 488–9).
5 See Wallace, 2004a: 117–18.
6 'There is no – or hardly any, ever so little – literature; that in any event there is no essence of literature, no truth of literature, no literary-being of literature' (Derrida, 1983: 223).
7 See also McCaffery, 2012: 21–52.
8 As Severs has noted, 'Wallace the reporter often eschewed the Q-and-A format of interviews, and he once built an entire character around the erasure of the Q's in deconstructed interviews. His essays become so long, meandering, and prone to doubts because, even when he has someone to profile, he seeks all the questions beneath the surface that cannot be volleyed back by a subject, per rigid media logic … . Thus it makes sense to call Wallace in his various nonfiction modes – reviews, reported journalism, memoirs – fundamentally an essayist' (Severs, 2018: 111).
9 The question of animal-machines (*bête-machine*) in Descartes has been long discussed. See Adam and Tannery, 1897–1913: 56, 158, 276; Descartes's letter to More on 5 February 1649, in Kenny, 1970: 243. For a deeper look see Cottingham, 1978: 551–9; Harrison, 1992: 219–27.
10 Also see Nagel, 1986.
11 Another story in *Oblivion*, 'Philosophy and the Mirror of Nature', openly refers to a famous essay on the pseudo-problematic, 'language game' – like nature of many long-standing philosophical questions. The work in question is Rorty (1979).
12 '"Contingency of language", the fact that there is no way to step outside the various vocabularies we have employed and find a metavocabulary which somehow takes account of all possible vocabularies, all possible ways of judging and feeling' (Rorty, 1989: XVI). See also 3–22.

References

Adam, C. and P. Tannery. eds. (1897–1913). *Oeuvres de Descartes*. Paris: Cerf.

Boswell, M. (2013). '"The Constant Monologue Inside Your Head": Oblivion and the Nightmare of Consciousness', 151–70. In Stephen J. Burn and Marshall Boswell, eds, *A Companion to David Foster Wallace Studies*. New York NY: Palgrave Macmillan.

Carlisle, G. (2013). *Nature's Nightmare. Analysing David Foster Wallace's Oblivion*. Austin TX: Sideshow Media Group Press.

Cohn, D. (1978). *Transparent Minds. Narrative Modes for Presenting Consciousness in Fiction*. Princeton NJ: Princeton University Press.

Cottingham, J. (1978). '"A Brute to the Brutes?": Descartes' Treatment of Animals', in *Philosophy* 53: 206, 551–9.

Derrida J. (1983). *Dissemination*, trans. Barbara Johnson. Chicago IL: University of Chicago Press.

Harrison, P. (1992). 'Descartes on Animals', in *The Philosophical Quarterly* 42: 167, 219–27.

Hering, D. (2018). '*Oblivion*', 97–110. In Ralph Clare, ed., *The Cambridge Companion to David Foster Wallace*. Cambridge: Cambridge University Press.

Kennedy, H. and G. Polk. (2012). 'Looking for a Garde of Which to Be Avant: An Interview with David Foster Wallace', 11–20. In Stephen J. Burn, ed., *Conversations with David Foster Wallace*. Jackson MS: University Press of Mississippi.

Kenny, A., ed. (1970). *Descartes' Philosophical Letters*. Oxford: Clarendon.

McCaffery, L. (2012). 'An Expanded Interview with David Foster Wallace', 21–57. In Stephen J. Burn, ed., *Conversations with David Foster Wallace*. Jackson MS: University Press of Mississippi.

Nagel, T. (1974). 'What Is It Like to Be a Bat?', in *The Philosophical Review* 83:4, 435–50.

Nagel, T. (1986). *The View from Nowhere*. Oxford: Oxford University Press.

Rorty, R. (1979). *Philosophy and the Mirror of Nature*. Princeton NJ: Princeton University Press.

Rorty, R. (1989). *Contingency, Irony, and Solidarity*. Cambridge MA: Cambridge University Press.

Severs, J. (2018). 'Wallace's Nonfiction', 111–24. In Ralph Clare, ed., *The Cambridge Companion to David Foster Wallace*. Cambridge: Cambridge University Press.

Tracey, T. (2009). 'Representations of Trauma in David Foster Wallace's *Oblivion*', 172–86. In David Hering, ed., *Consider David Foster Wallace*. Los Angeles CA: Sideshow Media Group Press.

Wallace, D. Foster. (1996). *Infinite Jest*. New York NY: Little, Brown.

Wallace, D. Foster. (2004a). *Oblivion*. New York NY: Little, Brown.

Wallace, D. Foster. (2004b). *Consider the Lobster and Other Essays*. New York NY: Little, Brown.
Wallace, D. Foster. (2012). *Both Flesh and Not*. New York NY: Little, Brown.

Internet sources

Karmodi, O. (2011). *A Frightening Time in America. An Interview with David Foster Wallace*. New York Books. www.nybooks.com/daily/2011/06/13/david-foster-wallace-russia-interview/ (accessed 30 June 2019).

10

The problem of other minds in 'Good Old Neon'

Matt Prout

David Foster Wallace's short story 'Good Old Neon' is about the philosophical problem of other minds. As we learn in the final pages, the bulk of the story, narrated by the depressed Neal, is in fact the attempt of his former classmate, the character David Wallace, to imagine what could have led to Neal's suicide.[1] The entire story has been the result of 'David Wallace trying, if only in the second his lids are down, to somehow reconcile what this luminous guy had seemed like from the outside with whatever on the interior must have driven him to kill himself' (Wallace, 2004: 181). David Wallace is attempting to imagine an 'interior' – another mind – on the basis of, *and* in spite of, an 'outside' that he knew.

Here is a definition of the problem of other minds by C. S. Chihara and J. A. Fodor from the collection *Wittgenstein and the Problem of Other Minds* (1967).

> Among the philosophical problems Wittgenstein attempted to dissolve is 'the problem of other minds.' One aspect of this hoary problem is the question: What justification, if any, can be given for the claim that one can tell, on the basis of someone's behavior, that he is in a certain mental state? To this question, the sceptic answers: no good justification at all. (Chihara and Fodor, 1967: 171)

I suggest that this passage provides us with evidence for reading Wallace's story in relation to Wittgenstein's treatment of the problem of other minds (as I will go on to do). We are told at the end of the story that David Wallace has been trying to reconcile Neal's interiority with what he had 'seemed like from the outside',

> With David Wallace also fully aware that the cliché that you can't ever truly know what's going on inside somebody else is hoary and insipid and yet at the same time trying very consciously to prohibit that awareness from mocking the attempt or sending the whole line of thought into the sort of inbent spiral that keeps you from ever getting anywhere. (Wallace, 2004: 181)

Hoary, originally referring to hair that is grey or white with age, also means ancient or time-honoured (it has also come to mean overused or trite). It is an unusual word to use to describe a philosophical problem; my contention is that Wallace's use of this phrase is an echo of, or allusion to, its use in the book about Wittgenstein and other minds.[2] In the essay by Chihara and Fodor, 'hoary' refers to the age of the problem of other minds (as Harold Morick points out in the introduction, some version of the problem can be found in Plato's *Theaetetus*) (Morick, 1967: xiii). Wallace's use of the adjective is less clear. David Wallace refers to the problem of other minds as a 'cliché' and as 'insipid', and yet the thrust of the passage seems to be that thinking about this problem is likely to derail his attempt to imagine Neal's interiority. The point seems to be that, if he thinks about this problem, and about how long it has been around, then he is likely to side with the sceptic's claim that we cannot 'truly know' what's going on inside someone else (and that this awareness would foil his attempt to imagine Neal's interiority).

Throughout his career Wallace conceived of the task of writing fiction in terms that evoke the problem of other minds: 'I guess a big part of serious fiction's purpose is to give the reader, who like all of us is sort of marooned in her own skull, to give her imaginative access to other selves' (McCaffery, 2012: 21–2). What is dramatized at the close of this story is David Wallace's attempt to 'leap over the walls of self' (as Wallace elsewhere described the task of fiction) (Wallace, 1998: 51). What's at stake in the story's close is whether (or to what extent) David Wallace has managed to overcome or avoid the problem of other minds, and, therefore, how he (and, by implication, the real author, David Foster Wallace) has fared as a fiction writer.

Wallace can, therefore, be seen to stage his literary practice as an attempt to overcome a philosophical problem. However, this is complicated by the fact that he also makes this problem a central thematic concern of his story; as I will show, Neal's problems can be understood with reference to the problem of other minds, and specifically with the treatment of this problem that emerges from the later philosophy of Wittgenstein. As noted above, Wittgenstein's aim was to dissolve the problem of other minds by exposing it as a pseudo-problem; however, more relevant to 'Good Old Neon', I argue, is the view of one of Wittgenstein's foremost interpreters, Stanley Cavell, who sees the problem of other minds as a real, albeit ultimately confused, threat.[3] Wallace once studied with Cavell during his brief time at Harvard in 1989, an encounter that went memorably badly.[4] None the less, Wallace's engagement with Cavell's reading of Wittgenstein can be observed in a number of places in his work, most notably in 'The Empty Plenum: David Markson's *Wittgenstein's Mistress*' (1990) – an essay that uses a comment of Cavell's about Wittgenstein as an epigraph, and which also discusses the philosophical problem of scepticism (explicitly connecting the philosophical notion of solipsism with a more existential or affective idea of loneliness).[5]

Like Wittgenstein, Cavell thinks that something has gone wrong when the question of whether we can know anything about another person's interior state is raised as a philosophical problem. However, Cavell stresses that the problem of other minds is not simply a pseudo-problem but rather a perennial threat. For Cavell, scepticism is a way of relating to the world, or to others around us, that can occur when we fall out of a natural attunement with others (or the world) and start to conceive of our relationship with others (or the world) in epistemic or intellectual terms. I will argue that Neal is a character who has succumbed to the threat of scepticism as Cavell describes it.

Cavell draws extensively on literature to make his case for scepticism as a real human possibility rather than an abstract philosophical problem (in fact, it is the tendency to treat all problems as abstract and philosophical that Cavell sees as the threat). By looking at literary texts, Cavell is able to point to examples of scepticism as an embodied reality rather than as a theoretical problem. Like Cavell Wallace also uses the literary form to make vivid the consequences of treating the human or existential problem of our relation to others as an abstract philosophical or epistemological problem. However, the literary form of Wallace's writing both complements and complicates any philosophical insights it might seem to offer. I conclude by considering a final complication posed by Wallace's story which undercuts any straightforward Cavellian message through a formal metafictional manoeuvre that appears to signal the story's own acquiescence to, rather than triumph over, the logic of the problem of other minds.

Pain behaviour

As Neal explains it, his central problem is his fraudulence. We can read Neal's sense of his fraudulence as the result of his perception that there is a mismatch between how he appears to others on the outside and what he knows to be his motivation or intent from the perspective of his interiority. To be a fraud is to deceive others by successfully conveying an outward appearance that does not match your inner intentions – it involves denying others knowledge of your interiority. And yet Neal simultaneously displays a desire to be known; being a fraud means that 'you simultaneously want to fool everyone you meet and yet also somehow always hope that you'll come across someone who is your match or equal and can't be fooled' (Wallace, 2004: 155). This dynamic plays out in the central relationship between Neal and his analyst, Dr Gustafson, who Neal hopes will be able to know him and therefore help him (even though Neal simultaneously hopes to deceive Dr Gustafson).

Neal's time in analysis and relationship with Dr Gustafson provide a central framing device for the story; it is in these sessions that Neal fills Dr Gustafson in on his history of fraudulence. Questions about how much either character can understand and know the other therefore constitute much of the narrative's drama. At stake in this relationship is the extent to which each character can know the other's mind.

The sections of Wittgenstein's *Philosophical Investigations* (1953) that are taken to deal with the problem of other minds involve his discussion of 'pain behaviour'.[6] References to pain behaviour, and questions about the possibility of knowing another's pain, occur throughout 'Good Old Neon'. For example, at the end of the story,

The problem of other minds in 'Good Old Neon'

David Wallace's attempt to overcome (or avoid) the problem of other minds is described as his attempt to imagine 'what sorts of pain or problems' (Wallace, 2004: 180) could have led Neal to commit suicide (thereby framing the entire story as an attempt to know another's pain). Relatedly a number of the examples Neal gives of his own fraudulence can be seen to involve deceiving others about the pain he is in. For instance Neal sits in his meditation class with the appearance of being 'quiet and mindful', despite feeling 'what felt like bright blue fire going up my spine and shooting invisibly out of the top of my head' and wanting to 'jump up screaming and take a header right out the window' (159–60).

Further evidence of the story's engagement with Wittgenstein's discussion of pain behaviour can be found in the moment in which David Wallace blinks – the moment during which the forty pages of this story is imagined – and Neal's sister 'stirs a boiling pot for dinner' (180). Wittgenstein has a remark about a boiling pot in the middle of his discussion of pain behaviour: 'Of course, if water boils in a pot, steam comes out of the pot, and also a picture of steam comes out of a picture of a pot. But what if one insisted on saying that there must also be something boiling in the picture of the pot?' (Wittgenstein, 2009: §297). This puzzling remark is about the relation between inner and outer and what an outward appearance allows us to infer about an 'interiority' (and about the limitations of such a concept). Cavell claims that 'the correct relationship between inner and outer, between the soul and its society, is the theme of the *Investigations* as a whole' (Cavell, 1979: 329). I see this as the theme of 'Good Old Neon', which explores the question of what we can know about another person's inner state through a sustained discussion of pain and pain behaviour.

The discussion of pain behaviour in the *Investigations* begins in §244 with the question: 'How do words refer to sensations?' (Wittgenstein, 2009: §269). The idea that words refer to sensations already entails the notion of a gap between language and the sensations it attempts to 'name'; Wittgenstein hopes to get us to see that there is something problematic in this formulation. In contrast to this referential explanation of language, Wittgenstein offers an alternative picture of words as naturalistic *expressions* of behaviour. He asks us to imagine a child learning the meanings of the names of sensations: 'a child has hurt himself and he cries; then adults talk to him and teach him exclamations and, later, sentences. They teach the child new pain-behaviour' (§244). Part of becoming socialised into the use of language involves using words in the place of howling or crying. Keeping this history in mind can help us to see the sentence 'I am in pain' as an *expression* of pain rather than as a *reference to* pain.

Immediately following this discussion of the child learning new pain behaviour Wittgenstein asks the question: 'How can I even attempt to interpose language between the expression of pain and the pain?' (§245). This question might seem to present a picture of human beings as wholly transparent to one another – and thereby to evaporate the problem of other minds, along with the Cartesian picture of a split between the mind and body that supports it.[7] Wittgenstein's view is ultimately more nuanced, but, none the less, a very intuitive anti-sceptical point is made here: most of the time, the problem of other minds is no problem at all. 'If we are using the word "know" as it is normally used (and how else are we to use it?), then other people very often know if I'm in pain' (§246); this is the case even given the fact that the only criterion we have for this knowledge is a person's pain behaviour. Consider the case of a man who is knocked over by a car who then tells us that he is in immense pain: the person who asks 'but can we really know he is in pain?' would strike us as psychotic.[8] And yet the sceptic is struck (rightly, it seems) by the fact that human beings are not always wholly transparent to one another: I *can* lie to you about how I feel. The possibility of simulation (or dissimulation) leads the sceptic to the conclusion that I can never know (for certain) what sensations you are feeling – I can never know on the basis of your outward behaviour what is going on inside you.

Stanley Cavell has noted that Wittgenstein's 'obsessive emphasis on the publicness of language and on the outwardness of criteria' can make it seem as though he wants to 'deny privacy' (Cavell, 1979: 329). This is not the case; Wittgenstein wants to get clear on what it means to say that our sensations are private. §248 states that 'the sentence "sensations are private" is comparable to "One plays patience by oneself"'. This is to say that it sets out the rules governing our use of the word 'sensation' – it states what it is we mean when we talk of sensations. Wittgenstein calls these kinds of sentences 'grammatical': they both describe and delimit the rules of a particular language game.⁹ The sceptic mistakes 'grammatical' propositions (which cannot coherently be doubted) for empirical propositions. When sceptics insist on the privacy of our sensations, they *are* right, but they are wrong to make a problem of this fact since it couldn't be otherwise. The sceptic overreacts to the fact of our separateness; this fact does not mean that human beings are necessarily (or always) obscure to each other. This is what Stanley Cavell means when he says that the sceptic experiences 'a metaphysical finitude as an intellectual lack' (Cavell, 1969: 242) – he is disappointed with a human limitation as though it could be overcome.[10]

The cause of scepticism

For Cavell the sceptic's refusal to accept human finitude goes hand-in-hand with both a kind of mania for knowledge and an over-reliance on the powers of the intellect. Cavell describes 'the cause of skepticism' as 'the attempt to convert the human condition, the condition of humanity, into an intellectual difficulty, a riddle' (Cavell, 1979: 493). An overly empirical view of our relationship to our world and an excessive faith in the powers of the intellect can lead us to be frustrated with our finitude (with the extent to which we can know the pain of others, for example). For this reason, overcoming scepticism is seen to require 'crucifying the intellect' (Cavell, 1969: 298).

Neal is a smart narrator who flaunts his intelligence. Through the lucidity and rigour of his sentences, his ability to navigate a range of different discourses, and his high regard for (and facility with) logical analysis, Neal performs his intelligence for the reader. This performance is mostly convincing, and Neal's self-understanding is, for the most part, impressive.[11] However, when he converts Dr Gustafson's idea that we can either love or fear the world into a logical formula, his performance of his intelligence seems absurd, or even comic.[12] Neal values intellectual analysis and is attached to intellectual ways of solving his problems; he wants to show Dr Gustafson 'that I was at least as smart as he was and that there wasn't much of anything he was going to see about me that I hadn't already seen and figured out' (Wallace, 2004: 143). Recalling a moment from childhood when he figured out how to deceive his stepdad (about having broken an expensive bowl), Neal says: 'I felt powerful, smart. It felt a little like looking at part of a puzzle you're doing and you've got a piece in your hand and you can't see where in the larger puzzle it's supposed to go' before, 'in a flash', seeing that 'it will fit' (149). The idea of a 'puzzle' can be seen to stand for an intellectual problem: it is something to be figured out.

Neal has a tendency to treat his interpersonal problems as puzzles, or intellectual problems. A former girlfriend, Beverly Elizabeth Slane, describes Neal as an expensive piece of 'diagnostic equipment that can discern more about you in one quick scan than you could ever know about yourself — but the equipment doesn't care about you, you're just a sequence of processes and codes' (165). In other words a calculating inhuman machine. Beverly says that 'she'd never felt the gaze of someone so penetrating, discerning, and yet totally empty of care, like she was a puzzle or problem [Neal] was figuring out' (165). Neal's tendency to relate to others as intellectual puzzles stops him from relating to them as people.

The term 'Problem' is used to describe the psychological difficulties for which people attend therapy. It can also be used to describe a common topic for philosophical or logical analysis (as in the *problem of other minds*).[13] Neal tells us that he 'tried analysis' to deal with his 'problems', a phrasing that also evokes the act of subjecting a logical or philosophical problem to (philosophical) analysis.[14] This is an apt equivocation, since Neal has a tendency to treat his psychological problems as though they were logical or philosophical problems. He describes the basic 'problem' of his fraudulence as a paradox: 'The fraudulence paradox was that the more time and effort you put into trying to appear impressive or attractive to other people, the less impressive or attractive you felt inside – you were a fraud' (147).[15] Paradoxes are logical puzzles that are a source of fascination for Neal and provide him with a model for understanding his (psychological) problems.

In a conversation with Michael Goldfarb on the release of *Oblivion*, Wallace was asked to discuss some of the paradoxes in the story. 'The basic paradox ... [is the] famous "I am lying" paradox ... . This is making the story seem very cerebral – this is actually supposed to be kind of the saddest story in the book – but one of the things about the narrator is, he's had enough sort of education to drive himself crazy with the surface of these certain paradoxes' (McCaffery, 2012: 147).

Here Wallace acknowledges that people might not think these cerebral concerns would result in an emotional story, but he goes on to link cerebration and sadness: it is Neal's education that leads him to 'drive himself crazy'. The liar paradox plays a crucial role in Neal's relationship with Dr Gustafson because of Neal's decision 'to be supposedly "honest" and to diagnose myself aloud' – that is, to be honest about his fraudulence (Wallace, 2004: 154).[16]

Dr Gustafson offers Neal what he hopes is a revelatory insight: 'but if you're constitutionally false and manipulative and unable to be honest about who you really are, Neal ... how is it that you were able to drop the sparring and manipulation and be honest with me a moment ago ... about who you really are?' (153). In more logical terms Dr Gustafson suggests that Neal's 'ability to be honest with him about [his fraudulence] logically contradicted [Neal's] claim of being incapable of honesty' (154). Neal is disappointed with this 'insight' for two reasons. The first is that he sees it coming: Neal makes it clear that he had anticipated 'his big supposed insight' (154) seven pages earlier. The second reason is that it fails to follow through on the logic of this insight which is that 'the fact that I had chosen to be supposedly "honest" and to diagnose myself aloud was in fact just one more move in my campaign to make sure Dr. Gustafson understood that as a patient I was uniquely acute and self-aware' (154).

Dr Gustafson fails to consider that Neal's honesty about his fraudulence may be just a further extension and expression of that fraudulence. In fact Neal is clear about this: he *owns up* to the reader that his honesty with Dr Gustafson is a further example of his fraudulence.

Neal's disclosure to the reader of facts about himself that he conceals from Dr Gustafson forces the reader to consider her own relationship (as reader) to Neal (as narrator). Neal is being open to us about the fraudulence of his honesty towards Dr Gustafson. Should we trust him? It is not clear what trusting him here would mean. Neal's description of his openness with Dr Gustafson as fraudulent is based on the idea that he is not *really* opening up to Dr Gustafson but merely presenting the image of opening up or being honest in order to give an impression of himself as 'acute and self-aware'. The question for the reader then is whether to apply this recursive logic to Neal's narration. Could this narrator just be trying to impress us with his self-knowledge or self-awareness rather than simply giving us an account of his life? What would this even mean? Whatever we decide as readers, it is clear that, if we try to understand Neal's honesty or fraudulence through the circular logic of the liar paradox, then we can never discount the possibility of his ultimate fraudulence. What is stranger is that Neal understands his *own* integrity through this logic. Any steps Neal takes towards honestly coming to terms with his problem can always be brought back under his interpretative model of 'fraudulence'. Cavell describes 'the cause of skepticism' as 'the attempt to convert the human condition, the condition of humanity, into an intellectual difficulty, a riddle' (Cavell, 1979: 493). Neal treats the human problem of his *own* honesty or integrity as an intellectual riddle, a paradox that cannot be resolved.

Firepower and acknowledgement

Central to Cavell's response to the problem of other minds, scepticism is his concept of 'acknowledgement'. Because, as the sceptic is right to point out, my relation to other minds is not one of knowledge – when knowledge is construed as certainty.[17] Rather, in order to overcome the problem of other minds, I must stop trying to know you and instead '*acknowledge*' you.[18] Cavell says that 'acknowledgment goes beyond knowledge. (Goes beyond not, so to speak, in the order of knowledge, but in its requirement that I *do* something or reveal something on the basis of that knowledge.)' (Cavell, 1969: 237). It moves us beyond a purely epistemological (or intellectual) relation to others and towards an ethical relation, one that requires practical involvement – I must *do something*. If scepticism requires a human (and humane) response, rather than an intellectual or epistemological one, it is also true that scepticism itself is a human problem – a perennial 'threat, or temptation'.[19] It is a threat that arises out of a tendency to intellectualize one's relation to the world (or to others), and overcoming it might require 'crucifying the intellect' (298). When attempting to overcome scepticism, we must ask: 'how do we stop? How do we learn that what we need is not more knowledge but the willingness to forgo knowing?' (298). The (infinitely) circular logic of the liar paradox makes it difficult to stop: the 'recursive inbent spirals' Neal finds himself in as a result of conceiving of his fraudulence through this model are an example of an inability to stop.

Cavell develops his idea of 'acknowledgement' in an essay on *King Lear* titled 'The avoidance of love', in which he claims that 'there are no lengths to which we may not go in order to avoid being revealed, even to those we love and are loved by' (261). Neal's interpretation of his honesty with Dr Gustafson as an expression of fraudulence ensures that there is an inner part of Neal that Dr Gustafson cannot know – it ensures that Neal's outward behaviour is ultimately a bad guide to his interiority. This victory of concealment is also an intellectual victory. As Neal explains it, Dr Gustafson's 'insight' about Neal's honesty with regards to his fraudulence 'actually had as its larger, unspoken point the claim that he could discern things about my basic character that I myself could not see or interpret correctly' (Wallace, 2004: 154). The fact that Dr Gustafson's insight is 'not only obvious and superficial but also wrong' is, for Neal, 'depressing, much the way discovering that somebody is easy to manipulate is always a little depressing' (154–5). It proves that DrGustafson 'didn't have the mental firepower' to get Neal out of his 'trap' (155). Somewhat confusingly, Neal thinks that Dr Gustafson's point is both 'obvious' and 'wrong'. For Cavell, as for Wittgenstein, it is the idea that the obvious is necessarily superficial that leads to scepticism: overcoming scepticism requires rejecting sophistication in favour of an acceptance of the ordinary. None the less, from the standpoint of Neal's narrative (what we, as readers, have access to), Dr Gustafson *has* failed to grasp the complexity of Neal's problem.

Neal repeatedly uses the military metaphor of 'firepower' to denote intellectual ability and, more specifically, the capacity to analyse or deal with problems. In an early description of Dr Gustafson, Neal says that 'he did have a talent for putting you at ease, there was no question about it', before making it clear that 'I had no illusions that this was the same as having enough insight or firepower to find some way to really help me, though' (147). This distinction makes it clear that Neal values intellectual firepower over the interpersonal comfort of being put at ease – and that he sees only an intellectual path out of his problems.

During a period that Neal describes as 'pretty much the zenith of my career of my analysis' (166), Dr Gustafson does briefly provide

Neal with an analysis of his problem that he finds useful. The idea is that 'one of the worst things about the conception of competitive, achievement-oriented masculinity that America supposedly hardwired into its males was that it caused a more or less constant state of fear that made genuine love next to impossible' (164). Neal is temporarily convinced that 'the real root of my problem was not fraudulence but a basic inability to really love' (165) – until an episode of *Cheers* reveals to him that this problem is a cliché. Neal's response is then to double down on his sense of his intellectual superiority over Dr Gustafson: 'I was able to analyse his own psychological makeup so much more accurately than he could analyse mine' (169). Neal re-enters the intellectual arms race rather than admitting that his 'competitive achievement-oriented' attachment to intellectual superiority might be part of the problem.

An intellectual riddle

David Wallace shows himself to be wary of sceptical intellectual reasoning in a way that distinguishes him from Neal. By attempting to imagine Neal's story David Wallace is 'trying very consciously to prohibit' his awareness of the problem of other minds 'from mocking the attempt or sending the whole line of thought into the sort of inbent spiral that keeps you from ever getting anywhere' (181).[20] David Wallace is 'trying very consciously' to stop himself from embarking on the kind of reasoning that has confirmed Neal's sense of his separateness from others. Indeed, the story ends, in a moment that might seem like triumph, with David Wallace refusing to take up a sceptical line of thinking:

> (considerable time having passed since 1981, of course, and David Wallace having emerged from years of literally indescribable war against himself with quite a bit more firepower than he'd had at Aurora West), the realer, more enduring and sentimental part of him commanding that other part to be silent as if looking it levelly in the eye and saying, almost aloud, 'Not another word'. (181)

This seems like a victory for the 'realer, more enduring' part of David Wallace over the part that would allow sceptical thoughts to spiral away – the victory emphasized by David Wallace's command, 'not another word', successfully ending the story's stream of words. This is also an apparent victory for David Wallace in overcoming the problem of other minds by imagining 'what sort of pain or problems' led his former classmate to commit suicide: the preceding forty pages of the story are a testament to his having overcome this problem. Or are they?

In the short section of 'Good Old Neon' describing David Wallace's internal struggle, there are a several signs that David Wallace shares important personality traits with Neal. For example the use of the word 'firepower' to denote a concept of mental resilience or ability to deal with problems; a sense of the insufficiency of language to capture inner experience (in his reference to his 'literally indescribable inner war'); or his reference to 'inbent spirals' (Neal mentions 'inbent fractals') (181). If David Wallace has been attempting to imagine Neal's interiority, and if such an attempt must involve overcoming the problem of other minds – and the leap 'over the walls of self' that is required to write fiction – then the similarities between David Wallace and Neal spell trouble. Could it be that, instead of genuinely imagining another person's interiority, David Wallace has simply projected his own problems on to Neal, and therefore failed to overcome the problem of other minds?[21]

This idea has led Cory M. Hudson to argue that

> though the generally accepted reading of 'Good Old Neon' maintains that it is a metafictional experiment that illustrates a storyteller's ability to mediate a meaningful relationship between two people, perhaps it would be more correct to read the short story as an exhaustive attempt to demonstrate the impermeability of the bonds of consciousness. (Hudson, 2018: 304)

Here we have the two most obvious ways of making sense of the story's extradiegetic frame. One reading would see the story's conclusion as celebrating a successful attempt to overcome our privacy, while the other sees it as cementing a sense of our separateness from one another. Reading the story alongside Cavell's discussion of other-minds scepticism can help us to take both of these readings seriously. In his role as a sceptic, Neal is right: there are limitations to our ability to express our interiority (or to know another's interiority) – this is what Cavell calls the 'truth of skepticism'. Scepticism is a constant (fateful) human possibility; it is what can happen when we intellectualize our relation to others (or ourselves, or the world). Neal's narrative is an evocation of the truth of scepticism.

For Cavell the upshot of recognizing the 'truth of skepticism' is that it teaches us that overcoming human privacy requires human action.[22] David Wallace shares Neal's sense of the insufficiency of language to convey inner experience and also shares his temptation to entertain sceptical lines of reasoning; but, in 'trying very consciously' to avoid the kind of reasoning that torments Neal, he demonstrates a willingness to *do something* to overcome his own scepticism. However, if we view David Wallace as heroically confronting his scepticism, it is also true that the text itself can be seen to undermine this attempt with its suggestion of the paucity of David Wallace's imagination. The ending of 'Good Old Neon' presents the reader with a puzzle – not just the narratological puzzle of figuring out exactly who has been talking to whom but also something like a philosophical puzzle: what does the story's performative failure to overcome the problem of other minds tell us? I would like to close by considering a number of interpretative possibilities.

Firstly, we could take the view that the 'realer, more enduring and sentimental part' of David Wallace triumphs over the sceptical logic of Neal by issuing what Patrick Horn has called 'a moral rebuke at the end of the story' (Horn, 2014: 253). In this reading the story's closing words successfully shift from an epistemological to an ethical frame – and therefore allow Wallace to display, in Horn's words, 'the true empathy that he thought was impossible' (248). Similarly Lee Konstantinou has argued that the purpose of the story's ending is 'to cause the reader to experience a form of connection with the writer' (Konstantinou, 2012: 98). However, these readings appear to overlook the similarities between David Wallace and Neal that force us to question the true empathic potential of David Wallace.

In contrast to these 'naive' readings, we could take 'Hudson's view': the story tells us that the problem of other minds cannot be overcome. If we take this reading, then the story's way of delivering its message is cruel: you thought the problem was being overcome? Think again! Since the ending might, on first reading, seem triumphant, then the message of defeat that is revealed on further inspection has sharp, ironic talons. In this reading it is the story's literary form – its exploitation of a kind of metafictional glitch in its own structure

The problem of other minds in 'Good Old Neon'   233

– that allows it to collapse any positive philosophical move beyond Neal's sceptical logic. In this reading the literary form of Wallace's writing would act as destructive, sceptical force against the anti-sceptical philosophy it seems at times to endorse.[23]

The next reading comes from Jon Baskin: the story shows us an unhealthy way of thinking so that we can learn to avoid it; it therefore functions therapeutically and negatively – it shows us how not to think (Baskin, 2019).[24] But doesn't this reading flounder on the same issues that led to the Hudson view? Isn't the sceptic ultimately proved right? What basis do we have for reading this story against the grain of its own conclusion (just because that conclusion seems unpleasant, or even unhealthy)? These are legitimate concerns to raise against the Baskin view, but it is a surprisingly resilient position. It is possible to repeat the Baskin view at a higher level: the story's failure (the failure revealed in its extradiegetic frame) is an extra warning – it reinforces the danger of this way of thinking. In this reading the story becomes a strange sort of self-refuting thing, a warning against itself. This view has now come close to two other popular readings of Wallace: Clare Hayes-Brady's view that Wallace's texts perform their own failure (to productively 'keep the conversation going'), and the view that Wallace's texts 'dialogically' grant agency to the reader in interpreting and therefore fulfilling the meaning of the text (Hayes-Brady, 2016; Hering, 2016). If we combine these three readings, we arrive at something like this: the story performs its own failure in order to make the point that the cerebral world of writing and reading short stories is never one in which we can meaningfully overcome the problem of other minds, since, as Cavell explains, this would require that we *do* something – put down the book (put down cerebral things) and return to our life. Following this logic would lead us to the view that a story's role can only be negative; it can only show us 'how exhausting and solipsistic it is to be like this' (Wallace, 2004: 155). And yet, like an attempted resolution of a philosophical paradox, this reading feels unsatisfying. Could the only role of reading and writing stories really be just to point us towards their inadequacies? The paradox here is one that is also present in Wittgenstein's *Investigations* – a philosophical masterpiece that urges us to turn away from philosophy.

Viewing the story as a purely negative repudiation of literature's promise of empathetic connection is as unsatisfying as relapsing to a naive reading according to which it is the reader's role to 'acknowledge', in Cavell's sense, the characters of Neal and David Wallace. Whether the reader feels more inclined to one or the other of these opposing readings will depend on her own degree of scepticism. In this story Wallace uses literary presentation to show us the limitations and absurdities of a certain sceptical mode of thought; he then uses that very same literary form to provoke the reader's scepticism towards the ability of literature to overcome such scepticism. 'Good Old Neon' shows us both the dangers and the enticements of sceptical thinking. Tantalizingly, it leaves it to us to unpick the puzzle of its capitulation to these ways of thinking.

Notes

1 I will hereafter refer to the Wallace character as 'David Wallace'.
2 Aside from the appearance of this word, and Wallace's long-standing interest in Wittgenstein, I have no evidence that Wallace encountered *Wittgenstein and the Problem of Other Minds*. However, the phrase 'the hoary problem of other minds' is also quoted in the first paragraph of the book's introduction, so Wallace would only need to have opened this book to come across it (Morick, 1967: xiii).
3 Wittgenstein's importance for Wallace has been established as far back as the first in-depth study of Wallace (Boswell, 2003). Recently there has also been growing recognition of the importance of Cavell (Chodat, 2017; Baskin, 2019). Baskin claims that Wallace's fiction is therapeutic in the sense that Wittgenstein's philosophy is. There is much agreement between my reading and Baskin's. However, by focusing on Cavell's account of 'the truth of skepticism', I am better able to account for the strong constitutive role that scepticism plays in Wallace's fiction and for the tendency of his texts to undercut their own therapeutic messages.
4 'Wallace, one student remembers, interrupted the professor and asked him to "make himself intelligible please," a snarl on his face. Shortly afterward, he stopped going' (Max, 2012: 133).
5 For an analysis of how this essay helps to explain Wallace's broader interest in the space *between* philosophy and literature see Ryerson (2011).
6 The themes of mental and psychic pain are obviously a broad interest of Wallace's work and have received much attention. For another analysis of Wittgenstein's discussion of pain behaviour in relation to Wallace see Den Dulk (2015: 145–50).

The problem of other minds in 'Good Old Neon' 235

7   Cavell spends some time on this puzzling remark before stating that 'I understand Wittgenstein's teaching to be something like this: My references to my pain are exactly my expressions of pain itself; and my words refer to my pain just because, or to the extent, that they are (modified) expressions of it' (Cavell, 1979: 342).
8   Cavell calls the idea that nothing is going on inside another person 'more or less psychotic on the face of it' (1979: 335).
9   These kinds of sentences might be thought of as 'a priori', since they are statements that cannot be doubted or that we cannot imagine the opposite of, unlike empirical propositions (§251).
10 This project of drawing the limits to knowledge (or reason) goes back to Kant. As Cavell points out, 'both Wittgenstein and Heidegger continue, by reinterpreting, Kant's insight that the limitations of knowledge are not failures of it' (Cavell, 1979: 241).
11 As Lucas Thompson has pointed out, Tolstoy's *The Death of Ivan Ilyich* is an important intertext to the story. Having lacked self-knowledge during his life, Ivan Ilyich has a realisation about the fraudulence and emptiness of his life in a spiritual conversion on his death bed. Neal is like a reverse Ilyich, in the sense that he is too acutely aware of his fraudulence – Neal could be viewed as possessing too much self-knowledge (Thompson, 2017: 106-11).
12 '$(\forall x) ((Fx \rightarrow \sim (Lx)) \& (Lx \rightarrow \sim (Fx))) \& \sim ((\exists x) (\sim (Fx) \& \sim (Lx)))$' (Wallace, 2004: 164).
13 In an early draft of the story Wallace changed all uses of the word 'therapy' to 'analysis'. Neal's job was changed from 'creative director' to 'senior analyst'; it eventually became 'creative associate' (Wallace, container 24.2, HRC).
14 Neal's assertion that 'it didn't really work, although it did make everyone sound more aware of their own problems and added some useful vocabulary and concepts to the way we all had to talk to each other to fit in and sound a certain way' (Wallace, 2004: 142) can also be read as a comic description of the fate of the philosophical analysis of (philosophical) problems.
15 This is more of a double bind than a paradox. Later Neal describes the fact that 'high beams don't work in fog' since they only 'light up the fog so it seems even denser' as 'kind of a minor paradox', though this is really just irony (Wallace, 2004: 177). Neal's ascription of paradoxical status to such mundane and diverse occurrences reveals his tendency to understand the world in logical terms (and to fixate on things that are logically irresolvable).
16 An early draft contained a reference to Dr Gustafson catching Neal in 'a Cretan-liar style paradox' (Wallace, container 24.2, HRC).

17 Cavell calls this 'the truth of skepticism', and it holds for external-world scepticism as much as for other-minds scepticism: 'the human creature's basis in the world as a whole, its relation to the world as such, is not that of knowing, anyway not what we think of as knowing' (Cavell, 1979: 241).

18 'The world is to be *accepted*; as the presentness of other minds is not to be known, but acknowledged' (1969: 298, original italics).

19 'Wittgenstein's *Investigations* is not written – as it had in my experience uniformly been taken – as a refutation of skepticism (as if the problem of skepticism were expressed by a thesis) but as a response to what I have come to call the truth of skepticism (as if the problem of skepticism is expressed by its threat, or temptation, by our sense of groundlessness)' (Cavell, 1988: 5).

20 More precisely, he is trying to 'prohibit his awareness' of the fact 'that the cliché that you can't ever truly know what's going on inside somebody else is hoary and insipid'. But I take this to be his thrust.

21 The logic of this metafictional move compels us to ask the same question of Wallace the author of 'Good Old Neon'.

22 There is significant overlap here with the Buddhist themes that Christopher Kocela notes in the story. Kocela states that Wallace 'is skeptical about the possibility of overcoming solipsism through spiritual or intellectual insight alone'; instead, his fictions reinforce the claim that overcoming solipsism 'requires a sustained imaginative and compassionate engagement with the others in one's environment – an engagement he likens to the writing process itself' (Kocela, 2017: 62). However, it is the very question of whether 'the writing process' is an adequate tool for overcoming the problem of other minds that is thrown into doubt at the story's close.

23 Hudson's reading could be seen to mirror the structure of David Rando's argument that the 'ironic form' of Wallace's work 'can itself be viewed as a kind of lovelessness [which] complicates the common view of affect's place in Wallace's fiction' (Rando, 2013: 577). In both these readings, it is the formal qualities of Wallace's writing that serve to undercut their oft perceived affirmative message.

24 Baskin does not discuss this story specifically, but I think it can be profitably understood through his analysis of Wallace's work.

References

Baskin, J. (2019). *Ordinary Unhappiness: The Therapeutic Fiction of David Foster Wallace*. Stanford CA: Stanford University Press.

Boswell, M. (2003). *Understanding David Foster Wallace*. Columbia SC: University of South Carolina.
Cavell, S. (1969). *Must We Mean What We Say?* Cambridge MA: Cambridge University Press.
Cavell, S. (1979). *The Claim of Reason*. Oxford: Oxford University Press.
Cavell, S. (1988). *In Quest of the Ordinary: Line of Skepticism and Romanticism*. Chicago IL: University of Chicago Press.
Chihara, C. S. and J. A. Fodor. (1967). 'Operationalism and Ordinary Language: A Critique of Wittgenstein', 170–205. In Harold Morick, ed., *Wittgenstein and the Problem of Other Minds*. New York NY: McGraw-Hill.
Chodat, R. (2017). *The Matter of High Words: Naturalism, Normativity, and the Postwar Sage*. New York NY: Oxford University Press.
Den Dulk, A. (2015). *Existentialist Engagement in Wallace, Eggers and Foer: A Philosophical Analysis of Contemporary American Literature*. London and New York NY: Bloomsbury.
Hayes-Brady, C. (2016). *The Unspeakable Failures of David Foster Wallace: Language, Identity, and Resistance*. London and New York NY: Bloomsbury.
Hering, D. (2016). *David Foster Wallace: Fiction and Form*. London and New York NY: Bloomsbury.
Horn, P. (2014). 'Does Language Fail Us? Wallace's Struggle with Solipsism', 245–70. In Robert K. Bolger and Scott Korb, eds, *Gesturing Toward Reality: David Foster Wallace and Philosophy*. London and New York NY: Bloomsbury.
Hudson, C. M. (2018). 'David Foster Wallace Is Not Your Friend: The Fraudulence of Empathy in David Foster Wallace Studies and "Good Old Neon"', in *Critique* 59:3, 295–306.
Kocela, C. (2017). 'The Zen of "Good Old Neon": David Wallace, Alan Watts, and the Double-Bind of Selfhood', 57–72. In Beatrice Pire and Pierre-Louis Patoine, eds, *David Foster Wallace: Presences of the Other*. Brighton: Sussex Academic Press.
Konstantinou, L. (2012). 'No Bull', 83–112. In Samuel Cohen and Lee Konstantinou, eds, *The Legacy of David Foster Wallace*. Iowa IA: Iowa University Press.
Max, D. T. (2012). *Every Love Story Is a Ghost Story: A Life of David Foster Wallace*. London: Granta.
McCaffery, L. (2012). 'An Expanded Interview with David Foster Wallace', 21–57. In Stephen J. Burn, ed., *Conversations with David Foster Wallace*. Jackson MS: University of Mississippi Press.
Morick, H., ed. (1967). *Wittgenstein and the Problem of Other Minds*. New York NY: McGraw-Hill.

Rando, D. (2013). 'David Foster Wallace and Lovelessness', in *Twentieth Century Literature* 59:4, 575–95.

Ryerson, J. (2011). 'Introduction.' In David Foster Wallace, *Fate, Time, and Language: An Essay on Free Will*. New York NY: Columbia University Press.

Thompson, L. (2017). *Global Wallace*. London and New York NY: Bloomsbury.

Wallace, D. Foster. (2004). *Oblivion*. London: Abacus.

Wallace, D. Foster. (1998). *A Supposedly Fun Thing I'll Never Do Again: Essays and Arguments*. London: Abacus.

Wittgenstein, L. (2009). *Philosophical Investigations*, 4, ed. and trans. P. M. S. Hacker and Joachim Schulte. Oxford: Wiley-Blackwell.

Archival sources

Wallace, D. Foster (undated). 'Good Old Neon', *Handwritten drafts*, David Foster Wallace Papers, container 24.2, Harry Ransom Center, University of Texas (TX).

PART III

Embodiment, gender, and sexuality

11

'I am in here': David Foster Wallace and the body as object

Clare Hayes-Brady

There is no doubt that Wallace was a writer deeply embedded in questions of language. Text, voice, communication, narrative, dialogue, dialectic: these are words that dominate critical and casual discussions of Wallace's work. Numerous scholars, including myself, have written extensively about Wallace's immersion in language as the protean, troubled home of experience – an unsteady bridge between my world and yours. From dazzled first-time readers through seasoned reviewers to outright jaded academics, we return again and again to the fizzing sentences, Wallace's expansive, explosive search for the magic words to convey a truth about what it is to be a human being.

In this chapter I am interested in moving this discussion on to address how Wallace roots the rooting of all that linguistic experience in the body. Specifically I will explore the ways in which Wallace, I argue, uses embodied experience as a counterpoint to Derrida's interpretation of the metaphysics of presence. I will explore the ways in which our embodied experiences, as represented in Wallace's writing, shape and often foreclose our linguistic engagement with the world. Wallace's focus on the body under various kinds of duress, from labour to violence to manipulation, I think posits the fundamental antecedence of embodied experience as communication. I am not at all suggesting that Wallace did not consider human connection the ultimate goal – one would certainly have to ignore a fair quantity of evidence to the contrary to sustain that position – but it's interesting, and instructive, to consider the way Wallace approaches the thorny issue of the connection of mind and body in his fiction, since we know it occupied him at a philosophical level as well. The concept of connection – of reaching beyond solipsism, irony and alienation – are well-worn paths in the development of Wallace scholarship, and over the pages that follow I wish to expand and complicate these discussions by approaching the texts through the lens of affect theory, discussing how an understanding of affect theory can enrich existing understandings of Wallace's philosophical entanglement with the mind and the body. In discussing several representations of embodiment in Wallace's writing I will outline the textual representations of affect in both body and language and explain how I see these presentations as inflecting the philosophical engagement with language and communication that consistently animated his writing.

In recent years critical attention to Wallace's representation of the body has increased dramatically, with several theses and book-length projects devoted to the topic. Peter Sloane's 2019 book *David Foster Wallace and the Body* remains probably the widest-ranging consideration of the topic at a general level, while Jamie Redgate's exceptional *Wallace and I* from the same year focuses more explicitly on the above-mentioned dualism of self and others. Also relevant for the exploration offered in this chapter is Mary Shapiro's 2020 *Wallace's Dialects*, which considers language as a material phenomenon and greatly enriches existing discourses around language in Wallace's work, which have hitherto focused largely on the philosophical elements of language and communication – guided in part by Wallace's clear and sustained engagement with Wittgenstein and with various forms of the legacies of modal logic. While Shapiro's book is not explicitly engaged with the body as a mediator of experience, its material and social instantiation of language bears upon much of the same ground as my work here.

Affecting a self

Over the lifetime to date of Wallace scholarship there has been a sustained exploration of the connections between Wallace's writing about language and communication and the work of various philosophers, ranging from Nietzsche and Levinas to Taylor, Barthes, and Derrida. A consistent focus of these critical engagements, including my own work, has been on the means by which language as an intangible system constructs – and constricts – our experience and understanding of reality. This critical coverage dates back to the beginning of Wallace studies, including for example Lance Olsen's essay 'Termite Art, or Wallace's Wittgenstein', which appeared alongside the now-famous interview with Larry McCaffery in the Summer 1993 issue of the *Review of Contemporary Fiction*. Olsen, and numerous critics after him, positioned Wallace as a writer working in the wake of postmodernist pyrotechnics, searching amid the wreckage for the human connection he believed was possible even within the self-consciousness and trickery of experimental fiction. Olsen's essay is chiefly interested in the sincerity of Wallace's writing – the ends of the games he played – and is an important way point in the development of our critical imagination of Wallace as a writer whose dominant concern is sincerity. This image of Wallace, of course, has been greatly influenced by his propensity for directionalist writing, which endeavours – and succeeds, to a remarkable degree – to guide and shape its own reading (the McCaffery interview and publication of 'E Unibus Pluram', both clear examples of this directionalism, constitute, as Kelly has noted, a 'nexus' from which the dominant strains of Wallace criticism have largely grown).

I do not dispute the significance of sincerity as a theme, or the centrality of language as a philosophical and conceptual element of experience – quite the contrary – but it seems to me that there remains a gap in our reading of Wallace's world-building that is key both to interpreting the work and to accounting for its popularity, and which might in part be explained or explored by affect theory. Scholars have long noted the affective goals of Wallace's writing, but in general this affective work has been rendered as abstract, disembodied, or at least cerebral in nature. This tendency is shifting in recent criticism; besides the specifically focused critical works I've already mentioned, we might look to Ralph Clare's recent *Cambridge Companion to David Foster Wallace*, which offers a rich sense of the evolving critical landscape, where Matthew Mullins, for instance, engages explicitly with the 'affective, non-cognitive practices and desires' (Mullins, 2018: 196) that shape our experience, picking up on Clare's own introductory reference to an 'affective charge' (Clare, ed., 2018: 2) that he connects with Wallace's imagined heads that 'throb heartlike' (Wallace, 2012: 74). Clare's introduction, interestingly, is titled 'An Exquisite Corpus: Assembling a Wallace Without Organs', and in its first lines notes 'words lodge in guts; that they change them and are changed there' (Clare, ed., 2018: 1). The role within Wallace's work of the body and its responses thus seems to be coming to the fore organically, so to speak, as the body of critical work evolves and expands. But how might affect theory specifically be relevant to this work?

In terms of timing, affect theory is an attractive proposition for Wallace scholars, given the way its growth parallels Wallace's own career; we might see affect theory's challenge to the Derridean rejection of the extratextual mirrored in Wallace's self-described move away from 'univocal solutions' (McCaffery, 2012: 32) towards a body of work that seeks to eff the ineffable, as it were. Both emerging in the mid-1990s, it is tempting to see something of a parallel between the development of affect theory and the arc of Wallace's career as he grew ever more interested in how the embodied self operates in the world. Considering the body as a point of focus for Wallace, Sloane points out that its centrality is announced at both ends of Wallace's career: in the opening paragraph of *The Broom of the System* (1987) and the final paragraph of Michael Pietsch's 'sensitive edit of Wallace's simultaneously premature and overdue final "novel"' (Sloane, 2019: 1). In both cases the focus is on the body as social signifier: the (ugly) feet of pretty women in the former text, and the self-consciousness that comes with having a body at all in the latter.

This irreducibility of affect, the fact of being 'never in a state entirely free from feeling' (Wundt, 1897, qtd in Barrett and Bliss-Moreau, 2009: 169) – and the twin fundamentals of that state being *both* deeply embodied *and* deeply social – is a recognizable feature of the deeply embodied characters of Wallace's worlds, as well as of the experience of reading his work. Writing about feeling late in the nineteenth century, Wilhelm Wundt argued that 'internally-generated sensations were as important to mental life as externally-driven sensations, so that affect (what he called "simple feelings") and sensation were two sides of the same mental coin' (Wundt, 1897, qtd in Barrett and Bliss-Moreau, 2009: 169) – a line of argument that would become significant to the development of affect theory a century later. In other words, how we are affected by reading – what

Wallace called the 'feeling in the stomach which is why we read' (Miller, 2012: 61) – has as much to do with our reading experience as does our cognitive engagement. While affect theory encompasses a wide range of different perspectives, largely emerging from either a Massumian or a Sedgwickian backdrop, Eszter Timár notes that 'Despite their differences, both legacies rely on the idea of a live, organic body as their foundation as well as perhaps their telos; and both use in part the authority of biology as a science to ground their claims about the affective body' (Timár, 2019: 197). Massumi's foundational work takes affect as 'immediately embodied', which is to say existing coterminously with the experience of the body. For Sedgwick and Frank it is grounded similarly (to an extent) in the same live, organic body, though one of the primary points of departure for their essay is that 'Human language is assumed to offer the most productive, if not the only possible, model for understanding representation' (Sedgwick and Frank, 1995: 496). In other words, for Sedgwick and Frank, while affect may be immediate, its connection with the external world is mediated through language.

This seems closer to Wallace's connection of the mind and the body, with its persistent return to the idea of connection between selves – which in his writing is grounded in a largely pragmatic view of language as communicative exchange. As Redgate notes in *Wallace and I*, Wallace is deeply interested in how the mind mediates – and, more pertinently, then communicates – experience as an embodied organ, or an 'embrained, embodied mind' (Redgate, 2019: 22), 'rejecting the fantasy of the bodiless mind and the limitless narrator' (22). Indeed the two obvious narrative instances in his fiction where this disembodiment occurs are at the point of death – Lucien Antitoi in *Infinite Jest* (1996) and Neal in 'Good Old Neon' (collected in *Oblivion*, 2004) – and both are inflected by a kind of sublime terror, the glancing horror of the infinite scope of thought untethered from expression through the body-mind. Both the preconscious, or the wholly affective, and the supraconscious, or the wholly cognitive, then, entail a departure from the kind of connective communication Wallace's work is engaged in seeking, a dizzying freedom-from that is almost abyssal.

As is almost always the case with Wallace, *Infinite Jest* seems a good point of departure. The novel's opening phrase 'I am in here' (Wallace, 1996: 3) has been insightfully read as a response to the question 'Who's there?', asked at the opening of *Hamlet*. This connection, as Burn (2012) argues, positions *Infinite Jest* as specifically addressing questions of identity, instability, and presence. Building on that work, I would like to attend more closely to the novel's opening line. As a direct response to 'Who's there?', we might expect to hear 'I am here' (or indeed, more simply still, 'I am'); instead, we get the grammatically rather jarring 'I am *in* here' (emphasis added), which goes on to refer specifically to the heads and bodies of the others present.[1] This added preposition makes Hal's a physical response – locational, at one level – in here, in the room – but also existential – inside, in this space of articulation. By following this with the heads and bodies reference, Hal's self-identification poses the mind–body problem, further destabilizing the 'I' in question by positioning it as one among many objects. The passage's dismemberment of the Deans moreover positions them as also subject to the splitting of identity and bodily presentation – particularly the decontextualizing detail that Hal does not know which face is whose.

On the one hand, the intertextual relationship with *Hamlet* is immediately established by the phrase 'I am in here', and, on the other, the 'I' that is speaking is not the 'he' that is seen, which is to say that the linguistic and physical self are distinct and at odds (this is true of any first-person narrative but is stylized and highlighted here). As we see him at the beginning, Hal is a precise incarnation of Cartesian dualism: his mind is lively, eloquent, and controlled, while his body is described as barely animalistic, brutal, and awkward. All human life is here, in *Jest*: we think of Hal, the iteration of the mind–body problem; of Orin, the epitome of the athletic, hypersexual heteronormative male body (although it is still grotesque, incarnating the problematic extremes of success in these areas); of Mario, a rebuke to the neo-Platonic ideal of beauty as virtue per se; and of the body as an object of will among the ETA students and of appetite among the half-way-house addicts. In this constellation we can confidently place the tennis students and the addicts as Schopenhauerian opposites orbiting the centre of the novel – and, still further out, we see the body as an object of ostentatious display among the separatists and the ostentatious concealment that takes place among Joelle and UHID. Indeed the often-fraught relationship between the cognitive and the physical self seems to me to form a kind of metonymic or metaleptic relationship between private body and public speech. Specifically I am interested in investigating the degree to which Wallace's bodies-in-distress and the attendant physical difficulties communicating mirror the ways in which his cognitive selves struggle with the boundaries between thought and speech, interior and exterior, self and world.

This opening scene of *Jest* merits specific attention to certain elements in the scene for our purposes in this chapter. Taking Schopenhauer as a framing paradigm for thinking about suffering and the mind–body connection is useful.[2] In particular it is instructive to keep in mind Schopenhauer's insistence that the body is both agent *and* object: 'the body is an object among objects, and is conditioned by the laws of objects' (Schopenhauer, 1995: 21). I argue that this phrasing goes to the heart of Wallace's engagement with subjectivity, both physical and metaphysical; we frequently see characters whose whole arcs are a journey from self-absorption to balanced identity through recognition of themselves as also-always objects – here we might consider Lenore (in *The Broom of the System*) and Cusk (in *The Pale King*) in particular, but this is a recurrent motif. We also often find characters who fail in that journey – as Bombardini, in *Broom*, gives clear example.[3] The body acts as a mediator; it is an immediate object, in the sense that experiential sensation is unmediated – that is to say, we experience the world through our bodies – but also a space of negotiation and translation, of individual and social struggle.

This, perhaps, is why Hal offers such a fruitful example of this tension: he dramatizes both aspects, the individual and the social. In the first scene we see Hal's struggle with himself: the dissonance between his eloquent mind and his ungovernable, animal body; the anguish it causes him to be unable to express himself. We also see the social side of this struggle, the horror engendered in his interlocutors (or internonlocutors, more accurately), which is rendered greater precisely because, until he attempts to communicate with a smile (or mediate between his thoughts and the world), Hal looks like the Platonic ideal of a young man: a good-looking, well-presented young athlete; a paragon, but a statue. The impression dissolves when he moves. Cohen has described Hal as 'a soul trapped inside a body' (Cohen, 2012: 67); we might consider Hal in this moment as a sort of reversal of the Pygmalion myth, or even as a version of the Daphne myth – moving away from the marriage of physical and cognitive, enacting a horrifying separation of the self.

This dissonance is the primary thrust of the opening scene and the understandable focus of most critical work, but I would like to look more closely at the language of the body used throughout the scene, with two purposes in mind. Firstly, while the scene does foreground this dissonance, it is striking how very physical the action of the scene is. As I have mentioned, Hal's monologue carves up not only his own body but also the bodies of the other men in the room – heads, bodies, biceps, laps, and so forth – in such a way as to effectively disembody them, mirroring the discombobulation of Hal's own subjectivity. The foregrounding of the role of perception – of the body as object among objects – is especially significant here, balancing its focus on perception and dissonance with Hal's own meditations on perception (both his and others'). Having established his self-consciousness through the deliberateness of his decisions and actions throughout the scene, things devolve: 'The familiar panic at being misperceived is rising. I expend energy on remaining utterly silent in my chair, empty, my eyes two great pale zeros ... I would yield to the urge to bolt for the door ahead of them if I could know that bolting for the door is what the men in this room would see' (Wallace, 1996: 8). These lines highlight the social struggle to control the body; whereas the earlier lines mentioned above dramatize the individual exercise of will on the body, here we see the interaction of that exercise with other subjects and how the disjunction between physical intent and interpretation engenders not just misunderstanding but horror. So, in the context of public/private boundaries, here we see both Hal as a subject perceiving the Deans as fragmented objects and Hal as a subjective object, perceiving the Deans as a subject perceiving him as an object – and an object of horror, at that.

Redgate notes that the whole of *Infinite Jest* is 'governed ... by a pattern of physical containment and entrapment' (Redgate, 2019: 26), anticipating the 'tiny skull-sized kingdoms' Wallace would speak of with such horror almost a decade later in the commencement speech published as *This Is Water* (Wallace, 2009: 117). It seems to me that the disembodiment of the scene as a whole, and especially the dramatization of Hal's struggle as a physical one, in some way reflects the struggle to articulate felt experience, to step beyond the containment, the difficulty in connecting with another self – the challenge of which echoes in that phrase 'I cannot make myself understood' (Wallace, 1996: 10). Here the text presents the boundary between physical and cognitive action as mediated through voice – voice as a physical, embodied thing; an act rather than an attitude or style. Critical scholarship has a tendency to conflate language and voice, discussing an author's voice or use of voice, register, and so forth. Similarly, talking about embodiment, we tend to use the term 'embody' when what we mean is 'enact or reflect a motif or trait in a literary context'. But here Wallace returns us to the voice as always fundamentally physical, as the text literally embodies the fundamental challenge of connection that we also see him explore as a philosophical question. Moreover the challenge of articulation – the process of connection, of witness and return – is external to both the mind and the body, so it is the translation of thought into language, of experience into speech, that we see incarnated in the struggling bodies of Wallace's work. It is in the voice, very specifically, that we see the liminal spaces between interior and exterior, private and public, self and world. Shapiro points out – importantly, I think – that Wallace's preoccupation with communication is 'reflected in the number of characters who lose their voice, who speak words others have crafted for them, who think about and speak about and judge each other's ways of speaking, who speak but are not heard, and so on' (Shapiro, 2020: 4). In other words there are physical iterations of de-voicing in Wallace's writing that mirror the fundamental difficulties of communication as a philosophical question. This mirroring is typical of Wallace's tendency to radical literalism, whereby he renders absurdly literal the philosophical or ethical problems that his fiction works out – from Norman Bombardini as an incarnation of solipsism in *The Broom of the System* to *The Pale King*'s Shane Drinion, whose tendency to levitate depicts the epitome of concentration, or even *Infinite Jest*'s own Entertainment, the literal instantiation of deadening screen time. Imagining the voice and its many representations as another radical literalization of a question brings together the physical and metaphysical realities of speech as a bridge to the world. The voice is both an approximation of thought and a strong locus of affect; the quality of a voice adds layers of information to its content. Properly rendered, the voice tells us a great deal beyond words. In attempting to read Wallace's work through this lens of embodied voicing and affect, there is a connection to be made, I think, with the more obvious theoretical influences on Wallace's work, chiefly including the Rortian or neopragmatist angle of approach. Specifically, if Rortian thinking suggests that our articulation of experience is the only way we have of fully experiencing the world as social animals, Wallace seems to suggest that there is a prelinguistic experientiality that cannot be ignored; we can see this particularly in the *Oblivion* story 'Philosophy and the Mirror of Nature', which is perhaps the key text for a Rortian reading of Wallace.

I have written elsewhere (Hayes-Brady, 2016) about the fundamentally gendered violence Wallace enacts when he robs his female characters of voice, but here we see a more nuanced imagining of the physicality of communication. Hal's body is troubled, but it is (broadly speaking) the body of a cisgendered, heterosexual, athletic white male. Interestingly, however, Hal's self-image is curiously alienated from this identity both through racialization and gendering: he is described as 'the only extant Incandenza who looks in any way ethnic [due to Native American heritage]' and 'worrie[d] secretly that he looks half-feminine' (Wallace, 1996: 101). Prior to his disability, though, he was externally an amalgam of all the possible forms of embodied privilege, and for most of the novel we see him in this form. His body, therefore, inscribes the actions and experiences of the Western male body – an object that is for better or worse the normative version of itself in the world – until his 'something I ate'. Hal's physical trauma in the first scene is most likely self-originating rather than externally imposed, as trauma typically is with Wallace's non-normative (female, homosexual, non-white, disabled) characters.[4] It's worth noting that often – though not always, of course – this pattern repeats itself: while the traumas and bodily obstacles of white male characters are not specifically self-inflicted, they originate in at least the *illusion* of agency; while they are victims of circumstance and expectation, these characters are less inclined to be the objects of the individual agency of others. We see white men in the roles of wounded insurrectionists, addicts, self-loathing film directors, criminals, rapists, accountants, ascetics, suicides – agentic bodies, in other words. We do not typically see them as patients, rape victims, objects of art. Characters like Hal are – relatively speaking – as unfettered as a body can be, living in a society designed to cater to them. Yet, even within this context, the pursuit of embodied subjectivity is fraught, painful, and lonely.

The heteronormative and relatively able male body is a useful place to begin considering Wallace's complex engagement with the body as a distinct site of boundary-negotiation. Orin, the quintessential sexually attractive (though not handsome, really, and in fact rather grotesque in his extreme conditioning) athlete, like Hal, acts as a kind of rebuke to the Platonist idea of beauty as a reflection of truth, while Joelle's membership in the UHID reinforces suspicion of beauty as a virtue – a kind of antithetical mirror of Mario's virtuous ugliness. Thus no form of bodily existence comes without its difficulty. A brief outline of these other bodily forms would also include Joelle's and Mindy's hegemonic femininity; the many dysfunctional bodies (we might think of LaVache and the AFR veterans, of Drinion and his ungovernable levitation); the specific iterations of disembodiment we encounter in Hal, Gately, and the Wraith in *Infinite Jest*, and more broadly in Neal from 'Good Old Neon', the Granola Cruncher in 'B.I. #20', and in *The Pale King*'s Toni and projected ghosts; the body in extreme situations of distress and duress in the short fiction; and, recurrently, the body as an object of the attention of other gazes, be they human or technological. All of the experiences attendant upon these bodily forms demonstrate aspects of embodied subjectivity, of Schopenhauer's conception of the body as an object among objects, and, I think, the struggles faced by the individual self as it attempts to connect. We might usefully conceive of Wallace's ethics of embodiment in this Schopenhauerian vein, in terms of the roles of the body as both locus of subjectivity and focus of objectification.

Affecting an other

These non-normative bodies, I think, are some of the most interesting of Wallace's creations, particularly those which, as Shapiro put it, speak but are not heard. There are, in this respect, two figures of particular significance in – or rather *not* in – Wallace's writing: the Granola Cruncher from 'B.I. #20' and Q, the muted interviewer of the Brief Interviews. These two figures embody what I wish to draw attention to here on a larger scale. The Granola Cruncher, whose narrative is the centrepiece of the story, is both physically and metaphysically silenced in the text by the physicality of her rapist and, subsequently, by the male narrator of the story. Simultaneously, Q is silenced by the text itself: we see her speech but not its content, so she is not physically silenced in the way the Granola Cruncher is but rather textually muted and contextually read on to. In this respect Q is a precise textual mirror of the absent protagonist, whose body is violently constrained by an external force and thereafter subjected to the projections of her assailant's desires – specifically physical control and sexual release. Then, in the context of the narrative, the woman is constrained by her narrator, who erases her from the narrative, divests her of her name, and appropriates her experience – projecting his own vocabulary and interpretation on to it. Visually we might think of the Granola Cruncher as the central frame of the story, with the male interviewee framing that narrative at a first remove, and Q at a second. Q is the closest, then, to the reader: a silent, physical or textual stand-in for the woman, who is visually constrained into the terse Qs, periods, and ellipses that make up her textual presence and invite the reader to metaleptically take the place of both the assailant and the narrator in reading our desires on to her textual body – only to have that reading interrupted by the narrator's violent reappropriation of the narrative with that slide into what we might call violent textual assault that closes the story. Where with Hal we see the internal struggle between presentation and perception, thought and speech, with these characters we see three struggles over power – one physical, two textual – all centring on the external violation (as opposed to internal disruption) of a body. One interesting element of the texts is how the women respond to their constraints: the protagonist inverts the anticipated dynamic of physical struggle and ultimately (it is suggested) positions the rapist as the one without power, which leads to him (it is again implied) executing his desire for physical mastery on his own body by suicide. In the middle layer, the narrative that we hear, we find the speech of the woman who is silenced come to dominate the narrative of the man working to silence her, until finally the obtuse textual figures of Q – whatever they may represent – enrage him to the point of simple (though violent) incoherence.

This swing at the end of the story invites us to read the text as one fundamentally concerned with affect at all three levels of struggle: the Granola Cruncher's attunement to her rapist's affect, the developing rage of the narrator, and Q's own elided affect. In this vein it is important to note the affective rendering of the male voice throughout the narrative: the voice is highly stylized, using clearly coded language of contempt grounded in socio-economic and intellectual insecurity – 'As someone who worked himself through both college and two years of postgraduate school I have to confess to an almost blanket – these rich kids in torn jeans' (Wallace, 1999: 247, *sic*) – and then more specifically the idiom of male rage and violence – 'she was like some kind of smooth blank perfect piece of pseudo-art you want to buy so you can take it home and sm–' (248, *sic*). The interruptions here are two of several throughout the story, in each case resulting in a slight ratcheting up of irritation and aggression in tone that is met with a repeated iteration of the interviewee's purported awareness of Q's reception of his words, creating the vicious circle of self-conscious aggression that culminates in his final, violent tirade of misogyny. In parallel with the interviewee's loss of lexical control of the surface narrative, we see his fascination with the rapist at the heart of the narrative, and indeed Rachel Himmelheber explicitly ties the development of the narrative voice to rape culture, noting that he 'takes pains to align himself with the rapist and to point out ways in which their behavior is similarly predatory yet fundamentally different, as if his acknowledgment and subsequent rejection of a characterization guarantee sufficient evidence for the interviewer and the reader' (Himmelheber, 2014: 523). To Himmelheber's point I would add emphasis on the affective trajectory of the narrative, its movement from an apparently benevolent – though clearly sexually oriented – opening through developing aggression and pressure (the repeated offers of refills, the directive conversation, and the mock-combativeness that slides into genuine irritation as the protagonist's control of the conversation slips away) that then finally becomes a burst of profanity, and which mirrors the affective trajectory of the rapist himself from apparent benevolence (picking up a hitchhiker) through developing aggression (the woman's growing awareness of threat) to his response to her assuming control of the situation (violence that is both self- and other-directed). In other words, as I suggested earlier, we can read the interview as a metaleptic echo of the rape at its narrative centre, with the affective content of the voice – especially its interruptions – guiding this connection. In the end the loss of mastery in both cases is met with rage and violence, sexual and then textual. The Granola Cruncher's story, as we hear it, seems to offer a Massumian inflection: the prelinguistic, visceral immediacy of fear being the grounding affect, with much of the narrative developing through unspoken moments of cathexis. The interview, by contrast, offers a more clearly Sedgwickian focus: the alteration of the interviewee's affect from seduction to rage is legible most clearly in the increasing fragmentation of his language, the factor mediating between him and Q, and between the text and the reader. In this way, again, an affective reading of the text mirrors the layered struggle for mastery described by the text, with the reader metaleptically put in the masculine position of imposing desire.

While both layers of struggle result in the failure of the masculine desire for mastery, I would caution very strongly against reading this as a story of female empowerment or reversal of power struggle. A violent rape is no less a violent rape because the victim exhibits an unanticipated response; a verbal assault remains a verbal assault regardless of its cause, and the silencing we see in the narrative is still an exercise in patriarchal power, even if it does not quite come off. Still it is certainly interesting to observe the subversion of those dynamics simultaneously at play in that narrative. One of the things that keeps returning me to this story as in some way emblematic of Wallace's work in general is exactly this complex sense of a narrative unravelling itself from the inside, with feminine silence and the female body as the seeds of the text's deconstruction. I would suggest that the framing of the story, with the physical experience at its centre and textual iterations at progressive removes, enacts this struggle between private and public by foregrounding embodied experience as the primary locus of narrative; the experience of the body is always antecedent, always prior to communication, which is the only means by which experience can be shared and so contextualized outside of the shadow of solipsistic reflexivity. In this respect another way of reading the same set of framings is to suggest that the ethical foregrounding of corporeality or intercorporeality – the relationship of bodies to each other with which the text is concerned – acts as a direct challenge to Derrida's interrogation of the metaphysics of presence: it is a sort of literalization of the ineluctability of embodied experience that precedes linguistic expression and has meaning or significance – or effect, at least – that may in fact *be*, or function as, a form of textual outside. Here we may also find some tools in the work of Husserl, another figure in the constellation of influences on Wallace (we know that he read Husserl, but I am not aware of much critical work explicitly connecting them apart from Kozin's essay on 'Derivative Sport' (2017), which engages his work on elementality and the ludic body in dialogue with the wind). As Dermot Moran wrote recently, 'Husserl, Merleau-Ponty and the phenomenological tradition more generally, reject the classical, dualistic descriptions of human beings in terms of soul and body' (2017: 271). Indeed both Husserl's conception of the *touching-touched* and Merleau-Ponty's of the body as *sujet-objet* seem to furnish useful framing devices for approaching Wallace's depiction of the pretextual entrapment of the embodied subject, wherein the body, both touching and experiencing touch, is mirrored in the mediated experience of the linguistic or textual self – simultaneously endlessly establishing and reaching beyond its own boundaries.

The deliberate framing I have outlined of sexual or physical violation superimposed with textual violation means that the affective reading I am suggesting works alongside this more traditionally textual investigation to show how voice is, for Wallace, both embodied and disembodied, both intrinsic and open to appropriation. The shifting affects at work in the layers of the story, as a prelinguistic form of awareness (in the case of the Granola Cruncher), and as vocal communication (in the case of the interviewee, his increasing rage signalled by the interruptions that precede his final turn to violent profanity). While the interviewee's vocal development highlights the latter, the vital, embodied, prelinguistic affect of the story is visible through the woman whose story he has appropriated – in the Granola Cruncher's growing, physically coded awareness of her danger ('something about his aspect, eyes, the quote energy field in the car') (Wallace, 1999: 251). The danger is not coded verbally or even through behaviour as such, but through a kind of intuition, a precognitive physical response. Interestingly the interviewer again provides a connection between the interviewee's declamatory affect and the woman's subtle physical understanding; we witness her responses changing typographically, but not verbally, mirroring the subtlety of the Granola Cruncher's changing disposition, while the effect of this affect is refracted through the interviewee's growing hostility (as is the case with the Granola Cruncher's assailant). In

'Brief Interview #20', then, we see one full expansion of the process of affective abstraction, from experience through narration and witnessing to appropriation and recasting. The narrative evolves from being purely private (experiential) through being shared (with the narrator) to finally being abstracted away from its original locus altogether – at which point it becomes operative as pure text within a different, but also physically vocalized, power dynamic.

To conclude, then, it seems to me that both the opening scene of *Jest* and (perhaps more richly) 'B.I. #20' operate at the critical nexus of philosophy of communication and affect theory, inviting a new perspective on the standard question of the dynamic exchange between the body of text and the body as text. Here the embodied or pretextual body offers a bridge between the thinking of Schopenhauer and that of Wittgenstein (and later Rorty), all three of whom are obviously major figures in Wallace's work, while affect theory can help to ventilate the experience of reading through this bridge. There is, as I have briefly suggested, an argument to be made for reading this balance of body and text through a pragmatic lens, or more specifically a Rortian neo-pragmatic lens, if we consider this focus on the body as a pre-emptive strike of sorts *against* Rorty's dismissal of everything before textual exchange as (literally, I suppose) insignificant. On the whole, however, it seems that we cannot speak of the body's relationship with language and communication in Wallace's writing without engaging meaningfully with affect theory and the power of 'the quote energy field' in a text predating and shaping what we try to say. And so we come back to Hal's tentative opening reply, 'I am in here', finding in it both a declaration of Husserlian subject–objecthood and the cry of a voice trapped in a body, a text with no way out.

Notes

1 The text goes on 'Three faces have resolved into place above summer-weight sportscoats and half-Windsors ... . These are three Deans ... I do not know which face belongs to whom' (Wallace, 1996: 3).
2 Vermeule and Bennett have written extensively about Schopenhauer as a presence in Wallace's writing, most notably in *Gesturing Toward Reality: David Foster Wallace and Philosophy* (2014) – a useful starting point for considering Schopenhauer's general influence on Wallace's writing.

3 These three characters differ widely in their significance to the text, as do the results of their journeys into identity. Lenore's journey is largely grounded in narrative rather than embodiment – she moves from an understanding of herself as a character in a story to one of herself as the heroine of a story. Meanwhile Cusk's awareness of himself is all physical; indeed, the centrality of sweat to his self-awareness suggests the porousness of borders between the internal self and the external world. Bombardini opposes Cusk in that, where Cusk is preoccupied by the externalization of his bodily experience, Bombardini's focus is on internalizing the external world.
4 It is hinted in the text that that Hal may have been forced to watch 'The Entertainment,' which changes the dynamic here; however, even in that case, the trauma is absorbed rather than inflicted directly.

References

Barrett, L. F. and E. Bliss-Moreau. (2009). 'Affect as a Psychological Primitive', in *Advances in Experimental Social Psychology* 41, 167–218.

Bennett, A. (2014). 'Inside David Foster Wallace's Head: Attention, Loneliness, Suicide and the Other Side of Boredom', 69–84. In Robert K. Bolger and Scott Korb, eds, *Gesturing Toward Reality: David Foster Wallace and Philosophy*. London and New York NY: Bloomsbury.

Burn, S. J. (2012). *David Foster Wallace's Infinite Jest: A Reader's Guide*. London and New York NY: Bloomsbury.

Clare, R., ed. (2018). *The Cambridge Companion to David Foster Wallace*. Cambridge: Cambridge University Press.

Cohen, S. (2012). 'To Wish to Try to Sing to the Next Generation: *Infinite Jest*'s History', 59–79. In Samuel Cohen and Leo Konstantinou, eds, *The Legacy of David Foster Wallace*. Iowa City IA: University of Iowa Press.

Himmelheber, R. H. (2014). '"I Believed She Could Save Me": Rape Culture in David Foster Wallace's "Brief Interviews with Hideous Men #20"', in *Critique* 55, 522–35.

McCaffery, L. (2012). 'An Expanded Interview with David Foster Wallace', 21–57. In Stephen J. Burn, ed., *Conversations with David Foster Wallace*. Jackson MS: University Press of Mississippi.

Miller, L. (2012). 'Interview with David Foster Wallace', 58–65. In Stephen J. Burn, ed., *Conversations with David Foster Wallace*. Jackson MS: University Press of Mississippi.

Moran, D. (2017). 'Lived Body, Intersubjectivity, and Intercorporeality: The Body in Phenomenology', 269–310. In Luna Dolezal and Danielle

Petherbridge, eds, *Body/Self/Other: The Phenomenology of Social Encounters*. New York NY: SUNY Press.

Mullins, M. (2018). 'Wallace, Spirituality, and Religion', 190–204. In Ralph Clare, ed., *The Cambridge Companion to David Foster Wallace*. Cambridge: Cambridge University Press.

Olsen, L. (1993). 'Termite Art, or Wallace's Wittgenstein', in *Review of Contemporary Fiction* 13.2, 199–215.

Redgate, J. (2019). *Wallace and I: Cognition, Consciousness, and Dualism in David Foster Wallace's Fiction*. New York NY: Routledge.

Schopenhauer, A. (1995). *The World as Will and Idea*. London: Everyman.

Sedgwick, E. K. and A. Frank. (1995). 'Shame in the Cybernetic Fold: Reading Silvan Tomkins', in *Critical Inquiry* 21:2, 496–522.

Shapiro, M. (2020). *Wallace's Dialects*. London and New York NY: Bloomsbury.

Sloane, P. (2019). *David Foster Wallace and the Body*. London: Routledge.

Timár, E. (2019). 'The Body of Shame in Affect Theory and Deconstruction', in *Parallax*, 25:2, 197–211.

Vermeule, B. (2014). 'The Terrible Master: David Foster Wallace and the Suffering of Consciousness (with Guest Arthur Schopenhauer)', 103–20. In Robert K. Bolger and Scott Korb, eds, *Gesturing toward Reality: David Foster Wallace and Philosophy*. London and New York NY: Bloomsbury.

Wallace, D. Foster. (1996). *Infinite Jest*. London: Abacus.

Wallace, D. Foster. (1999). *Brief Interviews with Hideous Men*. London: Abacus.

Wallace, D. Foster. (2009). *This Is Water*. Boston, MA: Little, Brown.

Wallace, D. Foster. (2012). *Both Flesh and Not: Essays*. Boston MA: Little, Brown.

Wundt, W. (1998). *Outlines of Psychology*, trans. C. H. Judd. Bristol: Thoemmes Press (original work published 1897).

Internet sources

Kelly, A. (2010). 'David Foster Wallace: The Death of the Author and the Birth of a Discipline', *Irish Journal of American Studies* 2. http://ijas.iaas.ie/article-david-foster-wallace-the-death-of-the-author-and-the-birth-of-a-discipline/ (accessed 10 April 2021).

Kozin, A. (2017). 'On the Elementals and Their Qualities in David Foster Wallace's *Derivative Sport in Tornado Alley*', in *Palgrave Commun* 3, 18. https://doi.org/10.1057/s41599-017-0022-3 (accessed 24 March 2022).

12

'The interstices of her sense of something': David Foster Wallace, the quest for affect, and the future of gendered interactions

Mara Mattoscio

> Now it occurs to you that you could simply ask her. The reader. That you could poke your nose out of the mural hole that '6 isn't working as a Pop Quiz' and 'Here's another shot at it' etc. have already made and address the reader directly and ask her straight away whether she's feeling anything like what you feel.
>
> Wallace, 1999: 131

As Adam Kelly remarked in his opening lecture for the conference *David Foster Wallace between Philosophy and Literature*, held in Pescara, Italy, in 2018, little attention had been dedicated to David Foster Wallace's understanding and literary treatment of gender (or race) until the last few years. An increasing number of studies on these subjects, inaugurated by the seminal works by Clare Hayes-Brady (2016) and Mary Holland (2017), have by now managed to signal that these are no marginal aspects of the writer's production and reception.[1] On the contrary, the constitutive character of gender categories and their derivative dangers seem crucial to Wallace's understanding of the limits and the potential of human life. Given that this author was so committed to philosophy to have often been characterized as a philosopher in his own right (Den Dulk, 2015; Scarlato, 2020), such acute awareness of the violent nature of gender structures, and his formal and informal explorations of this in writing, should be addressed as an essential aspect of his intellectual system and as central to his convictions in respect to the fundamental truths and principles of living.

A key text in this regard is the short-story collection *Brief Interviews with Hideous Men*, Wallace's most explicit engagement with gendered and sexed relationships and one of his works that have proved most difficult for critics to fully decipher. This chapter proposes to read *Brief Interviews*, and particularly its central stories 'Datum Centurio' and 'Octet', as explorations of the socio-structural nature of affects, which reveal Wallace's concern with and philosophical attitude towards the violently gendered structure of society. I maintain that, in contrast to Lauren Berlant's notion of 'cruel optimism' – i.e., our attachment to 'fantasies of the good life that are no longer sustainable in the present' and that turn out to be 'an obstacle to [our] flourishing' (2011: 1) – Wallace's attitude in this book is one of 'wry pessimism', predicated on the need to explicitly point out our societal crisis and on the refusal to take for granted a linear idea of future progress. Through the following sections my analysis foregrounds *Brief Interviews*'s chasing of affect, both embodied and narrated, and its invitation to readers to 'invest' in their own structural affective inadequacies so as to begin tracking apparently irretrievable emotions down in the 'interstices' of our gender-constrained world.

Gender imbalances, writing anxieties, and *Brief Interviews with Hideous Men*

Much recent scholarship on gender in Wallace has highlighted the extent to which the writer's preoccupation with power imbalances and communication failures in gendered interactions was intertwined with his meditations on the limits and fallibility of language and the inescapable prison of selfhood. As Mary Holland first remarked, it is easy to trace in Wallace's fictional and non-fictional writing pressing 'anxieties about masculinity and its seemingly inherent tendency to co-opt, disempower, or manipulate the female other in the service of its own needs', as well as a preoccupation with 'the limited capacities for language to ameliorate those anxieties – and his anxieties about the ways in which he might be complicit in them' (Holland, 2017: 68). Wallace's 'complicity' in an inherently masculinist culture and his somehow ambiguous gendering of the act of writing itself have been partly explained by Clare Hayes-Brady as a tendency to treat gender and the body as an exploration of absolute alterity or of the 'inaccessible selfhood of the other' (Hayes-Brady, 2016: 191). From this perspective, Wallace's attitude is understood as generically dramatizing what he saw as the 'unbreachable distance between individuals' (191) and the consequent fear of solipsism that characterizes so much of his work. Even while producing feminist-oriented critiques of other writers' novels – as in 'The Empty Plenum' (1990) on David Markson's *Wittgenstein's Mistress* or in his (1998) famous essay on John Updike as the 'Great Male Narcissist' – Wallace seemed unable to avoid conceiving the problem of self-definition as 'fundamentally masculine, beyond the purview of women' (Holland, 2017: 67), who instead enter the frame merely as objects of knowledge for essentially male subjects. For Daniela Franca Joffe, Wallace thus paradoxically ended up 'simultaneously and wholeheartedly … affirm[ing] and reject[ing] feminist objections' to macho literature (2018: 167).

Brief Interviews with Hideous Men, Wallace's most explicit engagement with gendered interactions and sexed selfhood, has also been seen as one of his most earnest attempts at repairing the structural fractures in the intimate relationship between reader and writer that seemed so crucial – and so crucially gendered – in his literary endeavour. The fact that in this text the reader is always referred to as 'she' or 'her', whereas the writer is invariably characterized as male, points, according to Hayes-Brady, to Wallace's 'almost-pathological consciousness of gender politics' (2013: 132) and particularly to his awareness of the inherently gendered structure of intellectual authority in the Western philosophical tradition. And yet, while such consciousness has been seen by Joffe as a 'political response to the social and cultural climate in which he was writing' (2018, 164), the socio-structural implications of Wallace's attitude to gender in writing have not yet been fully explored. My contention in this chapter is that they can be illuminated through an examination of *Brief Interviews* based on feminist takes at affect theory, and in particular Laurent Berlant's meditations on a 'cruel optimism' that hinders individual and social advancement, especially for women. The collection's concern with the present and the future of gendered interactions thus unveils an aspect of Wallace's work which has often been overlooked by scholars.

Even if we heed Cory Hudson's (2017) warning not to take Wallace's mediatic *persona* necessarily at face value, it is no marginal point that Wallace himself publicly qualified *Brief Interviews* as a text trying to locate a doorway to 'affect', or true emotional connection. Describing it in a radio interview in 1999, the year it was published, Wallace stated that the book is centred on 'a certain kind of loneliness that is constituted out of situations that are supposed to be … about love' (Wallace, 1999). Next to the discourse of love and loneliness is Wallace's focus on the philosophical viability of honesty (in expressing emotions) against the constructedness of language, and what appear to be the affective and philosophical implications of this conundrum for both the individual and society at large. Considering the formal and thematic centrality of philosophy in Wallace's work, and the suggestion by several scholars that his writing might be taken as an autonomous philosophical discourse, such call for attention to affects and how to convey them in language clearly indicates an in-depth engagement with the mediated nature of emotions as a constitutive aspect of the present and a central concern of his universe of thought. Wallace's meditations in *Brief Interviews* on the social and trained qualities of affective life thus seem to qualify as a systematic elaboration of principles about the workings of current society.

In order to better illuminate such principles, this chapter turns to theories of affect and particularly to Berlant's notion of a 'cruel optimism', or the tendency to remain stubbornly attached to 'compromised conditions of possibility' (2011: 1) even though they hinder the subject's and/or society's chances of flourishing. In the wake of Berlant's meditations, I read *Brief Interviews* as an exploration of the socio-structural nature of affects: in particular I suggest that the collection can be seen as a narrative performance of what I term 'wry pessimism' – a pessimism that, in contrast to the common understanding of Wallace as obsessed with the individual's solipsism, seems to point to a relentless preoccupation with the social and the political, especially in his perception of gendered interactions. Central to this analysis is my examination of the multi-sectional piece 'Octet', which famously stages a writer's experience of impasse and fantasy of interrogating his female reader about the effectiveness of his efforts at communication, as well as of 'Datum Centurio'. The latter story has been surprisingly neglected in critical scholarship on Wallace and yet proves an intriguing attempt at the genre of speculative fiction that effectively advances the writer's warnings about gendered society at large.

The politics of affect

Brief Interviews gathers 23 pieces of various lengths, spanning from the 79 words of 'A Radically Condensed History of Postindustrial Life' to the convoluted 28 pages of 'The Depressed Person'. Roughly half of the narratives are made up of the eponymous interviews with 'hideous men', structured so as to give readers only the male interviewees' answers, without the female interviewer's questions; the rest of the book is made up of short stories of disparate structures and styles, varying from a realist tale of socio-emotional growth ('Forever Overhead') to vertiginously experimental pieces that mimic a writer's reworking of consecutive drafts ('Octet'). As has been often remarked (Smith, 2009; Holland, 2013; Williams, 2015), the collection shows a relentless concern for the rhetorical mediatedness and painfully constructed language that permeate everyday life. In his various public statements on the book, Wallace famously insisted on pointing out the tyranny inherent in such inescapable linguistic posturing. In a radio conversation with Michael Silverblatt he remarked that

> It's a time in America when we're intensely self-conscious in terms of our own presentation, and in terms of other people's analysis of us and the sophistication of that, and of our awareness of their awareness of our awareness that they're interpreting... and yeah, it can all get kind of climberish, but... it also seems to me to be very *sad*. (Silverblatt, 2000, emphasis added)

In contrast with such hyper-sophistication of interpretation and judgement in the social arena, Wallace's choice of the affectively charged adjective 'sad' signals his attempt to redirect attention towards emotions as a respite from rhetorical narration. His dispiriting analysis implies that the search for (and absolute need of) 'authentic' affect remain his biggest drives in writing. Thus, while warning against the dangers of our frantically self-conscious times, he goes on to articulate his 'great fantasy-wish' that, 'in complication and in layer-upon-layer of sort of excruciating-detail-jagged-into-psychological-mirrors-staring-at-each-other stuff, ... there's the possibility of great and profound emotional, and spiritual, and existential *affect*' (Wallace in Silverblatt, 2000, emphasis added).[2]

In affect studies, as Naomi Greyser reminds us, a crucial distinction is usually made between affect and emotion, with affect mostly regarded as 'embodied' and emotion as 'social and narrated' (Greyser, 2012: 86). While this is a 'slippery distinction' because of the porousness between 'bodily 'intensities' and social categories of feeling', Greyser rightly sees it as productive, because 'slips between the self and the social animate the field and are crucial to feminism's investment in complicating the public/private divide' (86). Interestingly, while Wallace wrote his *Brief Interviews* at a time when only a few of the foundational texts in affect studies had been published and the 'affective turn' in the humanities was still to come, he seemed to employ a similar distinction at several points in his collection. 'Forever Overhead', for example, is entirely predicated on the contrast between the adolescent protagonist's *embodied* experience of emotional growth – including the pain of his physical transformation and the emotional intensity of placing his growing body in proximity to the social body itself – and the *narrated* social experience of adults acknowledging his presence for the first time. 'The Depressed Person', on the other hand, re-enacts and literally reproduces the linguistic performances of distress of a woman suffering from depression, who proves unable to move beyond her solipsism despite being acutely aware of it. The narrated quality of her emotions, which exist entirely in her discursive rehearsal of them in front of her 'Support System', means that she cannot effectively clear space for 'affect attunement with others' (Frantzen, 2018: 262) and that, while we learn all the medications she takes and see the obsessive recursiveness of her mental takes on her emotional states, her embodied experience itself remains squarely out of frame. As Zadie Smith has remarked, however, unlike in most postmodern writers, Wallace's employment of linguistic recursion does not simply highlight the fact that the narrative is mediated – as if to say 'this is not neutral, it is being written, I am writing it, but who am I?' (Smith, 2009: 276). Rather, she writes,

> what's 'recursive' about Wallace's short stories is ... the way these stories *run*, like verbal versions of mathematical procedures, in which

at least one of the steps of the procedure involves rerunning the whole procedure. And it's *we* who run them. Wallace places us *inside* the process of recursion, and this is why reading him is so often emotionally and intellectually exhausting. (276)

Indeed, as draining and demanding as they can be, these recursive procedures rerun the thoughts and signs of emotional life of another person through the reader's mind. Smith is right in pointing out that the reader is thus not simply provided with a verbal *description* of the fictional subject's mental world but is rather put in a condition to '*feel it* and know it' (279, emphasis added).

'Datum Centurio': linguistic authorities, affective bias, and entrenched misogyny

The framework delineated so far is useful when turning to 'Datum Centurio', a 'story' written in the form of a list of encyclopaedic entries whose slippage between mathematical-style verbal procedures and subtle evocations of embodied and narrated feelings is central to the text's thematization of gendered interactions. Compared to other stories in *Brief Interviews*, 'Datum Centurio' has received surprisingly little attention from scholars so far, and yet, as we will see, seems to offer a contrapuntal (un)affective integration of the subsequent, more widely studied 'Octet'.

'Datum Centurio' is essentially a condensed dystopia set in a future in which all (hetero)sexual contacts, disciplined by highly advanced technologies, have been rigidly categorized as either strictly reproductive activity or merely pornographic pleasure for men. Despite its reduced size and apparently 'aseptic' narrative structure, the story manages to conjure up an entire world in which interactions between men and women are supposed to be totally impersonal. The piece is composed of encyclopaedic entries for the word 'date' from a futuristic dictionary whose copyright year is reported as 2096, and which is significantly titled *Leckie & Webster's Connotationally Gender-Specific Lexicon of Contemporary Usage* and includes 'Contextual, Etymological, Historical, Usage and Gender-Specific Connotational Notes' (Wallace, 2001: 106). The repetition of the term 'gender-specific' immediately alerts the reader to the social scenario with which Wallace's text is concerned. The paragraph in small type that constitutes the story's opening, and which provides the lexicon's copyright data, also strategically introduces readers to the evolution of digital technologies and text coding languages that has apparently taken place in the story's world, including the 'Hyperavailable Hot Text Keyed' format of the dictionary itself. Reading modalities seem to have evolved as well, since the *Lexicon* is available in 'All 5 Major Sense-Media' and its readers are encouraged to 'affix [a] neural plug' if they want to use the 'pentasensory illustrative support' that comes with the text.[3] The graphic layout of the story itself reproduces a fragment from the dictionary, listing supposedly objective explanations of two different meanings (as well as various sub-meanings) of the word 'date', integrated with (or interrupted by) a series of contextual and historical notes, including samples taken from 2096 everyday language and historiographical and sociological excursions into the word's evolution through time.

Crucially, the two main definitions of 'date' we are given characterize women as merely objects or tools for reproduction in a world designed around men's sexual needs. The first definition speaks of 'the process of voluntarily submitting *one*'s nucleotide configurations' (as if the grammatically neutral, non-marked subject should always be male) 'to an agency empowered by law to identify an optimal female neurogenetic *complement* for the purposes of Procreative Genital Interface' (106, emphasis added). The second meaning of 'date', mimicking the contemporary one referring to the *person* one is going to see, instead refers to a 'living female P.G.I.-*complement*'. In other words women here are so understood to be objects or tools ('complements') that they end up being indiscernible from the virtual sex toys called 'V.F.S.A.' ('Virtual Female Sexual Arrays') that have become men's companions in all cases that do not involve procreation. In fact V.F.S.A.s seem to be so central in this 2096 universe that, paradoxically, they are reported to be sometimes assigned proper names and personal characteristics by 'overwrought' men who are the 'users' or 'consumers' of such 'depersonalized simulacra of genital interface' (109). Through a long historical note on twentieth-century understandings of the word 'date', the *Lexicon* reproduces the stereotypical notion that, in the reader's extradiegetic present, women's expectations of heterosexual social engagements invariably coincide with establishing family-oriented, long-term relationships, whereas men instead aim solely at sex. It is by insisting on this misunderstanding that the dictionary explains the invention and commercial distribution of interactive pornography, which appears to have been legally approved by the futuristic state, so that in 2096 heterosexual encounters are either devoted to reproduction (under state control) or merely virtually re-enacted (by men only and with digital sex toys).[4] In other words, in this dystopian heteronormative universe, sexual gratification is possible only for males and exclusively through pornography and masturbation. Women, on the other hand, are so dehumanized as to be reduced to objects (in the entries describing the diegetic world of 2096) or cast as victims of men's fraudulent sexual intentions (in the depictions of our own extradiegetic present).

In the *Lexicon*'s mediation of our understanding of this dystopic world, references to (mostly male) human subjects are rare compared to mentions of impersonal, seemingly automatized agents, such as the 'agency empowered by law' that is supposed to match women and men willing to meet for reproduction purposes (106). Readers might thus expect this universe to unveil a total emotional void and entail a complete unreadability of affective states. And yet, as Lauren Berlant remarks, the key to our analysis is not to 'see what happens to aesthetically mediated *characters* as equivalent to what happens to people' but rather to 'see that in the affective *scenarios* of these works and discourses we can discern claims about the situation of contemporary life' (Berlant, 2011: 9). It is thus noteworthy that, starting from the initial list of 'technical information', Wallace manages to position his readers to 'physically *sense*' how their reading experience would be in this imaginary 2096. Not only are we given the idea of reading this lexicon through all five 'sense-media' but we are even made to visualize the bodily movement of 'affix[ing our] neural plug' in the 'pentasensory illustrative support' of the text. Though the borders between the 'human' and the 'machinic' body are clearly blurred, everything in the text points towards 'sensing' and the sensorium. Indeed a closer look at the language of the story suggests that Wallace's 2096 is in fact far from un-affective; rather, it is filled with negative affects that (re)produce a culture of entrenched misogyny on the national scale.

The language used in the encyclopaedia is scientific and pretentious, starting from the text's very title, 'Datum Centurio', whose literal translation from Latin ('organizing what is given into 100-soldier military formations') is likely less relevant than more popular phonetic associations with the words 'data', 'date', and 'century' – with the latter, etymologically deriving from the Latin 'centuria' and 'centum', also alluding to the fact that the story is set in one hundred years from the moment it was written. In an apparent mockery of scientific texts, the language is also replete with capitalized words later recurring as acronyms. For example, in the first paragraph, we meet the 'Procreative Genital Interface' (apparently, the 2096 definition of reproductive sex), which later becomes simply 'P.G.I.' (Wallace, 2001: 106). Even the examples of 'real usage' provided by the *Lexicon* sound stilted and annoyingly technical, as if automatically generated.[5] See for instance the first contextual note for the word 'date':

> date[3] 1.a USAGE/CONTEXTUAL NOTE: 'You are too old by far to be the type of man who checks his replicase levels before breakfast and has high-baud macros for places like Fruitful Union P.G.I. Coding or SoftSci Deoxyribonucleic Intercode Systems in his Mo.SyS deck, and yet here you are, parking the heads on your V.F.S.A. telediddler and checking your replicase levels and padding your gen-résumé like a randy freshman, preparing for what appears for all the world to be an attempt at a soft date' (*McInerney et seq. {via OmniLit TRF Matrix}*, 2068). (107)

Here the ironic rebuke directed at an older man apparently determined to seduce a hypothetical date is conveyed through such tech-savvy language that the reading experience becomes particularly taxing.[6] And yet the interpolation of colloquial expressions – such as 'yet here you are' or 'for all the world' – signals to readers that they should remain wary of the supposed objectivity of such linguistic authority. In fact, when the encyclopaedic idiom of the dictionary is integrated with lists of words in block letters meant to function as intertextual links or references to further entries, the presumed neutrality of these keywords is rendered ambiguous, as we get glimpses of a paternalistic or decidedly ideological attitude on the part of the editor. For example, after describing the allegedly conflicting views on social engagements of twentieth-century men and women, the *Lexicon* proposes the following intertextual references:

> (KEY at MISCODINGS, INTERGENDER; Secondary KEYS at Historical Notes for MISOGYNY, *OSTENSIBLE* PROJECTED FORMS OF; for VICTIMIZATION, CULTURE OF; for FEMINISM, *MALEVOLENT* SEPARATIST OF EARLY U.S. 21C; for SEXUAL REVOLUTION OF LATE 20C, *PATHETIC DELUSIONS OF*). (109, emphasis added)

As the choice of the adjectives 'ostensible', 'malevolent', and 'pathetic' demonstrates, the supposedly neutral voice of the dictionary editor(s) actually betrays a strong cultural bias against women and their political movements, as well as an obvious intention to ideologically orientate readers. The paragraph thus provides a narrative articulation of Wallace's later remark that

> issues of English usage are fundamentally and inescapably political, and that putatively disinterested linguistic authorities like dictionaries are always the product of certain ideologies, and that as authorities they are accountable to the same basic standards of sanity and honesty and fairness as our political authorities. (Wallace, 2005: 69)[7]

Most importantly, for this analysis, the strongly opinionated voice of the *Lexicon* editor(s) also conveys passive-aggressive and negative affects, in the form of contempt, hostility, and spitefulness. In other words, in conjuring up a world of human–machine entanglements, automatized sex, and fully institutionalized misogyny, Wallace implies that sexism and power abuse are never the automatic result of an *objective* status quo but rather always the product of ideological and affective bias. The fact that this bias and the associated negative affects are so normalized as to be considered 'general knowledge' for the *Lexicon* readers to acquire is further proof that affect is trained and socially- constructed.[8]

As Berlant remarked in her study of sentimentality, 'affective atmospheres are shared, not solitary, and … bodies are continuously busy judging their environments and responding to the atmospheres in which they find themselves' (Berlant, 2011: 15). In other words, despite how spontaneous and individual they might seem, affects are always situated or inextricably linked to political ideologies and social environments. For Berlant this social constructedness of affect is so crucial as to also provide an interpretative key for creative works: if our understanding of the present is strongly dependent on socially circulated and publicly filtered feelings, it follows that 'aesthetically mediated affective responses' can be said to 'exemplify a shared historical sense' (3). In this context, Wallace's literary portrayal of misogyny as culturally entrenched not only in the present world but also in its future projection speaks of a profoundly political, as well as historical, analysis. By presenting readers with a dystopic world that is, despite its technical coding, still affectively experienced and ideologically oriented towards misogyny, Wallace signals not only an acute awareness of the violence and gender imbalances of his own society but also a fundamental pessimism with respect to any hope of future progress. If we read this stance against the backdrop of that 'cruel optimism' Berlant warns us against – i.e., the stubborn attachment to unattainable 'fantasies of the good life' that hinder the subject's chances of well-being – we might maintain that Wallace's attitude in 'Datum Centurio' is one of '*wry* pessimism': a disillusioned yet ironic stance predicated, on one hand, on the need to consciously and explicitly stress the societal crisis in terms of gender and language and, on the other, on the refusal to take for granted a linear idea of future progress. The ingenious linguistic mechanisms by which Wallace reveals the fundamental biases of the cultural and political authorities of both the present and the hypothetical future are key to his pragmatic poetics that shows the violence at work by foregrounding the operation of language itself.

Embodied affect and interstitial meaning in 'Octet'

Wallace's fundamental pessimism about the communicative potential of inter-gender exchange seems further confirmed by the next story in the collection, 'Octet', which follows a very nervous male writer as he tries to accomplish what he calls 'a cycle of very short belletristic pieces'. Mid-way through this creative process, however, the protagonist/narrator ends up abandoning his unfinished project and textually addressing, instead, his unmistakably female reader. As several scholars have pointed out (Holland, 2013; Williams, 2015; Kelly, 2018), this gender dynamic is complicated by the fact that, when the writer deviates from work on his 'pop quizzes' and embarks on metafictional reflection, the neutral third-person narrative voice of the first pages gives way to a more intimate second-person narration. This you-voice at first seems to directly address the writer himself, as we elicit from the first lines of this section: 'You are, unfortunately, a fiction writer. You are attempting a cycle of very short belletristic pieces, pieces which as it happens are not *contes philosophiques* and not vignettes or scenarios or allegories or fables, exactly, though neither are they really qualifiable as "short stories"' (Wallace, 1999: 123). However, later in the story the reader is somehow gradually drawn through this second person into the position of the writer addressing himself. Indeed, towards the end of the piece, after an incredibly self-conscious and yet desperate self-debate, the narrative voice declares feeling

> more like a reader ... down here quivering in the mud of the trench with the rest of us, instead of a *Writer*, whom we imagine to be clean and dry and radiant of command presence and unwavering conviction as he coordinates the whole campaign from back at some gleaming abstract Olympian HQ. (136)

The 'us'/'we' now seemingly includes the narrative voice itself and is thus differentiated from the initial 'you' of the fiction writer, though the narratorial – and thus epistemological – positions keep changing throughout the story. In other words, both the reading process and the instability of the narrative voice have the effect of somehow conflating reader and writer, and thus female and male consciousness, into the same performative space.

The meaning of writing – and more precisely the sense of the specific pieces this writer is trying to craft – is apparently 'hard to describe', but it seems to him akin to 'a certain sort of "*interrogation*" of the person reading them, somehow – i.e. palpations, feelers into the interstices of her sense of something, etc.' (123). Using a language that seems to claim a position of superiority for the writer over the reader (since, if taken literally, interrogations, palpations, and feelers are all instances of exerting control over somebody or something, in a judicial, medical, or general way), the narrative voice here betrays the manipulative attitude that Wallace seems to ascribe to both men and writers. However, insisting on the gaps (the 'interstices') of the reader's unknown reactions, the narrator puts the reader's consciousness centre stage, in a gesture that seemingly calls for her active participation in the production of meaning. As Hayes-Brady has noted, for Wallace Self and Other – the two poles of a communicative process – are never purely oppositional but rather 'interdependent and mutually defining' (Hayes-Brady, 2016: 104), and the material conditions for communication are never sufficient if they are not accompanied by an act of will on both ends. In other words, what the fictional writer of 'Octet' seems to be enacting through his 'interrogation' is Wallace's aspiration to 'encourage the reader to choose to be engaged' (105).

Most importantly, the choice of words such as 'palpations' and 'feelers' (and to a certain extent 'interrogation' with regard to the auditory field), as well as the 'quivering' of the reader 'down here ... in the mud of the trench', all signal Wallace's attempt to characterize both reader's and writer's understanding of the text as something which is physically *felt* before it is known. The search for a meaning that reader and writer share seems to be embodied and affectively structured by their respective frustrations and tentative movements. As the narrator himself explains, in fact, a *textually* mediated address to the reader 'runs the risk of compromising the queer *urgency* about whatever it is you feel you want the pieces to interrogate in whoever's reading them' (Wallace, 1999: 124). In other words, overt exposure of the fictionality of the text would make the reader question the authenticity of the fiction writer's communication, in a perpetual contradiction between self-conscious sophistication and genuine attempts at connection that the narrator seems to find despairing but apparently cannot avoid. The 'return to the scene of fantasy that enables you to expect that *this* time, nearness to this thing will help you or a world to become different in just the right way' is what Berlant identifies as the affective structure of an optimistic attachment, one that is 'cruel' in so far as it is not sustainable for the desiring subject (Berlant, 2011: 2). In this sense Wallace's 'Octet' seems related to an affective fantasy of 'authentic' exchange with the reader, in which, to use Berlant's words, 'the very pleasures of being inside a relation have become sustaining regardless of the content of the relation' (2).

And yet the fictional writer of the piece seems well aware of the affective costs of his loops. His surviving unfinished 'pop quizzes'

> all seem to be trying to demonstrate some sort of weird ambient *sameness* in different kinds of human relationships, some nameless but inescapable 'price' that all human beings are faced with having to pay at some point if they ever want truly 'to be with' another person instead of just using that person somehow. (Wallace, 1999: 131–2)

In other words the melancholic homogeneity that appears to link all human relationships proves to be an affective *structure* of social life that, in being 'shared, not solitary' (Berlant, 2011: 15), speaks to the corporeal, intimate, and political dimensions all at the same time. This 'ambient *sameness*' evokes an affective atmosphere that is fully social in dimension and implications and, through its patterning, constitutes what Berlant would call a 'theory-in-practice of how a world works' (16).

The 'weird univocal urgency' repeatedly evoked by the fiction writer has been seen by Adam Kelly as a potential reiteration of the tendency in traditional Western philosophy to reduce female difference to conformity with the phallocentric principle of identity. At the same time, since 'the question of sameness is being put by a male writer to a female reader, *as a question*', Kelly maintains that 'Octet' expresses a desire to place decisions over language firmly in the hands of women, with *Brief Interviews* as a whole qualifying as a 'potentially feminist text' (Kelly, 2018: 92). Yet since it is not possible to determine who will have the decisive power over this issue (given the referential ambiguity of the 'you' in the final 'So, decide' that brings the story to a close), this analysis seeks to redirect attention to the affective intensities determining the impact of the piece. It is worth noting that, while the 'sameness' is 'overwhelming and elemental' but its nature is never exactly determined ('the same question – whatever that question exactly is'), the fiction writer feels it is 'urgent, truly urgent, something almost worth shimmying up chimneys and shouting from roofs about' (Wallace, 2001: 132). Here the sheer urgency of the undetermined revelation of sameness is embodied in the physical movements of shaking and shouting, which are moreover both articulated in the social spaces of chimneys and roofs. In other words, whatever makes all human relationships similar, it is the affective tension of communicating it that potentially saturates the social atmosphere in a palpable and audible way.

Wallace's pragmatic poetics, which comments on the present by exposing its inner mechanisms (his 'theory-in-practice of how a world works'), is in fact most apparent in the narrator's attitude towards language. In 'Octet' most attempts to locate the meaning of the pop quizzes are semantically related to *interstices*, *gaps*, or spaces *in between* the pieces, as if suggesting that sense is created and conveyed most easily in the pauses in language, rather than in crafted expression.[9] Resembling the muddy 'trench' in which the community of readers feels itself to be in opposition to the writer, these interstices are the most common affective infrastructures of the ordinary and appear to materialize Wallace's view of the present as structured by a cultural and political impasse, rather than by movement towards any future. Again the writer's disillusioned yet ironic attitude towards the possibilities of 'authentic' contact between genders is one of 'wry pessimism', by which the violence produced by fixed gender hierarchies is denounced and yet no future improvement seems to be in sight. Wallace's humorous exposure of the mechanisms of creative writing and of the writer's own mental processes constitutes a sort of philosophical 'theory-in-practice' of the linguistic and political impasse the story identifies as structural to our affective life.

As mentioned earlier, Wallace's chase after sincere affect in *Brief Interviews* is particularly relevant when considering the collection's temporal frame. Written in the late 1990s, this work in fact anticipates some of the philosophical concerns and political implications of affect studies, premised as they are on the analysis of emotions and their operations at the juncture of the private and public realms. *Brief Interviews* even seems to somehow foresee the 'affective turn' that reshaped feminist scholarship in the 2000s, after foundational works by Berlant and Ann Cvetkovich urged reflection on the epistemic reach and limitations of a (feminist) politics of emotions, especially at the scale of the nation. One of the merits of *Brief Interviews* is to underscore how not only narrated emotions but also embodied affects are always situated and socially trained. In this way the collection emphasizes the collective responsibilities and complicities in both the current state of violent hierarchies and the practical or political impasse that seems to obstruct future improvements. In revealing a more conscious awareness of the structural dynamics of society than is usually ascribed to Wallace, an affective reading of the stories under examination also contributes to reinterpret Wallace's literary practice as a pragmatic philosophy centred on unveiling the mechanisms of communication and aligning the consciousnesses of readers and writer through the performative recursiveness of the latter's mental processes.

Notes

1 This is especially true if one considers such aspects in the context of the #metoo and #timesup movements and in the wake of the renewed debate

'The interstices of her sense of something'   275

regarding the contemporary engagements with race and gender by white male authors that these recent trends have stimulated. As David Hering (2018) remarks, the alarm raised by some commentators regarding the frequent chauvinism and sexism of Wallace's male readers has dovetailed with the accusations of Wallace's own misogyny raised by critics such as Jonathan McAloon (2017) and Deirdre Coyle (2017). Amy Hungerford, in particular, is noted for having made the case for 'not reading David Foster Wallace' altogether (2016), on the basis of worrying details found in the writer's biography and of the ambiguous constructedness of the contemporary literary market.

2   Statements such as these, seen in the context of Wallace's literary corpus, have in fact been instrumental in the scholarly tendency to read Wallace as champion of a 'New Sincerity' in contemporary American literature (Kelly, 2010).

3   The apparent blurring of the human–machine borders implied by words such as 'sense-media' has been linked by Hayes-Brady to Wallace's intimate fear of finding himself 'just a 98.6° calculating machine', unable, despite his erudition and mastery of language, to connect with a larger human community (Hayes-Brady, 2016: 152).

4   The idea of virtual pornography has been seen by Chiara Scarlato as central to Wallace's later production. In her examination of *Sir John Feelgood*, the unpublished draft novel on pornography that formed the basis for his later *The Pale King*, Scarlato finds that sex morphs into a voyeuristic practice in which the material body is replaced by its virtual representation, bypassing the imperfections of a *real* female partner while preserving the fascinating image of sex itself (Scarlato, 2020: 169).

5   This choice is particularly apparent if one compares Wallace's microdystopia with earlier American speculative fiction concerned with gender and sexual relations, such as Philip Dick's *Do Androids Dream of Electric Sheep?* (1968) or Margaret Atwood's *The Handmaid's Tale* (1985), where (ambivalent) notions of human empathy and desire remain the driving forces. In Dick's novel the ambiguous borders between humans and androids are particularly relevant to (heterosexual) sex and romance. Yet, though the story is set in a futuristic 2019 with private flying vehicles, individual 'mood modulators', and 'empathy boxes' for praying, these technological references are blended into everyday language in a way that makes dystopic and realistic features of the plot blur into one another. Even more strikingly, in Atwood's *The Handmaid's Tale*, arguably the most famous speculative-fiction narrative centred on gender relations, the story's temporal setting references a near future in which, according to the author, nothing happens 'that human beings had not already done in some other place or time, or for which the technology did not already

exist' (Atwood, 2018). The technological innovations in the novel, all clearly predictable at the time of writing, do not perform a central role in the institutionalized power abuses suffered by women in the dystopic universe of Gilead.

6 Zadie Smith defended Wallace's parodic engagement of advanced technology as a case of extreme 'realism', or the refusal to ignore the mutual entrenchment and irreversible coexistence of the human and the technological. She writes of 'Datum Centurio' that 'using extreme specialization to create little worlds was another, far more complicated way of saying THIS IS WATER, of reminding us that wherever we have language, we have the artificial conditions, limits and possibilities of our existence' (Smith, 2009: 288).

7 The essay containing this quotation, 'Authority and American Usage', is entirely devoted to analysing the ideological orientation and need for accountability of linguistic authorities, including dictionaries and other language repositories. It is no coincidence that, similarly to what happens in 'Datum Centurio', the cover page of this essay is also designed to graphically reproduce a standard dictionary page.

8 In Wallace's literary universe such excerpts would have dangerous effects, for example on *Infinite Jest*'s protagonist Hal Incandenza, who is reported to have the habit of memorizing entire pages of the *Oxford English Dictionary* (Wallace, 2007).

9 Gaps also both graphically and narratively structure the eponymous interviews with hideous men, which, despite being conducted by a woman, only report the male interviewees' answers, while signalling the presence of a question merely through a journalistic capital Q. In reference to the interviewer Wallace stated that he 'was far more interested in the interlocutor than in the people who are speaking', i.e. the 'hideous men', and that he 'heard these guys through the sensibility of a particular kind of woman who was very real to me but then didn't exist', so that in the book 'she is defined almost exclusively through what she, in her transcription process, allows men to direct toward her' (Silverblatt, 2000).

References

Atwood, M. (1985). *The Handmaid's Tale*. Toronto: McClelland and Stewart.
Berlant, L. (2011). *Cruel Optimism*. Durham NC and London: Duke University Press.
Den Dulk, A. (2015). *Existentialist Engagement in Wallace, Eggers and Foer. A Philosophical Analysis of Contemporary American Literature*. London and New York NY: Bloomsbury.

Dick, P. (1968). *Do Androids Dream of Electric Sheep?* New York NY: Doubleday.

Frantzen, M. K. (2018). 'Finding the Unlovable Object Lovable: Empathy and Depression in David Foster Wallace', in *Studies in American Fiction* 45:2, 259–79.

Greyser, N. (2012). 'Beyond the "Feeling Woman": Feminist Implications of Affect Studies', *Feminist Studies* 38:1, 84–112.

Hayes-Brady, C. (2013). '"…": Language, Gender, and Modes of Power in the Work of David Foster Wallace', 131–50. In Marshall Boswell and Stephen J. Burn, eds, *A Companion to David Foster Wallace Studies*. New York NY: Palgrave Macmillan.

Hayes-Brady, C. (2016). *The Unspeakable Failures of David Foster Wallace. Language, Identity, and Resistance.* London and New York NY: Bloomsbury.

Holland, M. K. (2013). 'Mediated Immediacy in *Brief Interviews with Hideous Men*', 107–30. In Marshall Boswell and Stephen J. Burn, eds, *A Companion to David Foster Wallace Studies*. New York NY: Palgrave Macmillan.

Holland, M. K. (2017). '"By Hirsute Author": Gender and Communication in the Work and Study of David Foster Wallace' in *Critique* 58:1, 64–77.

Hudson, C. M. (2018). 'David Foster Wallace Is Not Your Friend. The Fraudulence of Empathy in David Foster Wallace Studies and "Good Old Neon"', in *Critique* 295–306.

Hungerford, A. (2016). *Making Literature Now*. Stanford CA: Stanford University Press.

Joffe, D. F. (2018). 'No Man's Land: David Foster Wallace and Feminist America', in *The Journal of David Foster Wallace Studies* 1:1, 151–84.

Kelly, A. (2010). 'David Foster Wallace and the New Sincerity in American Fiction', 131–46. In David Hering, ed., *Consider David Foster Wallace: Critical Essays*. Los Angeles CA: Sideshow Media Group Press.

Kelly, A. (2018). '*Brief Interviews with Hideous Men*', 82–96. In Ralph Clare, ed., *The Cambridge Companion to David Foster Wallace*. Cambridge: Cambridge University Press.

Scarlato, C. (2020). *Attraverso il corpo: Filosofia e letteratura in David Foster Wallace*. Milan: Mimesis.

Silverblatt, M. (2000). *Brief Interviews with Hideous Men (2)*, KCRW podcast (audio episode of *Bookworm*).

Smith, Z. (2009). *Changing My Mind: Occasional Essays*. London: Penguin.

Wallace, D. Foster. (1990). 'The Empty Plenum: David Markson's *Wittgenstein's Mistress*', 243–75. In David Markson, *Wittgenstein's Mistress*. Champaign IL: Dalkey Archive Press.

Wallace, D. Foster. (2001). *Brief Interviews with Hideous Men*. London: Abacus.
Wallace, D. Foster. (2005). 'Authority and American Usage', 66–127. In Wallace, *Consider the Lobster and Other Essays*. Boston MA: Little, Brown.
Wallace, D. Foster. (2007). *Infinite Jest*. London: Abacus.
Williams, I. (2015). '(New) Sincerity in David Foster Wallace's "Octet"', in *Critique* 56:3, 299–314.

Archival sources

Atwood, M. (2018). 'Margaret Atwood on How She Came to Write *The Handmaid's Tale*. The Origin Story of an Iconic Novel', in *Literary Hub*. https://lithub.com/margaret-atwood-on-how-she-came-to-write-the-handmaids-tale/ (accessed 20 March 2020).

Internet sources

Coyle, D. (2017). 'Men Recommend David Foster Wallace to Me. Late to the Party: Reading *Brief Interviews with Hideous Men* for the First Time', in *Electric Lit*. https://electricliterature.com/men-recommend-david-foster-wallace-to-me/ (accessed 30 March 2020).
Hering, D. (2018). 'Thinking about David Foster Wallace, Misogyny and Scholarship', in *Literary Studies*. http://bloomsburyliterarystudiesblog.com/continuum-literary-studie/2018/02/thinking-david-foster-wallace-misogyny-scholarship.html (accessed 30 March 2020).
McAloon, J. (2017). 'Can Male Writers Avoid Misogyny?', in *The Guardian*. www.theguardian.com/books/booksblog/2017/may/04/can-male-writers-avoid-misogyny (accessed 30 March 2020).
Wallace, D. Foster. (1999). 'Brief Interviews Radio Interview', *The David Foster Wallace Audio Project*. www.dfwaudioproject.org/wp-content/uploads/interviews-profiles/Brief-Interviews-Radio-Interview.mp3 (accessed 20 March 2020).

13

'You are loved': race, love, and language in early Wallace

Lola Boorman

It might seem an understatement to say that David Foster Wallace's work has 'something to do with love' (McCaffery, 2012: 50). In his interview with McCaffery in 1993 Wallace placed love at the centre of his aesthetic mission, claiming that true art is about 'having the discipline to talk out of the part of yourself that can love instead of the part that just wants to be loved' (148). In Wallace's writing and his political and social philosophy, love is irrevocably bound up with the problem of communication, with, as Clare Hayes-Brady argues, the 'simultaneous renunciation and reinforcement of the boundaried self' (Hayes-Brady, 2016: 95). Taking a slightly different view, Daniel P. Rando suggests that Wallace's oeuvre is more preoccupied with the 'horror of lovelessness' (Rando, 2013: 579) than it is with exploring any viable manifestations of love as an interpersonal and civic concept. Wherever the critical emphasis is placed – on the giving of love or on its absence – Rando, Hayes-Brady, and others are united in diagnosing a discordance between Wallace's philosophy of love and his tendency to represent sex and sexuality as violent and dysfunctional, most notably and controversially in *Brief Interviews with Hideous Men* (1999). While Wallace's fictional explorations of love have been important for working through Wallace's troubling relationship to women and gender (in his biography as well as his writing) critics have tended to overlook how race shapes the exploration of love in his early work, most notably in *Girl with Curious Hair* (1989) and his co-authored essay *Signifying Rappers* (1990). In these texts racial difference presents a destabilizing challenge to communication on both an interpersonal and a political level. Nevertheless, these encounters with difference are essential to what Hayes-Brady calls 'the paradox of distance' (Hayes-Brady, 2016: 97) which lies at the heart of Wallace's philosophy of communication.

In these early works Wallace negotiates the unstable boundaries between private and public acts of love, where individual and cultural difference are sacrificed for a wider political vision that privileges communication and consensus. Race becomes, in both *Girl with Curious Hair* and *Signifying Rappers*, a crucial way of working through and understanding 'distance' as a political and ethical concept. Recentring our understanding of Wallace's early work as profoundly engaged with questions of racial difference sheds light on his faith in unfashionable models of consensus and universality that characterise his later writing, most explicitly in his essay 'Authority and American Usage' (2001), where he makes a case for Standard English as a viable solution for America's cultural and political fracture. In an oft-cited and uncomfortable passage in the essay Wallace explains at length his rejection of a black student's use of 'Standard Black English (SBE)' and his insistence that she/he embrace 'Standard Written English (SWE)', which Wallace admits 'we might as well call "Standard White English"' (Wallace, 2005: 109). The sublimation of cultural difference in order to achieve consensus is, for Wallace, a necessary act of love, as the essay's epigraph proclaims, '*Dilige et quod vis fac*': love and do what you will. It is clear that love and race are defining factors in Wallace's complex formulation of his political and aesthetic vision and in the development of his writing, a trajectory that ends, as Jorge Araya (2015) has observed, in the overwhelming 'whiteness' of *The Pale King* (2011).

Beginning with *Girl with Curious Hair*, this chapter examines how Wallace uses race to develop a logic of distance and separation across two stories: 'Girl with Curious Hair' and 'Lyndon'. Lyndon's exploration of race, sexuality, and the intersection between personal and political love play out against the backdrop of the civil rights movement. Reading the story alongside James Baldwin's evocation of love in *The Fire Next Time* (1963), I align Baldwin's concept of white lovelessness and his metaphor of interracial love as political action with Wallace's interrogation of love and distance. While *Girl* represents an attempt to work through the nuances of difference, in *Signifying Rappers* Wallace's vision for love as a logic through which to articulate and incorporate difference is compromised by his anxieties around race as a closed system. This chapter asks a crucial question: what does Wallace's whiteness have to do with love?

'Arrangements of distance': *Girl with Curious Hair*

Kathleen Fitzpatrick (2006), Samuel Cohen (2015), Lucas Thompson (2017; 2018), and Jorge Araya (2015) have considered how racial difference operates within Wallace's broader commitment to 'connect to [the] reader across the barriers that divide individuals from each other' (Cohen, 2015: 30). Central to these discussions is an attempt to understand how Wallace responds to and manifests racial difference in his work, which Araya and Thompson present as a complex oscillation between 'emphasis' and 'erasure'. Araya considers racial otherness in Wallace's earlier fiction as functioning as a means of 'emphasizing difference' (Araya, 2015: 240), a strategy that affords him opportunities to dramatize and work through the problems of communication that arise from social and cultural stratification. Wallace's anxieties about the potentially irreconcilable failures of language and communication are common across his oeuvre. Adding race to this equation, however, helps us to understand and work through Wallace's complex but flawed consideration of political consensus in his later work. At the core of this idea is what Thompson reads as Wallace's impulse towards the 'erasure of difference', a phrase he takes from an interview Wallace gave in 2000 in which he praises the Jewish-American writer Cynthia Ozick, claiming that when he reads her fiction he experiences 'an utter erasure of difference, which does not happen to me with a lot of other writers from different cultural backgrounds' (qtd in Thompson, 2017: 197). Thompson identifies this erasure as a central aspect of Wallace's treatment of race, stating that Wallace believed 'specific cultural content [to be] a mere surface-level dissimilarity that should not distract from a text's instantiation of universal truths and themes' (197). The tension between 'emphasis' and 'erasure' speaks to a broader aesthetic dilemma in Wallace's writing, one that is irrevocably intertwined with love as a political and ethical concept. In *Girl with Curious Hair* Wallace explores this push and pull through an explicit logic of spatial and linguistic separation, one that establishes 'distance' as a guiding principle for Wallace's philosophy of communication.

'Girl with Curious Hair', the title story in Wallace's first collection, makes visible Wallace's complex interlinking of racial difference with problems of communication and solipsism. It also begins to develop an interplay between love and distance that becomes a defining philosophical and political concept in 'Lyndon'. The story's action unfolds during a concert by jazz pianist Keith Jarrett and is narrated by Sick Puppy, an overtly racist and sexually perverse sociopath (a would-be precursor to Bret Easton Ellis's Patrick Bateman) who is accompanied by his lover, Gimlet, and a drug-fuelled crew of punks sporting an array of exaggerated hair styles. The eponymous 'curious hair' belongs to a young girl seated directly in front of Sick Puppy and his cronies. Gimlet's fascination with the girl's 'blonde and curled hair' (Wallace, 1989: 63) – features that suggest whiteness – is juxtaposed with Sick Puppy's overt racialization of Keith Jarrett's hair: 'all I could see of Keith Jarrett was the back of him and his hair's afro while he played' (60). In the auditorium the audience all faces one direction, looking directly at Jarrett's back as he turns away from the audience. Jarrett's face, like the girl's, is actively concealed from Sick Puppy's point of view, his 'afro' standing in as an all-consuming signifier for his racial identity. Similarly, the description 'his hair's afro' amplifies Jarrett's hair – and, by extension, his misconstrued blackness – to almost mythical proportions, serving to further distance Jarrett from Sick Puppy as both racially other and culturally illegible. But the focus on hair rather than faces serves only to blur the boundaries of racial identity. The girl's blondness does not *de facto* signify her whiteness, just as Jarrett's afro falsely marks him as black (Jarrett is white, of Hungarian descent, but commonly mistaken as black).[1] While Jarrett's performance provides the potential for a communal and communicative encounter between the story's characters, their one-directional gazes foreclose any mutual recognition and instead serve only to emphasize their racial difference.

The story's (misdirected) racial gaze underscores Sick Puppy's persistent failures of empathy, which manifest most clearly in his perverse sexual appetites, which the reader learns are the product of a childhood defined by incest and abuse. These details, while fitting into a broader pattern of sexual dysfunction in Wallace's work, also present Sick Puppy's lovelessness as a fundamental flaw. Cheese, one of Sick Puppy's crew, is the only character who seems to transcend the hollow, drug-induced self-involvement displayed by the other characters. He is set apart from the other members of Sick Puppy's crew because of his baldness and is later revealed to be in an interracial relationship. He is characterized by his openness, not only as an empathetic listener when Sick Puppy opens up about his disturbing childhood, but also by fulfilling a didactic role, explaining Jarrett's music to Sick Puppy in a way that momentarily seems to break through the latter's sociopathic apathy. Configuring Jarrett's improvisational jazz to be 'a line instead of a composed and round circle' (66), Cheese interprets the 'line' as antithetical to the recursive feedback-loop that Wallace saw as the primary aesthetic effect of postmodern fiction. The line projects outwards, foregrounding individual expression while still soliciting response. The line also implies distance and separation. Sick Puppy recognizes the line as expressing something alien to his experience, claiming that the 'line was like a little life story of the Negro's special experiences and feelings' (66). His appreciation of Jarrett's music as racially distinct nevertheless allows Sick Puppy to access his interior, dysfunctional self, 'without me even noticing the fact that Cheese took us from discussing musical genres and Keith Jarrett's negro experiences and emotions to no music and my white experiences and emotions' (67). The success of 'the line' in penetrating Sick Puppy's sinister, vacant persona demonstrates a model of empathy and mutual understanding that is generated through a logic of separation (or an emphasis on difference) that ultimately results in the erasure of the racial other, as Sick Puppy's 'white experiences' are realized both through and at the expense of black ones.

'Girl with Curious Hair' demonstrates how race becomes a central factor in Wallace's early mediations on communication, one that manifests in a complicated push and pull between emphasis and erasure. The problems of empathy and communication raised in 'Girl' find greater expression in 'Lyndon', where 'love' and 'distance' point to a broader political and civic vision that was beginning to develop in Wallace's fiction. As Jeffrey Severs notes, 'Lyndon' presents 'a rare opportunity to scrutinize Wallace in terms of race, gender, and sexual identity' (Severs, 2017: 78). Taken alongside the story's thematic concern with Lyndon B. Johnson's Great Society, 'Lyndon' represents an important stage in the evolution of Wallace's political philosophy, one that works through questions of civic love and responsibility via the obstacle of cultural identity. The juxtaposition of sexual and racial difference with a vision of American political collectivity allows love – as both a democratic concept and an embodied, sexual act – to come to the fore as a defining concept for the collection and as an aesthetic statement for Wallace's early fiction.

'Lyndon' tells the fictional account of David Boyd, a closeted gay man who is hired as an aide to Lyndon B. Johnson. Over the course of the story, Boyd's political apathy is wholly transformed into an obsession with the President (and his work) that consumes his life. The story plays with layers of public and private selves and the blurred boundary between Boyd's public commitment to Johnson and the deeper familial bond between the two men. This personal attachment verges, at times, into the romantic as Boyd is suspected, by characters and readers alike, of conflating duty with desire. Boyd's public, professional relationship with Johnson is contrasted with his private and, crucially, secret life with René Duverger, a Haitian immigrant who later dies of what seems to be an anachronistic case of HIV/AIDS. At the story's surreal conclusion, the gravely ill Duverger disappears, and it is revealed to Boyd that he has been taken to be 'presented to the President who is dying' (Wallace, 1989: 114). In a passage that Severs describes as the 'rhetoric of the Great Society and civil rights legislation given flesh' (Severs, 2017: 79), Boyd finds the two men in bed together, embracing, alongside a set of policy documents that Boyd thought he had lost. Critical accounts of this story have tended to focus on the figure of LBJ as the predominant means by which the dynamics of love play out. Focusing instead on Duverger as a character who both facilitates the exchange of love – with Boyd and LBJ, but also *between* Boyd and LBJ – and who brings together an embodied, erotic understanding of love with its broader civic definition, recentres race as essential to how Wallace was formulating these ideas in his early writing. Against the submerged backdrop of the civil rights movement, Duverger becomes a complex analogy for blackness, whiteness, and love that further complicates

Wallace's exploration of empathy, communication, and political responsibility.

As Hayes-Brady has argued, Wallace frequently engages issues of difference (particularly gender difference) as problems of language (Hayes-Brady, 2016: 171). While 'Lyndon' is not particularly explicit in its treatment of race until the final scene – an unusual fact in and of itself, given the centrality of the Civil Rights Acts to LBJ's presidency – Duverger's marginalization is realized through his limited English, which enforces a destabilizing separateness between him and Boyd, who speaks 'a kind of pidgin when alone' (Wallace, 1989: 99). Linguistically, pidgin languages are defined as having a 'simplified grammar and a smaller vocabulary than the languages from which [they are] derived, [and are] used for communication between people not having a common language' (*OED*, s.v. 'pidgin', 2018). Therefore, while a pidgin's grammatical simplicity renders it unrefined and clumsy, it also offers the potential to bridge important gaps in communication: in this case Boyd and Duverger's conflicting definitions of love. In the following exchange Duverger's and Boyd's disagreement about the best way to give each other love is further warped by the disruption that plagues the articulation of their love in language:

> '*Ce n'est pas moi qui tu aimes*.' 'Of course I love you. We share a life, René'. He was having difficulty breathing. '*Ce n'est* not I.' 'Whom, then?' I asked, rolling him off. 'If you say I do not love you, whom do I love?' '*Tu m'en a* besoin', he cried, rending dark bedroom air with his nails. 'You *need* me. You feel the responsibility for me. But your love it is not for me.' 'My love is for you, Duverger. Need, responsibility: these are part of love, in this nation.' (Wallace 1989: 99)

This passage is undoubtedly indebted to James Baldwin's 1956 novel *Giovanni's Room*, a heavily annotated copy of which can be found in Wallace's personal library at the Harry Ransom Centre in Austin (TX). In Baldwin's novel the protagonist, who is also called David, converses with his lover, Giovanni, in a mix of French and English, but the characters' proficiency in both languages means that the encounter does not lead to the kind of misunderstanding that occurs between Boyd and Duverger. In one scene Giovanni and David have a conversation similar to Boyd and Duverger's, with Giovanni asking David '*Je t'aime, tu sais?*' and David replying '*Je le sais, mon vieux*' (Baldwin, 2000: 110). The scene from 'Lyndon' is almost a direct inversion of this exchange. Whereas Giovanni affirms that he loves David, Duverger accuses Boyd of loving another: '*Ce n'est pas moi qui tu aimes*'. When Boyd assures him that he does not, Duverger repeats his statement '*Ce n'est* not I.' His mid-sentence shift into English is meant to emphasize the part of the sentence that Boyd has glossed over – a conflation of Boyd's dismissal with an assumption of his limited linguistic competence. In this translation Duverger underscores the negative aspect brought out in the French 'ne ... pas' construction, resulting in a statement that doubly enforces his negation of self: 'not I'. Unlike the reciprocal affirmation of love in *Giovanni's Room*, in which the answer is returned in the same language that the question is asked, Duverger and Boyd engage in continuous, disruptive code switching which defers the realization of communal meaning. Boyd's conception of love is inherently bound up in notions of duty and responsibility. His emphasis on 'this nation' displaces the private, erotic valence of Duverger's definition, transforming it into a social and civic act. It also reorients the focus away from personal conceptions of love in order to show how these opposing definitions are bound up with their social context. The evocation of national love not only serves to sublimate the private into the public but also further marks Duverger's marginal position in the American way of life. This intimate exchange echoes the broader political themes of the story, which presents LBJ's politics as a model of American civic responsibility at odds with what Wallace viewed as the destructive self-gratification of the 1960s. In one scene Johnson expresses his disconnection from the 'youth of America' (Wallace, 1989: 106), who he believes have substituted 'feelings' for 'responsibility'.

Wallace's appropriation of *Giovanni's Room* opens up an alternative philosophical, political, and historical context through which to interrogate his interpretation of 'love' in this story. In 'Letter from a Region in My Mind' (1962), republished later in *The Fire Next Time* (1963), Baldwin proposed love as a viable and necessary political solution to America's destructive race relations:

> If we – and now I mean the relatively conscious whites and the relatively conscious blacks, who, like lovers insist on, or create, the consciousness of the others – do not falter in our duty now, we may be able, handful

that we are, to end the racial nightmare, and achieve our country, and change the history of the world. (Baldwin, 1990: 89)

Baldwin situates interracial love at the centre of his political and social vision. His depiction of love as 'consciousness' here and elsewhere across his work positions it as a powerful tool in dismantling white 'innocence', which is configured as a kind of lovelessness. As Grant Farred (2015) suggests, in Baldwin's work love is inextricably tied up with the notion of responsibility, and this responsibility manifests in the political imbalance between blackness and whiteness, an asymmetrical experience of love. Following Derrida, Farred argues that 'Love is only love, comes into – as – itself – when there is inequality. Love can only be said to exist when the Self's commitment to the Other exceeds the Other's commitment to the Self' (293). This account of asymmetrical love in Baldwin's racial politics chimes with Hayes-Brady's (2016: 99) reading of Derrida's notion of *se render*, where the 'giving of the self' inherent in *rendre* is in tension with the reflexivity of *se*. What is gained from Baldwin's articulation of this self-sacrificial love is its interrogation of whiteness as lovelessness:

> the white man came to the Negro for love. But he was not often able to give what he came seeking. The price was too high; he had too much to lose. And the Negro knew this, too. When one knows this about a man, it is impossible for one to hate him, but unless he becomes a man – becomes equal – it is also impossible for one to love him. (Baldwin, 1990: 87)

There are distinct echoes of Baldwin's analogy in the scene between Duverger and Boyd, where the inequality experienced by these two characters is multiform: in their status as a couple that is both interracial and homosexual, and in Boyd's specific difficulty in giving love to Duverger. Baldwin's demand that the racially conscious act 'like lovers' presents a view of love that is both self-sacrificing and transformative. A notable opponent to Baldwin's philosophy of love was Hannah Arendt who, in a letter to the editor of the *New Yorker* in November 1962, noted that 'In politics, love is a stranger, and when it intrudes upon it nothing is being achieved except hypocrisy' (Arendt, 2006). This sentiment is expressed more forcibly in *The Human Condition* (1958: 242), where she states that 'Love, by its very nature, is unworldly ... it is not only apolitical but antipolitical, perhaps the most powerful of all antipolitical human forces'. Love, for Arendt, threatens the character of plurality which, like Hayes-Brady's interpretation of *se rendre*, simultaneously unites and separates individuals. Action, which relies on the preservation of plurality (that is, a state which relies in equal measure on individuality and equality), can be achieved only through 'the in-between which relates us to and separates us from others' (242). Sean Butorac (2018: 4) makes a crucial distinction between Arendt's and Baldwin's formulations, emphasizing Baldwin's use of the simile 'like lovers', which operates as a crucial means of distancing that relinquishes the need to 'love all our fellow citizens' but instead asks 'that we engage with them – and ourselves – in ways that are informed by love'. Baldwin's interlinking of 'love' and 'duty' 'orients us toward a worldly responsibility' (8).

Unlike Hayes-Brady's (2016: 100) reading of Wallace's 'love' as a 'radically disembodied and desexualised' means of communicating with the reader, and unlike Arendt's staunch separation of intimate love from the realm of politics, Baldwin offers a sensual and embodied philosophy of love that explicitly addresses problems of race. It also provides an illuminating metaphor through which to read the peculiar ending of 'Lyndon' and Wallace's enduring political struggle with difference. Throughout the story Boyd conflates and confuses private and public love (or responsibility) in his obsession with LBJ. This is compounded by his closeted sexuality, as he is trapped first in a sham marriage to a woman and then in a secret union with Duverger. As the above exchange between Boyd and Duverger makes clear, Boyd sees love as synonymous with duty, but he cannot reconcile it with more intimate experiences of love.

In the final sections of the story, while Boyd is searching both for Duverger and for the lost policy documents, he is summoned by Ladybird Johnson who informs him that Duverger has been taken to keep Johnson company on his deathbed. Perplexed, Boyd expresses concern first for Duverger's health and then for his poor English, doubting his ability to communicate with the President. Despite this, Ladybird discloses that Lyndon and Duverger manage to have 'conversations of great length' (Wallace, 1989: 114), and she confirms that 'M. Duverger has impressed Lyndon as a truly singular Negro, Mr. Boyd. They have discussed such issues close to Lyndon's heart as suffering, and struggles between sides, and Negroness' (115). Not only do Lyndon and Duverger, then, inexplicably transcend linguistic barriers, but they also enter into a dialogue which expresses Duverger's racial marginalization, a subject that is otherwise unvoiced in the story. The union of Johnson and Duverger introduces a definition of 'love' alternative to the one outlined by Boyd previously. As Ladybird expresses to Boyd, 'love is simply a word. It joins separate things' (115). 'Love' and 'responsibility' are, for Johnson, 'arrangements of distance' like 'a federal highway, lines putting communities, that move and exist at great distance, in touch' (115). Facilitating empathy, consensus, and connection is – like building federal highways – central to the mission of national government.

This grand structural metaphor can also be interpreted as a more intimate, syntactical one. Ladybird's description of love as a 'word' that 'joins separate things' reduces it to its grammatical function, a verb that links together subject and object. Significantly, in 'Lyndon' tension arises in the conversations between Duverger and Boyd precisely because of their grammatical confusion over what subject and object the word 'love' or '*aimer*' joins – a tension that is enhanced through the repeated objectification of Duverger throughout the story and his questioning of precisely where, or towards whom, Boyd's love is directed. But 'love' can operate as both a transitive and an intransitive verb: it can mediate the relationship between two separate things while also conveying the 'action' or feeling of love, the latter of which (intransitive) does not require a direct object. As Baldwin (1990: 82) asserts, love can surpass the personal and become instead 'a state of being, or a state of grace'. Love's dual grammatical function, which is central to the ways 'Lyndon' equates public and private, resonates with Baldwin's call to act 'like lovers' – a political position that is generated through 'arrangements of distance'. Love functions both as an instrument of direct exchange and as a wider, unattributed 'action' or way of being. The outward projection of love that expects no reciprocation informs the contract between writer and reader and reaches its full realization in *Girl with Curious Hair*'s final story, 'Westward the Course of Empire Takes Its Way', which ends by assuring the reader that 'You are loved' (Wallace, 1989: 373).

While love emerges in 'Lyndon' as a Baldwinian model of political transformation and civic communication, the story's ending complicates this notion in ways that threaten to undermine Wallace's consideration of difference. Duverger's position as triply marginalized – as a black, homosexual, immigrant – embodies the vast societal changes that occurred under LBJ's presidency and, at the same time, reflects the fraught social conservatism of the 1980s when Wallace was writing the collection. Despite the promise of social reconciliation at the end of the story, the final image of Duverger and Johnson in bed 'like lovers' calls into question the distance that is so crucial to both Arendt's and Baldwin's theories. The distance between Duverger and Johnson allows them to achieve genuine, uninhibited communication in spite of obvious linguistic barriers. This distance is achieved through Duverger's 'singularity', which is also implicitly tied to his political equality through the evocation of the Civil Rights and Voting Acts of 1964–65 – the 'Negroness' which is so close to Johnson's heart. But despite Duverger's effect on Johnson, there is no full disclosure of Duverger as a distinct and individuated subject.

In the final scene the distance sought after by both Wallace and Baldwin disappears in the literalization of Duverger and Johnson's act of love, a move that actively stages a shift from emphasis to erasure. Duverger's disease causes his 'brown' skin to fade to 'grey' (Wallace, 2005: 103), while elsewhere Boyd notices Lyndon's age-spotted 'brown-freckled fingers' (106) – as though Lyndon were taking on Duverger's lost pigmentation. In the story's final image Boyd looks at Duverger 'curled stiff on his side, a frozen skeleton X ray, impossibly thin, fuzzily bearded, his hand outstretched with dulled nails to cover, partly, the white face beside him, the big white face attached to the long form below the tight clean sheets' (117). The emphasis on Lyndon's whiteness here is counterposed with Duverger's near-invisibility. Finally Boyd hears 'lips that kissed the palm of a black man as they moved together to form words' (118). This peculiar juxtaposition of race, love, and language plays out in the wake of Duverger's depersonalization and, crucially, the dissolution of his racial difference. The physical proximity of Johnson and Duverger leads to a grotesque closeness that obscures both racial and linguistic expression. The resolution of 'Lyndon' is indeterminate: on the one hand, it preaches a model of empathetic distance, a kind of civic 'love' that facilitates the inclusion, coexistence, and communication of the other; on the other, the story portrays the sublimation of Duverger's racial otherness to Lyndon's wider political purpose. The story plays out the political and ethical tensions inherent in a philosophy of love, tensions which inevitably involve linguistic work and the struggle for communication on the level of word and sentence. 'Lyndon', and *Girl with Curious Hair* more broadly, represent Wallace's attempts to work through and incorporate racial and sexual difference into his civic vision. Significantly, while Wallace interrogates the boundaries between the personal and private, and the possibilities for difference and plurality, his depiction of blackness and queerness are transmuted and subsumed into his national allegory. In its ambiguous ending Wallace's anxieties about this model of political and communicative engagement are palpable. In his later work, 'Authority and American Usage' in particular, his fascination with difference moves more resolutely towards a desire for consensus – a political sentiment that can also be located in the figure of LBJ. In *Signifying Rappers*, the text that immediately follows *Girl with Curious Hair*, 'love' and 'distance' come to mediate and define Wallace's racial anxiety and subsequently to alter his belief in the possibility of genuine communication.

'No Less Love?' *Signifying Rappers* and the perversion of distance

Signifying Rappers continues to explore (or, rather, fret over) the aesthetic and political questions laid out in *Girl with Curious Hair* and marks an important transition to a period in which Wallace begins to recognize the limitations of the exploration of difference in his early writing. Central to this shift is, again, the interlinking of whiteness and lovelessness, but this time it is Wallace who feels his love is not – and cannot – be returned. Written in the summer before Wallace started a graduate programme at Harvard and while living with his college roommate, Mark Costello, *Signifying Rappers* poses itself as a love letter, of sorts, to 1980s hip hop. The essay's frenetic energy is driven by the problem of accessibility, an awareness that rap is '*by* urban blacks *about* same *to* and *from* same' (Wallace and Costello, 2013: 25). Their emphasis on the form's exclusion of the white spectator plays into the essay's broader positioning of Wallace and Costello as culturally marginal. Indeed the essay fetishizes the incongruity of its authors' interest in the subject, provocatively naming its first section 'Entitlement' and continuously asking the question: 'What business have two white yuppies trying to do a sampler on rap?' (21). The essay is filled with images of distance and division, frequently evoking the metaphor of the 'window' in order to emphasize their outsider position. In doing so, it casts their appreciation for rap, and their 'ethnic distance' (22) from it, as a culturally transgressive form of love, asking whether the 'unease and ambivalence with which the rare white at the window loves rap renders that love no less love. Is this perverse?' (32).

Wallace's repeated formulation of his own positionality with regards to rap – although rarely in relation to the communities or artists it emerges from – demonstrates that he is less interested in how it might represent black experience and instead how it manifests both aesthetic potential and isolation. More specifically he is interested in how it excludes him. Recalling a rap concert that he and Wallace attended, Costello describes Wallace's sheer disappointment when, rather than being hassled, dissed, or confronted, the pair are completely ignored by the other members of the predominantly black audience. Wallace and Costello's configuration of their own invisibility, which Tara Morrissey and Thompson (2015: 91) read as a coy reference to Ralph Ellison's *Invisible Man*, reveals their misguided exaggeration of the antithetical role of whiteness in rap's construction of blackness. Wallace's racial anxiety is compounded by sexual insecurity, as the tenderness of 'Lyndon' gives way to the overt masculinity of 1980s hip hop. His affected marginality does not, however, bring him closer to an understanding of and appreciation for rap as a black art form that speaks to a specific cultural and historical positioning. Instead, he expresses anxiety for rap's cultural inaccessibility, its 'closed' nature, and its refusal to communicate outside of its cultural context:

> What if the artists are not influencing or informing but rather just *reflecting* their audience, holding up a mirror their world can see itself as world in? … What if cutting-edge rap really *is* a closed music? Not even pretending it's promulgating anything controversial or even unfamiliar to its young mass audience? What if rap scares us because it's really just preaching to the converted?' (Wallace and Costello, 2013: 47)

Here Wallace's 'us', in opposition to 'their world', firmly demarcates his and his audience's whiteness and speaks to the cultural and legal backlash against rap during the period (details of which are discussed in more detail in Costello's sections of the essay). Wallace's desire to be 'converted', to be communicated to, eclipses his ability to recognize rap's 'signifying' as something more than a 'Closed System', as just another example of the kind of postmodern, ironic self-reference that he sought to counter in texts like *Girl with Curious Hair*. As Rando (2013) suggests, Wallace's fiction repeatedly engages with irony as a kind of 'lovelessness'. Here, in Wallace's encounter with 'signifyin(g)', lovelessness as both whiteness and irony come into close, uncomfortable proximity. What Wallace and Costello seem to miss is the political valence of 'signifyin(g)', theorized in Henry Louis Gates Jr.'s *The Signifying Monkey* published a year before *Signifying Rappers* in 1988. In Gates's (1988: xxv) formulation, black texts are always 'double-voiced', produced simultaneously and self-consciously for a white and black audience while also 'signifyin(g)' on other black texts. Wallace (McCaffery, 2012: 48) recognizes this intricate doubleness as just another version of postmodern irony that 'splits things apart' in unproductive and damaging ways and which, in telling phrasing, has 'gone from liberating to enslaving'.

While Wallace views rap as culturally inaccessible – if only because his anxiety about whiteness operates as its own 'Closed System' – he finds possibility in its grammatical and poetic legibility. Wallace finds possibility in rap's formal and linguistic innovation irrespective of its cultural valence: its 'complicated prosodic innovations – disordered but effective enjambment, stresses alternated between standard feet, wild combinations of iamb with trochee and both with spondee, the kind of metrical libertinism that spells f-r-e-e-v-e-r-s-e but is here required by *exactly* the sort of tight aural walls free verse was all about knocking down' (110–11). For Wallace, rap's cultural 'doubleness' reads as political solipsism, but its ability to produce art out of formal and linguistic contradiction holds a wider social and civic potential: 'the same verbal skills and enthusiasms rap values (and values enough to let rap-dissing stand symbolically for fighting or killing) can obviously be applied in mainstream approved, "productive" ways – G.E.D.s, college, Standard Written English ... perhaps someday even ad copywriting!' (114). Despite his caustic edge, Wallace's image of kids 'hunched over notebooks on their own time trying to put words together in striking and creative ways' (114–15) projects a genuine belief in the potential for culturally specific forms of art to work towards bridging gaps between communities, even if this means ultimately subscribing to standard forms. Appealing to rap's linguistic elements, therefore, facilitates its cultural transfer into larger, and distinctly more homogeneous, cultural institutions.

In *Signifying Rappers* Wallace's philosophy of love falters. While *Girl with Curious Hair* dramatized the inherent difficulties of self-disclosure, its logic of distance as a necessary precondition for love attempted to make space for the other's profound unknowability. As I have shown, the tensions and fault lines in Wallace's approach are always visible. His work is, as Hayes-Brady (2016: 2) suggests, characterized by its resistance to closure. Focusing on race as a determining factor in Wallace's exploration of love and communication makes visible his complex attitude to questions of difference and accounts for a perceptible shift in his writing and political philosophy towards a model of consensus that tilts the balance from 'emphasis' towards 'erasure'. Reading *Signifying Rappers* alongside 'Lyndon' also offers an alternative way of understanding Wallace's anxieties about irony, communication, and political consensus that takes his whiteness into account. *Signifying Rappers* signals a moment when, faced with the reality of the other rather than its abstraction, Wallace cannot accept the possibly irreconcilable distance between them. Understanding rap as a linguistic system becomes a means of tangibly expressing and acting on his love for the form. But in his treatment of rap as linguistic code, Wallace begins to consider how the problems of cultural exclusion might be rectified by the consideration and adoption of the linguistic practices of the other – namely, how cultural otherness might be rendered as merely a different grammatical system whose rules can be studied and mastered like a foreign language. In texts like 'Solomon Silverfish' and the Wardine episode in *Infinite Jest* (1996) Wallace's attempts to represent blackness are associated with an uncomfortable linguistic mimicry that collapses the distance between the self and other and which results in a difficult, unsuccessful proximity. To speak of Wallace's 'philosophy of love', then, is perhaps to assign too rigid a schema. We might consider it more like a series of sustained attempts, worked over again and again on the level of language, in an effort to stave off lovelessness.

Note

1 See James Lincoln Collier (1979), 'Jazz in the Jarrett Mode'.

References

Araya, J. (2015). 'Why the Whiteness? Race in *The Pale King*', 238–51. In Philip Coleman, ed., *Critical Insights: David Foster Wallace*. Ipswich MA: Salem.
Arendt, H. (1958). *The Human Condition*. Chicago IL: University of Chicago Press.
Baldwin, J. (1990). *The Fire Next Time*. London: Penguin Books.
Baldwin, J. (2000). *Giovanni's Room*. New York NY: Delta Trade Paperbacks.
Butorac, S. K. (2018). 'Hannah Arendt, James Baldwin and the Politics of Love'. *Political Research Quarterly* 71:3, 710–21.
Cohen, S. (2015). 'The Whiteness of David Foster Wallace', 228–43. In Len Platt and Sara Upstone, eds, *Postmodern Literature and Race*. Cambridge: Cambridge University Press.
Farred, G. (2015). 'Love Is Asymmetrical: James Baldwin's *The Fire Next Time*'. *Critical Philosophy of Race* 3:2, 284–304.
Fitzpatrick, K. (2006). *The Anxiety of Obsolescence: The American Novel in the Age of Television*. Nashville TN: Vanderbilt University Press.
Gates Jr., H. L. (1988). *The Signifying Monkey: A Theory of Afro-American Literary Criticism*. Oxford: Oxford University Press.
Hayes-Brady, C. (2016). *The Unspeakable Failures of David Foster Wallace: Language, Identity, and Resistance*. London and New York NY: Bloomsbury.
McCaffery, L. (2012). 'An Expanded Interview with David Foster Wallace', 21–57. In Stephen J. Burn, ed., *Conversations with David Foster Wallace*. Jackson MS: University Press of Mississippi.
Morrissey, T. and L. Thompson, (2015). '"The Rare White at the Window": A Reappraisal of Mark Costello and David Foster Wallace's *Signifying Rappers*'. *Journal of American Studies* 49:1, 77–97.
Oxford English Dictionary. (2018). Oxford: Clarendon Press.
Rando, D. P. (2013). 'David Foster Wallace and Lovelessness'. *Twentieth Century Literature* 59:4, 575–95.
Severs, J. (2017). *David Foster Wallace's Balancing Books: Fictions of Value*. New York NY: Columbia University Press.
Thompson, L. (2017). *Global Wallace: David Foster Wallace and World Literature*. London and New York NY: Bloomsbury.

Thompson, L. (2018). 'Wallace and Race', 204–19. In Ralph Clare, ed., *The Cambridge Companion to David Foster Wallace*. Cambridge: Cambridge University Press.

Wallace, D. Foster. (1989). *Girl with Curious Hair*. London: Abacus.

Wallace, D. Foster. (2005). *Consider the Lobster and Other Essays*. London: Abacus.

Wallace, D. Foster and M. Costello. (2013). *Signifying Rappers*. New York NY: Back Bay Books.

Internet sources

Arendt, H. (2006). 'The Meaning of Love in Politics. A Letter by Hannah Arendt to James Baldwin'. *HannahArendt.Net* 2(1). www.hannaharendt.net/index.php/han/article/view/95 (accessed 28 March 2022).

Collier, J. L. (7 January 1979). 'Jazz in the Jarrett Mode'. *The New York Times*. www.nytimes.com/1979/01/07/archives/jazz-in-the-jarrett-mode-jarrett.html (accessed 26 March 2022).

14

'They remain just bodies': on pornography in David Foster Wallace (1989–2006)

Chiara Scarlato

One of the most recurrent topics in David Foster Wallace's oeuvre is pornography. This issue emerges again and again in both his fiction and non-fiction writings.[1] Pornography is also mentioned by Wallace in several personal notebooks and drafts kept at the Harry Ransom Center (HRC); these archival documents include notes, projects, and ideas for essays, novels, and stories. Finally Wallace lingered extensively on this topic in the interviews with Schecter (1989), Lipsky (1996), and Borrelli (2006). I will argue that Wallace's recurring attention to pornography may shed light on important themes that are highly relevant to his oeuvre: addiction and entertainment and their challenging juxtaposition.

As Allard den Dulk pointed out in his essay 'Wallace and Philosophy' (2019), Wallace's 'exploration of philosophical themes, rather than being conceptual or theoretical, is driven by a clear desire to express, and thereby allow the reader to experience, some of the most existentially urgent and painful aspects of contemporary human experience' (Den Dulk, 2019: 155). Building upon this perspective, it may be argued that Wallace considered pornography not merely as a theme but as a device or vehicle prompting *literary conversation* by addressing how the entanglement of addiction and entertainment can ensnare human beings through fatal viewing practices. In pornography the aim of being entertained and need for immediate satisfaction have a strong connection with technology predicated on progressive disconnection from the outside world.

Wallace started his research on pornography concurrently with the advent of porn home videos in the late 1980s: his attention was drawn to the dangerous potential of adult movies whose combination of technology, entertainment, and (eventually) erotic pleasure was enhanced by the possibility of viewing them in a private setting. In particular Wallace thought this viewing practice increased viewers' loneliness, while exacerbating forms of social disease, particularly forms of hatred for women. In an interview with Borrelli in 2006, he claimed that people addicted to pornography conceal an awkward disease tied to the disturbing form of misogyny resulting from private viewing of porn home movies and DVDs (Borrelli, 2015). I contend that Wallace reached this conclusion as a result of the long-term and continuous research that he conducted from 1989 to 2006.

The chronology I trace highlights how Wallace, when he first began focusing on porn home movies, was also aware of a radical change in both the general function of art and the particular function of literature. This emerges clearly from a passage of 'Fictional Futures and the Conspicuously Young' (1988) in which he claimed that the 'demise of Structuralism has changed a world's outlook on language, art, and literary discourse; and the contemporary artist can simply no longer afford to regard the work of critics or theorists or philosophers –no matter how stratospheric – as divorced from his own concerns' (Wallace, 2012: 63).

Given this, I would argue that, through his exploration of pornography, Wallace joined one of his main philosophical concerns – the loop between addiction and entertainment – to a particular matter: the impact of pornography on the American cultural system, especially in relation to issues concerning representation of the female body.[2] More specifically from 1989 to 2006 Wallace mobilized these themes within a writing practice premised in philosophical reflection that was deeply influenced by contemporary debates over the role played by pornography in the American cultural system. In this regard he mainly focused on the paradox of pornography – which he understood as entailing both the representation of sexual intercourse and the denial of any form of relationship among viewers and performers – in order to show that there was another way to experience intimacy through aesthetic practice: through the act of reading, which, as he often stressed, is characterized by a distinctive and powerful conversation between author and reader.

Indeed, during his road-trip interview with David Lipsky in 1996, Wallace declared that 'a fair amount of aesthetic experience is – is erotic. And I think a certain amount of it has to do with this weird kind of intimacy with the person who made it' (Lipsky, 2010: 72). Although other forms of art (like pornography) may provide this 'intimacy', the eroticism of the author–reader relationship is peculiar and unique, as Wallace further highlighted in another interview of the same year. In answering Laura Miller's question on what 'is uniquely magical about fiction', Wallace explained, 'I don't know what you're thinking or what it's like inside you and you don't know what it's like inside me. In fiction I think we can leap over that wall itself in a certain way' (Burn, ed., 2012: 62). Speaking about his personal experience of reading, Wallace claimed also that the author–reader relationship is 'very strange and very complicated and hard to talk about' (62), as it ties (at least) two human beings together in a way that is rarely fulfilled with the same degree of intensity in other human interactions, and, at the same time, allows us to overcome 'this existential loneliness in the real world' (62). In other words the act of reading enables a form of recognition that is inherently experiential.

As Wallace maintained in his interview with Larry McCaffery (1993), serious fiction may help us empathize with the suffering and pain of others: 'We all suffer alone in the real world; true empathy's impossible. But if a piece of fiction can allow us imaginatively to identify with characters' pain, we might then also more easily conceive of others identifying with our own. This is nourishing, redemptive; we become less alone inside' (Burn, ed., 2012: 22). This kind of 'true empathy' is precisely what the aesthetic experience of pornography denies: if the specific purpose of serious fiction is to empathize with other people's pain (or suffering) in order to develop a deeper understanding of our own despair, the main aim of pornography is to be a temporary 'distractor'. Metaphorically, pornography acts as an anaesthetic, while literature offers a viable means of diffusing loneliness. In this sense Wallace considered the act of viewing adult movies as in fundamental opposition to the act of reading: the former has dangerous effects, while the latter performs a 'nourishing' and 'redemptive' function.

In the following sections of this chapter I will analyse, respectively: firstly, the archival documents concerning Wallace's unpublished 1989 piece commissioned by *Playboy*; secondly, his treatment of pornography in the novel *Infinite Jest* (1996); thirdly, the stories 'Adult World (I)' and 'Adult World (II)' (Wallace, 1999: 161–89) in relation to the essay 'Big Red Son' (Wallace, 2005: 3–50). In the first section I will trace the initial phase of Wallace's research, focusing on the piece on pornography commissioned by *Playboy*. By reconstructing the composition of this piece through some archival documents I will argue that it constitutes Wallace's first attempt at combining philosophical themes with his reflection on the function of literature. By exploring the role of entertainment within the American cultural system Wallace dealt with problems of contemporary philosophy – i.e., addiction, entertainment, and, specifically, the consequences of pornography on human relationships – within the framework of a particular practice of writing seen as a conversation between author and reader. In the second section I will focus mainly on the film cartridge 'Infinite Jest', in order to show how this conversation between author and reader may be understood as an alternative to the aesthetic experience of pornography, a form of entertainment which tends to deny human pain and suffering. In the third and last section I will address further developments in Wallace's reflections around pornography, addiction, and entertainment and their interrelation. This chronological approach will help me to clearly assess firstly the development of Wallace's research, along with the development of the porn industry itself; secondly the ways in which this issue continuously influenced Wallace's writing; thirdly the association of pornography with other recurrent themes in Wallace's work, and, particularly with the issue of the overlap between addiction and entertainment.

Fiction versus non-fiction: writing on pornography (1989–93)

As Mark Costello notes in the preface to the second edition of *Signifying Rappers: Rap and Race in the Urban Present* (1990), Wallace started his research on pornography in 1989. Costello – co–author of the essay on rap music and Wallace's housemate in Somerville – declared that Wallace's project 'on the making and the watching of pornographic movies ... grew and swallowed others', while his friend was attempting 'to decode the awful yet addictive anti-fantasy of porn' that became 'a maze of paradox or simple contradiction' (Wallace and Costello, 2013: xi). Comparison of a series of archival documents and interviews makes clear that Wallace's research on pornography was troubled and complex, even before *Playboy* rejected his piece on the topic. At first Wallace's idea was to focus on the business of the adult film industry, but, during the initial phase of his research, he collected an enormous number of documents – including essays on pornography, interviews with porn performers and producers, and videotapes – that made it difficult to narrow down the most noteworthy aspects of this steadily changing phenomenon.[3]

Looked at in more detail, Wallace's interest in pornography was first signalled in a long letter written to Bonnie Nadell on 11 May 1989, in which Wallace expressed his desire to write a 'long piece of fiction that has something to do with the adult film industry', and, more precisely, with 'the 80's kind of almost made-for-video-rental films' collected 'in any tape outlet's adult selection' (Wallace, container 1.2, HRC). Wallace emphasized 'the paucity of material on the actual nuts and bolts (no pun) of the adult film business' (Wallace, container 1.2, HRC); then he reported that the only two books focused on the topic – Kenneth Turan's and Stephen F. Zito's *Sinema: American Pornographic Films and the People Who Make Them* (1974) and Stephen Ziplow's *The Film Maker's Guide to Pornography* (1977) – did not explore 'the illusion of realism/narrative familiarity' (Wallace, container 1.2, HRC) resulting from the vision of porn home movies.

Since drafts of this (supposed) long fiction piece have been lost, we can only extrapolate from the letter the aspects that initially interested Wallace, namely: firstly, matters concerning the scripting of movies and times of shooting; secondly, choices related to both artistic issues (like the assignment of acting roles) and technical issues (like the use of lighting and choice of a particular camera-technology); thirdly, getting 'explanations of certain curious conventions' (Wallace, container 1.2, HRC), such as some sexual practices frequently performed by the actresses and actors; fourthly, the meaning of the 'ritual about sexual interactions of these films' (Wallace, container 1.2, HRC); fifthly, the economic flux generated by the distribution of adult industry home videos in the US market (production, distribution, taxation); and sixthly, the differences and similarities between the US and European markets. However, when Wallace actually started this research, he became increasingly interested in elaborating the role of pornography in American culture and the 'humanness' of the performers involved in porn production – as evidenced by the frequent references he made to his contacts and interviews with *Caballero Home Video* productors, directors, actresses, and actors.

Although Wallace's initial purpose was to explore some aspects of pornography in a piece of fiction – and this was also the genre agreed upon with *Playboy* editor Alice Turner – he decided to change form as he was writing, as some letters to Turner and Nadell testify. More specifically, in July 1989 he wrote to Turner: 'I didn't decide I really wanted to do a piece of non–f[iction] until after I'd gotten out there and done all these interviews' (Wallace, container 1.2, HRC); a month later, in August, he told Nadell that the 'porn essay is horribly long ... I've got ab[o]ut 200 pages and am only half done' (Wallace, container 1.2, HRC). This switch from fiction to non-fiction is confirmed by a 1989 interview in which Wallace explained to Martin Schecter that he was working on a non-fiction piece focused on the meanings of conventional gestures in adult movies (Schecter and Wallace, 2018).

Bearing in mind that Wallace conducted this research on pornography before enrolling in the doctoral programme in Aesthetics at Harvard (Kennick papers, box 1, folder 4), it is also interesting to note that Wallace added:

> I don't want fiction to become work; the times I feel like I have to do it, I don't enjoy it. I want another job so that fiction remains my play – serious play. And I don't want to be part of the literary world; I'm scared of it. Writing is a lot like sex; I love to do it, but you've got to be in the mood, you can't do it for hours and hours, and I don't want to fuck for a living. (Schecter and Wallace, 2018)

Despite an occasional metaphor between writing and sex (probably influenced by the research he was conducting), Wallace's schema was clear: fiction was 'serious play', philosophy a 'profession', and non-fiction served as the 'mediation' between fiction and philosophy. Indeed, after the publication of *Girl with Curious Hair* (1989) and his enrolment at Harvard, Wallace decided to leave the 'literary world' – yet without abandoning his purpose of performing an authentic conversation with other human beings through the act of writing. Along the same lines he explained to Lipsky that 'Westward the Course of Empire Takes Its Way', the final story of his 1989 collection *Girl with Curious Hair*, should be read as 'a kind of suicide note', as he figured that he 'wasn't going to write anymore' (Lipsky, 2010: 61).

As far as Wallace's double allegiance to fiction and philosophy is concerned, it is worth noting that – in reflecting on fiction, aesthetics, and criticism – Wallace asserted that 'I leave the planet when I'm writing: I don't think critically about what I'm doing until it's done. But it's hard to do once you're published. Once your stuff starts getting talked about by other people, how do you deal with that? How do you keep from developing a hard aesthetic line? The story has got to write me' (Schecter and Wallace, 2018). Thus, in addition to the more common concerns of reader reception and interpretation, here Wallace expressed his difficulty in decoupling fiction writing and its critical appraisal: on the one hand, there was the act of writing; on the other hand, there was the fear of being misunderstood. This interrelation always remained a given in Wallace's experience of his craft.[4] From this perspective, the 1989 piece on pornography can be read as Wallace's first attempt to link together fiction, philosophy, and non-fiction – an attempt further developed in the subsequent phases of his research on the relationship among pornography, addiction, and entertainment.

Fiction: pornography, addiction, and the entertainment (1993–97)

As mentioned above, Wallace's initial purpose was to frame the function of pornography within the American entertainment system with particular reference to the case of porn home movies. In the second phase of his research Wallace focused on the relationship between performers and viewers using the case of virtual pornography, which he further elaborated within the structure of the novel *Sir John Feelgood* (described as a 'porn novel' or 'Π – novel' in the drafts kept at the HRC) – a text whose main subject is the consequence of virtual pornography on perceptions of the body.[5]

The technology of virtual pornography is also mentioned in a dialogue between Randy Lenz and Bruce Green in *Infinite Jest* (Wallace, 1996: 560) and in 'Datum Centurio', a brief story published in *Brief Interviews with Hideous Men* (Wallace, 1999: 125–30). Speaking about his 1996 novel with Lipsky, Wallace directly linked virtual pornography and entertainment:

> In ten or fifteen years, we're gonna have virtual reality pornography. Now, if I don't develop some machinery for being able to turn off pure unalloyed pleasure, and allow myself to go out and, you know, grocery shop and pay the rent? I don't know about you, but I'm gonna have to leave the *planet. Virtual. Reality. Pornography.* I'm talking, you know what I mean? The technology's gonna get better and better at doing what it does, which is seduce us into being incredibly dependent on it, so that advertisers can be more confident that we will watch their advertisements. And as a technology system, it's amoral. (Lipsky, 2010: 83)

Here Wallace might be seen as suggesting a deep correspondence between the infinite pleasure provided by the cartridge 'Infinite Jest' in the eponymous novel and the one conveyed by the technology of virtual pornography, since both induce the subject to abandon reality in favour of a representation on a screen. The content of the cartridge is indirectly described through the separate accounts given by four characters in the novel: Joelle van Dyne (the main female character of 'Infinite Jest'), her friend Molly Notkin, James Orin Incandenza (the auteur of the cartridge), and, partially, Donald Gately.

Referring to the main (and supposedly lethal) scene of the cartridge, Molly Notkin explains that Joelle van Dyne performed the role of 'Madame Psychosis, as some kind of maternal instantiation of the archetypal figure Death', who had to tell 'in very simple childlike language to whomever the film's camera represents that Death is always female, and that the female is always maternal' (Wallace, 1996: 788). Molly Notkin then adds that this was 'the alleged substance of the Death-cosmology Madame Psychosis was supposed to deliver in a lalating monologue to the viewer, mediated by the very special lens' (788). Joelle herself affirms that there 'was nothing coherent in the mother-death-cosmology and apologies she'd repeated over and over, inclined over that auto-wobbled lens propped up in the plaid-sided pram' (230). None the less, as its catatonic effects on viewers prove, this 'cosmology', characterized by the vision of Joelle's body in association with hearing her monologue, creates a *system of addiction and entertainment* very similar to the enjoyment provided by the technology of virtual pornography.[6]

In other words the technology of virtual pornography and that of 'Infinite Jest' share the same potential to captivate human beings in a continuous practice of viewing: this is why pornography (like 'Infinite Jest') might be considered a 'failed entertainment', since it triggers a recurring demand to watch while simultaneously destroying the humanity of spectators. The resulting interrelation between addiction and entertainment can be seen to derive from Wallace's overarching view that any kind of detachment from reality causes pain and loneliness: if pornography corrupts the humanity of its viewers, literature offers a figurative cure to recover from this closed, circular loop.

This cure coincides with Wallace's idea that fiction has got 'something to do with loneliness and something to do with setting up a conversation between human beings'. In particular, speaking about the composition of *Infinite Jest* in his interview with Michael Silverblatt, Wallace declared: 'I know that when I started this book ..., I wanted to do something really sad. ... I wanted to do just something really sad and I wanted to do something about what was sad about America' (Silverblatt and Wallace, 1996). Pornography seems to occupy a prominent position among the sad things – as several scenes of *Infinite Jest* prove.

For instance, in a crucial passage near the end of the book, Hal Incandenza affirms that adult movies 'are too downright sad to be truly nasty, or even really entertainment, though the adjective *adult* is kind of a misnomer' (Wallace, 1996: 955). In this scene Hal is commenting on a dialogue between his brother Orin and their father James Orin Incandenza (JOI) in which JOI expresses doubts about Orin's choice to watch the Mitchell brothers' *Behind the Green Door* (1972). Clearly here Hal is not only expressing his lack of interest in pornography but is also stating that adult movies are 'sad' and 'nasty', because they do not provide any form of entertainment. Further on Hal adds that his father believes movies like *Behind the Green Door* represent sex as 'nothing more than organs going in and out of other organs, emotionless, terribly lonely' (Wallace,

1996: 956).[7] This controversial relationship among the denial of pleasure, entertainment, and the feeling of loneliness is properly exemplified by Joelle in the cartridge 'Infinite Jest'.

The central message of the 'Entertainment' is not Joelle's body – which is not clearly visible because of Incandenza's optical effects – but the words she pronounces (as mother for each spectator). As Hamilton Carroll argues in his essay 'Desire, Self, and Other: Wallace and Gender' (2019), Joelle van Dyne is the 'most important figure of male desire in all of Wallace's fiction' (Carroll, 2019: 170), where 'the female object of desire is often a location – or trajectory – that allows the relationship of the sexually mature adult male to his mother-centric infant self to be worked through' (171). In the cartridge Joelle's body is perceived only through the mediation of 'an infantile visual field' (Wallace 1996: 940) that reproduces the visual of a newborn: to put it bluntly, Joelle's naked (or veiled) body is the technological device fostering a regression to the neonatal period – to the period in which there is no knowledge of suffering, and pleasure is crucially bound up with the satisfaction of basic needs.[8]

By reading the content of 'Infinite Jest' in light of Wallace's remarks on virtual pornography I therefore suggest that the cartridge exemplifies the anti-fictional strategy of pornography. As Wallace claimed in his interview with Lipsky,[9] if 'entertainment lies on the addictive continuum' (Lipsky, 2010: 83), the purpose of 'Infinite Jest' is 'to sort of shake the reader awake about some of the things that are sinister in entertainment' (79). The opposition of 'entertainment versus art' (80) mirrors the challenge pornography produces vis-à-vis literature: given that pornography and the 'Entertainment' exemplify the consequences of the addiction–entertainment loop, the task of art – or, more specifically, the task of *Infinite Jest* – is to raise questions around human engagement with entertainment itself. That is the revelational function of *Infinite Jest*, in which the author–reader relationship seems to be 'anti-Entertainment', or rather, the 'remedy or antidote' (Wallace, 1996: 126) to entertainment's lethal power.

Fiction and nonfiction: pornography, addiction, and entertainment (1997–2006)

This kind of revelation is addressed in a different way in the brief stories 'Adult World (I)' and 'Adult World (II)', which depict the character Jeni Roberts going through a process of self-recognition triggered by the vision of female bodies in pornographic movies. As Glenn Kenny has argued, these stories are complementary to the essay 'Big Red Son' (Neyfakh, 2008); this is confirmed by the fact that a draft of the essay contains excerpts from the two stories (Wallace, container 29.1, HRC). Moreover, considering Wallace's larger interest in pornography, I would contend that these writings complete Wallace's research cycle on pornography, since, taken together, they provide a critical insight on the role of pornography in American culture.

Mary K. Holland has observed that Wallace's treatment of pornography in the non-fiction journalism of 'Big Red Son' constitutes 'a merciless look at the still shocking ways in which the porn industry objectifies women physically and psychically, encouraging them to transform their bodies into plasticized machines to accommodate men's bodies and desires' (Holland, 2017: 138). Objectification of the female body as an expression of male sexual desire is also described in 'Adult World (I)' and 'Adult World (II)'. These two stories from *Brief Interviews with Hideous Men* focus on the main characters' different ways of relating to porn videotapes: the husband (unnamed, like the other anonymous 'hideous' men of the collection) is addicted to pornography; the wife (Jeni) experiences a process of recognition about her own sexuality.

Significantly Jeni is referred to in three different ways: firstly, she is the 'wife', before learning about her husband's addiction; secondly, she is presented as 'Jeni Roberts' when she is about to learn of it; and, thirdly, after her realization of the situation, she is called 'Ms. Jeni Orzolek Roberts' (J.O.R.). These changes signal the progression of her process of recognition: when the 'wife' discovers that her husband – 'the Secret Compulsive Masturbator' (Wallace, 1999: 186) – is addicted to watching X-rated movies, she '[r]ealizes/gradually accepts that hsbnd loves his secret loneliness & "interior deficits" more than he loves {/is able to love} her; accepts her "unalterable powerlessness" over hsbnd's secret cmplsions' (187). Jeni thereafter never speaks with her husband about his 'S.C.M. [Secrete Compulsive Masturbation] or interior pain/loneliness/"deficits"' (187). Comparing these stories with *Infinite Jest*, we see a strong coherence in Wallace's characterization of pornography as a nasty relief from loneliness that does not provide entertainment.

More precisely, when Jeni herself starts watching the X-rated movies 'to study and compare the sex techniques of the women in the video' (167), she promptly notices that the eyes of the actresses 'were empty and hard' as if 'they weren't experiencing any intimacy or pleasure and didn't care if their partners were pleased' (168). Jeni's insight recalls JOI's (and Hal's) description of porn movies as staging an 'impoverished, lonely idea of sexuality' (Wallace, 1996: 956). The reason for this feeling is described in a footnote in 'Big Red Son' in which Wallace explains that the unattractiveness of adult movies derives from the performers' faces, which 'usually appear bored or blank or workmanlike' but actually are 'simply *hidden*, the self locked away someplace far behind the eyes. Surely, this hiddenness is the way a human being who's giving away the very most private parts of himself preserves some sense of dignity and autonomy – he denies us true expression' (Wallace, 2005: 17 n14). Stressing a deep association between the eyes and the self, Wallace observes that the actresses and actors are suffering from what viewers understand as a mix of embarrassment, awkwardness, and bother. Yet if adult movies are so unappealing, why do people watch them?

One answer to this question, given by Harold Hecuba, is quoted in the same footnote to 'Big Red Son' as Wallace's explanation above. Recounting his conversation with an LAPD detective who was a 'hard-core fan' of porn, Hecuba reports what the detective replied when asked about the reasons for his interest in pornography.

> The detective confessed that what drew him to the films was 'the faces,' i.e. the actresses' faces, i.e. those rare moments in orgasm or accidental tenderness when the starlets dropped their stylized 'fuck-me-I'm-a-nasty-girl' sneer and became, suddenly, real people. 'Sometimes—and you never know when, is the thing —sometimes all of a sudden they'll kind of reveal themselves' was the detective's way of putting it. 'Their what-do-you-call . . . humanness.' It turned out that the LAPD detective found adult films *moving*, in fact far more so than most mainstream Hollywood movies, in which latter films actors – sometimes very gifted actors – go about feigning genuine humanity, i.e.: 'In real movies, it's all on purpose. I suppose what I like in porno is the accident of it.' (Wallace, 2005: 16 n14)

The search for these instants of 'humanness' provides strong motivation to keep watching adult movies because the interest of viewers is enhanced by those 'rare moments' in which they experience an illusory form of intimacy with the performers, namely when 'the porn performer's whole face change as self-consciousness (in most females) or crazed blankness (in most males) yields to some genuinely felt erotic joy in what's going on; the sighs and moans change from automatic to expressive' (Wallace, 2005: 17 n14). When the 'self' is hidden, the bodies of the performers 'remain just bodies' (17 n14); when the 'self' appears, these bodies become a sort of instrument through which viewers can experience a form of self-pleasure.

To a certain extent this process recalls the evolution of the character of Jeni, who, in 'Adult World (II)', reaches what Wallace (probably ironically) calls an '"authentic responsibility for self"' (Wallace, 1999: 188). This happens precisely when she recognizes both her husband's addiction and her own body as a potential 'sexual object', and, in this respect, it is significant that, near the end of 'Adult World (II)', Jeni and her husband become 'one flesh' (189) – as though, together, they might embody the entanglement of addiction and entertainment.

As I have claimed throughout this chapter, pornography played a prominent role in Wallace's reflections from 1989 on. By focusing on the overlaps between addiction and entertainment, Wallace explored the relationship between pleasure and technology, analysing some of their most dangerous effects. Although the themes of sex and sexuality have been broadly analysed according to a gender-oriented perspective in the field of Wallace studies (Hayes-Brady, 2013; Holland, 2013; Holland, 2017; Jackson, 2020), I hope to have showed that a chronological account of Wallace's treatment of pornography offers useful grounds for exploring the relationship between addiction and entertainment and functions as a 'case study' on the fusion of philosophy and literature in his work.

Notes

1 The list is rather long. i.e.: the essay *Signifying Rappers: Rap and Race in the Urban Present* (1990), co-written with Mark Costello; the novel *Infinite Jest* (1996); the stories 'Adult World (I)', 'Adult World (II)', and 'Datum Centurio' (all collected in *Brief Interviews with Hideous Men*, 1999); the articles and short essays 'David Lynch Keeps His Head'

(*Premiere*, 1995; republished in *A Supposedly Fun Thing I'll Never Do Again*, 1997), 'Back in New Fire' (originally appeared as 'Impediment to Passion' in *Might Magazine*, 1996; republished in *Both Flesh and Not*, hereafter *BFN*, 2012), 'Big Red Son' (originally appeared as 'Neither Adult nor Entertainment' in *Premiere*, 1998; republished in *Consider The Lobster*, 2005), 'The (As It Were) Seminal Importance of *Terminator 2*' (originally appeared as 'F/X Porn' in *Might Magazine*, 1998; republished in *BFN*), 'Federer Both Flesh and Not' (appeared as 'Federer as Religious Experience' in the *New York Times* in 2006; republished in *BFN*).

2 Moreover, as Adam Kelly points out in his reading of *Brief Interviews with Hideous Men* (1998), the interest on 'the question of the feminine – and particularly the question of how the feminine can and should be represented in writing' on Wallace's part derived from so–called French feminism, whose theories 'combined training in the psychoanalysis of Jacques Lacan with an interest in the new poststructuralist approaches to language pioneered by Jacques Derrida' (Kelly, 2018: 84).

3 Wallace's research followed the developments of the adult industry itself as it emerges, for instance, from a footnote of 'Big Red Son' in which Wallace suggests that some 1990s adult productions such as 'Dark's and Black's movies are not for men who want to be aroused and maybe masturbate. They are for men who have problems with women and want to see them humiliated' (Wallace, 2005: 27 n23). A little further on he adds something crucial on the developments of the adult industry, stating: 'The thing to recognize is that the adult industry's new respectability creates a paradox. The more acceptable in modern culture it becomes, the farther porn will have to go in order to preserve the sense of unacceptability that's so essential to its appeal' (28 n23).

4 Many interviews show that Wallace held this view throughout his career. During a conversation with Richard Powers and John O'Brien in 2000, for example, Wallace claimed: 'One of the biggest problems in terms of learning to write, or teaching anybody to write, is getting it in your nerve endings that the reader cannot read your mind. That what you say isn't interesting simply because you, yourself, say it. Whether that translates to a feeling of obligation to the reader I don't know, but we've all probably sat next to people at dinner or on public transport who are producing communication signals but it's not communicative expression. It's expressive expression, right? And actually it's in conversation that you can feel most vividly how alienating and unpleasant it is to feel as if someone is going through all the motions of communicating with you but in actual fact you don't even need to be there at all' (Burn, ed., 2012: 114). Other crucial passages on this issue can be found in 'The Nature of Fun' (1998, collected in *BFN*) and in the conversation with Bryan A.

Garner in which Wallace mainly spoke about his teaching experience (Wallace and Garner, 2013).
5 On *Sir John Feelgood* see Hering, 2016: 127–35, 140–1; Scarlato, 2020: 155–70.
6 This similarity seems to be confirmed by Wallace in an interview in which he declared: 'the book is about a culture deciding that the meaning of life consists in experiencing as much pleasure as much of the time as possible and what are the implications of that' (Wallace and Wiley, 1997).
7 The relationship between the vision of pornography and the reaction of the viewer is also addressed by JOI in a 'Pornography–parody' titled 'Möbius Strips', whose main character is Hugh G. Rection (the name is a comic pun frequently used in those years), 'a theoretical physicist ("Rection"), who can only achieve creative mathematical insight during coitus' and 'conceives of Death as a lethally beautiful woman (Heath)' (Wallace, 1996: 990 n24).
8 To a certain extent this regression is mentioned in the Q&A section of 'Big Red Son' in which pornography is addressed as that complex landscape in which 'you get to be a kid again. You roll around and get dirty. It's the adult sandbox' (Wallace, 2005: 35). On Wallace and pornography, see also Sloane, 2019 (77–80). Here the analysis of 'Big Red Son' and of some stories from *Brief Interviews with Hideous Men* (including 'Adult World (I)') is set against the broader issue of the function of the body in Wallace's oeuvre. Sloane's analysis of 'Big Red Son' touches up the following themes: firstly, the relationship between sex and desire, secondly, male power over the female body; thirdly, the function of the male gaze in the objectification of the female body.
9 This issue was somehow addressed also in the interview with Wiley. In reference to the relationship between technology and pleasure Wallace said to Wiley: 'all that stuff is now pulling against what I think in my generation and yours is very different from, say, our grandparents' – an immense, gnawing, craving hunger for pleasure, and a real feeling of deprivation when we're not experiencing it. I don't think that I would do it, but I think what I would do is I would arrange to have a lot of friends around me who would keep me from doing it' (Wallace and Wiley, 1997).

References

Borrelli, F. (2015). *Maestri di finzione*. Macerata: Quodlibet.
Burn, S. J., ed. (2012). *Conversations with David Foster Wallace*. Jackson MS: University Press of Mississippi.

Carroll, H. (2019). 'Desire, Self, and Other: Wallace and Gender', 169–79. In Stephen J. Burn and Mary K. Holland, eds, *Approaches to Teaching the Works of David Foster Wallace*. New York NY: The Modern Language Association of America.

Den Dulk, A. (2019). 'Wallace and Philosophy', 155–68. In Stephen J. Burn and Mary K. Holland, eds, *Approaches to Teaching the Works of David Foster Wallace*. New York NY: Modern Language Association of America.

Hayes-Brady, C. (2013). '"…": Language, Gender, and Modes of Power in the Work of David Foster Wallace', 131–50. In Marshall Boswell and Stephen J. Burn, eds, *A Companion to David Foster Wallace Studies*. New York NY: Palgrave Macmillan.

Hering, D. (2016). *David Foster Wallace. Fiction and Form*. London and New York NY: Bloomsbury.

Holland, M. K. (2013). 'Mediated Immediacy in *Brief Interviews with Hideous Men*', 107–30. In Marshall Boswell and Stephen J. Burn, eds, *A Companion to David Foster Wallace Studies*. New York NY: Palgrave Macmillan.

Holland, M. K. (2017). '"By Hirsute Author": Gender and Communication in the Work and Study of David Foster Wallace', 128–50. In Beatrice Pire and Pierre-Louis Patoine, eds, *David Foster Wallace: Presences of the Other*. Brighton: Sussex Academic Press.

Jackson, E. (2020). *David Foster Wallace's Toxic Sexuality: Hideousness, Neoliberalism, Spermatics*. London and New York NY: Bloomsbury.

Kelly, A. (2018). '*Brief Interviews with Hideous Men*', 82–96. In Ralph Clare, ed., *The Cambridge Companion to David Foster Wallace*. Cambridge: Cambridge University Press.

Lipsky, D. (2010). *Although of Course You End Up Becoming Yourself: A Road Trip with David Foster Wallace*. New York NY: Broadway Books.

Scarlato, C. (2020). *Attraverso il corpo: Filosofia e letteratura in David Foster Wallace*. Milan: Mimesis.

Sloane, P. (2019), *David Foster Wallace and the Body*, New York NY: Routledge.

Wallace, D. Foster. (1996). *Infinite Jest*. Boston MA: Little, Brown.

Wallace, D. Foster. (1999). *Brief Interviews with Hideous Men*. Boston MA: Little, Brown.

Wallace, D. Foster. (2005). *Consider the Lobster and Other Essays*. Boston MA: Little, Brown.

Wallace, D. Foster. (2012). *Both Flesh and Not: Essays*. Boston MA: Little, Brown.

Wallace, D. Foster and M. Costello. (2013). *Signifying Rappers. Rap and Race in the Urban Present*. New York NY: Back Bay Books.

Wallace, D. Foster and B. A. Garner. (2013). *Quack This Way. David Foster Wallace & Bryan A. Garner: Talk, Language and Writing*. Dallas TX: RosePen Books.

Wallace, D. Foster and D. Wiley. (27 February 1997). 'An Interview with David Foster Wallace', in *The Minnesota Daily*.

Internet sources

Neyfakh, L. (18 September 2008). 'Premiere Editor Glenn Kenny Remembers Wallace: "Dave Was the Greatest Bargain in Magazine Publishing"', *Observer*. https://bit.ly/2KTdevK (accessed 4 December 2020).

Schecter, M. and D. Foster Wallace. (12 October 2018). 'Lost David Foster Wallace Interview from 1989', ed. Andrea Laurencell Sheridan, *The David Foster Wallace Society*. https://bit.ly/2A7r2id (accessed 4 December 2020).

Silverblatt, M. and D. Foster Wallace (11 April 1996). 'Bookworm. David Foster Wallace: Infinite Jest', *KCRW*. www.kcrw.com/culture/shows/bookworm/david-foster-wallace-infinite-jest (accessed 4 December 2020).

Archival sources

Wallace, D. Foster. (29 March 1989). 'Letter to William E. Kennick', William E. Kennick Papers, box 1, folder 4. Amherst College Archives and Special Collections, Amherst College Library (MA).

Wallace, D. Foster. (10 May 1989). 'Letter to Bonnie Nadell', container 1.2, Bonnie Nadell Collection of David Foster Wallace, Harry Ransom Center, University of Austin (TX).

Wallace, D. Foster. (22 August 1989). 'Letter to Bonnie Nadell', container 1.2, Bonnie Nadell Collection of David Foster Wallace, Harry Ransom Center, University of Austin (TX).

Wallace, D. Foster. (7 November 1989). 'Letter to Alice Turner', container 1.2, Bonnie Nadell Collection of David Foster Wallace, Harry Ransom Center, University of Austin (TX).

Wallace, D. Foster. (27 June 1998). 'Neither Adult nor Entertainment. Letter of David Foster Wallace to Glenn Kenny', David Foster Wallace Papers, container 29.3, Harry Ransom Center, University of Austin (TX).

Wallace, D. Foster. (undated). 'Neither adult nor entertainment', David Foster Wallace Papers, container 29.1, Harry Ransom Center, University of Austin (TX).

15

'Something staring back at you': an anamorphic reading of *Infinite Jest*

Angelo Grossi

Several critics have pointed out the relevance of the problem of Descartes's mind–body dualism in David Foster Wallace's oeuvre. What has been ignored is that Wallace's critique of the dualities implied in the Cartesian model involves not only the field of discursivity but also the field of visuality. In this chapter, which will focus on Wallace's magnum opus *Infinite Jest* (1996) – a novel famously oversaturated with references to visual culture – I will discuss how the text thematizes a radical questioning of the philosophical dualities implied in the Cartesian subject by evoking two rival models of modern visuality: Renaissance perspectivalism and the baroque.

As Martin Jay, author of *Downcast Eyes* (1993) – a study on the anti-ocularcentric discourse in twentieth-century French thought – points out, Cartesian perspectivalism and the baroque are two of the three main visual regimes of modernity (along with the descriptive mode of the Northern European Renaissance). Each one of these models of visuality presupposes a different epistemological rhetoric. Cartesian perspectivalism is the visual model of the Southern European Renaissance, as well as the hegemonic model of modernity. It can be identified with Renaissance notions of perspective in the visual arts and Cartesian ideas of subjective rationality in philosophy. The Cartesian model assumes a separation between subject and object (as well as between mind and body) and understands the subject's gaze as a transcendent, coherent, and objective one and the object as inert to the subject's mastery. The baroque model of vision, on the contrary, involves a radical rejection of these dualities and a tension towards a transcendence of the fixedness of the subjective point of view implied in Renaissance perspective. As Jay explains, the baroque is inclined towards a 'confusing interplay of form and chaos, surface and depth, transparency and obscurity' (Jay, 1993: 47). One of the most salient features of the baroque is, as Omar Calabrese points out, 'experimentation with the elasticity of the borders of a total system *starting from its most extreme consequences*' (Calabrese, 2017: 50 emphasis in the original) – a stylistic tendency that produced 'a series of models beyond which perspective destroyed itself, such as trompe-l'oeil, illusionist architectural scenes (*quadratura*), anamorphosis and foreshortening' (50). The overloading of images present in the baroque visual regime disorients the subject instead of presenting a clear and rationalized view of the external world. As Jay notes, 'the typical mirror of the baroque was not the flat reflecting mirror, which is often seen as vital to the development of rationalized perspective, but rather the anamorphic mirror, either concave or convex, that distorts the visual image' (Jay, 1993: 48). In her influential study on the phenomenological aesthetics of the baroque *La folie du voir* (1986), the French philosopher Christine Buci-Glucksmann characterizes the baroque paradigm as a 'madness of vision' (a term borrowed from Maurice Merleau-Ponty) offering an immersive visual experience that turns the mirror of representation against itself, unmasking the limits of subjectivity and representation and ultimately constructing 'a mimesis of nothingness [une mimétique du rien]' (Buci-Glucksmann, 2013: 14).

An aspect that has been overlooked by the scholarship on David Foster Wallace is how his oeuvre, and especially *Infinite Jest*, function as an expression of the twentieth-century recovery of the baroque, generally referred to as the 'neo-baroque'. The proliferation of iconic baroque landmarks in *Infinite Jest* includes both overt and hidden references. One of the most blatant instances is the almost leitmotif-like recurrence of Gianlorenzo Bernini's *The Ecstasy of St Teresa*. The statue takes centre stage in one of James O. Incandenza's fictional films, *Pre-Nuptial Agreement of Heaven and Hell*, where it serves to evoke a longing for transcendence of the fixedness of a subjective point of view (a standpoint belonging to an 'alcoholic sandwich-bag salesman' (Wallace, 1996: 742) in case of the fictional film). The fictional film portrays a transcendence of the limits of the fixed subject position of Cartesian perspectivalism, where '[t]he statue, the sensuous presence of the thing, let the alcoholic sandwich-bag salesman escape himself, his tiresome ubiquitous involuted head' (742). Another indicator of the centrality of baroque to *Infinite Jest* is the title of the earliest-written section of the novel, which Wallace composed as an independent short story during his MFA in creative writing at the University of Arizona between 1985 and 1986: 'Las Meniñas' (Wallace, 'Las Meniñas', HRC). With hardly any alteration, the two-page draft became a section of *Infinite Jest* (37–8) set in the Year of the Trial-Size Dove Bar and narrated by a minor character, Clenette Henderson, an African American woman and future Ennet House Resident. The link between the section (arguably one of the novel's most controversial sequences, as it is narrated in a 'mock Ebonics' slang) and Velasquez's self-reflexive masterpiece *Las meniñas* is mysterious and much debated.[1] Still, it offers another valuable clue to the novel's willingness to appropriate baroque's visual rhetoric.

Wallace's use of imagery drawn from the baroque in a novel portraying a fictional near-future age that is an exaggerated version of the 1990s can be considered in keeping with Omar Calabrese's proposal to adopt the term 'neo-baroque' instead of 'postmodern' to define the prevailing taste of that period (Calabrese, 2017: 12–17). Leaving aside the equation between baroque and postmodernity, Wallace's work invites us to explore the peculiar nature of baroque visuality in its deeper implications.

In this chapter I will argue that Wallace in *Infinite Jest* both thematically and formally deploys a baroque and anamorphic understanding of the gaze and seems to conceive it as a device to undermine the ideological construct portrayed in the novel. The conception of the gaze that emerges in the mature phase of Jacques Lacan's thought will be helpful for analysing the model of visuality employed by Wallace. In Lacan's formulation the 'gaze' does not concern the subject's vision but pertains to the way the object looks back at the viewer. This encounter with the gaze dismantles the rationalist sense of mastery of the subject postulated by Cartesian perspectivalism. From a philosophical standpoint the decentring of the fixed subject position of Cartesian perspectivalism also acts as a way out of the self-reflexive game of the neo-capitalistic ideology represented in the novel. As Nicoline Timmer points out, 'the ideology promoted in this fictional U.S. that is presented in *Infinite Jest* is a decadent form of Western utilitarian liberalism, or at least a form of liberalism tested to its limit' (Timmer, 2010: 128). On the one hand, this ideological apparatus seems to deconstruct monolithic ideological systems; on the other hand, it perpetuates in the subject an illusion of autonomy and autarchic accomplishment. It is a neocapitalistic ideology 'committed to *the appearance of freedom*' (Wallace, 1996: 1031 n164). The resulting subjectivities can be described as atomized, self-contained, and solipsistic, which amounts to saying that the self becomes its own ultimate authority. The decentring of such a subject involves the realm of both visuality and of discursivity/vocality. Therefore in the second part of the chapter I will discuss how an experience of the limits of representation informs the theme of aphasia in *Infinite Jest*. I will show how aphasia can be interpreted as a break within language's possibility of symbolizing everything, another illusion that characterizes the transcendent Cartesian subject.

In this sense *Infinite Jest* will prove to be a literary *Vexierbild* – a term designating the picture-puzzles typical of the baroque era, containing riddles and concealed images. Sometimes these images (or messages) are concealed in the verbose proliferation of information that characterizes the novel, other times they are found in the recesses of the novel: the endnotes. And it is indeed from an endnote that this analysis will start, namely endnote 129.

The baroque and anamorphism in *Infinite Jest*

Endnote 129 is attached to a passage (333) which is in turn buried amongst the intricate set of details that accompany the narration of the Eschaton game. Eschaton is a convoluted nuclear war-simulation based on an interplay between tennis and calculus that some ETA students embark on about one-third through the novel. I am quoting it at length because of its valuable theoretical implications:

> M. Pemulis is, in the best Allston MA tradition, a good friend and a bad-news enemy, and even E.T.A.s who don't like him are careful not to do or even say anything that might call for score-settling, because

Pemulis is a thoroughgoing chilled-revenge gourmet, and is not one bit above dosing someone's water-jug or voltaging their door-knob or encoding something horrid in your E.T.A. med-files or dickying with the mirror over the bureau in the little recessed part of your subdorm room so that when you look in the mirror in the A.M. to comb or tend to a blackhead or something you see *something staring back at you* that you'll never entirely get over, which is what took over two years to finally happen to M. H. Penn, who afterward wouldn't say what he'd seen but stopped shaving altogether and, it's agreed, has never been quite himself since. (1025 n129, emphasis added)

Immediately after endnote 129, we find a key moment which, according to Stephen Burn, introduces 'a crisis point' that will instigate 'a number of chains of cause and effect that lead into the novel's climactic last days' (Burn, 2003: 23). This moment revolves around a quarrel about the game triggered by the intrusion of the 'real' element of snow. Nevertheless, an equally relevant detail is contained – or better, given the surrounding bombardment of elaborate information, 'hidden' – in the apparently trivial content of the endnote devoted to explanation of Pemulis's penchant for pranks. The last-mentioned of the pranks listed in the endnote, the 'dickying with the mirror over the bureau', produces in M. H. Penn, Pemulis's 'sworn foe' (333), a traumatic effect. The 'something' that triggers such a reaction remains unknown to the reader as well as to the other characters, given that we read that Penn himself has been unable ever since to put it into words: he 'afterward wouldn't say what he'd seen'. This amounts to further concealment, since the bureau is already concealed 'in the little recessed part of your subdorm room' (as well as in the endnotes, the 'recessed part' of the novel). This concealment supposedly triggers, just as it frustrates, the reader's desire to know that 'something' which is not only hidden in the mirror but also left unrevealed in the text. What we know is what this 'something' does: it is 'staring back at you'. The 'thing' seems able to exceed the mirror's passive act of pure reflection, which insinuates an uncanny feeling of loss of control.

A possible explanation of Penn's trauma, as well as of the fact that he 'has never quite been himself since', is that he experienced an encounter with the 'gaze' as it was conceived by Jacques Lacan during the mature phase of the development of his thought. Lacan discusses the gaze extensively in *Seminar XI: The Four Fundamental*

Concepts of Psychoanalysis, a sequence of four lectures delivered in 1964 and published in 1973. Of these the sessions entitled 'Of the Gaze as Objet Petit a' are especially important to understanding how Lacan conceives of a difference between the eye and the gaze that is in keeping with the scopic regime of the baroque. The former (the eye) belongs to the subject and corresponds to the self-reflexive sense of mastery that we have over what we see as long as we are in control of where and how to look. Lacan describes it as 'that form of vision that is satisfied with itself in imagining itself as consciousness' (Lacan, 1978: 74), a consciousness that, in this process, 'may turn back upon itself' (74) – a choice of words that is echoed in *Infinite Jest* by Marathe's refusal of everything that 'bends back in on the self' (107).

Influenced by Maurice Merleau-Ponty's essay *The Visible and the Invisible*, by Jean-Paul Sartre's *Being and Nothingness*, and by the Lithuanian art historian Jurgis Baltrušaitis, Lacan came to conceive the gaze as something belonging not to the subject but to the object. As Todd McGowan explains, the Lacanian gaze is 'something that the subject (or spectator) encounters in the object' (McGowan, 2007b: 5). Inside the scopic field the gaze is the visual version of what Lacan terms, using an untranslatable neologism, 'objet petit a'. Situated outside the field of visibility, the 'objet petit a' is the impossible object of desire: an object that is permanently out of reach. It is not the goal of desire but the cause of it. Its loss inaugurates the process of desiring and constitutes the subject as desiring. The subject desires because of the lack of this impossible object, but this object exists only in so far as it is missing. Its unattainability supports the real goal of desire, which in Lacan's conception is not to reach the object but to perpetuate desire itself. The name 'objet petit a' indicates it is a 'little other' (*petit autre*), as opposed to the 'big Other' that stands for signification, the collective symbolic order. It is something that exceeds signification and cannot be signified. Therefore it belongs to the order of the Real. For Lacan the Real is the indication of the limits of the Symbolic order, of the inability of language and signification to speak the whole truth. It is the point at which language and signification break down, or, as Slavoj Žižek puts it, it 'is not an external thing that resists being caught in the symbolic network, but the fissure within the symbolic network itself' (Žižek, 2006: 72).

Being the 'objet petit a' of a scopic drive (the drive that prompts us to look at something), the gaze is not a positive entity that the subject sees as much as a gap in the subject's looking, something that is irreducible to the visual field and exceeds representation. As Joan Copjec explains, 'This point at which something appears to be *in*visible, this point at which something appears to be missing from representation, some meaning left unrevealed, is the point of the Lacanian gaze' (Copjec, 1994: 34). Therefore the gaze is not only different from the omnipotent eye of Cartesian perspectivalism. It is its exact obverse, in so far as it is the point that marks the failure of the seemingly transcendent Cartesian subject to perceive everything. As McGowan puts it, the gaze is 'the gap within the subject's seemingly omnipotent look' (McGowan, 2007b: 6).

In *Seminar XI*, Lacan provides a much-quoted example of the gaze by discussing Hans Holbein the Younger's painting *The Ambassadors* in the National Gallery, London (1533) (Lacan, 1978: 85–90). The painting depicts two wealthy-looking ambassadors surrounded by the intricate and detailed array of objects accumulated during their travels. In the foreground of the painting, in a position that seems to defy the laws of gravity, stands an oblong and deformed figure. Looking directly at the figure, one does not see anything discernible – only an unintelligible blot. Yet looking at the painting from the left side at an angle, one sees distinctly that the mysterious figure is a skull staring back at the viewer. Not only does the skull represent a *memento mori* that underscores the fugacity of the riches displayed in the painting, it also indicates the site of the gaze. The viewer experiences a point that resists the mastery of vision: instead of exerting control over that point, the subject becomes involved in what she sees, because the object cannot be looked at directly but requires movement of the body and a turning of the head in order to be seen. At the same time it cannot be integrated into the rest of the visual field. This is an experience of how the spectator's perspective distorts the field of the visible: once the viewer turns her head and makes sense of what, from her default perspective, was unintelligible, all the other represented objects become distorted and undecipherable. In this sense the gaze shows the objective absence of a safe distance from which to look at the object: the subject is inscribed in the object in the form of the stain (or the disruption) implicated in the picture (or in the text) itself. Thus this uncanny experience functions as a form of loss of mastery which, as Lacan puts it, 'makes visible for us here something that is simply the subject as annihilated' (Lacan, 1978: 88). Such an experience ultimately leads to a reflection concerning ideology. The subject is founded by the act of recognizing the point where a void hidden by ideology manifests itself because, as Slavoj Žižek explains, 'this original void, this lack of symbolic structure, is the subject' (Žižek, 1989: 175).

Now let us return to *Infinite Jest* and to endnote 129. Although the text does not explain how Pemulis had been able to prompt Penn to encounter the gaze, the described experience seems to be the one discussed by Lacan. If the reason of Penn's trauma is that the hidden and undescribed 'something' was 'staring back' (Wallace, 1996: 1025) at him, which is exactly what Lacan's gaze does, the 'something' is left undescribed (and Penn will never be able to describe it) precisely because it is impossible to describe it, to account for it symbolically: it is a blind spot in the visual field, irreducible to signification as well as to representation. Therefore, after this traumatic experience Penn 'has never quite been himself since' (1025), because what he experienced was a traumatic encounter with the Real that undermined his sense of mastery. Although we learn that he has tried to avoid that experience ever since ('stopped shaving altogether'), the loss of stability produced by that moment results in a marginalization inside the social order of ETA: during YDAU, when Penn is 21 (333),[2] his position in the field of tennis is particularly low, given that he is 'flailing away on the grim Third-World Satellite pro tour, playing for travel-expenses in bleak dysenteric locales' (333).

Aphasia and the limits of representation

References to *memento mori* are ubiquitous in Wallace's novel. The most conspicuous reference is the title itself, which quotes the moment of Hamlet's recognition of Yorick's skull, a *memento mori* belonging to the same tradition as the one contained in Hans Holbein's painting. The terminology related to optical deformations also recurs throughout the novel. This frequency is motivated by plot reasons, as one of the novel's main characters, the suicide experimental filmmaker James O. Incandenza, is an expert of optics. He is the director of 'The Entertainment', the novel's eponymous, lethally addictive film, in which deforming lenses play a crucial role. 'The Entertainment' is a representation of maternal plenitude, reproducing an encounter with an impossible object of desire. Joelle van Dyne plays an archetypal maternal figure seen from a deformed lens positioned in a crib. The lens is designed to reproduce the wobbly vision of a very young infant. The novel mentions twice that the peculiar optical deformations deployed in 'The Entertainment' involve the phenomenon of anamorphosis. In Molly Notkin's (pretty unreliable) account of 'The Entertainment', the fictional film scholar, abducted and interviewed by the Wheelchair Assassins, describes the film as deploying 'anamorphic fragmentation' (791) as one of its aesthetic features. In addition the same account claims that Joelle's face in the film is 'either veiled or blanked out by undulating computer-generated squares of color or *anamorphosized* into unrecognizability as any kind of face by the camera's apparently very strange and novel lens' (788, emphasis added).

Terminology concerning optical effects is also often used in the novel to delineate characters' appearance. Hal's nickname is 'halation' (97), described as 'the most angelic of distortion' (97). Halation is the result of light reflecting off a highly reflective surface – an effect that is deployed also in 'The Entertainment', where the wobbly lens is characterized by a 'milky blur' (939). Moreover, Mario is described as being not 'retarded or cognitively damaged' but 'more like *refracted* ... a pole poked into mental water and just a little off and just taking a little bit longer, in the manner of all *refracted* things' (314, emphases added). Refraction is an optical illusion that concerns transparency, as it involves the bending of light when it passes from one transparent medium to another. As David Hering underscores, this optical effect in *Infinite Jest* can be read as the possibility to 'refractively pass through the "reflective" surface and dialogically communicate with whoever is through or outside that surface' (Hering, 2016: 87). Another description involving an optical distortion concerns Hal and Mario's half-uncle Charles Tavis. We read that 'Charles Tavis is physically small in a way that seems less endocrine than perspectival. His smallness resembles the smallness of something that's farther away from you than it wants to be, plus is receding' (Wallace, 1996: 519). Endnote 218 explains that Tavis's peculiar 'perspectival smallness' inspired James in the invention of 'weird wide-angle rear-view mirrors on the sides of automobiles that so diminish the cars behind you that federal statute requires them to have printed right on the glass that Objects In Mirror Are Closer Than They Appear' (note 218, p. 1036) – the only invention attributed to James that actually exists. Moreover, due to this 'weird appearance of recessive drift' (519), Tavis is described as 'looking as usual oddly foreshortened and small' (519), adjectives that assume the weight of an epithet: 'the mirrors had been inspired by the *always-foreshortened* Charles Tavis' (note 218, p. 1036, emphasis added). The abundance of references to optical distortions implies a constant questioning of the subject's capacity to be in control of the objects of its perceptions. Images appear distorted and ambiguous, and, more importantly, are not inert. Tavis's perceived 'recession' is related not to his movement but to an agency of the image itself.

Just as optical distortions are able to dismantle the subject's illusory sense of mastery over the object in the realm of visuality, a similar lack of control is revealed in the realm of language by an experience that exposes language's failure to symbolize and 'say' everything – defying language's seemingly omnipotent symbolic power. If, as we have seen, in the realm of visuality the object-gaze is a blind spot in the visual field, in the realm of vocality the object-voice par excellence is silence. As Jacques-Alain Miller stressed in his article 'Jacques Lacan and the Voice' (2007), the object-voice is, by way of analogy with the object-gaze, that which is subtracted from the field of the audible and which the ear cannot grasp. As Miller explains, 'potential considerations on the voice [as objet petit a] ... can only be inscribed in a Lacanian perspective if they are indexed on the function of the voice as *a-phonic [a-phone]*' (Miller, 2007: 139).

In *Infinite Jest* Hal is the character that epitomizes language's illusory omnipotence. His seemingly infallible ability with language and signification is repeatedly stressed by the narrator: he has 'for a long time identified himself as a lexical prodigy' (Wallace, 1996: 155), 'reads like a vacuum' (15), has memorized the whole *Oxford English Dictionary* in its integral version, etc. Towards the end of the novel there is a meaningful episode in which this mastery of language starts revealing some cracks. The episode involves Hal trying to find a concise word to define an optical distortion produced by a particular position. In the following paragraphs I will show how this episode can be read as one of Hal's first contacts with the possibility that language may be less precise than he had previously assumed. The episode occurs when Hal is experiencing a very advanced stage of marijuana withdrawal. One symptom of this process is increased inability to communicate, which will (probably) culminate in aphasia in front of the admissions committee of the University of Arizona narrated in the novel's first section – set in the year of Glad (the last event of the novel in terms of chronology). In the second to last section Hal appears to be lying on the floor, almost completely unable to move, with a glass labelled 'NASA' – which he always carries with him to spit into – on his chest. This section of the novel, like other sections towards the end, are narrated by Hal, who as a narrator demonstrates a surprising awareness of several details about his parents and relatives and thus contradicts what the reader has previously learned about him from the omniscient narration – above all, that he has an 'odd blankness about his family' (517) or that, when asked about family members (besides Mario), his 'mind will go utterly blank … as if the names were words on the tip of his tongue' (516). What occurs is a kind of Möbius-strip-like reversal between inside and outside whereby the 'odd blankness', or void of Hal's interiority, becomes external, invading every relationship with the exterior and transforming it into an exteriorized version of his interior blankness. This is a process that does not only involve his voice, in so far as he refers to himself at the beginning of the novel as 'staring with all the blankness I can summon' (13). Simultaneously the blankness about his family gets replaced deep within him by unsuspected awareness, in a process that coincides with his promotion to narrator of his story. While Hal is lying on the floor with the NASA glass on his chest, his first-person narration follows his reconsideration of many aspects of his family and general story, demonstrating an unsuspected knowledge of the many secrets scattered throughout the novel. For instance it mentions his mother's affairs with John Wayne and with her half-brother Charles Tavis and, more explicitly, hints at the fact that Mario was born from that semi-incestuous relationship. As Hal's reflection on his family unfolds, it is often disrupted by attempts to recall the 'concise term' for the 'optical perspective' distorting 'glass's round mouth' into a 'narrow slot' (953). His guesses are '*specular* is what refers to optical perspective; it came to me after I stopped trying to recall it' (953) and 'the word that best connoted why the glass mouth looked slotty was probably *foreshortened*' (954). While 'specular' is certainly not the word Hal is looking for – as the visual distortion does not involve any mirroring effect – 'foreshortened' seems appropriate, although it is not devoid of problematic implications. Foreshortening (i.e.: perspective on an object's head that makes it looks compressed) is an optical distortion adopted in Renaissance art to convey an illusory sense of three-dimensionality that imitates the way the human eye perceives objects in space. Such a realistic – yet artificial – effect is often created by deploying proportions that differ dramatically from those of the real world.[3] Therefore the term 'foreshortened' is appropriate to describe the fixed subject implied in the perspectivalism of the Renaissance[4] but does not perfectly grasp the real vision of a human eye. In addition to Hal's unprecedented word-finding difficulty, what the episode shows is that the character is experiencing the limits of the precision of language: words can approximate meaning but not completely exhaust it. Therefore what is at stake in this passage is a double experience of the Real, which simultaneously involves the gaze and the voice.

Hal's confrontation with the limits of his own control over objects was anticipated by another moment of significance for the thematic economy of the novel. Half-way through *Infinite Jest* Hal, while waiting for his official scolding for the Eschaton debacle outside the Headmaster's office, stares at blue wallpaper that communicates an increasingly uncanny feeling to him. This unsettling feeling is provoked by the fact that the wallpaper scheme is composed of 'fluffy cumuli arrayed patternlessly against an overenhancedly blue sky' (509), a feature that contributes to making the wallpaper 'incredibly disorienting' (509). This sense of disorientation drives Hal to the point of loathing the sky-and-cloud wallpaper. We read that 'Hal loathes sky-and-cloud wallpaper because it makes him feel high-altitude and disoriented and sometimes plummeting' (509). The unpleasantness of this object is more easily linked to Hal's inability to make 'fluffy cumuli' fit a pattern than to the actual depiction of the sky: it is not coincidental that the narration, focalized on Hal, introduces the description with the words 'the wallpaper's scheme'. The clouds are formless spots that defy a scheme (they are 'arrayed patternlessly') and therefore disturb Hal's sense of mastery, which requires a pattern. In this respect it is worth noting that the wallpaper scene occurs in a section which opened with Hal's attempt to provide an exhaustive catalogue of all the blue-coloured objects present in the waiting room: 'The following things in the room were blue. The blue checks in the blue-and-black-checked shag carpet ...' (508). The section's opening, internally focused on Hal, therefore portrays his subjectivity as prone to mapping, categorization, and, ultimately, control of the external world (in a nutshell, a 'Cartesian' subjectivity), while simultaneously introducing the unsettling possibility of an undermining of this sense of mastery.

In the realm of language and signification, an analogous loss of control is at stake in the issue of aphasia. In fact Hal's aphasia in the first section can be read as an imposition of the 'silence of the Real' (McGowan, 2007b: 208) on ideology's capacity to symbolize and 'say' everything. If his contact with the limits of language, epitomized by the difficulty in finding the concise term for 'optical perspective', is the turning point of this process, this moment was also anticipated. In the section (not much earlier in the novel) where Hal drives to what he thinks is a Narcotics Anonymous meeting, but which will turn out to be a surreal gathering focused on nurturing the 'Inner Infant' (Wallace, 1996: 795–808), Hal is trying to kill the time of the 'dull drive' (Wallace, 1996: 796) by attempting to reconstruct 'the probable etymological career of the word *Anonymous*' (796). We read that

> all the way he supposed from the Æolic ὄνμγα through Thynne's B.S. 1580s reference to 'anonymall Chronicals'; and whether it was joined way back somewhere at the Saxonic taproot to the Olde English on-ane, which supposedly meant All as One or As One Body and became Cynewulf's eventual standard inversion to the classic anon, maybe. (796–7)

Two aspects of this passage are particularly meaningful in relation to the process I want to emphasize. On the one hand, this etymological excursus links the word 'name' with a concept of the illusion of integrity that is founded on misrecognition (the 'Olde English' word 'on-ane' means 'All as One or As One Body'). It also links the word with self-reflexivity, given that 'on-ane' is a blatant homophone of ONAN – the name of the political configuration portrayed in the novel, which encompasses the United States, Mexico, and Canada – and, needless to say, is a reference to the onanistic essence of the solipsistic neo-capitalist ideology satirized in the novel. These connections, although overtly fictional and parodic, are crucial in pointing out a radical correlation between language, misrecognition, and self-reflexivity that leads us to Louis Althusser's idea of interpellation, which contends that it is through its name that a subject is ideologically constituted 'As One Body'.

The other element of this passage worth noticing concerns the Greek word mentioned by Hal, which is completely misspelled: he refers to the nonexistent ὄνμγα (onmga) instead of the Aeolic ὄνυμα (onyma). On the one hand, this misspelling is certainly a demonstration of the way Wallace plays parodically with the ostentation of erudition, blurring the boundaries between elements that are based on actual research and others that are utterly made up. On the other hand, it can also be read as indicative of Hal's incipient loss of linguistic mastery: he fails to pronounce the name of a word whose meaning is precisely 'name'. And it is exactly this progressively receding mastery over words that leaves room for contact with the Real.

A comparison of the beginning and ending of the novel makes particularly clear how the above-mentioned imposition of what McGowan calls 'the traumatic silence of the Real' (McGowan, 2007a: 218) constitutes the very centre not only of Hal's experience but also of the novel. As a matter of fact, if there is a specularity linking Hal's aphasia before the admission committee and Gately's awakening on a cold beach in Gloucester (the novel's ending, following Gately's loss of consciousness the night before during the episode of Fackelman's horrific punishment), this specularity concerns precisely the issue of aphasia.

Keeping this in mind, it is important to pay attention to the novel's final sentence ('And when he came back to, he was flat on his back on the beach in the freezing sand, and it was raining out of a low sky, and the tide was way out', Wallace, 1996: 981). As a matter of fact there is only one other passage in the novel in which this 'hitting the bottom' moment experienced by the then-twenty-four-year-old Gately is mentioned. While Gately lies immobilized and mute in a bed at St Elizabeth Hospital and is heroically fighting to refuse Demerol (the drug he was addicted to) as a pain killer, he stoically tries to evade the temptation by recalling previous episodes of his life, which gives way to a series of flashbacks that constitute the main bulk of the narration concerning him as the novel draws to an end. Most of these flashbacks seem to parallel his present condition by exposing episodes in which Gately failed to be more than a spectator, or 'figurant', when confronted with oppression and abuse (his mother being beaten by the MP, the suicide of his neighbour Mrs Waite, the bullying of the 'North Shore violin-playing kids' (829) and of a 'so-called homosexual kid', 973). Only one flashback originates from a reflection on the mutism rather than on the stasis that Gately is forced into. It occurs in a passage where we learn that Gately had experienced this inability to speak only once before, which is also the passage that points to what happens in the novel's final lines. The passage reads 'This is the only time he's ever been struck dumb except for a brief but nasty bout of pleuritic laryngitis he'd had when he was twenty-four and sleeping on the cold beach up in Gloucester, and he doesn't like it a bit, the being struck dumb' (833). The cold beach where Gately slept on that occasion is clearly the one mentioned by the novel's last sentence; this anticipation of the ending thus makes it possible to project what happened afterwards. Immediately after sleeping on the 'freezing sand' (981), Gately fell ill with pleuritic laryngitis, which left him unable to speak for a while. This detail is important, because it shows how traumatic contacts with the Real – often coinciding with cathartic and positively life-changing hitting-the-bottom moments – are often meaningfully accompanied in *Infinite Jest* by the inability to speak, and therefore by the annihilation of language. Or at least that is what happens with the two main protagonists of the novel, whose hitting-the-bottom moments coincide with the beginning and ending of the novel.

Therefore Gately's past condition of being 'struck dumb' (833) after awakening on the cold beach of Gloucester can be helpful, by way of analogy with Hal's aphasia, in projecting a possible positive continuation of Hal's incident with the University of Arizona admissions committee. Considering the mirroring of the two moments (given that they do not occupy the two extreme poles of the novel incidentally), it is possible to conceive of Hal's aphasia as both temporary and the precursor of a rebirth – which is also what happened to Gately who, shortly after recovering from pleuritic laryngitis, will join the recovery residence of Ennet House. This is also what happened to the ex-addicts who report their testimonies in the narration devoted to Ennet House when they, as the novel's AA lexicon puts it, 'Surrender' (465). This experience, which constitutes a transformation of the ideological subject into a free subject (therefore the 'actual' birth of the subject, symbolized by Hal's promotion to narrator), involves the characters' contact with the silence of the Real, the possibility of existing outside language and its signifying ability. Furthermore, on a more formal level, this silence is conveyed through a literary device that tries to construct the *'mimétique du rien'* that Buci-Glucksmann attributes to baroque art, which deploys an overflow of signs and representations to create contact with the point where the void concealed by the symbolic network manifests itself.

In this respect it is also meaningful that page 982 – the last page of *Infinite Jest* (if one reads the endnotes in conjunction with the text), which separates the ending from the 'Notes and Errata' – is completely blank, devoid not only of content but also of a page number. This intentionally blank page may certainly be the simple result of a printing convention. None the less, in light of what we have seen so far, it may also be interpreted as an immersion in the silence of the Real that the novel intentionally leads to. It is that silence that, as Todd McGowan puts it, allows us to experience 'the moment of loss that generates subjectivity itself and yet which all the actions of the subject attempt to escape' (McGowan, 2007a: 218) – namely, the moment of loss of the privileged object (objet petit a) that gives birth to the subject and constitutes it as a desiring being. Sustaining contact with this moment would entail for McGowan a freedom from 'the illusory promises of ideology and the blandishments of capitalist accumulation' (218), in so far as it would show us that 'enjoyment derives from not having the object rather than having and thus avoid the struggle to have more' (218–19). In fact it is significant that the blank page immediately follows the novel's very last words: 'way out' (Wallace, 1996: 981). It may be read as representing a point outside of ideology, which ideology prompts us to perpetually escape from – the point of pure loss that indicates the incompleteness of the symbolic structure. And it is precisely contact with this lack that frees the subject.

To sum up we have seen how *Infinite Jest* embraces the baroque model of vision to challenge the epistemological model of Cartesian perpectivalism. The fixed subject position implied in the Cartesian visual regime coincides with the hyper-rational and self-reflexive subjectivities portrayed in the novel, which are characterized by an illusory sense of mastery over the external word. The baroque visual model is, as we have seen, at the basis of Lacan's conception of the object gaze, which allows him to theorize a radical decentring of the Cartesian subject that shutters her illusory sense of control. By considering the issue of the anamorphic 'gaze' – the object looking back at the viewer – in endnote 129, we have seen how the novel thematizes the uncanny possibility of shuttering the subjective sense of mastery through a viewer who experiences the distortion (and incompleteness) of her own vision. This represents a contact with something that remains irreducible to representation, as well as to signification. We have also seen how a similar experience is represented in the novel in the realm of language. While in the realm of images the anamorphic object prompts the subject to experience the reality of her own distortion, in the realm of symbols and language the real of the subject is revealed by an experience of silence that points at language's inability to symbolize everything. In this respect I have paid particular attention to the novel's initial and final parts: Hal and Gately's experiences of hitting rock bottom, which both revolve around the inability to speak. Learning from the baroque model, Wallace experiments with the elasticity of the borders of the systems of representation and language. What he ultimately achieves is a contact with their limits, which reveals ideology's constitutive incompleteness.

Notes

1 See David Hering's discussion of the importance of *Las meninas* as a model of reflection in Wallace's work.
2 Endnote 129 describes a flashback, because the Eschaton game is set in YDAU when Penn is no longer a student at the Enfield Tennis Academy.
3 A pivotal example of these unreal yet realistic-looking proportions can be found in Andrea Mantegna's *Lamentation over the Dead Christ* (1480), where the viewer is positioned at Christ's feet. However, Christ's feet are unnaturally small so as not to cover the rest of the foreshortened figure, with an effect that looks natural but is radically different from the way the human eye would have seen a real figure from the same position.
4 The skull in *The Ambassadors* is also severely foreshortened, but it is not integrated into the rest of the visual field like the glass's mouth

described by Hal. This is one of the ways it challenges the Renaissance perspectivalism and is not what occurs with the NASA glass.

References

Althusser, L. (2011). 'Ideology and Ideological State Apparatuses (Notes towards an Investigation)', 204–22. In Imre Szeman and Timothy Kaposy, eds, *Cultural Theory: An Anthology*. Hoboken NJ: John Wiley & Sons.
Baltrušaitis, J. (1977). *Anamorphic Art*, trans. W. J. Strachan. Cambridge: Chadwyck-Healey.
Buci-Glucksmann, C. (2013). *The Madness of Vision: On Baroque Aesthetics*, trans. Dorothy Z. Baker. Athens OH: Ohio University Press.
Burn, S. J. (2003). *David Foster Wallace's Infinite Jest: A Reader's Guide*. New York NY: Continuum.
Calabrese, O. (2017). *Neo-baroque: A Sign of the Times*. Princeton NJ: Princeton University Press.
Copjec, J. (1994). *Read My Desire: Lacan against the Historicists*. Cambridge MA: MIT Press.
Hering, D. (2016). *David Foster Wallace: Fiction and Form*. London and New York NY: Bloomsbury.
Jay, M. (1993). *Downcast Eyes: The Denigration of Vision in Twentieth-Century French Thought*. Berkeley CA: University of California Press.
Lacan, J. (1978). *The Four Fundamental Concepts of Psychoanalysis*, trans. Alan Sheridan. New York NY: Norton.
McGowan, T. (2007a). *The Impossible David Lynch*. New York NY: Columbia University Press.
McGowan, T. (2007b). *The Real Gaze: Film Theory after Lacan*. Albany NY: State University of New York Press.
Merleau-Ponty, M. (1968). *The Visible and the Invisible: Followed by Working Notes*, trans. Alphonso Lingis, ed. Claude Lefort. Evanston IL: Northwestern University Press.
Miller, J.-A. (2007). 'Jacques Lacan and the Voice', 137–46. In Veronique Voruz and Bogdan Wolf, eds, *The Later Lacan: An Introduction*. Albany NY: SUNY Press.
Sartre, J.-P. (2001). *Being and Nothingness: An Essay in Phenomenological Ontology*. New York NY: Citadel Press.
Timmer, N. (2010). *Do You Feel It Too? The Post-Postmodern Syndrome in American Fiction at the Turn of the Millennium*. Amsterdam: Rodopi.
Wallace, D. Foster. (1996). *Infinite Jest*. New York NY: Little, Brown.
Žižek, S. (1989). *The Sublime Object of Ideology*. New York NY and London: Verso.

Žižek, S. (1992). *Looking Awry: An Introduction to Jacques Lacan through Popular Culture*. Cambridge MA: MIT Press.
Žižek, S. (2006). *How to Read Lacan*. New York NY: W. W. Norton.

Archival sources

Wallace, D. Foster. (undated). 'Las Meniñas', *Handwritten and Typed Drafts*, David Foster Wallace Papers, container 15.7, Harry Ransom Center, The University of Austin (TX).

Index

Note: literary works and illustrations can be found under authors'/artists' names.

absorption 9, 19–23, 25–9, 31–3, 37–44, 95, 149–51, 154, 158, 169
   reflective absorption 39–40
   refractive absorption 9, 23, 33, 37, 40–2
   see also selfhood, self-absorption; solipsism
acknowledgment 13, 26, 39, 116, 130, 134, 228–9, 234, 236, 253, 264
addiction 14, 41, 62, 64–5, 143, 171–2, 175, 246, 250, 297–8, 300–1, 303, 305–9, 321, 327–8
Aeschylus 57
aesthetic(s) 7, 9, 11–12, 20–8, 32–3, 40–3, 56, 138–42, 148, 153–8, 173, 182, 191, 197, 213, 215, 267, 269, 279–84, 291–2, 298–303, 315, 322
affect 13, 192, 194–7, 236, 242–5, 249, 251–6, 259–74
alienation 11, 51, 63, 95, 116, 140–1, 145, 149, 161–73, 242, 250, 310
   see also selfhood, self-alienation

allegory 6, 54, 212, 270, 291
ambiguity 3, 6, 72, 84, 115, 117, 134, 182, 196, 201, 260, 268, 273, 275, 291, 323
Anscombe, Elizabeth 173
Antiseri, Dario 174
anxiety 92, 96–7, 120, 192, 210, 260, 281, 291–4
Aquinas, Thomas 57
Arendt, Hannah 184, 287–90
Aristotle 2, 196
art (artwork) 7, 21–45, 48–9, 57–8, 61–5, 106, 131, 134, 138, 140, 155–6, 188, 250, 253, 279, 292–4, 298–9, 306, 325, 329
Artaud, Antonin 61–4
attention 26, 35, 75, 95, 133, 134, 1934, 197, 251
Aufhebung see absorption
Austin, J.L. 51
authenticity 26–8, 49, 56, 61, 69, 73–4, 85, 92, 173, 202, 204, 263, 272, 274, 303, 309
author 4, 6–7, 11, 14, 40, 44, 72, 74–5, 78–80, 84–5, 86, 95, 140–2, 148, 152–7,

175, 180, 188–90, 196, 220, 299–300, 306
authoriality 78, 75, 78–80, 83–5, 151, 155, 158
authorial self 40, 78, 151, 155
author-reader relationship 11, 14, 40, 54, 104, 155, 299, 300, 306
authorship 71, 75, 79, 140, 153, 157
avant-garde 31–2, 61–3
awareness *see* consciousness

Badiou, Alain 50
Bakhtin, Mikhail 50, 54–5, 183, 191–4, 197
Baldwin, James 14, 280, 285–90
baroque 14, 33, 43, 314–19, 329–30
Barrett, Lisa Feldman 244
Barth, John 94
Barthes, Roland 152, 158, 243
Bartley III, William Warren 174
Baskin, Jon 42, 120, 233, 234, 236
de Beauvoir, Simone 117–18
Beckett, Samuel 50, 61, 63
Bennett, Andrew 174, 176, 256
Benzon, Kiki 120
Berlant, Lauren 13, 260–2, 267–74
Bernini, Gianlorenzo 33–40, 43–4, 315
  Ecstasy of St Teresa, The 33–6, 44, 315
Blake, William 37
Bliss-Moreau, Eliza 244
Boddy, Kasia 174
body 13, 64, 154, 158, 163, 193–4, 202, 210, 216, 224, 241–56, 261, 264, 267, 275, 298, 304–9, 311, 314, 320, 326–7
  disembodiment 245, 248, 251
  embodiment 9, 13, 242, 249, 251, 257

female body 254, 298, 307, 311
male body 246, 250–1
see also gender; sexuality
boredom 82, 120, 308
Borges, Jorge Luis 79
Borrelli, Francesca 297–8
Boswell, Marshall 29–30, 89, 115, 119, 123, 131, 133, 134, 147–8, 150–1, 171
Bourdieu, Pierre 32
Brando, Marlon 64–5
Brecht, Bertolt 25, 50–1
Bres, Jacques 83
Brook, Peter 64
Bruno, Giordano 212
Burn, Stephen 141, 176, 189, 246, 318
Buci-Glucksmann, Christine 315, 329

Camus, Albert 20, 50, 189
Calabrese, Omar 315–16
Carlisle, Greg 83
Carroll, Hamilton 306
Carson, Johnny 59
Cavell, Stanley 12–13, 32, 43–4, 79, 221–5, 228–36
Chardin, Jean-Baptiste-Siméon 26
child (children, childhood) 12, 56–7, 124, 164–5, 173, 185, 187, 201–14, 215, 223–5, 283
Chodat, Robert 20–1, 40, 42
choice 61, 98–9, 102, 104, 122
  see also freedom
Cioffi, Frank Louis 51
Civil Rights movement 280, 284–5, 290
cliché 82, 220, 230, 236
Cohen, Robert 64
Cohen, Samuel 247, 281
Cohn, Dorrit 81
communication 2, 6, 8, 13, 22, 24, 28–33, 40, 44, 58–9, 69, 75, 95, 114–16, 125, 130–2, 138–56, 157–8,

165–6, 175, 192, 194, 201–2, 207–11, 241–50, 254–6, 260–2, 270–4, 279–85, 288–94, 310, 322–5
incommunicability 12, 208–10
see also connection; dialogue; dialogism; language
compassion 72–4, 77, 80–5, 236
connection (interpersonal, interconnection) 107, 130, 132, 140, 143, 145–8, 154, 169, 232–3, 242–6, 249, 262, 272, 286, 289
consciousness 9–12, 31, 42–3, 69, 80, 98–105, 123–5, 134, 162, 184, 194, 200–1, 207, 209–11, 214–15, 220, 230–2, 261, 270–2, 274, 286–7, 319, 327
hyperconsciousness 92, 114, 120, 122–6
self-consciousness (self-reflection, reflexivity) 11–12, 20, 24, 38–9, 58–65, 92–4, 120, 123–5, 132, 153–5, 201, 204, 243–4, 248, 253, 263, 271–2, 293, 309
see also selfhood
consensus 13, 193, 280–1, 289–91, 294
consubstantiality 11, 139–43, 151–2, 156
contradiction 20–5, 86, 123, 172, 272, 293, 301
Copjec, Joan 320
Costello, Mark 291–3, 300–1, 309
Cottingham, John 216
Courbet, Gustave 26
cynicism 49, 57, 63, 92–4, 175
see also irony

David, Jacques-Louis 26
death 54–61, 72, 76, 82, 84, 86, 126–7, 195

deconstruction 11, 115, 139–40, 149, 152, 154, 254, 317
Deleuze, Gilles 50
depression 22–4, 42, 96, 119–21, 124–5, 127–8, 134, 170, 219, 264
Derrida, Jacques 1, 50–1, 115, 190, 201, 204, 215, 241, 243–4, 254, 287, 310
Descartes, René 5, 14, 163, 169, 210, 216, 224, 246, 314–17, 320, 326, 329–30
desire 30, 39, 41, 104, 165, 170–2, 243, 252–4, 272–3, 275, 306–7, 311, 319, 322, 329
despair 12, 92, 96, 98, 102, 104, 114, 188, 124–5, 130, 200, 299
dialogue 3, 6, 10–12, 40, 49–55, 58, 63–4, 72, 74, 82–3, 106, 131, 133, 138–9, 152–5, 169–70, 180, 182, 191–7, 206, 233, 241, 289, 322
dialogism 50, 54, 83, 87, 192
Diakoulakis, Christoforos 115
Diderot, Denis 26–7, 39
den Dulk, Allard 10, 107, 146, 149, 161, 173, 175–6, 234, 259, 297
Dostoevsky, Fyodor 10–11, 21, 55, 113–33, 134, 214
drama 5, 10, 21, 48–51, 54–8, 62–6, 81, 163–4
dualism (mind body) 210, 246, 255, 314
see also subject
dystopia 265, 267, 269, 275–6

ego *see* selfhood
Ellison, Ralph 292
embodiment *see* body
emotion 3, 13, 29, 37–8, 44, 56, 65, 69–70, 75, 81, 92,

120, 122, 124, 128, 131, 133, 162, 169, 172, 194–5, 207, 210, 213, 227, 260–7, 274, 283, 305
empathy 11, 12, 59–60, 80–1, 114–15, 130–3, 134, 182, 207–8, 210–13, 232–3, 275, 282–5, 289–90, 299
emptiness (inner, spiritual) 91–2, 95–6, 103, 171–2, 235
Engel, S. Morris 173
Engelmann, Paul 174
entertainment ('The Entertainment') 14, 23, 27, 30–3, 42, 61, 64–5, 162, 249, 257, 297–300, 303–9, 321–2
see also addiction
epistemology 102–3, 105, 169–70, 209, 222, 228, 232, 271, 314, 329
ethics 7, 9, 10, 25, 52, 58, 94, 98–9, 101–5, 138, 140, 153, 156, 158, 161, 173, 191–2, 196, 209, 213, 228, 232, 249, 251, 254, 280, 282, 290
existentialism 20, 61, 99, 102, 107, 116–18, 120, 133
experimental (experimentation) 6, 8, 30, 52, 54, 80, 214, 230, 243, 263, 315, 321, 330

Felski, Rita 115
feminism 13, 261, 264, 268, 273–4, 310
film 9, 22–5, 27, 29–33, 36–44, 48–51, 61–4, 300–1, 304, 308, 315–16, 322
Foucault, Michel 14, 52
Frank, Joseph 113–14, 116, 118, 121, 125, 131–2
Frankl, Viktor 60

fraudulence 70, 72–5, 77–9, 84–5, 205, 222–3, 226–30, 235, 267
freedom 8, 20, 37, 43, 63, 90, 98, 100–2, 123, 152, 245, 317, 329
see also choice
Freudenthal, Elizabeth 175
Fried, Michael 21, 25–9, 31–4, 37–40, 43
Friedman, Milton 186

Gabor, Dennis 20, 41
Garner, Bryan A. 311
Gates Jr., Henry Louis 293
gaze 14, 40, 73–4, 77, 84, 87, 91–2, 201, 206, 226, 251, 282, 311, 315–25, 330
Geist (spirit) 20, 23–4, 158
gender 9, 13, 44–5, 56, 128, 186, 247–50, 259–65, 268, 270, 274, 275, 279, 284–5, 309
see also body; sexuality
genius 57–8, 189, 204–6, 208
Géricault, Théodore 26
Gombrich, E. H. 24
Greenberg, Clement 31–2, 38
Greuze, Jean-Baptiste 26
Greyser, Naomi 264

Habermas, Jürgen 12, 181, 183, 186, 190–4
Harry Ransom Center 89, 105, 113, 285, 297, 303
Hayes-Brady, Clare 13, 45, 69, 115, 196, 233, 259, 261, 271, 275, 279–80, 285, 287–8, 294, 309
Hayles, N. Katherine 175
Hegel, Georg Wilhelm Friedrich 5, 9, 20–32, 37, 40–3, 52, 158
Heidegger, Martin 235

Hering, David 30, 40, 79, 89, 152–3, 189, 275, 322
Himmelheber, Rachel Haley 253
Hobbes, Thomas 20
Holbein, Hans 320–1
Holland, Mary K. 89, 114–15, 134, 142, 174, 176, 193–4, 259–63, 270, 307
Horn, Patrick 115, 174, 232
Hudson, Cory M. 78–80, 231–3, 236, 262
Husserl, Edmund 255–6
Hyde, Lewis 93
hyperconsciousness (hyperawareness; hyperreflexivity) *see* consciousness

imagination 7, 10, 55, 71, 75, 77, 79–80, 84–5, 162, 210–13, 232, 243
individualism 96, 98–9, 101, 172, 175, 192
interconnection *see* connection
interiority 78, 80, 146–7, 171, 175, 185, 208, 220–3, 229, 231, 324
intertextuality 158, 246, 268
intimacy 14, 29, 43, 157, 298–9, 308–9
irony (and anti-irony) 28, 37, 44, 48, 52, 59–60, 83, 91–4, 98, 131, 138, 147, 149–50, 157, 175, 205, 207, 213, 232, 235–6, 242, 268, 270, 274, 293–4, 309
see also cynicism

Jacobs, Timothy 133
James, William 164
Jay, Martin 314–15
Joyce, James 11, 139–43, 148–57, 158

Ulysses 11, 55, 139–42, 151, 157
Judd, Donald 28

Kafka, Franz 61, 214
Kant, Immanuel 5, 7, 25–6, 39, 163, 235
Karmodi, Ostap 52, 214
Keane, Mark 173
Kelleher, Conor 173
Kelly, Adam 9, 54–5, 106, 158, 175, 183, 192–3, 243, 259, 273, 310
Kenny, Glenn 307
Kierkegaard, Søren 20, 50
Kocela, Christopher 236
Konstantinou, Lee 31, 232
Kozin, Alexander 255
Krasinski, John 48
Kripke, Saul 175

Lacan, Jacques 14, 310, 316–23, 330
Lamarque, Peter 15
language 6, 8, 12, 50–1, 69, 71, 87, 114–18, 125, 129, 134, 139–58, 160–75, 191, 201, 209–12, 216, 223–5, 231–2, 241–63, 267–76, 281, 285–6, 294–5, 298, 304, 317, 319, 323–30
aphasia 317, 321–8
communal language 115, 140, 145–7, 149, 151, 157–8, 171
failure of language 114–15, 125, 129, 134, 139, 147–8, 232, 323
see also Wittgenstein, Ludwig
Lasch, Christopher 10, 89–107, 174
Leavis, Frank R. 174
Levinas, Emmanuel 243
Lipsky, David 175, 187, 297, 299, 303–6

loneliness 11, 91–2, 95, 100, 103–4, 117, 120, 141, 147, 162, 168, 170, 172–4, 207, 221, 251, 262, 298–9, 305–8
  see also solitude
Louis, Morris 27
love 13, 34–5, 51, 78, 90, 99, 147, 165, 170–2, 225, 229–30, 236, 262, 280–95, 307
  erotic love 284, 286, 298–9, 309
  interracial love 280, 283, 287
  love as political action 282, 284, 288
  see also loneliness; race

McCaffery, Larry 138, 160, 190, 212, 243, 279, 299
McCarthy, Tom 62
McGowan, Todd 319–20, 327, 329
Malcolm, Norman 175
Manet, Édouard 26, 28
Mann, Thomas 55
Marat, Jean-Paul 63–4
Markson, David 161–4, 173, 175, 214, 261
masculinity 230, 254, 260–1, 292
Massumi, Brian 245, 254
Max, Daniel T. 65, 113, 173
Mayo, Rob 120, 134, 169, 174
mediation 23–4, 32, 37, 62, 79, 302, 306
medium 20, 28–9, 32–4, 37–8, 40, 43–4, 49, 322
Menzel, Adolphe 39
Merleau-Ponty, Maurice 255, 315, 319
metafiction 79–81, 90, 93, 106, 149, 222, 231–2, 236, 270
metaphysics 50, 117, 209, 241, 254
Miller, Jacques-Alain 323

Miller, Laura 299
misogyny 52, 54, 128–30, 253, 267–70, 298
modernism 24, 26–8, 32, 37, 50, 139, 157
Moi, Toril 1, 115–16, 134
Moran, Dermot 255
Morris, David 41
Morris, Robert 28
Morsia, Elliott 131
Mouffe, Chantal 196–7
Mulhall, Stephen 175
Mullins, Matthew 243
Murdoch, Iris 50

Nadell, Bonnie 173, 301–2
narrator 11, 51, 70, 77, 83, 87, 123, 129–30, 155, 203–5, 227, 245, 252–3, 256, 271–3, 329
narcissism 40, 59, 73, 75, 78, 87, 90–107, 114, 116, 119–21, 125–34, 142
Nagel, Thomas 12, 201, 210–11, 215–16
neoliberalism 182–6, 192, 197
Nietzsche, Friedrich 50, 57, 243
nihilism 98, 116
Nowakowska, Alexandra 83

O'Brien, John 310
Oedipus 56–7
Olitski, Jules 27
Olsen, Lance 243
omniscience 71, 76–7, 80, 84–5, 324
optics 30, 306, 321–6
  refraction 40, 71, 78, 86, 322
others 19–22, 39, 44, 69, 72, 77, 82, 86, 90–2, 103, 116–31, 147–8, 167, 173, 175, 184–5, 192, 213, 221–3, 232, 236, 242, 246–50, 264, 286, 288, 299

other minds 12, 39–40, 73, 79–80, 85, 219–36
Ozick, Cynthia 281

Palleau-Papin, Françoise 173
paradox 7, 70, 75, 84–6, 161, 167, 172, 175, 226–9, 233–5, 280, 298, 301
Parak, Franz 174
performance 10, 48–52, 57–65, 81, 99, 169, 225, 262, 264, 282
performativity 9, 51–2, 59, 65, 169–70, 191, 232, 271, 274
perspective 19, 34, 37, 76–80, 165, 167, 170, 175, 185, 190, 196–7, 201–5, 213–14, 222, 245, 256, 309
   Cartesian perspectivalism 314, 316, 320, 329
   foreshortening 315, 323–5, 330
   see also point of view
pessimism 211, 260, 262, 270, 274
Pippin, Robert B. 23–4, 30, 39
Pitcher, George 174
Plato 2–5, 10, 49–58, 204, 212, 220, 246–7, 251
poetry 5–6, 134
point of view 38, 77, 106, 172, 180, 315
porn (pornography) 14, 48, 265, 267, 275, 297–311
postmodernism 27–9, 62, 157
Powers, Richard 310
Prout, Matt 12–13, 79
psychoanalysis 310, 319
public sphere 12, 180–97
Puchner, Martin 49–50, 53–5
Putnam, Hilary 212

race 13–14, 186, 259, 279–94
   racial anxiety 291–4
   racial difference/otherness 250, 280–92
   whiteness 280–2, 284, 287, 290–4
Ramal, Randy 174
reader (reading) 8–14, 22, 25, 28, 40–4, 52–8, 65, 68, 71–6, 79–83, 93–5, 115–16, 120, 130–4, 140, 148, 152–8, 182, 187, 191–7, 204, 208, 210, 213, 220, 225–34, 224, 245, 252, 254, 259–75, 288–9, 299–303
   response of 3–6, 41, 128, 133, 190
   see also author, author-reader relationship
recognition 24, 29, 41, 44, 91, 102, 106, 143–4, 155, 170, 194, 247, 282, 299, 321
   misrecognition 326–7
redemption 97, 155
Redgate, Jamie 120, 242, 245, 248
reflexivity *see* consciousness, self-consciousness
religion 37, 45, 55, 74–7, 156, 158, 191
representation 317–22, 330
responsibility 99–105, 164–5, 173, 183, 284–9
Romanticism 24, 26, 32, 38–9, 43, 284
Rorty, Richard 5, 201, 211–15, 256
Rousseau, Jean-Jacques 20, 26, 39
Ryerson, James 107, 173, 175, 234

de Sade, Marquis Donatien Alphonse François 63–4
Sartre, Jean-Paul 102, 107, 123, 319
scepticism (skepticism) 50, 97, 114–15, 121, 124, 163–6, 221, 225, 228–36

Schama, Simon 33–4, 37
Schelling, Friedrich Wilhelm Joseph 26
Schopenhauer, Arthur 164, 173, 246–7, 251, 256
Scott, Anthony O. 60
Sedgwick, Eve Kosofsky 245, 254
self-consciousness *see* consciousness
self-reflection *see* consciousness
selfhood 55, 61, 65, 139, 145–52, 260–1
   ego (Ego) 132, 163–72
   fictional self 76–8, 82
   self and other 31, 40, 84, 96
   self-absorption 92, 95–7, 115, 123, 128–9, 247
   self-alienation 38–9, 120
   self-awareness *see* consciousness, self-consciousness
   selflessness 99–102
   self-loathing (self-disgust) 114, 121, 126–7, 130, 250, 325
   self-objectification 30, 123, 150
   self-transcendence 37–40
   see also subject
Severs, Jeffrey 10, 42, 188, 191, 216, 283–4
sex 59, 175, 252, 255, 266–9, 275, 279–84, 291–2, 301, 306–9, 311
   dysfunctional 279, 283
sexuality 44, 279, 307–9
   closeted 284, 288
   see also gender
Shapiro, Mary 30, 242, 249–51
Shakespeare, William 151
   Hamlet 22, 57, 151, 246, 321
   King Lear 229
Shaw, George Bernard 50
silencing 70, 254
Silverblatt, Michael 263, 305
sincerity (and insincerity) 9, 21, 26–32, 41, 44, 48, 58–60, 158, 243

Sloane, Peter 242, 244, 311
sociology 9–10, 90, 93, 96
solitude 14, 147, 165, 206–7
   see also loneliness
Sophocles 57
spirituality 52, 96, 98, 235–6, 264
Smith, Tony 27
Smith, Zadie 54, 107, 264–5, 276
Socrates 10, 50, 52–4, 63
solipsism 8, 11, 95, 104, 139–49, 160–75
Sophists (sophistry) 49, 51–7, 65
speech 6, 21–2, 48, 50–1, 56, 58, 66, 129, 169, 192, 204, 247–9, 252
spite (spitefulness) 114, 122, 126, 269
stage 48–64
Stella, Frank 27
subject 7, 15, 23, 30, 37, 43, 70, 74, 144, 147–51, 162, 165, 168, 170–4, 184–6, 193–4, 248, 255–6, 272, 289–90, 304, 314–30
   Cartesian subject 14, 169, 314, 317, 320, 326, 330
   subjectivity 23–4, 29–32, 117, 148, 150, 174, 184, 247–51, 315, 326, 329
   subject-object 20, 23, 25, 30, 31, 40, 151, 248, 256
   see also consciousness; selfhood
substance abuse 142–9, 158
   see also addiction
suffering 96, 98, 104, 119–21, 125–34, 172–3, 210, 247, 264, 288, 299, 300, 306, 308
suicide 29–30, 73–4, 81–4, 97, 161, 165, 174, 219, 223, 231, 250–2, 303, 321, 328

technology 41, 188, 197, 251, 265–6, 275–6, 298, 301, 304–6, 309, 311

temptation 128, 228, 232, 236, 327
theatre 49–66
theatricality 25–51, 58–62, 66
theology 11, 139, 142, 152
therapy (therapist) 41–2, 74, 96–9, 120, 123–6, 129, 131, 139, 152–3, 160, 166, 226, 233–5
Thompson, Lucas 63–4, 133–4, 235, 281, 292
Timár, Eszter 245
Toal, Catherine 120
transcendence 20–3, 37–40, 91, 96, 154, 315–16
Trilling, Lionel 21
trinity 11, 139–58, 171
Turan, Kenneth 301
Turner, Alice 302

utilitarianism 14, 97–100, 317

Vermeule, Blakey 256
violence 54, 63, 250, 253–4, 270, 274
visuality 14, 267, 306, 314–25, 329–30
voice 22, 48, 51, 55, 58, 64, 72, 74, 76–81, 85, 93, 95, 169, 201, 205, 241, 249, 250, 253, 255–9, 270–1, 293, 323–5
  de-voicing 249, 289
Voltaire 212
vulnerability 3, 10, 49, 61, 92–3, 175, 195

Wallace, David Foster
  Both Flesh and not: Essays 310
    'Back in New Fire' 310
    'The Empty Plenum: David Markson's *Wittgenstein's Mistress*' 50, 107, 160, 221, 261
    'Federer Both Flesh And Not' 310
    'Fictional Futures and the Conspicuously Young' 298
    'The (As It Were) Seminal Importance of *Terminator 2*' 310
    'The Nature of Fun' 310
  Brief Interviews with Hideous Men 13, 48, 97, 114, 174, 260–1, 279, 304, 307–11
    'Adult World (I)' 14, 300, 307, 311
    'Adult World (II)' 14, 300, 307, 309
    'Brief Interview #2' ('B.I. #2') 53
    'Brief Interview #20' ('B.I. #20') 13, 61, 129, 251, 256
    'Brief Interview #28' ('B.I. #28') 52
    'Brief Interview #46' ('B.I. #46') 60
    'Brief Interview #59' ('B.I. #59') 52, 56
    'Brief Interview #78' ('B.I. #78') 54
    'Datum Centurio' 13, 260, 262, 265, 267, 270, 276, 304
    'Death Is Not the End' 129
    'The Depressed Person' 10 97, 113–33, 263–4
    'Octet' 13, 41, 58–61, 79, 260–5, 270–3
    'On His Deathbed, Holding Your Hand, the Acclaimed New Young Off-Broadway Playwright's Father Begs a Boon' 56
    'Suicide as a Sort of Present' 161, 165
    'Tri-Stan: I Sold Sissee Nar to Ecko' 58

Broom of the System, The 51, 97, 102, 104, 162, 167, 175, 244, 247, 249

Consider the Lobster and Other Essays 310
  'Authority and American Usage' 50, 101, 172, 276, 280, 291
  'Big Red Son' 14, 300, 307–11
  'Certainly the End of Something or Other' 95
  'Consider the Lobster' 209–10, 310
  'Joseph Frank's *Dostoevsky*' 21, 113–14, 116–19, 121, 124, 131–2

Girl with Curious Hair 97, 280, 282, 289, 291, 293–4
  'Girl with Curious Hair' 14, 204, 280, 282–3
  'Lyndon' 14, 280–92
  'Westward the Course of Empire Takes its Way' 41, 94, 289, 303

Infinite Jest 9, 11–14, 19–44, 49, 51, 57, 62–5, 89, 97, 100, 114, 120, 133–4, 138–58, 162, 171–3, 208, 213, 215, 245–51, 256, 276, 294, 300, 304–6, 309, 314–15, 328–9

Oblivion 65, 97, 200, 205, 208, 211, 215–16, 226, 250
  'Another Pioneer' 12, 203–14
  'Good Old Neon' 41, 69, 71, 75, 79, 81–6, 97, 200, 205, 221–2, 231–6, 245, 251
  'Incarnations of Burned Children' 12, 200–16
  'Oblivion' 206

  'Philosophy and the Mirror of Nature' 206, 216, 250
  'The Soul Is Not a Smithy' 200
  'The Suffering Channel' 200, 206

Pale King, The 12, 49, 62–5, 180–97, 211, 247, 249, 251, 280

Signifying Rappers: Rap and Race in the Urban Present 13–14, 280–1, 291–4, 300, 309

Supposedly Fun Thing I'll Never Do Again, A 125, 310
  'David Lynch Keeps His Head' 309
  'E Unibus Pluram: Television and U.S. Fiction' 10, 21, 29, 49–50, 90–4, 243

This Is Water 97, 99, 100, 102, 248

Warren, Andrew 41, 63–4
Warwick, Genevieve 34
Weiss, Peter 63–4, 189
Widiss, Benjamin 79
Wilde, Oscar 50
Wittgenstein, Ludwig 1, 6, 11–12, 21, 52, 100, 115, 139–40, 144–57, 160–73, 214, 219–24, 229, 233–6, 242–3, 256
  family resemblances 11, 139, 144–8, 154, 157
  language games 4, 6, 11, 139–58, 175, 216, 225
  pain behaviour 222–4, 234
  Philosophical Investigations 145–6, 151, 160–1, 167, 175, 214
  private language 140–50, 158, 166, 172, 174
  Tractatus Logico-Philosophicus 144–5, 160–71, 175

worship 33, 44, 64, 96, 98–101, 205
Wundt, Wilhelm 244

Zeno of Elea 79
Zito, Stephen F. 301
Žižek, Slavoj 319, 321

EU authorised representative for GPSR:
Easy Access System Europe, Mustamäe tee 50,
10621 Tallinn, Estonia
gpsr.requests@easproject.com

www.ingramcontent.com/pod-product-compliance
Lightning Source LLC
Chambersburg PA
CBHW051556230426
43668CB00013B/1876